How Intimate Partner Violence Affects Children

How Intimate Partner Violence Affects Children

Developmental Research, Case Studies, and Evidence-Based Intervention

Edited by **Sandra A. Graham-Bermann and Alytia A. Levendosky**

American Psychological Association • Washington, DC

Published by
American Psychological Association
750 First Street, NE
Washington, DC 20002
www.apa.org

To order
APA Order Department
P.O. Box 92984
Washington, DC 20090-2984
Tel: (800) 374-2721; Direct: (202) 336-5510
Fax: (202) 336-5502; TDD/TTY: (202) 336-6123
Online: www.apa.org/pubs/books/
E-mail: order@apa.org

In the U.K., Europe, Africa, and the Middle East, copies may be ordered from
American Psychological Association
3 Henrietta Street
Covent Garden, London
WC2E 8LU England

Typeset in Goudy by Circle Graphics, Inc., Columbia, MD

Printer: Maple-Vail Book Manufacturing, York, PA
Cover Designer: Mercury Publishing Services, Rockville, MD

The opinions and statements published are the responsibility of the authors, and such opinions and statements do not necessarily represent the policies of the American Psychological Association.

Library of Congress Cataloging-in-Publication Data

How intimate partner violence affects children : developmental research, case studies, and evidence-based intervention / [edited by] Sandra A. Graham-Bermann and Alytia A. Levendosky. — 1st ed.
   p. cm.
  Includes index.
  ISBN-13: 978-1-4338-0930-9
  ISBN-10: 1-4338-0930-3
  1. Children and violence—Psychological aspects. 2. Intimate partner violence—Psychological aspects. 3. Family violence—Psychological aspects. 4. Children of abused wives. 5. Child development. I. Graham-Bermann, Sandra A. II. Levendosky, Alytia A.

  HQ784.V55H69 2011
  618.92'85822—dc22
                        2010031731

British Library Cataloguing-in-Publication Data

A CIP record is available from the British Library.

Printed in the United States of America
First Edition

doi: 10-1037/12322-000

CONTENTS

CONTRIBUTORS

Linda L. Baker, PhD, CPsych, Centre for Children & Families in the Justice System; Faculty of Education, University of Western Ontario, London, Ontario, Canada

G. Anne Bogat, PhD, Department of Psychology, Michigan State University, East Lansing

Alison Cunningham, MA, Centre for Children & Families in the Justice System, London, Ontario, Canada

William S. Davidson II, PhD, Department of Psychology, Michigan State University, East Lansing

Renee L. DeBoard-Lucas, MS, Department of Psychology, Marquette University, Milwaukee, WI

Manuela A. Diaz, PhD, Child Trauma Research Program, University of California, San Francisco; San Francisco General Hospital

Lauren Earls, MS, Department of Psychology, Eastern Michigan University, Ypsilanti, MI

Sandra A. Graham-Bermann, PhD, Department of Psychology, University of Michigan, Ann Arbor

John H. Grych, PhD, Department of Psychology, Marquette University, Milwaukee, WI

Kathryn H. Howell, MS, Department of Psychology, University of Michigan, Ann Arbor

Alissa C. Huth-Bocks, PhD, Department of Psychology, Eastern Michigan University, Ypsilanti, MI

Ernest N. Jouriles, PhD, Department of Psychology, Southern Methodist University, Dallas, TX

Jessica Latack, MS, Department of Psychology, Eastern Michigan University, Ypsilanti, MI

Alytia A. Levendosky, PhD, Department of Psychology, Michigan State University, East Lansing

Alicia F. Lieberman, PhD, Child Trauma Research Program, University of California, San Francisco; and San Francisco General Hospital

Laura Ann McCloskey, PhD, Department of Kinesiology & Community Health, University of Illinois at Urbana–Champaign

Renee McDonald, PhD, Department of Psychology, Southern Methodist University, Dallas, TX

Laura E. Miller, MS, Department of Psychology, University of Michigan, Ann Arbor

Laura C. Minze, MA, Department of Psychology, Southern Methodist University, Dallas, TX

Tova B. Neugut, MSW, MS, Department of Psychology and School of Social Work, University of Michigan, Ann Arbor

Patricia Van Horn, PhD, Child Trauma Research Program, University of California, San Francisco; San Francisco General Hospital

Alexander von Eye, PhD, Department of Psychology, Michigan State University, East Lansing

ACKNOWLEDGMENTS

This book is the culmination of many decades of research, development, and evaluation. It is a great pleasure to include among our colleagues both former and present graduate students. We thank them for their invaluable assistance, especially those who have contributed chapters to this volume.

We also thank the many families—women and children—who have contributed to this book through the generous sharing of their own lives. We dedicate this book to them and hope that it may further research and programs that will change the lives of families that have experienced intimate partner violence.

Finally, we thank our husbands, Eric Bermann and David Nacht, for their unwavering love and support not only during this project but also over the past few decades.

How Intimate Partner Violence Affects Children

1

INTRODUCTION

SANDRA A. GRAHAM-BERMANN AND ALYTIA A. LEVENDOSKY

Richard has stopped eating and has started biting his mother since he witnessed her being slashed with a bottle across the face by her boyfriend. He is 16 months old. Marrishia is usually very quiet, but she tells the group leader that she once called 911 after her father pushed her mother down the stairs. She is 7 years old. Casey, an 8-year-old girl, says she does not want to get married because she does not think that she can pick the right man. She is just going to adopt children. Adolescent Jerrold was suspended after students reported that he shoved and slapped his girlfriend in the hallway during an argument at the break between classes in his high school.

Each of these children has been an eyewitness to intimate partner violence (IPV) in their home. Yet the expression of their distress and their resulting problems in cognitive, physical, social, and emotional development are different. We know that children's exposure to IPV is not rare. Recent surveys and studies show that approximately 20% to 30% of married or cohabiting couples engage in physical violence annually (Kessler, Molnar, Feurer, & Applebaum, 2001). By extrapolation, at least 15.5 million children are estimated to be exposed to IPV, with 7 million exposed to severe IPV every year in the United States (McDonald, Jouriles, Ramisetty-Mikler, Caetano, &

Green, 2006). Children exposed to IPV also suffer disproportionately high levels of child abuse and physical injuries (Graham-Bermann & Howell, 2010; Johnsona et al., 2002; Smith Slep & O'Leary, 2005). As many as 40% of children exposed to IPV also experience overlapping child abuse (Finkelhor, Ormrod, & Turner, 2009; Herrenkohl, Sousa, Tajima, Herrenkohl, & Moylan, 2008).

We know much about the ways in which IPV affects children of different ages, and we know that these effects are pronounced and significant. Meta-analyses consistently report more than half of school-age children exposed to IPV have mental health problems in the clinical range, such as depression, anxiety, and conduct disorder (Chan & Yeung, 2009; Rhoades, 2008; Sternberg, Baradaran, Abbott, Lamb, & Guterman, 2006; Wolfe, Crooks, Lee, McIntyre-Smith, & Jaffe, 2003). For example, one meta-analysis of 61 studies by Evans, Davies, and DiLillo (2008) showed that IPV exposure predicted children's internalizing behavioral problems (effect size $d = 0.48$), externalizing problems ($d = 0.47$), and symptoms of traumatic stress ($d = 1.54$). The rates may be even higher for younger children because they are more likely to be exposed to IPV than children of other ages (Fantuzzo & Fusco, 2007). Teenagers have their own constellation of difficulties, including increased risk of delinquency, dating violence, substance use, or abuse. In sum, children exposed to IPV are many, and the need for clinical interventions on their behalf is great.

In this volume, we present a developmental perspective on the consequences of children's exposure to IPV and on interventions that have been designed to help them. More specifically, we provide a developmentally framed description of the heterogeneity of children's functioning in the context of exposure to IPV across childhood. We also provide state-of-the-art information on evidence-based practices that illustrate the challenges and successes of working with children exposed to IPV. Finally, we provide rich clinical case presentations that illustrate the central constructs of interest at each age period, as well as the methods and measures used in the assessments. Thus, this book melds basic research with clinical practice and demonstrates evidence-based practices at their best.

THE NEED FOR THIS BOOK

Previous books on the effects of children's exposure to IPV have made important contributions to the research and clinical work in this field. When these volumes were first produced (e.g., starting with Holden, Geffner, & Jouriles, 1998), the chapters generally introduced the field of research on violence against women and children. However, these volumes presented no clinical cases and described few interventions. Little was known about the effectiveness of interventions at that time. Since then, the field has advanced considerably so that today we have much more research on the effects of exposure to IPV for children of different ages, more sophisticated clinical insights on how to work with children exposed to IPV, and, most recently, a growing number of successful evidence-based intervention programs.

Moreover, we now have a set of important longitudinal studies addressing the mechanisms involved in effects of IPV on children, and some interventions for this population have been empirically validated. Thus, the current volume includes descriptions of the findings of these longitudinal studies and the data on effective interventions.

It is important to note that many of these advances have been spurred by national research centers that have called for the use of evidence-based treatments—that is, intervention programs that have been demonstrably effective with particular groups, or children of certain ages, or those with specific diagnoses, when providing services to children and adolescents, including children exposed to IPV (National Advisory Mental Health Council Workgroup on Child and Adolescent Mental Health Intervention and Development and Deployment, 2001; Office of the Surgeon General, 2004; President's New Freedom Commission on Mental Health, 2003). As of yet, however, few shelters and community clinics provide evidence-based services specifically designed to assist the abused women and their children who seek help. Meta-analyses have shown evidence-based treatments to be more effective than treatments as usual, with effect sizes that, although initially in the small to medium range, increase somewhat over time (Weisz, Jensen-Doss, & Hawley, 2006). Studies have also found minority and Caucasian groups to have similar rates of success with evidence-based treatments. As illustrated in this book, the most effective evidence-based treatments are produced when researchers work in collaboration with mental health providers to evaluate and adapt treatments for specific community contexts (Weisz, Sandler, Durlak, & Anton, 2005). Examples of such collaborations appear in this volume, along with accounts of age-specific intervention programs designed to address a given range of the developmental needs of children exposed to IPV.

DEVELOPMENTAL PATHWAYS OF IPV EFFECTS

There are multiple pathways of functioning that children may follow in response to IPV. The developmental perspective begins in this book with an understanding of the first possible effects of IPV on the child—in utero—and continues through late adolescence. The developmental pathways are in part determined by the age at which children are exposed to violence and their historical and concurrent risk and protective factors, which either promote or enhance vulnerability or resilience in the face of IPV. Effects of IPV may occur at the physiological, behavioral, and/or emotional level, and the effects may be seen in their relationships with peers, romantic partners, parents, other authority figures, and with society more generally.

Using a developmental psychopathology perspective to integrate the research findings presented in this book, we can imagine a tree with many branches, all leading in slightly different directions, as depicted by Sroufe (1997) in his seminal piece, "Psychopathology as an Outcome of Development." Successive branching may lead to maladaptive or adaptive development, following different paths along the way, some veering into dysfunction prior to adaptive development and others beginning with adaptive functioning eventually leading to maladaptation. Sroufe argues that there are at least five implications of the developmental psychopathology model, and these can be used to interpret the effects of IPV on children's developmental outcomes. First, psychopathology is a result of developmental deviations over time. For example, a deviation from normality in attachment during infancy puts the child at risk for problematic peer relationships during school-age. Second, there are multiple pathways that may lead to similar developmental outcomes: the concept of equifinality. Thus, exposure to IPV or being directly physically abused both put the child at risk for aggressive behavior during school-age and adolescence. Third, multifinality suggests that the same pathway, in this case exposure to IPV, can lead to heterogeneous outcomes. That is clear from the research chapters in this book, which show that some children have a more externalizing trajectory whereas others have a more internalizing trajectory and some appear to be resilient to the effects of IPV exposure. The fourth and fifth maxims are about change: Change can occur at any time, and change is simultaneously somewhat constrained by prior functioning. Thus, changes in the life circumstances of the child and/or developmental changes in the child can facilitate positive or negative trajectory changes in the context of risk. However, it is also true that developmental deviations build on each other so that prior maladaptation makes future adaptation less likely and more difficult.

In this context of developmental psychopathology, we can begin to understand developmental pathways as they begin during pregnancy through the adolescent period. This book uses this perspective to understand the particular vulnerabilities for children at each of the developmental eras. The effects of IPV may begin during pregnancy through the mother's representations of her unborn child. The effects of IPV play out in the parenting relationship and ultimately in the quality of the attachment relationship and begin even before the children witness the violence with their eyes. The attachment relationship, a fundamental block in early child development, which has been linked to later child and adult functioning (Carlson, Sroufe, & Egeland, 2004), is clearly affected by the prenatal IPV, and thus the child is placed on an at-risk developmental trajectory from this early exposure. If the child witnesses IPV during the formation of the attachment relationship, he or she is also placed on an at-risk developmental trajectory in response to the traumatic exposure. However, trajectories may also change at this point. For example, if mothers have more balanced representations by 1-year postpartum, they are more likely to use better parenting strategies than those who maintain disengaged or distorted representations. Thus, changes in the parenting behaviors due to changes in maternal mental health, income, or IPV can lead to a positive trajectory of change for the developing infant.

The child's exposure to IPV during the preschool years is further complicated by the beginning development of social relationships and normative aggressive behavior. These normal developmental milestones (capacity for both social relationships with nonfamily members and capacity for aggression) can become vulnerable to the effects of the traumatic exposure to IPV. Children's worldviews and social and emotional responses to the world begin to develop during this period and thus are vulnerable to the effects of violence within their family. Several risk and protective factors for this age group have been established, including resilient coping and positive parenting. These positive factors, among others at the level of the individual child or the family, are related to resilient functioning for these young children exposed to IPV. Thus, developmental trajectories begin to show quite heterogeneous outcomes for preschool-age children with some demonstrating positive functioning and others continuing down at-risk pathways, supporting at least three of the assumptions of the developmental psychopathology model: multifinality, constraint on change, and potential for change.

School-age children begin to show a wide variety of developmental trajectories in response to IPV, including internalizing behavior problems, externalizing behavior problems, both internalizing and externalizing, and resilience. Effects of IPV are evident in their social relationships, including reactive and proactive aggressive behavior with peers, as well as in their academic functioning, with many children exposed to IPV falling below grade level in their academic performance. While the trajectory of normative aggression decreases in the school-age years, children exposed to IPV are more likely to display higher levels of aggression in their peer relationships, thus placing them at risk for social developmental problems as they move into adolescence. This point illustrates the first assumption of the developmental psychopathology model, which is that psychopathology is a function of deviation over time.

Finally, during the transition to adolescence, a number of new at-risk developmental trajectories are possible, including early pregnancy, delinquent and criminal behavior, and drug abuse. The pathways, which began earlier in childhood, begin to come to fruition in adolescence, potentially sending these youth on negative trajectories into early adulthood, following caring for a child, dropping out of high school, and landing in the juvenile justice system. However, there remain a number of resilient adolescents, some of whom have followed positive developmental trajectories since birth and others who experience a positive change in their trajectories due to the presence of protective factors and/or in response to developmental change.

THEORETICAL UNDERSTANDING OF IPV EFFECTS ON CHILDREN

In addition to the attachment/psychodynamic theory described above, a number of sometimes overlapping theories help to explain the heterogeneous effects of IPV on children's developmental trajectories across these different levels of the individual. For example, social learning theory posits that children learn by imitation, role modeling, and reinforcement, the kinds of behaviors that are acceptable in relationships and used in response to conflict (Bandura, 1973). Thus, children raised in families with IPV might be expected to use aggression in response to stress and psychological maltreatment in their interpersonal relationships because that is what they have learned to do at home, through direct reinforcement or by inconsistent messages from parents (Fosco, DeBoard, & Grych, 2007; Patterson, 1982).

Not all of the effects of IPV are related to interpersonal aggression and inappropriate conflict resolution skills. Trauma theory has been used to explain some of the symptoms shown by children that are associated with exposure to traumatic violence that are not learned behaviors, such as nightmares, developmental regressions, hypervigilance, and heightened physiological reactivity (Graham-Bermann et al., 2008). Other theories hypothesize that how children think about and process the experience of violence determines their reactions to it and their coping. For example, the emotional security theory (Davies & Cummings, 1994; Cummings & Davies, 1995) posits that IPV threatens children's secure relationships with their parents and affects how they regulate their emotions. In turn, children's efforts to seek and achieve emotional security affect their adjustment. According to social cognition theory, children also develop social scripts, or social cognitions, over time from their earliest family experiences, including exposure to IPV. For example, studies have shown that children exposed to IPV have more extreme attitudes and beliefs about the acceptability of violence, particularly by males, relative to children in nonviolent families (Graham-Bermann & Brescoll, 2000; Graham-Bermann, Lynch, Banyard, DeVoe, & Halabu, 2007). As a consequence, these children's social relationships may be challenged and diminished with different consequences at each stage of their development.

These theories are used variously throughout this book to describe the effects of IPV on children of different ages and to frame the interventions designed to help them. There is little research evidence on the success of prevention programs for children of different ages, and clinical cases describing prevention are rare, given that clinical treatment usually involves addressing some aspect of dysfunction. We discuss the topic of prevention programs for children exposed to IPV as an area for future research in the concluding chapter.

FORMAT AND ORGANIZATION OF THIS BOOK

This book is divided into four sections by children's age group—from prenatal to infancy, children who are preschool-age, school-age children, and adolescents. Within each age group, there are three chapters highlighting (a) a review of research studies on the effects of IPV; (b) a description of intervention programs and their attendant evaluations, honed to address the children's developmental issues; and (c) a clinical case that illustrates age-specific concerns.

Hence, the research chapters describe the latest findings on the effects of IPV on children in each age group. Studies are presented using a developmental framework of risk and protective factors that can influence how children respond to family violence. Research scientists who are expert in studying the effects on children in particular age groups share what they have learned about the effects of family violence on children.

Each intervention chapter is written by a clinical researcher who has created and evaluated developmentally appropriate programs for children of specific ages exposed to IPV. These chapters include a description of the program, its theoretical underpinnings, and evidence for the program's efficacy, including effect sizes, as well as for who each program is most successful and suitable. The challenges of developing, testing, and implementing evidence-based practices for this field are highlighted throughout the intervention chapters.

The clinical case chapters illustrate the complexity of cases for each age group—these cases often include traumatic events other than IPV, such as child sexual abuse. Assessment techniques and theories of change are presented to provide a framework for understanding the treatment approach and its results. The cases presented in this book are amalgamated or combined cases to protect the identity of those women and children whose stories are included here. That is, the cases were based, in part, on actual clinical cases and, in part, on common issues presented during research interviews with women and children of particular ages.

Recommendations for future studies are found in the final, concluding chapter, while discussion questions related to each section of the book are provided in the Appendix.

Part I: Prenatal to Infancy

To locate the issues relevant to IPV during pregnancy and the neonatal period, Bogat, Levendosky, von Eye, and Davidson (Chapter 2) use research on attachment theory to explain the effects of IPV on the mother-infant relationship. A rich description of attachment theory is provided, including the theory about maternal representations developed during pregnancy. The empirical findings concerning attachment in the context of IPV are also reviewed, yet the primary focus of the chapter is the authors' longitudinal prospective study of IPV beginning during pregnancy. Results for the impact on the mother-child attachment relationship through age 4 are presented and discussed. This chapter highlights the role of maternal representations and parenting behavior on early attachment relationships and in doing so gives the reader a new perspective on the ways in which even the very youngest children can be affected by exposure to IPV.

Lieberman, Diaz, and Van Horn (Chapter 3) were the first to design and test the efficacy of an intervention for the perinatal period focusing on the parent-child relationship, beginning during pregnancy and continuing through at least age 6 months. They describe assessments of maternal and child functioning that are done at the beginning of treatment (pregnancy for the mother and postpartum for the infant) and are repeated at the end of treatment. This multimodal treatment includes psychoeducation about the effects of IPV on mothers and infants, practical aid to mothers around their needs for support during this period, mindfulness about parenting and infant massage, guidance about normal pregnancy and child development, and insight-oriented interpretations around maternal feelings and behaviors, and the child's responses. This chapter concludes with a presentation of the evidence for the effectiveness of their treatment program.

Huth-Bocks, Earls, and Latack (Chapter 4) describe the case of a 12-month-old boy who was having behavior problems, including aggressive behavior, and who appeared temperamentally difficult. His mother experienced IPV from his father during her pregnancy and in the first postpartum year. The mother had recently separated from the father and was living on her own with her infant son. She was seeking help for herself and her son because she wanted him to be happy again. The evaluation involved interviews with the mother, a semistructured interview to assess her maternal representations, and home and clinic observations of the mother and son interaction. The case conceptualization relied on attachment theory and treatment recommendations were for attachment-based therapy (parent–infant psychotherapy) for the mother–infant dyad with the goals of improving the attachment relationship between mother and son and maintaining a violence-free home.

Part II: Toddler to Early Childhood

Research on the effects specific to exposure to IPV during the preschool-age period is presented by Howell and Graham-Bermann (Chapter 5). The vulnerabilities during the preschool-age period are highlighted in terms of the amount of exposure and the child's limited capacity to understand and to modulate affect in response to IPV. A diverse range of outcomes is critically reviewed from studies of neurological damage, internalizing and externalizing behavior problems, cognitive functioning, physical health, and the newer field of posttraumatic stress disorder in preschool-age children exposed to IPV. The role of parents, including fathers, in children's adjustment following exposure to IPV is reported as well. This chapter contributes to our knowledge of young children's strengths and their resilient coping in the face of toxic family experiences. By identifying which risk factors contribute to dysfunction and which protective factors are associated with positive coping, the authors have attempted to provide a balanced and nuanced picture that incorporates both the complexities of the problem and state of the field.

McDonald, Jouriles, and Minze (Chapter 6) focus on interventions for preschool-age children exposed to IPV. They begin with a thoughtful presentation of the age-specific problems that interventions might address and then introduce a range of theories of what might contribute to the expression of those problems for young children. They illustrate how the theories on which interventions are based indicate the parameters of the treatments designed to assist these children. The chapter describes the ways in which one highly successful intervention program, Project Support, was developed and tested. This is an evidence-based treatment for preschool-age children diagnosed with conduct disorder following exposure to IPV. Results for the evaluation of this intervention are presented and include both a short-term and, more important, a long-term follow up analysis of change. Relative to those who did not participate in the intervention, young children with conduct disorder had fewer externalizing problems over time. They report that changes in mothers' parenting played a mediating role in the children's recovery—a finding that leads to a thoughtful discussion of what contributes to program success for this age group.

The clinical case presentation of Chris, age 5, by Neugut and Miller (Chapter 7) explores issues related to assessing the effects of IPV on young children, including the contribution of the intergenerational transmission of violence from the mother's family of origin. This chapter highlights the role that many ongoing risk factors can play in contributing to dysfunction and challenging the recovery of this mother and her children and frames the evaluation in terms of trauma theory. Detailed information on the assessments of the mother's violence experiences and mental health is provided with scores on standardized instruments that measure violence experiences, depression and posttraumatic stress. Results of the assessments that were conducted at various stages in Chris's evaluation and treatment are used to show whether and how the treatment he received was effective and what issues remained for further consideration.

Part III: School-Age Children

DeBoard-Lucas and Grych (Chapter 8) present findings from the research on consequences of exposure to IPV on school-age children. This is the most highly studied age group among children exposed to IPV; therefore; the evidence for a range of developmental challenges and disturbances is presented. The authors review the studies, focusing on their methodological differences—for example, longitudinal studies or person-centered approaches. In addition, they offer methodological critiques of these studies, including controversies over the conceptualization of IPV, the measurement of IPV, and questions about the specificity of IPV as a risk factor, given its common co-occurrence with other risk factors. Finally, the authors review the most common theoretical frameworks used to explain the effects of IPV on school-age children and offer ideas about future research directions.

Graham-Bermann's chapter on intervention for school-age children (Chapter 9) begins with a historical and critical review of research on group interventions for children and/or their mothers exposed to IPV. The chapter focuses primarily on a description and evaluation of the Kids' Club Program—a 10-week group intervention for school-age children exposed to IPV. This program focuses on helping children to process their traumatic experiences in the context of other children who have had similar experiences and addresses the most common consequences of exposure to IPV, such as self-blame, and use of aggression to solve interpersonal conflict. A detailed description of how the program was evaluated is provided, along with reference to the challenges and rewards of applying the highest evaluation standards used in clinical trials to the realities of community intervention studies. This program, along with the concurrent parenting program for mothers, was found to be effective in reducing externalizing and internalizing behavior problems and enhancing children's attitudes and beliefs about the acceptability of violence in their lives, with the best results found for children whose mothers also participated in the treatment.

Levendosky and Graham-Bermann (Chapter 10) describe the case of a 9-year-old girl who witnessed IPV between her parents, with suspected sexual abuse by her older brother. The case was complicated because her parents had recently separated due to IPV and her father, who favored the other children in the family over her, had rejected her. This traumatized girl was referred by her therapist from a group psychoeducational treatment program for children exposed to IPV. She was referred for evaluation and for possible individual treatment at a university-based clinic based on her noticeable difficulties in getting along with other children, her verbal aggression, name calling, and recent academic difficulties despite her above-average intelligence. The evaluation sessions are presented in rich detail, as well as considerations in the clinical formulation of the case that relied on rely on attachment and trauma theories. Treatment recommendations included play therapy for the girl and parent guidance for her mother, as well as continuation in the IPV treatment groups.

Part IV: Adolescents

McCloskey (Chapter 11) reviews the research on whether and how IPV affects adolescents. We are reminded that research on adolescents exposed to IPV remains at an early stage in contrast to the substantially larger body of research focusing on younger children. The review of outcome studies highlights both the commonalities of adolescents' experiences following exposure to IPV and the unique age-related features, such their heightened risk for delinquency, depression, substance abuse, and dating violence. The developmental differences in the meaning of common outcomes are also discussed. Methodological challenges in studying the effects of IPV in adolescents are also thoughtfully presented, including problems encountered when assessing and controlling for the diverse and associated array of risk factors that can accumulate and contribute to effects on adolescents over time.

The implications for intervention of adolescents' experiences with IPV are considered by Cunningham and Baker (Chapter 12). After describing the prevalence data, they suggest reasons why adolescents are underrepresented in research studies of children exposed to IPV and give evidence from research studies. They review key developmentally sensitive issues for adolescents and reframe them in terms of mechanisms of influence for the effects of IPV on teenagers. Among these issues are abusive male role models, erosion of the mother–child bond, isolation from helpful supports, co-occurring adversities, and problematic coping strategies. The authors also describe ways in which IPV can shape children's family roles. Specific intervention strategies for a range of individual teenagers' issues are presented.

The clinical case of an adolescent boy evaluated by Levendosky (Chapter 13) illustrates the complexity of some IPV cases and the range of issues they may present. This chapter shows the unfolding of the story of a teenager who was exposed to severe IPV and taken hostage by his stepfather. Presenting problems included uncharacteristic acting out in school, being truant from school, and displays of extreme anger at his mother. The comprehensive evaluation took place during several weeks and included individual sessions with the adolescent and the mother. A thoughtful recounting of the themes presented during the evaluation sessions, combined with the results of standardized assessments, revealed that this adolescent had been traumatized by his experiences. Fine details of the individual sessions, as well as a recounting of the risk and protective factors in this case, illustrate the ways in which the symptoms of teenagers' traumatic stress may be expressed.

CONCLUSION

We believe that the information provided in this book is needed by therapists, researchers, and graduate students in psychology, social work, marriage and family work, and children's health who work with IPV victims and their families. Professionals in settings where IPV is prevalent, such as outpatient clinics and battered women's shelters, will find the book particularly beneficial. Above all, we seek to impart the latest knowledge and demonstrate clinical science at its best.

REFERENCES

Bandura, A. (1973). *Aggression: social learning analysis*. Englewood Cliffs, NJ: Prentice-Hall.

Carlson, E. A., Sroufe, L. A., & Egeland, B. (2004). The construction of experience: A longitudinal study of representation and behavior. *Child Development, 75*, 66–83. doi:10.1111/j.1467-8624.2004.00654.x

Chan, Y. C., & Yeung, J. W. K. (2009). Children living with violence within the family and its sequel: A meta-analysis from 1995–2006. *Aggression and Violent Behavior, 14*, 313–322. doi:10.1016/j.avb.2009.04.001

Cummings, E. M., & Davies, P. T. (1995). The impact of parents on their children: An emotional security perspective. *Annals of child development: A research annual* (Vol. 10, pp. 167–208). London, England: Jessica Kingsley.

Davies, P. T., & Cummings, E. M. (1994). Marital conflict and child adjustment: An emotional security hypothesis. *Psychological Bulletin, 116*, 387–411. doi:10.1037/0033-2909.116.3.387

Evans, S. E., Davies, C., & DiLillo, D. (2008). Exposure to domestic violence: A meta-analysis of child and adolescent outcomes. *Aggression and Violent Behavior, 13*, 131–140. doi:10.1016/j.avb.2008.02.005

Fantuzzo, J. W., & Fusco, R. A. (2007). Children's direct exposure to types of domestic violence crime: A population-based investigation. *Journal of Family Violence, 22,* 543–552. doi:10.1007/s10896-007-9105-z

Finkelhor, D., Ormrod, R. K., & Turner, H. A. (2009). The developmental epidemiology of childhood victimization. *Journal of Interpersonal Violence, 24,* 711–731. doi:10.1177/0886260508317185

Fosco, G. M., DeBoard, R. L., & Grych, J. H. (2007). Making sense of family violence: Implications of children's appraisals of interparental aggression for their short- and long-term functioning. *European Psychologist, 12*(1), 6–16. doi:10.1027/1016-9040.12.1.6

Graham-Bermann, S. A., & Brescoll, V. (2000). Gender, power, and violence: Assessing the family stereotypes of the children of batterers. *Journal of Family Psychology, 14,* 600–612. doi:10.1037/0893-3200.14.4.600

Graham-Bermann, S. A., & Howell, K. H. (2010). Child abuse in the context of intimate partner violence. In J. E. B. Myers (Ed.), *APSAC handbook on child maltreatment* (3rd ed.). Thousand Oaks, CA: Sage.

Graham-Bermann, S. A., Howell, K. H., Habarth, J., Krishnan, S., Loree, A., & Bermann, E. A. (2008). Toward assessing traumatic events and stress symptoms in preschool children from low-income families. *American Journal of Orthopsychiatry, 78,* 220–228. doi:10.1037/a0013977

Graham-Bermann, S. A., Lynch, S., Banyard, V., DeVoe, E., & Halabu, H. (2007). Community based intervention for children exposed to intimate partner violence: An efficacy trial. *Journal of Consulting and Clinical Psychology, 75,* 199–209. doi:10.1037/0022-006X.75.2.199

Herrenkohl, T. I., Sousa, C., Tajima, E. A., Herrenkohl, R. C., & Moylan, C. A. (2008). Intersection of child abuse and children's exposure to domestic violence. *Trauma, Violence & Abuse, 9*(2), 84–99. doi:10.1177/1524838008314797

Holden, G. W., Geffner, R., & Jouriles, E. N. (Eds.). (1998). *Children and marital violence: Theory, research, and intervention.* Washington, DC: American Psychological Association.

Johnsona, R. M., Kotch, J. B., Catellier, D. J., Windsor, J. R., Dufort, V., Hunter, W., & Amaya-Jackson, L. (2002). Adverse behavioral and emotional outcomes from child abuse and witnessed violence. *Child Maltreatment, 7,* 179–186. doi:10.1177/1077559502007003001

Kessler, R. C., Molnar, B. E., Feurer, I. D., & Applebaum, M. (2001). Patterns and mental health predictors of domestic violence in the United States: Results from the National Comorbidity Survey. *International Journal of Law and Psychiatry, 24,* 487–508. doi:10.1016/S0160-2527(01)00080-2

McDonald, R., Jouriles, E. N., Ramisetty-Mikler, S., Caetano, R., & Green, C. E. (2006). Estimating the number of American children living in partner-violent families. *Journal of Family Psychology, 20*(1), 137–142. doi:10.1037/0893-3200.20.1.137

National Advisory Mental Health Council Workgroup on Child and Adolescent Mental Health Intervention Development and Deployment. (2001). *Blue-print for change: Research on child and adolescent mental health.* Rockville, MD: U.S. Department of Health and Human Services, Public Health Service, National Institutes of Health.

Office of the Surgeon General. (2004). *Report of the Surgeon General's Conference on Children's Mental Health: A national action agenda.* Rockville, MD: U.S. Department of Health and Human Services.

Patterson, G. R. (1982). *Coercive family process.* Eugene, OR: Castalia.

President's New Freedom Commission on Mental Health. (2003). *Achieving the promise: Transforming mental health care in America: Final report* (DHHS Publication No. SMA-03-3832). Rockville, MD: Author.

Rhoades, K. A. (2008). Children's responses to interparental conflict: A meta-analysis of their associations with child adjustment. *Child Development, 79,* 1942–1956. doi:10.1111/j.1467-8624.2008.01235.x

Smith Slep, A. M., & O'Leary, S. G. (2005). Parent and partner violence in families with young children: Rates, patterns, and connections. *Journal of Consulting and Clinical Psychology, 73,* 435–444. doi:10.1037/0022-006X.73.3.435

Sroufe, L. A. (1997). Psychopathology as an outcome of development. *Development and Psychopathology, 9,* 251–268. doi:10.1017/S0954579497002046

Sternberg, K., Baradaran, L., Abbott, C., Lamb, M., & Guterman, E. (2006). Type of violence, age, and gender differences in the effects of family violence on children's behavior problems: A mega-analysis. *Developmental Review, 26,* 89–112. doi:10.1016/j.dr.2005.12.001

Weisz, J. R., Jensen-Doss, A., & Hawley, K. M. (2006). Evidence based youth psychotherapies versus usual clinical care: A meta-analysis of direct comparisons. *American Psychologist, 61,* 671–689. doi:10.1037/0003-066X.61.7.671

Weisz, J. R., Sandler, I. N., Durlak, J. A., & Anton, B. S. (2005). Promoting and protecting youth mental health through evidence-based prevention and treatment. *American Psychologist, 60,* 628–648. doi:10.1037/0003-066X.60.6.628

Wolfe, D. A., Crooks, C. V., Lee, V., McIntyre-Smith, A., & Jaffe, P. (2003). The effects of children's exposure to domestic violence: A meta-analysis and critique. *Clinical Child and Family Psychology Review, 6,* 171–187. doi:10.1023/A:1024910416164

I

PRENATAL TO INFANCY

2

EFFECTS OF INTIMATE PARTNER VIOLENCE ON THE ATTACHMENT RELATIONSHIP BETWEEN MOTHER AND CHILD: DATA FROM A LONGITUDINAL STUDY BEGINNING DURING PREGNANCY

G. ANNE BOGAT, ALYTIA A. LEVENDOSKY, ALEXANDER von EYE, AND WILLIAM S. DAVIDSON II

This chapter reviews findings regarding attachment and intimate partner violence (IPV) from the Mother Infant Study, a longitudinal study of 206 women and children. We discuss attachment theory as it relates to both child attachment classifications and maternal representations of the child and the relationship with the child. Attachment is relevant to understanding the mother–child relationship in families with IPV. IPV occurs in the context of a significant attachment relationship in the mother's life (i.e., her romantic partner), thus likely influencing her internal working models of self and others, including the developing internal representations of herself as a mother and of her infant. In fact, the impact of IPV on mothers' representations may be particularly salient during pregnancy because this is the time in which women are forming and reorganizing representations of themselves and their infants (Cohen & Slade, 2000; George & Solomon, 1999). In addition, the chronic, ongoing trauma of IPV is likely to impair the woman's capacity for sensitive parenting after her child is born, another factor that is directly linked to child attachment (De Wolff & Van IJzendoorn, 1997). In this chapter, we first describe attachment theory, with a special focus on maternal representations and infant attachment. We then discuss the methodology of the longitudinal study and results relevant to attachment beginning during pregnancy through age 4.

ATTACHMENT THEORY

Overview

Attachment theory proposes that development occurs through transactions between the child and his or her caregiving environment (Bowlby, 1969/1982; Sroufe, Carlson, Levy, & Egeland, 1999). *Attachment* is the child's behavioral manifestation of internal working models or representations of the relationship with the primary caregiver, usually the mother, and focuses on the emotional security within the context of the parent–child relationship (Bowlby, 1969/1982; Sroufe et al., 1999). Attachment behavior becomes consolidated as predictable patterns of behavior within the mother–infant dyad, and these patterns of behavior serve to regulate emotions and emotional interactions. As the child ages, the dyadic emotional regulation system developed in the infant–mother relationship becomes increasingly internalized (Ainsworth, 1989). Thus, the initial working models developed in the context of the caregiving relationship serve as templates for the child's interactions with others, including peers and teachers (Bowlby, 1969/1982; Sroufe et al., 1999). The child then evokes particular, predictable behavior from others based on the internalized relationship with the primary caregiver; for example, hostility and aggression expressed by the child discourages teacher involvement and evokes negative behavior from peers (Sroufe et al., 1999). The function of the internal working models is to guide behaviors in close relationships by offering a template or heuristic for how individuals should anticipate and interpret the behavior of others with whom they have intimate relationships.

Individual differences in child attachment have been typically categorized into four types: secure, avoidant, ambivalent, and disorganized, most commonly measured through a procedure known as the Strange Situation (SS; Ainsworth, Blehar, Waters, & Wall, 1978). The SS is a 22-min laboratory procedure in which the child and mother participate in eight episodes of play, separation, and reunion. During the separation, the child is left with a stranger (the experimenter). The series of episodes is considered mildly to moderately stressful for the young child and, thus, induces particular attachment behaviors, such as crying, clinging, and withdrawal. Most children (approximately 65% in low-risk samples) are classified as securely attached (for a review, see Slade & Aber, 1992). Secure attachment is characterized by the child's confidence in the mother's emotional availability and responsiveness to his or her needs. During the SS, the securely attached child may be distressed when the mother leaves and will show preference for the mother (rather than the experimenter), when she returns, by seeking proximity and contact with her. This child is easily soothed and returns to play on being comforted (Carlson & Sroufe, 1995; Slade & Aber, 1992). The remaining children are categorized as insecurely attached through one of three attachment classifications. Children who lack confidence in their mother's caregiving and expect rejection from her are classified as having an avoidant attachment (approximately 20% to 25%). These children show little distress at separation, they actively avoid her on reunion, and they typically appear indifferent to her (Carlson & Sroufe, 1995; Slade & Aber, 1992). Children with an ambivalent attachment style (approximately 10% to 15%) are unsure about the likelihood of responsiveness from the mother, presumably because she has been inconsistently available to them. These children are preoccupied with the mother during the SS, are inconsolable when she leaves, and are not easily soothed when she returns. They may also show anger toward her by simultaneously seeking and resisting contact (Carlson & Sroufe, 1995; Slade & Aber, 1992). Finally, disorganized attachment (less than 10% in low-risk samples) is characterized by a lack of a coherent strategy for coping with the stress of separation from the mother (Van IJzendoorn, Schuengel, & Bakermans-Kranenburg, 1999). These children may show apprehensive, depressed, and bizarre behaviors, and even disorientation (Main & Solomon, 1990). This final classification has been associated with abusive and neglectful parenting (Carlson, Cicchetti, Barnett, & Braunwald, 1989) and is rarely found in low-risk populations.

There is also evidence for a genetic influence on attachment. A study conducted with adult adoptees found that the short variant of the 5-HTTLPR allele was related to more unresolved attachment during the Adult Attachment Interview (Caspers et al., 2009). (Unresolved/disorganized attachment is exemplified by adults who show momentary problems in reasoning and speech when discussing loss or abuse. This attachment status in caregivers is thought to predict infant disorganized attachment.) The authors note that their findings are consonant with explanations that relate attachment disorders to problematic changes in the emotion regulation system. Because the prefrontal cortexes and amygdala are involved with emotional experiencing, "the presence of the 5-HTTLPR short allele may influence the interconnectivity between these brain regions . . . thereby increasing susceptibility to the disorganizing effects of elevated affective intensity experienced during discussions of loss" (Caspers et al., 2009, p. 72).

Other associated research has focused on the dopaminergic system as it relates to a possible genetic susceptibility for disorganized attachment (Bakermans-Kranenburg, Van IJzendoorn, & Kroonenberg, 2004; Gervai et al., 2007; Lakatos et al., 2000, 2002; Van IJzendoorn & Bakermans-Kranenburg, 2006). Although the findings have not been consistent, researchers propose that disorganized attachment, in which infant behavior is erratic and characterized by freezing, wandering, and approach/avoidance of the mother, is a specific problem related to the regulation of fear.

The general stability of attachment behavior over time constitutes evidence for a genetic basis for attachment. However, because attachment is open to modification and can be influenced by changes in the environment (Bowlby, 1969/1982; De Wolff & Van IJzendoorn, 1997; Moss, Cyr, Bureau, Tarabulsy, & Dubois-Comtois, 2005; Waters, Merrick, Treboux, Crowell, & Albersheim, 2000; Weinfield, Whaley, & Egeland, 2004), environmental influences are still considered important. The attachment relationships with the primary caregivers can be modified in a positive or negative direction during infancy and childhood in response to changes in the family environment. In addition, the security of attachment has implications for the child beyond the family as attachment has been related to later child functioning, specifically social functioning (Carlson & Sroufe, 1995; Elicker, Englund, & Sroufe, 1992).

Recently, researchers have turned their attention to elucidating factors that influence the mother's contribution to the infant's attachment. In the next section, we discuss one of these factors, prepartum representations of the mother, and how these influence infant attachment once the baby is born.

Prepartum Representations

During the second trimester of pregnancy, mothers begin to develop specific representations/schemas of their unborn infants and their own, imagined parenting behavior (Stern, 1995). These are likely constructed from the mother's experiences of being parented (Cohen & Slade, 2000; Stern, 1995). While the caregiving behavioral system begins to develop during adolescence, interactions between the biological (including hormonal and neurological) and psychological changes (cognitive representations and affective responses) associated with pregnancy bring the caregiving behavioral system to maturity (George & Solomon, 1999). George and Solomon (1999) theorized that the caregiving behavioral system complements the attachment behavioral system. The focus of the attachment system is to maintain proximity to the caregiver; the complementary focus of the caregiving system is to provide protection to the infant. Thus, the mutuality of both systems, working in conjunction, ensures that the child will survive. The internal representations, which the mother develops at the time of quickening, is one element of the caregiving behavioral system.

Some research supports George and Solomon's theory. For example, maternal representations of the infant and of the self as a mother were complementary to each other (Ammaniti, 1991; Ammaniti et al., 1992). In addition, women's maternal prepartum representations were similar to the ways in which mothers viewed their relationships with their own mothers (Slade & Cohen, 1996). Pregnant women who reported emotional warmth from their mothers, compared with those who did not, also reported more affectionate relationships with their unborn child (Siddiqui, Hägglöf, & Eisemann, 2000). However, Pajulo, Helenius, and Mayes (2006) found that in addition to the woman's relationship with her own mother, contextual factors, such as number of young children or planned/unplanned pregnancies, also influence prepartum representations.

Maternal representations are commonly elicited from a structured interview, the Working Model of the Child Interview (Zeanah, Benoit, Hirshberg, Barton, & Regan, 1994). The interview asks questions about the mother's expectations about her child's behavior and personality, her relationship with her infant, and her sense of herself as a mother. Representations can be coded as either balanced or one of two types of nonbalanced: disengaged or distorted. Balanced narratives demonstrate an integration of negative and positive feelings about the child, are rich in their descriptions of the child, and give a sense of the mother's healthy absorption in her relationship with the child. Disengaged narratives are characterized by a cool emotional tone and the mother's lack of emotional involvement with her child. Distorted narratives tend to be inconsistent in content and process and demonstrate the mother's inability to focus on her child as an autonomous individual; they also are characterized by the mother's preoccupation with her child. While mothers develop these maternal representations during pregnancy, they may be modified over time as a result of the mother's relationship with her child after birth (Fava Viziello, Antonioli, Cocci, & Invernizzi, 1993; Theran, Levendosky, Bogat, & Huth-Bocks, 2005). Also, research indicates that there is stability in these representations from pregnancy to the 1st year of the infant's life (Benoit, Parker, & Zeanah, 1997; Slade & Cohen, 1996).

Importantly, the mother's internal representations affect both the mother and the infant after the birth of the child. For example, women's attachment representations (measured by the AAI) predict infant attachment after birth (Benoit & Parker, 1994; Fonagy, Steele, Moran, Steele, & Higgitt, 1993; Fonagy, Steele, & Steele, 1991; Fonagy, Steele, Steele, Moran, & Higgitt, 1991; Levine, Tuber, Slade, & Ward, 1991; Steele, Steele, & Fonagy, 1996; Ward & Carlson, 1995). Although there is little research examining how prepartum maternal representations influence parenting behavior once the infant is born (the notable exception is the work of the authors, discussed later), other research finds that concurrently assessed postpartum maternal representations influence the parent–child relationship as well as specific parenting behaviors (Benoit, Zeanah, Parker, Nicholson, & Coolbear, 1997; Button, Pianta, &

Marvin, 2001; Coolbear & Benoit, 1999; Messina Sayre, Pianta, Marvin, & Saft, 2001). Internal representations are an important way in which mothers regulate their affective and behavioral responses to their infants (Rosenblum, Dayton, & McDonough, 2006). These mother–infant interactions subsequently affect infant neurological development (see Fonagy, Gergely, Jurist, & Target, 2004; Schore, 2003) and infant behavior (e.g., Crockenberg & Leerkes, 2000).

IPV and Maternal Representations

Although there is little research on the relationship of IPV and maternal representations (the exception being the present authors' work, which is discussed in a subsequent section); there is research on the association between traumatic experiences, posttraumatic stress disorder (PTSD), and problematic attachment representations in adulthood. The prevalence of PTSD and IPV is high, ranging from 45% to 84% (Houskamp & Foy, 1991; Kemp, Green, Hovanitz, & Rawlings, 1995; Kemp, Rawlings, & Green, 1991; Vitanza, Vogel, & Marshall, 1995). PTSD is a syndrome of intrusive reexperiencing, avoidance and emotional numbing, and hyperarousal symptoms that occurs in some individuals in the aftermath of a traumatic event (American Psychiatric Association, 1994). A *traumatic event* is defined as experiencing or witnessing an event involving threat to life or physical integrity that results in feelings of fear, helplessness, or horror.

Among victims of chronic trauma (e.g., IPV), trauma symptoms are often more complex, diffuse, and long-standing. Herman (1992) noted that trauma experiences that occur in the context of relationships (e.g., IPV) can severely affect a victim's capacity for forming healthy relationships with others. Research with victims of trauma other than IPV (e.g., childhood sexual abuse) has found that large numbers of adults are unresolved on the AAI with a secondary classification of preoccupied (Stalker & Davies, 1995). In other research, unresolved representations have been associated with problematic caregiving behaviors (e.g., frightening, hostile, or withdrawn behaviors; Cassidy & Mohr, 2001; Main & Hesse, 1990; Jacobvitz, Hazen, & Riggs, 1997; Schuengel, Bakermans-Kranenburg, & Van IJzendoorn, 1999). In the only study of which we are aware (Sullivan-Hanson, 1990, as cited in Lyons-Ruth & Jacobvitz, 1999), women experiencing IPV, compared with women not experiencing IPV, were more likely to be classified as Preoccupied/Overwhelmed on the AAI.

IPV and Attachment

There is little research specifically examining how IPV experienced by the mother might influence infant attachment. Quinlivan and Evans (2005) found that women's experiences of prepartum IPV were related to poor mother–infant attachment (measured via a maternal self-report questionnaire about her feelings toward her infant) when the infants were age 1. What research exists regarding attachment (other than the authors' work discussed in the next section) measured with standard infant attachment protocols (i.e., the SS) suggests that these infants are more likely to have insecure attachments, particularly disorganized attachment (Zeanah et al., 1999). No doubt this is due to numerous factors, including problematic maternal representations and maternal unavailability. Maternal IPV experiences during the early years of a child's life are associated with reduced maternal warmth and support (Levendosky & Graham-Bermann, 2000, 2001), impaired mother–infant bonding (Huth-Bocks, Levendosky, Bogat, & von Eye, 2004), and inconsistency in parenting (Holden & Ritchie, 1991). It is likely that IPV disturbs the comfort and protective qualities within the home environment. In these homes, an infant's sense of well-being and safety—factors that are crucial for secure attachment—are lacking (Margolin, 1998). However, a longitudinal study by Sternberg, Lamb, Guterman, Abbott, and Dawud-Noursi (2005), examining exposure to child abuse and spousal abuse when children were ages 8 to 13 and assessing attachment 5 years later, found that witnessing IPV during childhood did not impair adolescents' attachment relationships with their parents. As the authors noted, the measure of attachment used (Inventory of Parents and Peer Attachment; Armsden & Greenberg, 1987) may not be sensitive to important aspects of the adolescent–parent relationship. Also, exposure to spousal abuse earlier in the children's lives was not measured but could have been influential.

In the following section, we focus on the Mother Infant Study and its contributions to the understanding of pre- and postpartum maternal representations, attachment, and IPV. The research presented in this chapter focuses on attachment; however, our longitudinal study has also investigated the effects of IPV on women and infant's health (Huth-Bocks, Levendosky, & Bogat, 2002) and women's mental health (Bogat et al., 2005; Bogat, Levendosky, DeJonghe, Davidson, & von Eye, 2004; Bogat, Levendosky, Theran, von Eye, & Davidson, 2003; Levendosky et al., 2004; Jones, Bogat, von Eye, Davidson, & Levendosky, 2005; Martinez-Torteya, Bogat, von Eye, Davidson, & Levendosky, 2009; Mourad, Levendosky, Bogat, & von Eye, 2008; von Eye, & Bogat, 2006; Weatherill, Almerigi, Levendosky, Bogat, & Harris, 2004). Other research has focused on infants' response to IPV (Bogat, DeJonghe, Levendosky, Davidson, & von Eye, 2006; DeJonghe, Bogat, Levendosky, von Eye, & Davidson, 2005), IPV and parenting (Levendosky, Leahy, Bogat, Davidson, & von Eye, 2006), and factors that influence children's resilience when living with IPV (Martinez-Torteya, Bogat, von Eye, & Levendosky, 2009).

THE MOTHER INFANT STUDY

Begun in 1999, the broad purpose of the Mother Infant Study[1] was to assess risk and protective factors for women and children living with IPV. An important innovation of the longitudinal study was to examine the effects of IPV on children at the earliest time they could be affected—in utero. Therefore, we began assessing women during their last trimester of pregnancy and then assessed women and their children yearly until the children were age 7 (we are currently collecting data now that the children are age 10). Research findings, based on data from pregnancy through the first 4 years of the child's life, are described later in this section. Overall, our results support the importance of considering the effects of IPV on the mother's internal representations of the child and the child's organization of attachment behavior.

Participants

The participants were 206 women recruited during their pregnancy. Demographic information about the sample can be found in Huth-Bocks, Levendosky, Bogat, et al. (2004). We oversampled for exposure to IPV during the pregnancy, such that 122 women had experienced one of the following types of IPV during their pregnancy: 86.5% had experienced a nonphysical incident of IPV (e.g., a verbal threat), 63.7% a mild or minor physical incident, 40.9% a moderate or severe physical incident, and 28.0% an incident of sexual violence. (The total exceeds 100% because participants are counted in more than one category.)

Participants were recruited in a Midwestern state, including urban, suburban, and rural areas, through contact with more than 50 settings relevant to pregnant women, such as obstetrician/gynecologist clinics, hospitals, WIC, maternal outreach programs, and IPV shelters. In addition, flyers were posted in public settings, such as grocery store bulletin boards and bus stop shelters.

Inclusion criteria for the study were as follows: (a) between ages 18 and 40; (b) in the third trimester of pregnancy; (c) at least a 6-week romantic relationship during the pregnancy; and (d) fluency in the English language. When women telephoned our offices, they were administered the Conflict Tactics Scale (Straus, 1979) to ensure that at least half of our participants had experienced IPV during pregnancy. After 3 months of conducting the pregnancy interviews, we found that 50% of the women who had screened negative for IPV during pregnancy had experienced IPV with a prior partner or with the

---

[1]The Mother Infant Study is a collaborative research investigation by Alytia Levendosky, G. Anne Bogat, Alexander von Eye, and William Davidson that was funded by National Institute of Justice, Centers for Disease Control, and Michigan State University (https://www.msu.edu/~mis/index.html).

pregnancy partner prior to pregnancy. Thus, we moved to a multinomial sampling strategy in which we considered two response categories: (a) IPV during current pregnancy and (b) duration of current intimate relationship. We assigned individuals to response categories when they contacted the project office; no filtering, based on responses, occurred. The advantage of this procedure was that it allowed for the best assessment of the continuum of violence/nonviolence that exists in the general population.

Over the course of the first six waves of data collection (through the child's 4th year of life), women moved in and out of violent relationships. From age 1 through age 4 of the child's life, between 31% and 45% of the women were in violent relationships at any given time. At each wave of data collection, approximately half of the women reporting violence also indicated that their children directly witnessed the abuse.

Measures

Numerous assessment instruments were administered at various waves of the Mother Infant Study. The ones listed here are those that appear in the findings we discuss later in this section. IPV was assessed with the Severity of Violence Against Women Scales (Marshall, 1992), which measure threats of violence, physical violence, and sexual violence ranging from mild to severe during the past year.

Child attachment at ages 1 and 4 was assessed by the SS procedure (Ainsworth et al., 1978). Based on patterns of child behavior toward the caregiver, children at ages 1 and 4 were classified into one of the following general attachment categories: Secure, Insecure-Avoidant, Insecure-Ambivalent, or Disorganized. When a secure/insecure dichotomy was used in data analysis, disorganized children were grouped with the two insecure categories.

Maternal representations were assessed by a semistructured interview, the Working Model of the Child Interview, prepartum (Zeanah & Benoit, 1995) and 1-year postpartum (Zeanah et al., 1994). The interview, administered to women during their last trimester of pregnancy and when their children were age 1, assesses mothers' caretaking representations. Mothers' narratives were audiotaped, transcribed, and coded on 15 five-point Likert scales that assess qualitative (e.g., intensity of involvement), content (e.g., fear for infant safety), and affective (e.g., joy) aspects of the mothers' representations. These scales were used to classify mothers' responses into one of three categories: balanced, disengaged, and distorted (Zeanah, Benoit, Barton, & Hirshberg, 1996). In several of our studies, the WMCI was also coded for the woman's representation of her competence and self-efficacy in the maternal role and her expectations of herself as a mother (Slade et al., 1994). This is not part of Zeanah and colleagues' original coding scheme.

Adult attachment was measured using the Perceptions of Adult Attachment Questionnaire (Lichtenstein & Cassidy, 1991), a 60-item self-report questionnaire that assesses the woman's childhood experiences, her perceptions of the caregiving provided by her mother, and her overall relationship with her mother.

Parenting was assessed using a videotaped mother–child interaction when the child was age 1. Six scales, adapted from Ainsworth (Ainsworth & Bell, 1974; Ainsworth, Bell, & Stayton, 1971; Ainsworth et al., 1978) and Crittenden (1981), were coded on the basis of observed maternal behavior: Sensitivity, Disengagement, Controlling, Covert Hostility, Warmth, and Joy.

The Beck Depression Inventory (Beck, Ward, Mendelson, Mock, & Erbaugh, 1961) was used to assess maternal depressive symptoms. Finally, social support was measured using the Norbeck Social Support Questionnaire (Norbeck, Carrieri, & Lindsey, 1983; Norbeck, Lindsey, & Carrieri, 1981), which assesses multiple dimensions of support. For the research reported in this chapter, we calculated the proportion of supporters who were women.

Procedures

After the woman agreed to participate in the study, she was scheduled for the first assessment. These took place at the participant's home or university offices, depending on the wave of data collection, the woman's preferences, and/or whether or not a videotaped observation was required. Interviews of children, ages 1 and 4, took place in project offices in order to videotape and administer the SS and the mother–child interaction in a standardized format. Interviews lasted between 1 and 3 hr, depending on the wave of data collection, and women were paid for their participation. The children were given a small gift for their participation. Between the yearly interviews, participants were contacted every 90 days to maintain their current address and telephone number for scheduling the subsequent assessments.

Results

Maternal Representations

Overall, our findings indicate that maternal representations are an important aspect of the caregiving relationship between the mother and child and are related to infant attachment. In addition, these representations are likely to be affected by experiences of IPV with the romantic partner. In one study examining the relationship between experiences of IPV during pregnancy and prepartum maternal representations (Huth-Bocks, Levendosky, Theran, & Bogat, 2004), we found that women who experienced IPV during their pregnancies had significantly more negative schemas of their unborn babies than those who did not. Specifically, after controlling for maternal education and current relationship status, the women experiencing IPV, compared with those who did not, were more likely to have lower scores on openness to change, coherence, sensitivity, acceptance, joy, and maternal self-efficacy. They were more likely to report infant difficulty, anger, anxiety, and depression. Furthermore, the women experiencing IPV were more likely to be classified as nonbalanced (either disengaged or distorted), rather than balanced. Notably, several of the women experiencing IPV during pregnancy attributed the fetal kicks and movement as abuse toward themselves from the fetus, including beliefs that the fetus wanted to break their ribs and that active movement of the fetus indicated that he or she would be physically aggressive and abusive in ways similar to the father of the unborn baby.

We also assessed maternal representations 1-year postpartum. Maternal representations, similar to other attachment-related working models, can be modified over time according to environmental influences and changing experiences. Thus, given that women move in and out of IPV relationships over time, we were interested in the predictors of stability and instability of maternal representations from pregnancy to 1-year postpartum (Theran et al., 2005). We found that most women's representations were stable (62%). However, for those women whose representations went from balanced prepartum to nonbalanced postpartum, significant predictive factors included lower income and single parenthood. There was a trend for IPV during pregnancy to influence this change.

Taken together, our findings indicate that pregnancy IPV influences both the mother's developing relationship with her as yet unborn child and her 1-year-old child. Pregnancy is a vulnerable time for women, during which they are reevaluating existing relationships in their lives as well as developing a new relationship (i.e., a caregiving relationship with a child about to be born; George & Solomon, 1999; Stern, 1995). IPV has a significant effect on the mother's representations while she is pregnant, that is, while the mother–child relationship is in its formative stage. The transition from an early maternal relationship with the fetus to an actual relationship with a child is complex and vulnerable to IPV exposure.

An important question is whether maternal representations are related to maternal parenting behavior, which is one of the clearest and strongest predictors of child attachment (see De Wolff & Van IJzendoorn, 1997). If maternal representations are, in fact, related to parenting behavior, pregnancy may be an important intervention point not only for prepartum health care, but for improving the developing relationship with the unborn child. Two of our studies addressed this relationship (Dayton, Levendosky, Davidson, & Bogat, 2010; Theran et al., 2005). Dayton et al. (2010) found that prepartum representations were significantly related to observed parenting of a 1-year-old. Balanced prepartum maternal representations were significantly associated with positive parenting. Mothers with distorted representations displayed significantly higher levels of hostile parenting than mothers holding balanced representations. Mothers with disengaged representations displayed higher levels of controlling parenting than mothers holding balanced representations.

Although the finding about the relationship between disengaged representations and controlling parenting may appear to be counterintuitive, in fact, controlling parenting behavior is characterized by an absence of emotional attunement. So, although the mother is physically present, she is not emotionally sensitive or responsive to her child and instead is attempting to control the interaction.

Theran et al. (2005) found that the pattern of stability and instability of maternal representations was also related to maternal parenting behaviors. Mothers with nonbalanced representations prepartum and 1-year postpartum were less sensitive and more controlling than mothers who became balanced postpartum. Findings from these two studies demonstrate that maternal representations are closely related to and even predict parenting behavior. Thus, our research supports the importance of assessing a mother's working model of her unborn child and perhaps intervening during pregnancy with programs that address these developing schemas (Cohen & Slade, 2000; Stern, 1995).

Finally, we tested a structural model of individual and contextual predictors of infant–mother attachment that proved to be a good fit with the data (Huth-Bocks, Levendosky, Bogat, et al., 2004). Characteristics of prepartum maternal representations, such as coherence, acceptance of the baby, richness of perceptions, and openness to change, mediated the relationship between the mother's attachment experiences as a child and her own infant's attachment, as measured by the SS at age 1. Maternal risk factors, including economic disadvantage and experiences of prepartum IPV, were significantly related to these prepartum representations, which were again related to infant attachment. Postpartum social support from other women also predicted infant attachment. Thus, not only are prepartum representations of the infant and the relationship with the infant important for later mother–infant attachment, they also are influenced by individual maternal characteristics and contextual factors in mothers' lives. This was the first study to empirically confirm these multiple associations, which have been speculated about in the theoretical literature for some time (e.g., Stern, 1995).

Our research demonstrates the wide-ranging effects on the mother–child relationship that stem from IPV exposure during pregnancy. Importantly, IPV affects parenting during pregnancy as measured by prepartum maternal representations. The experience of IPV during pregnancy may also cause an activation of the mother's unresolved experiences or feelings about her childhood relationships with her own significant others that may then negatively affect the ways in which she develops and organizes her schemas of herself as a mother and of her infant prior to birth. The experience of IPV during pregnancy may be psychologically and physically compromising for mothers and thus may overwhelm women's capacities to develop a sensitive and attuned relationship with their child after birth (Lieberman & Van Horn, 1998; Zeanah & Scheeringa, 1997). The influence of IPV on these maternal representations, both pre- and postpartum, has direct repercussions for the child in terms of the mother's parenting behaviors and the child's attachment security. One implication of our findings is that they suggest there are multiple "ports of entry" for modifying maternal prepartum representations for the better (e.g., through helping women resolve difficult childhood experiences, improving their socioeconomic status, providing social support from other women, or decreasing the occurrence and/or impact of partner violence during pregnancy).

Child Attachment

Other findings from our research explain factors that influence the child's attachment at age 1 as well as the stability of child attachment between ages 1 and 4 (Huth-Bocks, Levendosky, Bogat, et al., 2004; Huth-Bocks, Theran, Levendosky, & Bogat, 2009; Levendosky, Bogat, Huth-Bocks, Rosenblum, & von Eye, 2009). As noted earlier, attachment security is the behavioral manifestation of internal working models of the relationship with the primary caregiver, usually the mother (e.g., Bowlby, 1969/1982; Sroufe et al., 1999). Given that much of an infant's social development occurs within a dyadic context, the development of attachment with the primary caregiver in early childhood is a critical foundation for social and emotional development. This foundation begins with maternal responsiveness to physiological needs shortly after birth and the development of affect synchrony in face-to-face interactions with the mother at about age 2 months; this sets the stage for the type of attachment that develops by age 1. Throughout this time, the mother's ability to establish synchrony with her child and repair asynchrony, along with recognizing and understanding the child's needs, is critical to the normal social and emotional development of her infant (Schore, 2003). IPV is a stressor or traumatic event(s) that may disrupt this normative process of synchrony and repair and thus result in less than optimal infant attachment.

Furthermore, attachment stability and instability are of interest to researchers in child development because attachment with the primary caregiver is viewed as the template for future significant relationships. Studies of low-risk samples have demonstrated significant attachment stability (generally around 60%–70%; e.g., Frodi, Grolnick, & Bridges, 1985; Owen, Easterbrooks, Chase-Lansdale, & Goldberg, 1984). High-risk samples typically show lower rates of stability (about 40%–50%; e.g., Barnett, Ganiban, & Cicchetti, 1999; Belsky, Campbell, Cohn, & Moore, 1996; Vondra, Shaw, Swearingen, Cohen, & Owens, 2001). Instability has been associated with various stressors in the family environment (Moss et al., 2005; National Institute of Child Health & Human Development [NICHD] Early Child Care Research Network, 2001; Vondra, Hommerding, & Shaw, 1999). IPV may be one of those stressors.

As mentioned previously, we found an association between prepartum maternal representations and infant attachment (Huth-Bocks, Levendosky, Theran et al., 2004); in this study, infant attachment was assessed along a secure-insecure dimension. To explore further the relationship between prepartum representations and infant attachment, we examined the concordance and discordance between prepartum classifications of maternal representations (balanced, nonbalanced) and infant attachment classifications at age 1 (secure, insecure; Huth-Bocks et al., 2009). Overall, we found a 60% concordance rate; while this rate was statistically significant, a substantial amount of discordance was observed. A number of factors were related to discordance between maternal and infant classifications including demographic risk factors, high maternal depression, low social support, the presence of IPV, and negative maternal and infant interactions.

Most relevant to the current chapter, the Balanced/Insecure group was more likely to experience prepartum IPV than were women in the Balanced/Secure group, as was the Non-Balanced/Insecure group compared with the Non-Balanced/Secure group. These results indicate that prepartum experiences of IPV have enduring effects on the developing attachment relationship between mother and infant. And these effects exist over and above those of prepartum representations. That is, IPV may override prepartum representations' influence on 1-year-olds' attachment classifications. Future research will need to further elucidate the relationship between IPV and prepartum maternal representations. Given that the primary goal of the developing caregiving system is to provide care and protection to offspring (George & Solomon, 1999), it may be that IPV, which is a direct threat to the mother, and therefore her child, impedes the mother's capacity to develop appropriate maternal representations, which subsequently may affect her ability to be a secure base for her infant.

We also examined children's attachment stability at ages 1 and 4 (Levendosky et al., 2009) and how the trajectory of the mother's IPV experiences at five different times (pregnancy, age 1, age 2, age 3, and age 4) influenced stability and/or change. We found modest stability (57%) among our sample, which was not significant. Thus, instability is common. To examine which factors predicted stability or instability of attachment, we categorized children into four patterns based on attachment classifications at age 1 and age 4: secure–secure, secure–insecure, insecure–secure, and insecure–

insecure. Examining the polynomials, there was a significant quadratic effect of Time × Pattern, indicating differential curvature in the trajectories of these groups. The stable secure group (secure–secure) had relatively constant levels of low IPV over time. Movement toward security (insecure–secure) was related to low levels of IPV that decreased over time and then rose to previous levels. In contrast, the stable insecure group (insecure–insecure) started with the highest level of IPV during pregnancy and then decreased to low levels. Finally, movement toward insecurity (secure–insecure) was related to unstable levels of IPV characterized by low levels of IPV during pregnancy that then increased, decreased, and finally increased to the highest levels at age 4. For this group, the secure nature of the mother-infant relationship during the 1st year of the child's life appeared to be disrupted by the intermittent presence of IPV and the very high levels at the time the child was age 4.

These findings illustrate the complicated relationship between IPV and attachment. Importantly, the timing of IPV for attachment seems to matter. IPV is typically an intermittent social problem; there are few households in which IPV occurs on a daily basis. Furthermore, women move in and out of abusive relationships. Thus, across samples, children's exposure to IPV is probably quite heterogeneous. Unfortunately, little is known about how the timing of IPV exposure affects children.

Given the importance of the attachment relationship in developing templates for future significant relationships (e.g., Rutter, Kreppner, & Sonuga-Barke, 2009), our findings suggest that the attachment relationship may be one possible mechanism for the intergenerational transmission of violence. Research indicates that among young children, insecure–avoidant parent–child attachment is associated with aggression (e.g., Monks, Smith, & Swettenham, 2005; Renken, Egeland, Marvinney, Mangelsdorf, & Sroufe, 1989). Aggression normally declines somewhat as children get older. However, a recent study found that preoccupied attachment among youth was related to higher levels of aggressive behavior and significantly less decline in aggressive behavior over time compared with youth who were classified in other attachment categories (Kobak, Zajac, & Smith, 2009). Our findings reported here show that the young child exposed to IPV may develop an insecure or unstable attachment with his or her mother. The child experiences frustration and anger as his or her ploys to gain the mother's attention fail. These experiences create a template for later relationships based on distrust; thus, the child is expecting to be hurt and disappointed and may lash out proactively to avoid the pain of rejection (e.g., Troy & Sroufe, 1987) or may misinterpret benign situations and lash out reactively, as our recent findings with children exposed to IPV indicate (Huston, von Eye, Bogat, Levendosky, & Davidson, 2009). These patterns of social relationships that develop early in the life of the infant, as a result of the attachment relationship with the mother, may eventually result in the individual per-petrating IPV.

It is important, however, that many mothers and children in our study were resilient to the negative influences of IPV on the attachment relationship. More needs to be understood about what makes these mothers and children resilient. Our recent work finds that more than half of the children in our study show positive adaptation (based on externalizing and internalizing symptoms) over time. These children were characterized by easy temperaments and mothers who had few depressive symptoms (Martinez-Torteya, Bogat, von Eye, & Levendosky, 2009). Factors associated with secure attachment and IPV need further exploration.

CONCLUSIONS AND FUTURE DIRECTIONS

Overall, the findings from our longitudinal study indicate that for some mother–child dyads, the attachment relationship is damaged by IPV such that the mothers have disengaged or distorted maternal representations and the children have insecure attachments. However, our findings also indicate there are a number of additional protective and vulnerability factors within these families that may either increase the likelihood of damage from IPV or protect them from it.

Bowlby's theory, as well as a developmental psychopathology paradigm, suggests that attachment status is influenced by numerous contextual variables (Finkelhor & Kendall-Tacket, 1997; Masten, Best, & Garmezy, 1990). Prior research has found that stability and instability of child–mother attachment can be predicted from individual characteristics of the mother, the mother's relationship with her partner, and the demographic characteristics of the family (Egeland & Farber, 1984; Moss et al., 2005; NICHD Early Child Care Research Network, 2001; Vondra et al., 1999). However, little prior research is longitudinal. Our body of research makes a significant contribution to the literature by using a prospective, longitudinal design where factors that might influence attachment status and its stability are measured at the earliest time they can affect the child—in utero.

Pregnancy appears to be a particularly vulnerable period for IPV to affect the mother–child relationship. The mother's developing representations of her child and herself as mother may be negatively affected by the experience of IPV from her romantic partner. This damage is then transferred to her relationship to her child through the impairment in her parenting behaviors. Her impaired parenting, along with other family experiences, such as poor social support, low income, and/or maternal depression, may then influence the development of insecure attachment in her child. Without a positive change in environmental circumstances, the child may maintain an insecure attachment to the mother at age 4. However, some women, particularly those with healthy childhood relationships and/or available and emotionally supportive networks, develop balanced maternal representations, despite the experience of IPV. These women are then more likely to display sensitive parenting in the 1st year of life and to have infants with secure attachment.

Postpartum, IPV continues to play a role in the organization of child attachment. Children whose mothers continued to be exposed to IPV or were exposed for the first time during the 1st year of their children's lives were more likely to either maintain insecure attachments or develop them by age 4. However, children whose mothers left the abusive relationship were more likely to become securely attached by age 4. This finding illustrates the potential for positive change in the mother–child relationship. (This can also be seen in the change between prepartum and 1-year-postpartum maternal representations; women who leave the abusive relationship and/or do not develop depressive symptoms are more likely to demonstrate balanced postpartum maternal representations.)

The ability of the mother–child relationship to experience recovery has important implications for interventions with families experiencing IPV. First, our findings indicate that IPV does affect infants and the mother–infant relationship, including the developing relationship while the woman is pregnant. Second, ending an abusive relationship between pregnancy and when the child is age 4 can lead to recovery in the mother–child relationship. Thus, if mothers of young infants are able to, they should be encouraged to leave the abusive relationship.

The other important clinical implication from our research relates to the relationships between maternal representations and both caregiving behavior and child attachment. Our findings lend empirical support for interventions that target maternal representations both pre- and postpartum. In addition, our findings suggest that services targeted to battered women and their young children should include a component that emphasizes the mother–child relationship. Rather than focusing only on the mother's mental health or her parenting, interventions should also include targeted work with the mother–child dyad to increase the likelihood of secure attachment. One example of such work is the child–parent psychotherapy developed by Lieberman and colleagues (e.g., Lieberman & Van Horn, 2005). This relationship-based treatment highlights the importance of parent–child attachment as the context for addressing both the emotional and behavior problems during early childhood as well as early risk factors that are associated with IPV. In this approach, IPV is recognized as a traumatic stressor for both mother and young child, and the therapeutic relationship is viewed as a critical influence in the treatment (i.e., as a corrective interpersonal experience). The primary treatment goal is to promote a more secure and growth-promoting relationship between the child and parent.

Consistent with the findings from our longitudinal study, Lieberman and Van Horn suggested that these goals' may be met through a number of "ports of entry," depending on what is deemed most appropriate and salient at the time, including maternal representations of the self and the child, parenting behaviors, parent–child interaction sequences, and child behaviors. Indeed, these researchers have found empirical support that this model of intervention may reduce young child witnesses' behavior problems and trauma symptoms, as well as mothers' posttraumatic stress avoidance symptoms (Lieberman, Van Horn, & Ghosh Ippen, 2005).

The findings from our research also lead to new research questions for understanding the mechanisms through which IPV affects mothers and children. For example, the child's insecure attachment is understood to serve as a template for the child's interactions with others, including peers and teachers (Bowlby, 1969/1982; Sroufe et al., 1999). We find that the trajectory of IPV is a predictor of attachment security in 4-year-old children; however, as these children age, are their relationships with peers and teachers typified by hostility and aggression? Do stable, balanced maternal representations and/or positive caregiving behavior continue to buffer the mother–child relationship as the child gets older, even in the context of IPV? Does secure attachment buffer older children from the negative effects of IPV, especially the development of internalizing and externalizing behavior? We hope to answer some of these questions as we continue to analyze the data from the Mother Infant Study. However, more research on the role of attachment and IPV as the children move to adolescence and develop intimate friendships and romantic relationships remains to be done. For example, in what ways does the experience of IPV during childhood continue to affect the development of internal working models and attachment relationships as IPV exposed children become adolescents?

In conclusion, findings from the Mother Infant Study clearly demonstrate the negative effects of IPV on mothers' internal representations of their children both pre- and postpartum. Importantly, the attachment that children develop with their mothers at ages 1 and 4 is also influenced by maternal prepartum caretaking representations. However, as we have demonstrated, our findings also have implications for possible interventions and the timing of those interventions.

REFERENCES

Ainsworth, M. D. (1989). Attachments beyond infancy. *American Psychologist, 44,* 709–716. doi:10.1037/0003-066X.44.4.709

Ainsworth, M. D., Blehar, M., Waters, E., & Wall, S. (1978). *Patterns of attachment: A psychological study of the Strange Situation.* Hillsdale, NJ: Erlbaum.

Ainsworth, M. D. S., & Bell, S. M. (1974). Mother–infant interaction and the development of competence. In K. Connolly & J. Bruner (Eds.), *The growth of competence* (pp. 97–118). New York, NY: Academic Press.

Ainsworth, M. D. S., Bell, S. M., & Stayton, D. J. (1971). Attachment and exploratory behavior of one year olds. In H. R. Schaffer (Ed.), *The origins of human social relations* (pp. 17–52). New York, NY: Academic Press.

American Psychiatric Association. (1994). *Diagnostic and statistical manual of mental disorders* (4th ed.). Washington, DC: Author.

Ammaniti, M. (1991). Maternal representations during pregnancy and early infant–mother interactions. *Infant Mental Health Journal, 12,* 246–255. doi:10.1002/1097-0355(199123)12:3<246::AID-IMHJ2280120310>3.0.CO;2-8

Ammaniti, M., Baumgartner, E., Candelori, C., Perucchini, P., Pola, M., Tambelli, R., & Zampino, F. (1992). Representations and narratives during pregnancy. *Infant Mental Health Journal, 13,* 167–182. doi:10.1002/1097-0355(199223)13:2<167::AID-IMHJ2280130207>3.0.CO;2-M

Armsden, G. C., & Greenberg, M. T. (1987). The Inventory of Parent and Peer Attachment: Individual differences and their relationship to psychological well being. *Journal of Youth and Adolescence, 16,* 427–454. doi:10.1007/BF02202939

Bakermans-Kranenburg, M. J., Van IJzendoorn, M. H., & Kroonenberg, P. M. (2004). Differences in attachment security between African-American and White children: Ethnicity or socioeconomic status. *Infant Behavior and Development, 27,* 417–433. doi:10.1016/j.infbeh.2004.02.002

Barnett, D., Ganiban, J., & Cicchetti, D. (1999). Maltreatment, negative expressivity, and the development of type D attachments from 12 to 24 months of age. In J. I. Vondra & D. Barnett (Eds.), Atypical attachment in infancy and early childhood among children at developmental risk (pp. 97–118). *Monographs of the Society for Research in Child Development, 64* (Serial No. 258).

Beck, A. T., Ward, C. H., Mendelson, M., Mock, J., & Erbaugh, J. (1961). An inventory for measuring depression. *Archives of General Psychiatry, 4,* 561–571.

Belsky, J., Campbell, S. B., Cohn, J. F., & Moore, G. (1996). Instability of infant–parent attachment security. *Developmental Psychology, 32,* 921–924. doi:10.1037/0012-1649.32.5.921

Benoit, D., & Parker, K. C. H. (1994). Stability and transmission of attachment across three generations. *Child Development, 65,* 1444–1456. doi:10.2307/1131510

Benoit, D., Parker, K. C. H., & Zeanah, C. H. (1997). Mothers' representations of their infants assessed prenatally: Stability and association with infants' attachment classifications. *Journal of Child Psychology and Psychiatry, and Allied Disciplines, 38,* 307–313. doi:10.1111/j.1469-7610.1997.tb01515.x

Benoit, D., Zeanah, C. H., Parker, K. C. H., Nicholson, E., & Coolbear, J. (1997). Working Model of the Child Interview: Infant clinical status related to maternal perceptions. *Infant Mental Health Journal, 18*(1), 107–121. doi:10.1002/(SICI)1097-0355(199721)18:1<107::AID-IMHJ8>3.0.CO;2-N

Bogat, G. A., DeJonghe, E. S., Levendosky, A. A., Davidson, W. S., & von Eye, A. (2006). Trauma symptoms among infants who witness domestic violence toward their mothers. *Child Abuse & Neglect: The International Journal, 30,* 109–125. doi:10.1016/j.chiabu.2005.09.002

Bogat, G. A., Leahy, K. L., von Eye, A., Maxwell, C., Levendosky, A. A., & Davidson, W. S. (2005). The influence of community violence on the functioning of battered women. *American Journal of Community Psychology, 36*(1–2), 123–132. doi:10.1007/s10464-005-6237-2

Bogat, G. A., Levendosky, A. A., DeJonghe, E., Davidson, W. S., & von Eye, A. (2004). Pathways of suffering: The temporal effects of domestic violence on women's mental health. *Maltrattamento e abuso all'infanzia, 6*(2), 97–112.

Bogat, G. A., Levendosky, A. A., Theran, S., von Eye, A., & Davidson, W. S. (2003). Predicting the psychosocial effects of interpersonal partner violence (IPV): How much does a woman's history of IPV matter? *Journal of Interpersonal Violence, 18,* 1271–1291. doi:10.1177/0886260503256657

Bowlby, J. (1982). *Attachment and loss: Vol. 1. Attachment* (2nd ed.). New York, NY: Basic Books. (Original work published 1969)

Button, S., Pianta, R. C., & Marvin, R. S. (2001). Mothers' representations of relationships with their children: Relations with parenting behavior, mother characteristics, and child disability status. *Social Development, 10,* 455–472. doi:10.1111/1467-9507.00175

Carlson, E. A., & Sroufe, L. A. (1995). Contributions of attachment theory to developmental psychopathology. In D. Cicchetti & D. J. Cohen (Eds.), *Developmental psychopathology* (pp. 581–617). New York, NY: Wiley.

Carlson, V., Cicchetti, D., Barnett, D., & Braunwald, K. (1989). Disorganized/disoriented attachment relationships in maltreated infants. *Developmental Psychology, 25,* 525–531. doi:10.1037/0012-1649.25.4.525

Caspers, K., Paradiso, S., Yucuis, R., Troutman, B., Arndt, S., & Philibert, R. (2009). Association between the serotonin transporter promoter polymorphism (5-HTTLPR) and adult unresolved attachment. *Developmental Psychology, 45,* 64–76. doi:10.1037/a0014026

Cassidy, J., & Mohr, J. J. (2001). Unsolvable fear, trauma, and psychopathology: Theory, research, and clinical considerations related to disorganized attachment across the life span. *Clinical Psychology: Science and Practice, 8,* 275–298. doi:10.1093/clipsy/8.3.275

Cohen, L. J., & Slade, A. (2000). The psychology and psychopathology of pregnancy: Reorganization and transformation. In C. H. Zeanah (Ed.), *Handbook of infant mental health* (pp. 20–36). New York, NY: Guilford Press.

Coolbear, J., & Benoit, D. (1999). Failure to thrive: Risk for clinical disturbance of attachment? *Infant Mental Health Journal, 20*(1), 87–104. doi:10.1002/(SICI)1097-0355(199921)20:1<87::AID-IMHJ7>3.0.CO;2-M

Crittenden, P. M. (1981). Abusing, neglecting, problematic, and adequate dyads: Differentiating by patterns of interaction. *Merrill-Palmer Quarterly, 27,* 201–218.

Crockenberg, S., & Leerkes, E. (2000). Infant social and emotional development in family context. In C. H. Zeanah (Ed.), *Handbook of infant mental health* (2nd ed., pp. 60–90). New York, NY: Guilford Press.

Dayton, C. J., Levendosky, A. A., Davidson, W. S., & Bogat, G. A. (2010). The child as held in the mind of the mother: The influence of prenatal maternal representations on parenting behaviors. *Infant Mental Health Journal, 31*, 220–241.

DeJonghe, E. S., Bogat, G. A., Levendosky, A. A., von Eye, A., & Davidson, W. S. (2005). Infant exposure to domestic violence predicts heightened sensitivity to adult verbal conflict. *Infant Mental Health Journal, 26*, 268–281. doi:10.1002/imhj.20048

De Wolff, M. S., & Van IJzendoorn, M. H. (1997). Sensitivity and attachment: A meta analysis on parental antecedents of infant attachment. *Child Development, 68*, 571–591. doi:10.2307/1132107

Egeland, B., & Farber, E. A. (1984). Infant–mother attachment: Factors related to its development and changes over time. *Child Development, 55*, 753–771. doi:10.2307/1130127

Elicker, J., Englund, M., & Sroufe, L. A. (1992). Predicting peer competence and peer relationships in childhood from early parent-child relationships. In R. D. Parke & G. W. Ladd (Eds.), *Family–peer relationships: Modes of linkage* (pp. 77–106). Hillsdale, NJ: Erlbaum.

Fava Viziello, G., Antonioli, M., Cocci, V., & Invernizzi, R. (1993). From pregnancy to motherhood: The structure of representative and narrative change. *Infant Mental Health Journal, 14*, 4–16.

Finkelhor, D., & Kendall-Tackett, K. A. (1997). A developmental perspective on the childhood impact of crime, abuse, and violent victimization. In D. Cicchetti & S. L. Toth (Eds.), *Developmental perspectives on trauma: Theory, research, and intervention* (pp. 1–32). Rochester, NY: University of Rochester Press.

Fonagy, P., Gergely, G., Jurist, E., & Target, M. (2004). *Affect regulation, mentalization, and the development of the self.* New York, NY: Other Press.

Fonagy, P., Steele, M., Moran, G., Steele, H., & Higgitt, A. (1993). Measuring the ghost in the nursery: An empirical study of the relation between parents' mental representations of childhood experiences and their infants' security of attachment. *Journal of the American Psychoanalytic Association, 41*, 957–989. doi:10.1177/000306519304100403

Fonagy, P., Steele, H., & Steele, M. (1991). Maternal representations of attachment during pregnancy predict the organization of infant-mother attachment at one year of age. *Child Development, 62*, 891–905. doi:10.2307/1131141

Fonagy, P., Steele, M., Steele, H., Moran, G., & Higgitt, A. (1991). The capacity for understanding mental states: The reflective self in parent and child and its significance for security of attachment. *Infant Mental Health Journal, 12*, 201–218. doi:10.1002/1097-0355(199123)12:3<201::AID-IMHJ2280120307>3.0.CO;2-7

Frodi, A., Grolnick, W., & Bridges, L. (1985). Maternal correlates of stability and change in infant-mother attachment. *Infant Mental Health Journal, 6*, 60–67.

George, C., & Solomon, J. (1999). Attachment and caregiving: The caregiving behavioral system. In J. Cassidy & P. R. Shaver (Eds.), *Handbook of attachment: Theory, research, and clinical applications* (pp. 649–670). New York, NY: Guilford Press.

Gervai, J., Novak, A., Lakatos, K., Toth, I., Danis, I., Ronai, Z., . . . Lyons-Ruth, K. (2007). Infant genotype may moderate sensitivity to maternal affective communications: Attachment disorganization, quality of care, and the DRD4 polymorphism. *Social Neuroscience, 2,* 307–319. doi:10.1080/17470910701391893

Herman, J. L. (1992). *Trauma and recovery.* New York, NY: Basic Books.

Holden, G., & Ritchie, K. (1991). Linking extreme marital discord, child rearing, and child behavior problems: Evidence from battered women. *Child Development, 62,* 311–327. doi:10.2307/1131005

Houskamp, B. M., & Foy, D. W. (1991). The assessment of posttraumatic stress disorder in battered women. *Journal of Interpersonal Violence, 6,* 367–375. doi:10.1177/088626091006003008

Huston, P., von Eye, A., Bogat, G. A., Levendosky, A. A., & Davidson, W. S., II. (2009). *Domestic violence exposure and early behavior problems predict aggression subtypes in boys and girls.* Unpublished manuscript.

Huth-Bocks, A. C., Levendosky, A. A., & Bogat, G. A. (2002). The effects of domestic violence during pregnancy on maternal and infant health. *Violence and Victims, 17,* 169–185. doi:10.1891/vivi.17.2.169.33647

Huth-Bocks, A. C., Levendosky, A. A., Bogat, G. A., & von Eye, A. (2004). The impact of maternal characteristics and contextual variables on infant–mother attachment. *Child Development, 75,* 480–496. doi:10.1111/j.1467-8624.2004.00688.x

Huth-Bocks, A. C., Levendosky, A. A., Theran, S. A., & Bogat, G. A. (2004). The impact of domestic violence on mothers' prenatal representations of their infants. *Infant Mental Health Journal, 25,* 79–98. doi:10.1002/imhj.10094

Huth-Bocks, A. C., Theran, S. A., Levendosky, A. A., & Bogat, G. A. (2009). *Continuity and discontinuity between maternal caregiving representations during pregnancy and infant–mother attachment.* Unpublished manuscript.

Jacobvitz, D., Hazen, N., & Riggs, S. (1997, April). *Disorganized mental processes in mothers, frightening/frightened caregiving, and disoriented/disorganized behavior in infancy.* Paper presented at the biennial meeting of the Society for Research in Child Development, Washington, DC.

Jones, S. M., Bogat, G. A., von Eye, A., Davidson, W. S., & Levendosky, A. A. (2005). Family support and mental health in abused pregnant women: An analysis of ethnic differences. *American Journal of Community Psychology, 36*(1–2), 97–108. doi:10.1007/s10464-005-6235-4

Kemp, A., Green, B. L., Hovanitz, C., & Rawlings, E. (1995). Incidence and correlates of posttraumatic stress disorder in battered women: Shelter and community samples. *Journal of Interpersonal Violence, 10*(1), 43–55. doi:10.1177/088626095010001003

Kemp, A., Rawlings, E., & Green, B. L. (1991). Posttraumatic stress disorder (PTSD) in battered women: A shelter sample. *Journal of Traumatic Stress, 4*(1), 137–148. doi:10.1002/jts.2490040111

Kobak, R., Zajac, K., & Smith, C. (2009). Adolescent attachment and trajectories of hostile-impulsive behavior: Implications for the development of personality disorders. *Development and Psychopathology, 21,* 839–851. doi:10.1017/S0954579 409000455

Lakatos, K., Nemoda, Z., Toth, I., Ronai, Z., Ney, K., Sasvari-Szekely, M., & Gervai, J. (2002). Further evidence for the role of the dopamine D4 receptor (DRD4) gene in attachment disorganization: Interaction of the exon III 48-bp repeat and the 521 C/T promoter polymorphisms. *Molecular Psychiatry, 7,* 27–31. doi:10.1038/sj/ mp/4000986

Lakatos, K., Toth, I., Nemoda, Z., Ney, K., Sasvari-Szekely, M., & Gervai, J. (2000). Dopamine D4 receptor (DRD4) gene polymorphism is associated with attachment disorganization in infants. *Molecular Psychiatry, 5,* 633–637. doi:10.1038/ sj.mp.4000773

Levendosky, A. A., Bogat, G. A., Huth-Bocks, A. C., Rosenblum, K. L., & von Eye, A. (2009). *Contextual factors related to stability of attachment from infancy to preschool: The role of income, child gender, domestic violence, and mental caregiving representations.* Unpublished manuscript.

Levendosky, A. A., Bogat, G. A., Theran, S. A., Trotter, J. S., von Eye, A., & Davidson, W. S. (2004). The social networks of women experiencing domestic violence. *American Journal of Community Psychology, 34*(1–2), 95–109. doi:10.1023/ B:AJCP.0000040149.58847.10

Levendosky, A. A., & Graham-Bermann, S. A. (2000). Behavioral observations of parenting in battered women. *Journal of Family Psychology, 14,* 80–94. doi:10.1037/ 0893-3200.14.1.80

Levendosky, A. A., & Graham-Bermann, S. A. (2001). Parenting in battered women: The effects of domestic violence on women and children. *Journal of Family Violence, 16,* 171–192. doi:10.1023/A:1011111003373

Levendosky, A. A., Leahy, K. L., Bogat, G. A., Davidson, W. S., & von Eye, A. (2006). Domestic violence, maternal parenting, maternal mental health, and infant externalizing behavior. *Journal of Family Psychology, 20,* 544–552. doi:10.1037/0893-3200.20.4.544

Levine, L. V., Tuber, S. B., Slade, A., & Ward, M. J. (1991). Mothers' mental representations and their relationship to mother–infant attachment. *Bulletin of the Menninger Clinic, 55,* 454–469.

Lichtenstein, J., & Cassidy, J. (1991, April). *The Inventory of Adult Attachment (INVAA): Validation of a new measure of adult attachment.* Paper presented at the biennial meeting of the Society for Research in Child Development, Seattle, WA.

Lieberman, A. F., & Van Horn, P. (1998). Attachment, trauma, and domestic violence: Implications for child custody. *Child and Adolescent Psychiatric Clinics of North America, 7,* 423–443.

Lieberman, A. F., & Van Horn, P. (2005). *Don't hit my mommy! A manual for child–parent psychotherapy with young witnesses of family violence*. Washington, DC: Zero to Three Press.

Lieberman, A. F., Van Horn, P., & Ghosh Ippen, C. (2005). Toward evidence-based treatment: Child-parent psychotherapy with preschoolers exposed to marital violence. *Journal of the American Academy of Child and Adolescent Psychiatry, 44*, 1241–1248. doi:10.1097/01.chi.0000181047.59702.58

Lyons-Ruth, K., & Jacobvitz, D. (1999). Attachment disorganization: Unresolved loss, relational violence, and lapses in behavioral and attentional strategies. In J. Cassidy & P. R. Shaver (Eds.), *Handbook of attachment* (pp. 520–554). New York: Guilford Press.

Main, M., & Hesse, E. (1990). Parents' unresolved traumatic experiences are related to infant disorganized attachment status: Is frightened and/or frightening parental behavior the linking mechanism? In M. T. Greenberg & D. Cicchetti (Eds.), *Attachment in the preschool years: Theory, research, and intervention. The John D. and Catherine T. MacArthur Foundation series on mental health and development* (pp. 161–182). Chicago, IL: University of Chicago Press.

Main, M., & Solomon, J. (1990). Procedures for identifying infants as disorganized/disoriented during the Ainsworth Strange Situation. In M. T. Greenberg & D. Cicchetti (Eds.), *Attachment in the preschool years: Theory, research, and intervention. The John D. and Catherine T. MacArthur Foundation series on mental health and development* (pp. 121–160). Chicago, IL: University of Chicago Press.

Margolin, G. (1998). Effects of domestic violence on children. In P. K. Trickett & C. Schellenbach (Eds.), *Violence against children in the family and the community* (pp. 57–101). Washington, DC: American Psychological Association. doi:10.1037/10292-003

Marshall, L. L. (1992). Development of the Severity of Violence Against Women Scales. *Journal of Family Violence, 7*, 103–121. doi:10.1007/BF00978700

Martinez-Torteya, C., Bogat, G. A., von Eye, A., Davidson, W. S., & Levendosky, A. A. (2009). Women's perceptions of the stressfulness of intimate partner violence predict depression and trauma symptoms. *Violence and Victims, 24*, 707–722. doi:10.1891/0886-6708.24.6.707

Martinez-Torteya, C., Bogat, G. A., von Eye, A., & Levendosky, A. A. (2009). Resilience among children exposed to domestic violence: The role of protective and vulnerability factors. *Child Development, 80*, 562–577. doi:10.1111/j.1467-8624.2009.01279.x

Masten, A. S., Best, K. M., & Garmezy, N. (1990). Resilience and development: Contributions from the study of children who overcome adversity. *Development and Psychopathology, 2*, 425–444. doi:10.1017/S0954579400005812

Messina Sayre, J., Pianta, R. C., Marvin, R. S., & Saft, E. W. (2001). Mothers' representations of relationships with their children: Relations with mother characteristics and feeding sensitivity. *Journal of Pediatric Psychology, 26*, 375–384. doi:10.1093/jpepsy/26.6.375

Monks, C. P., Smith, P. K., & Swettenham, J. (2005). Psychological correlates of peer victimisation in preschool: Social cognitive skills, executive function and attachment profiles. *Aggressive Behavior, 31*, 571–588. doi:10.1002/ab.20099

Moss, E., Cyr, C., Bureau, J., Tarabulsy, G., & Dubois-Comtois, K. (2005). Stability of attachment during the preschool period. *Developmental Psychology, 41*, 773–783. doi:10.1037/0012-1649.41.5.773

Mourad, M., Levendosky, A. A.; Bogat, G. A., & von Eye, A. (2008). Family psychopathology and perceived stress of both domestic violence and negative life events as predictors of women's mental health symptoms. *Journal of Family Violence, 23*, 661–670. doi:10.1007/s10896-008-9188-1

National Institute of Child Health & Human Development Early Child Care Research Network. (2001). Child-care and family predictors of preschool attachment and stability from infancy. *Developmental Psychology, 37*, 847–862. doi:10.1037/0012-1649.37.6.847

Norbeck, J. S., Carrieri, V. L., & Lindsey, A. M. (1983). Further development of the Norbeck Social Support Questionnaire: Normative data and validity testing. *Nursing Research, 32*, 4–9. doi:10.1097/00006199-198301000-00002

Norbeck, J. S., Lindsey, A. M., & Carrieri, V. L. (1981). The development of an instrument to measure social support. *Nursing Research, 30*, 264–269. doi:10.1097/00006199-198109000-00003

Owen, M. T., Easterbrooks, M. A., Chase-Lansdale, L., & Goldberg, W. A. (1984). The relation between maternal employment status and the stability of attachments to mother and father. *Child Development, 55*, 1894–1901. doi:10.2307/1129936

Pajulo, M., Helenius, H., & Mayes, L. (2006). Prenatal views of baby and parenthood: Association with sociodemographic and pregnancy factors. *Infant Mental Health Journal, 27*, 229–250. doi:10.1002/imhj.20090

Quinlivan, J. A., & Evans, S. F. (2005). Impact of domestic violence and drug abuse in pregnancy on maternal attachment and infant temperament in teenage mothers in the setting of best clinical practice. *Archives of Women's Mental Health, 8*, 191–199. doi:10.1007/s00737-005-0079-7

Renken, B., Egeland, B., Marvinney, D., Mangelsdorf, S., & Sroufe, L. A. (1989). Early childhood antecedents of aggression and passive-withdrawal in early elementary school. *Journal of Personality, 57*, 257–281. doi:10.1111/j.1467-6494.1989.tb00483.x

Rosenblum, K. L., Dayton, C. J., & McDonough, S. (2006). Communicating feelings: Links between mothers' representations of their infants, parenting, and infant emotional development. In O. Mayseless (Ed.), *Parenting representations: Theory, research, and clinical implications* (pp. 109–148). New York, NY: Cambridge University Press. doi:10.1017/CBO9780511499869.005

Rutter, M., Kreppner, J., & Sonuga-Barke, E. J. (2009). Emanuel Miller lecture: attachment security, disinhibited attachment, and attachment disorders: Where do research findings leave the concepts? *Journal of Child Psychology and Psychiatry, and Allied Disciplines, 50*, 529–543. doi:10.1111/j.1469-7610.2009.02042.x

Schore, A. N. (2003). *Affect dysregulation and the disorders of the self.* New York, NY: Norton.

Schuengel, C., Bakermans-Kranenburg, M. J., Van IJzendoorn, M. H. (1999). Frightening maternal behavior linking unresolved loss and disorganized infant attachment. *Journal of Consulting and Clinical Psychology, 67*, 54–63. doi:10.1037/0022-006X.67.1.54

Siddiqui, A., Hägglöf, B., & Eisemann, M. (2000). Own memories of upbringing as a determinant of prenatal attachment in expectant women. *Journal of Reproductive and Infant Psychology, 18*, 67–74. doi:10.1080/02646830050001690

Slade, A., & Aber, J. L. (1992). Attachments, drives, and development: Conflicts and convergences in theory. In J. W. Barron & M. N. Eagle (Eds.), *Interface of psychoanalysis and psychology* (pp. 154–185). Washington, DC: American Psychological Association. doi:10.1037/10118-006

Slade, A., & Cohen, L. J. (1996). The process of parenting and the remembrance of things past. *Infant Mental Health Journal, 17*, 217–238. doi:10.1002/(SICI)1097-0355(199623)17:3<217::AID-IMHJ3>3.0.CO;2-L

Slade, A., Dermer, M., Gibson, L., Graf, F., Grunebaum, L., Reeves, M., & Sitrin, A. (1994). *The pregnancy interview coding system.* Unpublished manuscript.

Sroufe, L. A., Carlson, E. A., Levy, A. K., & Egeland, B. (1999). Implications of attachment theory for developmental psychopathology. *Development and Psychopathology, 11*, 1–13. doi:10.1017/S0954579499001923

Stalker, C. A., & Davies, F. (1995). Attachment organization and adaptation in sexually-abused women. *Canadian Journal of Psychiatry, 40*, 234–240.

Steele, H., Steele, M., & Fonagy, P. (1996). Associations among attachment classifications of mothers, fathers, and their infants. *Child Development, 67*, 541–555. doi:10.2307/1131831

Stern, D. N. (1995). *The motherhood constellation: A unified view of parent–infant psychotherapy.* New York, NY: Basic.

Sternberg, K. J., Lamb, M. E., Guterman, E., Abbott, C. B., & Dawud-Noursi, S. (2005). Adolescents' perceptions of attachments to their mothers and fathers in families with histories of domestic violence: A longitudinal perspective. *Child Abuse & Neglect, 29*, 853–869. doi:10.1016/j.chiabu.2004.07.009

Straus, M. A. (1979). Measuring intrafamily conflict and violence: The Conflict Tactics Scales. *Journal of Marriage and the Family, 41*, 75–81.

Theran, S. A., Levendosky, A. A., Bogat, G. A., & Huth-Bocks, A. C. (2005). Stability and change in mothers' internal representations of their infants over time. *Attachment & Human Development, 7*, 253–268. doi:10.1080/14616730500245609

Troy, M., & Sroufe, L. A. (1987). Victimization among preschoolers: Role of attachment relationship history. *Journal of the American Academy of Child and Adolescent Psychiatry, 26*, 166–172. doi:10.1097/00004583-198703000-00007

Van IJzendoorn, M. H., & Bakermans-Kranenburg, M. (2006). DRD4 7-repeat polymorphism moderates the association between maternal unresolved loss or trauma and infant disorganization. *Attachment & Human Development, 8*, 291–307. doi: 10.1080/14616730601048159

Van IJzendoorn, M. H., Schuengel, C., & Bakermans-Kranenburg, M. J. (1999). Disorganized attachment in early childhood: Meta-analysis of precursors, concomitants, and sequelae. *Development and Psychopathology, 11*, 225–250. doi:10. 1017/S0954579499002035

Vitanza, S., Vogel, L. C., & Marshall, L. L. (1995). Distress and symptoms of posttraumatic stress disorder in abused women. *Violence and Victims, 10*(1), 23–34.

Vondra, J. I., Hommerding, K. D., & Shaw, D. S. (1999). Stability and change in infant attachment in a low-income sample. *Monographs of the Society for Research in Child Development, 64*(3), 119–144. doi:10.1111/1540-5834.000.36

Vondra, J. I., Shaw, D. S., Swearingen, L., Cohen, M., & Owens, E. B. (2001). Attachment stability and emotional and behavioral regulation from infancy to preschool age. *Development and Psychopathology, 13*, 13–33. doi:10.1017/S0954 57940100102X

von Eye, A., & Bogat, G. A. (2006). Mental health in women experiencing intimate partner violence as the efficiency goal of social welfare functions. *International Journal of Social Welfare, 15*(Suppl. 1), S31–S40. doi:10.1111/j.1468-2397. 2006.00442.x

Ward, M. J., & Carlson, E. A. (1995). Associations among adult attachment representations, maternal sensitivity, and infant–mother attachment in a sample of adolescent mothers. *Child Development, 66*(1), 69–79. doi:10.2307/ 1131191

Waters, E., Merrick, S., Treboux, D., Crowell, J., & Albersheim, L. (2000). Attachment security in infancy and early adulthood: A twenty-year longitudinal study. *Child Development, 71*, 684–689. doi:10.1111/1467-8624.00176

Weatherill, R. P., Almerigi, J. B., Levendosky, A. A., Bogat, G. A., & Harris, L. J. (2004). Is maternal depression related to side of infant holding? *International Journal of Behavioral Development, 28*, 421–427. doi:10.1080/01650250444000117

Weinfield, N. S., Whaley, G. J. L., & Egeland, B. (2004). Continuity, discontinuity, and coherence in attachment from infancy to late adolescence: Sequelae of organization and disorganization. *Attachment & Human Development, 6*, 73–97. doi:10.1080/14616730310001659566

Zeanah, C. H., & Benoit, D. (1995). Clinical applications of a parent perception interview in infant mental health. *Child and Adolescent Psychiatric Clinics of North America, 4*, 539–554.

Zeanah, C. H., Benoit, D., Barton, M. L., & Hirshberg, L. (1996). *Working model of the child interview coding manual.* Unpublished manuscript.

Zeanah, C. H., Benoit, D., Hirshberg, L., Barton, M. L., & Regan, C. (1994). Mothers' representations of their infants are concordant with infant attachment classifications. *Developmental Issues in Psychiatry and Psychology, 1,* 9–18.

Zeanah, C. H., Danis, B., Hirshberg, L., Benoit, D., Miller, D., & Heller, S. S. (1999). Disorganized attachment associated with partner violence: A research note. *Infant Mental Health Journal, 20,* 77–86. doi:10.1002/(SICI)1097-0355(199921)20:1<77:: AID-IMHJ6>3.0.CO;2-S

Zeanah, C. H., & Scheeringa, M. S. (1997). The experience and effects of violence in infancy. In J. D. Osofsky (Ed.), *Children in a violent society* (pp. 97–123). New York, NY: Guilford Press.

3

PERINATAL CHILD–PARENT PSYCHOTHERAPY: ADAPTATION OF AN EVIDENCE-BASED TREATMENT FOR PREGNANT WOMEN AND BABIES EXPOSED TO INTIMATE PARTNER VIOLENCE

ALICIA F. LIEBERMAN, MANUELA A. DIAZ, AND PATRICIA VAN HORN

Pregnancy and the perinatal period make up a particularly vulnerable developmental stage for the baby and the parents due to the infant's biological immaturity, the pregnant woman and new mother's changing physical condition, and the emotional demands posed by the transition to parenthood. The risks to mother and baby are exacerbated in situations of intimate partner violence (IPV), which poses physical and emotional dangers to both the mother and the child. This chapter describes perinatal child–parent psychotherapy (Perinatal CPP) as a treatment model designed to prevent or ameliorate the short- and long-term consequences of IPV on child and maternal safety and well-being. Perinatal CPP is an adaptation to pregnancy and the postpartum period of child–parent psychotherapy, an evidence-based treatment for infants, toddlers, and preschool-age children exposed to IPV and other traumatic stressors (Lieberman & Van Horn, 2005, 2008).

IMPACT OF IPV ON PREGNANT WOMEN
AND THEIR OFFSPRING

A pregnant woman has a 35.6% greater risk of being the victim of violence than a nonpregnant woman (Gelles, 1988). With documented prevalence rates equal or greater than routinely screened complications of pregnancy
(Gazmararian et al., 1996; Taillieu & Brownridge, 2010), IPV during pregnancy
has been consistently linked to adverse maternal–fetal outcomes that extend
beyond the perinatal period. Exposure to IPV in pregnancy is associated with
maternal low weight gain, hemorrhage, infections, anemia, predelivery hospitalization, and cesarean sections as well as infant prematurity, low birth weight,
susceptibility to infectious diseases, and state dysregulation manifested in excessive crying and feeding and sleeping problems (Coker, Sanderson, & Dong,
2004; Jasinski, 2004). There is an estimated 50% to 70% overlap between IPV
and child abuse (Kitzmann, Gaylord, Holt, & Kenny, 2003), posing ongoing
threats to the baby immediately after delivery and during infancy. One third of
maltreated infants under age 1 are injured during their 1st week of life, and 44%
of child abuse mortalities occur during the 1st year of the baby's life (Child
Welfare Information Gateway, 2008).

The physical and emotional hardships experienced by pregnant women
in violent relationships take a toll on the mother–infant relationship. Due to
the increased prevalence of depression (Golding, 1999), posttraumatic stress
disorder (PTSD; Jones, Hughes, & Unterstaller, 2001), and other emotional
disturbances triggered or aggravated by IPV, battered women have greater difficulty bonding with their infants and engage in higher rates of punitive parenting and child abuse, with minority mothers particularly vulnerable because of
their more adverse socioeconomic circumstances and access to fewer resources
(Osofsky, 1999; Roberts, 2002). The risk of child abuse increases because infants
exposed to IPV may be more challenging to care for due to greater irritability,
feeding and sleeping problems, and illness risk, while battered women and their
violent partners often lack the personal resources to face the stresses associated with parenting and may respond with anger and withdrawal of physical and emotional care (Osofsky, 2003). Pregnancy and the perinatal period
offer important opportunities for intervention to prevent child abuse and
alleviate the negative impact of IPV on infant development, both directly
and through its effect on the mother–infant relationship.

PERINATAL CHILD–PARENT PSYCHOTHERAPY
AS TRAUMA-FOCUSED TREATMENT

Perinatal CPP represents an extension into pregnancy of Child–Parent
Psychotherapy (CPP), a trauma-focused treatment for children—from birth to

age 5—that involves meeting with parent and child jointly and using play, caregiving routines, and spontaneous interactions as the basis to build safety and restore reciprocity (Lieberman & Van Horn, 2005, 2008). CPP is rooted in Fraiberg's (1980) pioneering clinical focus on enhancing the mother–child relationship with the goal of curtailing the intergenerational transmission of psychopathology. As with Fraiberg's model, CPP is based on the premise that the quality of caregiving is a reflection of how the parent was cared for as a child, but it expands on this understanding by focusing also on the impact that violence and other stressors have on the parent's state of mind and capacity to empathize with the child's experience (Lieberman & Van Horn, 2008). Perinatal CPP is based on theoretical premises and clinical strategies that have empirical evidence of efficacy on a range of conditions that affect the emotional well-being of infants, toddlers, and preschool-age children, including anxious attachment (Lieberman, Weston, & Pawl, 1991), maltreated infants (Cicchetti, Rogosh, & Toth, 2006), toddlers of depressed mothers (Toth, Rogosch, Manly, & Cicchetti, 2006), maltreated preschool-age children (Toth, Maughan, Manly, Spagnola, & Cicchetti, 2002), and preschool-age children who witnessed IPV (Lieberman, Ghosh Ippen, & Van Horn, 2006; Lieberman, Van Horn, & Ghosh Ippen, 2005). Exposure to IPV is the most frequent stressor reported for infants and mothers referred for treatment at our clinic, the Child Trauma Research Program (CTRP) at San Francisco General Hospital, and it is often associated with other family adversities, including poverty, low parental education, absent fathers, maternal depression, and child neglect (Lieberman, Van Horn, & Ozer, 2005). IPV in the present can be a source of traumatic stress both for the mother and for the child, regardless of the mother's childhood experiences. For this reason, the hallmark of CPP is simultaneous clinical attention to present trauma for the parent and the child as well as to the childhood sources of parental dysfunction. The therapist intervenes to address maladaptive perceptions, beliefs, and behaviors in the both child and the parent and to foster role-appropriate mutuality between the parent and the child. This therapeutic attitude is based on the premise that modeling affect regulation and interpersonal attunement can be instrumental in generating these frames of mind in the parent and the child.

INTEGRATED MODEL OF MENTAL HEALTH CARE WITH PRIMARY CARE

Addressing the nexus between maternal and child safety and well-being in IPV situations during pregnancy and the perinatal period calls for coordination of services across health care providers, integrating primary obstetrical and pediatric care with family support and mental health treatment. To address these clinical needs, we launched a model of collaboration linking CTRP's trauma-trained infant mental health providers, obstetrical providers, and pediatrics. Referrals to the program come from social workers in the obstetrician–gynecologist (OB-GYN) department who ask pregnant women coming for prenatal care about environmental adversities such as IPV and other traumatic stressors. When a woman reports stress or violence with her partner, the social worker briefly describes the intervention, and if the mother agrees to a referral, the CTRP clinician meets with her at the next prenatal care appointment to offer weekly counseling through pregnancy, delivery, and until the baby is at least 6 months old. After the baby's birth, the pediatric care provider is also linked into the service team. All of the providers are located at our county general hospital, which facilitates collaboration.

The importance of linking primary health care with mental health services is supported by the stark statistics of the population we treat. Data from 41 pregnant women referred for treatment show that more than half (52%) experienced pregnancy complications, with vaginal bleeding and hypertension as the most frequent problems. The women were highly symptomatic, reporting symptoms of both depression (73%) and PTSD (60%). About half of the women (48%) reported living with the baby's father. Only 26% reported using birth control, and 69% reported that the pregnancy was unplanned, representing an additional stress in already difficult socioeconomic circumstances. All the women were publicly insured, their average monthly income was $1,075 ($SD = \$645$), and only 24% of them were employed. About half of the women (40%) were expecting their first child, and approximately one third of them had left older children in their countries of origin to pursue greater economic stability in the United States.

IPV perpetrated by the woman was an unexpected early finding as we implemented the treatment model. Approximately 30% of the women reported that they engaged in physical violence against their partners by slapping, shoving, or throwing objects at them. Use of knives, guns, or other lethal objects was infrequent, but a few women reported engaging in violence that led to their partner's severe injury and hospitalization. This finding underscores the importance of assessing and treating maternal and mutual violence in addition to violence perpetrated by the male partner when working with battered women and their infants.

IPV exposure influences women's choices for primary care. They tend to use the emergency room rather than regular pediatric appointments for their infants' care, resulting in less appropriate pediatric care and posing a burden for the increasingly stressed public health system. When asked about their reasons for choosing the emergency room, the mothers said that they associated the need for medical care with serious health problems and often avoided regular contact with the medical system for fear of legal problems due to being undocumented or medical reports of family violence. Cultural factors, including unfamiliarity with the U.S. health care system, also lead to frequent misunderstandings between mothers and pediatric providers. For example, some mothers worried that vaccinations could cause AIDS or that bringing healthy babies to the pediatric clinic could make them sick from exposure to pathogens. Many mothers believed that their pediatric providers discriminated against them by not offering the treatment expected by the mother, for example by not prescribing antibiotics to treat a baby's flu symptoms, a widely accepted approach to treatment in their countries of origin. The health providers at times also voiced negative perceptions of the mothers. Even medical providers, who are committed to underserved populations, may believe that the mothers are neglectful when they do not comply with medical recommendations, especially if language and cultural barriers make it difficult for them to understand the reasons for the mothers' behavior.

Maternal descriptions of attitudes toward medical care highlight the importance of understanding the cultural background for their choices. This understanding enabled the CTRP clinicians, who belong to a range of cultural and ethnic groups and many of whom are bilingual in Spanish and English, to serve as cultural mediators between the mothers and pediatric care providers. The clinicians take the time to understand the specifics of mutual misconceptions between mothers and pediatric care providers and frame them in a cultural context that avoids blaming either side. Active engagement in promoting well baby care has become an integral component of our intervention as a result of this experience.

IMPLEMENTING PERINATAL CHILD–PARENT PSYCHOTHERAPY

When CPP treatment begins during pregnancy, as is the case with Perinatal CPP, the woman's experiences of her pregnancy are linked with her fantasies, fears, attributions, and hopes for her unborn child. After the birth, the therapeutic focus turns to the mother's experience of labor and delivery, her perception of her newborn baby, and the harmonies and dissonances of the rhythm that is being cocreated between mother and baby. To guide and monitor the effectiveness of the intervention, the clinician collects data at three points during treatment, as described next.

Intake Assessment

Intervention begins with a 3-week assessment designed to foster the therapeutic alliance, collect demographic information, and ascertain the mother's psychological functioning. The clinician administers the following psychometric instruments:

- Abuse Assessment Screen (AAS; McFarlane & Parker, 1994). The AAS is used to determine the frequency, severity, perpetrator, and body sites of injury within a stated period of time. It is well received by respondents, has a high rate of response, and has been validated in multiethnic samples.
- Adult–Adolescent Parenting Inventory-2 (AAPI-2; Bavolek & Keene, 2001). The AAPI-2 measures parents' attitudes about corporal punishment, role reversal, expectations of the child, and empathy. It is found to differentiate between abusive and nonabusive parents. In this sample, the psychometric properties of this scale were acceptable at the two assessment periods, with internal consistencies of .91 and .85, respectively.
- Center for Epidemiological Studies Depression Scale (CES-D; Radloff, 1977). The CES-D has validity screening for depression among Spanish- and English-speaking populations in large-scale national studies. The CES-D was found to have excellent internal consistencies throughout the two assessment periods (coefficient alphas ranging from .90 to .92).
- Davidson Trauma Scale (DTS; Davidson et al., 1997). This DTS contains 17 items that mirror the diagnostic criteria of PTSD and has strong validity and reliability. The reliability of the DTS for this sample was high (Cronbach's coefficient alphas were .93 and .95, respectively).
- Life Stressor Checklist-Revised (LSC-R; Wolfe, Kimerling, Brown, Chrestman, & Levin, 1996). The LSC-R measures caregivers' lifetime exposure to stressful life events. Scores are significantly correlated with a PTSD diagnosis.
- Parenting Stress Index-Short Form (PSI-SF; Abidin, 1995). The PSI-SF yields a Total Stress score from three subscales—Parental Distress, Parent–Child Dysfunctional Interaction, and Difficult Child—and has a validity subscale to determine the amount of response bias (defensive responding). The PSI-SF has been shown to have good reliability and validity.

Childbirth and Neonatal Assessment

The clinician is notified of the baby's birth by the mother or the OB-GYN social worker, and he or she makes a visit to mother and child while they are still in the hospital. This visit is an opportunity to welcome the baby into the clinical partnership with the mother as well as to gather data from the medical chart and from maternal reports about the labor and delivery.

The clinician administers the Newborn Behavioral Observations System (NBO; Nugent, Keefer, Minear, Johnson, & Blanchard, 2007) to assess the newborn and promote maternal understanding and joy in the baby's capacities. The NBO is a relationship-building tool that encourages the parent's capacity for reflective functioning and helps to promote a positive bond between parent and child. Its administration helps clinician and parent discover together the full richness of the newborn infant's behavioral repertoire, including capacity for self-regulation and response to stress. Mothers are taught that their babies are born with a repertoire of skills to adapt to their environment and are well equipped to communicate their needs to their parents. Through the administration of a set of 18 infant behavioral observations using two stimuli (i.e., a rattle and a flashlight), the clinician and the mother obtain individualized information about the infant's preferences and the areas in which the infant may need support in adapting to his/her environment. This process of *discovering the infant* is also used to strengthen the mother–infant relationship. This is particularly helpful for new parents whose posttraumatic preoccupations with their own emotional states may interfere with their capacity to deploy their attention to focus on their infant's signals.

Treatment Outcome Assessment

Treatment is provided until the baby is 6 months old. At this time, the measures administered at intake are readministered to assess treatment outcome. In addition, infant development is assessed using the Mullen Scales of Early Learning-AGS Edition (MSEL; Mullen, 1995), which assess early development in the domains of gross motor, fine motor, visual perception, receptive language, and expressive language functioning. It has good test–retest reliability and good construct validity.

Perinatal CPP Treatment Modalities

Perinatal CPP employs a range of therapeutic modalities to address maternal emotional problems and promote the mother–infant relationships during pregnancy and after the baby's birth. Therapy sessions are geared to providing appropriate support, guidance, and opportunities for emotional growth as the pregnant woman transitions to motherhood. Both during pregnancy and after childbirth, interventions are consistently geared to two main goals: (a) promoting the mother's self-care, attunement to the fetus, and responsiveness to the baby's signals through caregiving practices that are appropriate to the infant's developmental needs and individual characteristics; and (b) targeting negative maternal attributions to the baby and maladaptive caregiving practices by guiding the mother in elucidating their roots in her experiences of adversity and trauma. Cultural considerations guide every aspect of the treatment because of the mother's values, attitudes and beliefs about gender roles, child-rearing practices, and culturally acceptable behaviors. The therapeutic modalities deployed toward these goals are described below.

Psychoeducation About IPV

Clinicians provide psychoeducation about the impact of IPV and life adversities on the pregnant woman's and baby's physical and emotional well-being. This treatment modality aims at normalizing the woman's symptoms of depression, anxiety, and traumatic stress by framing them as a predictable and understandable response to her circumstances. Our program library contains written materials and DVDs that are made available to expand the knowledge of clinicians as well as mothers. Clinicians give the mothers written material on parenting during the 1st year with developmental tips and information about how babies change, what they like to do, crib safety, safe use of car seats, building healthy sleeping and feeding habits, and other topics (Riley, Shatell, Nitzke, & Ostergren, 2006). We wrote a Resource Guide for Pregnant Women in San Francisco that clinicians use as a guide to refer mothers to programs that offer basic resources and other services. The guide is also distributed to staff of our OB-GYN and pediatrics collaborators and to community family resource centers.

Body-Based and Mindfulness-Promoting Interventions

Traumatic stress derails normative patterns of affect regulation, resulting in symptoms of hyperarousal, numbness, exaggerated stress responses, muscular tension, and somatic symptoms (American Psychiatric Association, 1994; van der Kolk, 1996). Based on the concept that the body is the repository of traumatic memories and sensations, we have incorporated practices that help mothers become aware of and tolerate negative body sensations in themselves. This greater self-awareness is then used as a link to their becoming more attuned to their baby's physical sensations and emotions. As the mother speaks and interacts with the baby, the clinician tracks the mother's affect and its manifestation in body postures and movements and, when appropriate, directs the mother's attention to her body and asks her to describe how she is feeling in the moment. This tracking of the mother's affective and somatic experience in the moment becomes an opportunity to understand how the present themes and concomitant bodily responses are influenced by memories from childhood or from the more recent past. This technique facilitates the retrieval of past memories, often with an immediate effect on the mother's body sensations and emotional state. Mindfulness practices involve bringing the mother's attention to the present to help her practice awareness that she is in a safe space in the moment and that remembering the trauma need not entail reliving it in the form of emotional and somatic dysregulation. Relaxation techniques are used to reinforce this message, including deep breathing, graduated relaxation, grounding, and the creation of visualized safe spaces.

Infant massage is incorporated in Perinatal CPP to promote maternal attunement to the baby's biological rhythms. Infants are responsive to manifestations of stress in their mothers and may respond with seemingly unpredictable crying; difficulty soothing; and feeding, sleeping, and digestive problems. There is research evidence indicating that teaching mothers to massage their infants is efficacious in improving maternal mood, infant sleep patterns and fussiness, and mother–infant interaction (Field, 2000). A CTRP staff member is a certified infant massage therapist whose services are offered to mothers who have difficulty holding or touching their babies or whose babies have difficulty with homeostasis and self-regulation. Infant massage is particularly useful as a concrete intervention for mothers who find physical contact aversive as the result of coercive sexual experiences and physical abuse. Massaging the baby offers these mothers a developmentally acceptable framework that makes it possible for them to feel safe when touching their babies with the protective guidance of the clinician. The infant's increased relaxation and pleasure in response are powerful sources of positive reinforcement for the mother. Clinicians report that mothers who use infant massage to soothe their distressed babies describe feeling more competent in their daily caregiving.

Reflective Developmental Guidance

Clinicians provide guidance on pregnancy, delivery, and parenting during the perinatal period and the first months of the baby's life. Developmental guidance is offered not in didactic fashion but couched in the effort to help the mother become attuned to her baby's subjective experience. This modality is employed in response to two clinical situations: (a) when it is clear that the mother lacks accurate information about her own or the baby's developmental stage and (b) when the mother has a negative interpretation of her baby's or her own motives and behavior. Reflective developmental guidance is intended to promote in the mothers a "theory of mind" attitude where interest and compassion for her baby's and her own experiences becomes the mother's prevailing frame for reading interpersonal and intrapsychic signals.

The mothers referred to our program have as a rule only rudimentary knowledge about the changes in their bodies as the result of pregnancy. They frequently report being afraid of labor and delivery, and this is particularly true among immigrant mothers who are unfamiliar with childbirth medical practices in the United States. The clinician elicits the mother's description of what is happening to her body and provides reflective developmental information about the meaning of these changes. After the baby's birth, the clinician engages the mother in conversations about feeding, sleeping, bathing, and other caregiving routines that provide the opportunity to offer reflective developmental information as needed.

Insight-Oriented Interpretations

These kinds of interpretations are used to link current emotional states to early experiences and present traumatic triggers, with a dual emphasis on elucidating the "ghosts in the nursery" that interfere with the mother's emotional claim on the baby (Fraiberg, 1980) and on retrieving loving early memories that can serve as "angels in the nursery" that guide the mother's plans for how to care for her child (Lieberman, Padron, Van Horn, & Harris, 2005). The clinician listens to the mother's description of her adverse relationship experiences both in childhood and as an adult with the goal of understanding how these experiences shed light on the mother's present difficulties in parenting, including negative attributions (e.g., being manipulative, aggressive, or greedy) that lead to ignoring the baby's needs or responding in ways that exacerbate those needs. Once these processes are uncovered and understood, the mother can be guided to create and practice appropriate ways of responding to the baby's signals that become self-sustaining because the baby's positive response reinforces the mother's pleasure in her competence and in her growing intimacy with her baby.

Concrete Assistance With Problems of Living and Crisis Intervention

The mothers referred for treatment often live in precarious financial circumstances. Poverty, inadequate housing, lack of a steady income, and the threat of deportation among undocumented immigrants are frequent sources of stress. Clinicians define their role as attending to the basic needs of the mother and infant in addition to their emotional needs, and intervene when necessary by making referrals for needed services, making phone calls to facilitate problem solving, explaining how systems work, and intervening as needed to ensure safety for mother and child.

Fathers' Participation in Treatment

The increased risk of IPV during pregnancy is a powerful but undervalued indicator of the stress that impending fatherhood may pose for a man. While a woman's pregnancy sets in motion prenatal and perinatal care for the mother-to-be, there are no formal services to educate men about the emotional challenges that they are likely to experience during their partner's pregnancy and to help them plan for their new responsibilities. Men are often ignored or actively excluded from services offered to pregnant women.

The general neglect of fathers as active participants in their partner's pregnancy becomes much more pronounced when men perpetrate IPV, and there is much debate about the desirability of including them in treatment (Groves, Van Horn, & Lieberman, 2007). We developed a set of assessment procedures designed to evaluate the safety and clinical appropriateness of engaging the father in treatment, including the questions of whether, when, and how to do so. The first consideration is whether the mother wants her partner to be involved. Many mothers in violent relationships use treatment as a private opportunity to safely explore whether they want to remain in the relationship and how they want the relationship to change now that there is a baby at stake. It is important to honor the mother's motivations and enable her to use the treatment as a tool to plan for a safer future for herself and her baby. The second consideration is safety for the mother, the baby, and the clinician if treatment is offered. Many of the fathers are described by the mothers as unpredictably violent; others stalk the mothers after the relationship ends. Court orders may be in place restricting the father's access to the mother and/or the child. Each one of these situations needs careful evaluation in the decision to extend fathers an invitation to treatment.

If the mother wants the father to be involved in treatment, the clinician makes clear that before treatment can be offered, the father needs to participate in an initial assessment to ascertain his capacity for self-reflection and remorse, potential for violence and lethality, and commitment to parenting prior to offering treatment. We adopted five criteria for offering treatment to a violent father: (a) the mother wants to include the father in the treatment; (b) the father acknowledges that he engages in violent behavior; (c) he expresses the wish to change and makes a commitment to refrain from violence during the treatment; (d) he is willing to participate in an anger management program in tandem with starting treatment; and (e) he signs releases of information that enables the clinician to gain access to information about him from all relevant sources, including mental health providers, probation officers, child welfare workers, and the courts (Groves et al., 2007). The format of treatment when the father is involved can be adapted in response to clinical needs, but the focus remains on the safety and well-being of the baby and the mother. In some situations, the father attends every session; in other situations, he attends at regular intervals but there are also separate sessions with the mother or, after the baby's birth, with the mother and the child. When fathers are included, safety remains a primary focus, and the Perinatal CPP therapeutic modalities described earlier are deployed flexibly to help the father grow in his capacity to become a safe partner and a competent parent.

A CLINICAL ILLUSTRATION

Rosalind, a 21-year-old, was referred for treatment when she was 4 months pregnant after disclosing that her husband of 1 year had hit her on the face during an argument and was regularly violent with her. The couple had recently been evicted from their apartment and had moved in with Rosalind's in-laws, with whom she reported a "terrible" relationship. She reported feeling "all alone" without the support of her family and friends, who lived out of state.

Intake Assessment

At intake, Rosalind was in the clinical range for depression and traumatic stress, and she endorsed attitudes that placed her at risk of abusing her child. She showed little interest in the fetus, as demonstrated both in the fetal attachment instrument and in clinical observations. She tended to be dismissive of her pregnancy and showed no interest or pleasure in how the baby was growing or in the physical sensations associated with fetal movement.

Rosalind grew up in a closely knit family that suffered from extreme poverty. There was recurrent IPV between Rosalind's parents as well as frequent physical abuse of their four children. Rosalind often tried to intervene to protect her mother from her father's violence, and she was physically attacked by the father in return. She met her future husband at work and married him after a 2-month relationship when she found out that she was pregnant. The violence in their relationship began a month after the marriage when the young couple began having severe financial problems. Rosalind's husband slapped her, pushed her, pinned her against the wall, and called her names. The police were called during one incident of violence resulting in Rosalind's husband being mandated to attend a perpetrator treatment program. Rosalind reported that he attended the group meetings regularly.

Prenatal Therapy Sessions

The early pregnancy sessions focused on helping Rosalind construct a coherent narrative of the traumatic events she had endured. The intervention made use of all the Perinatal CPP therapeutic modalities. Psychoeducation was provided about perinatal depression and traumatic stress and their impact on the mother–infant relationship. Body-based techniques were used to strengthen her bond to her fetus and help her manage her anxiety and PTSD symptoms. Reflective developmental information was offered when Rosalind made derogatory or dismissive remarks about her body changes. Insight-oriented interpretation was employed to help Rosalind make links between her terror as an abused young child, her expectation that her husband's violence would never change in spite of his conscientious attendance to his class for batterers, and her feelings of depression and despair. The clinician also made referrals to appropriate community programs for assistance with the family's concrete needs.

In a typical early session, Rosalind told the therapist about her worries that her baby would suffer from the poverty and hardship that she experienced while growing up. The therapist said, "It sounds like you wish to give your baby what you didn't have," and went on to briefly mention some of Rosalind's early difficult experiences. As Rosalind recalled specific childhood events that made her feel frightened and uncared for, the therapist supported Rosalind's wish to give her baby a different life where the child would have "enough to eat, a place where he can play and feel safe."

Although Rosalind spoke in this session about her concern for the baby's future, she did not show any behavior indicating an emotional tie to the fetus. The therapist took action to make the baby real by looking at Rosalind's belly and saying, "Your mother is telling me that she wants to give you what you need . . . what you deserve. . . . Your mother worries when she feels that she won't be able to give you that . . . but she is trying very hard to figure out ways to give you a nice place where to live when you come to this world, give you enough food for you to grow healthy . . . a place where you feel safe and cared for." The therapist then asked Rosalind whether she had ever talked to her baby, for example, when the baby moved. Rosalind responded that she had never thought about doing that and "wouldn't know how to do it." The therapist asked Rosalind whether she would like to try it and see how she felt. With a smile of interest and curiosity, Rosalind nodded in agreement. The therapist instructed mother to gently place her hand on her belly and to either simply observe her belly as she took deep breaths in and out or if she felt like it, she could say something to her baby girl, whom the parents had already named "Sofia" after a beloved aunt. Rosalind initially observed her belly while she took deep breaths with the therapist. After the breathing exercise and while caressing her belly, Rosalind said to the therapist, "My baby . . . You know, I want her to have a good life." The therapist reinforced Rosalind's behavior and said, while looking at the mother's belly, "Your mom loves you very much and wants to make sure she can give you a life that has everything that you need and deserve so you can grow up to be a healthy little girl!"

As treatment continued, Rosalind began to describe in greater detail her experiences of being physically abused as a child. The therapist directed her attention to her bodily sensations and demonstrated deep breathing and muscular flexing and tensing exercises to regulate her bodily sensations. Rosalind showed remarkable ability in incorporating these exercises into her daily routine, and she reported that she found them useful in managing her responses to traumatic reminders.

As Rosalind's due date approached, the therapy sessions focused increasingly on helping her manage her anxiety about giving birth. Although Rosalind had been able to use body-based interventions and exercises effectively to manage her distress at memories of past events, as her pregnancy advanced, she reported that she was feeling very anxious and worried about the actual labor and delivery and that sometimes these feelings were overwhelming. The therapist acknowledged the appropriateness of these feelings, telling Rosalind that her anxiety was very common among first-time mothers and asking her to describe what she noticed when she worried about giving birth. Rosalind replied that whenever she thought about going into labor, she felt pain on her neck and shoulders, her palms began sweating, and at times she had difficulty breathing. The therapist used this opportunity to provide psychoeducation about how the body reacts to stress and to help Rosalind practice the grounding and relaxation techniques she had already learned to manage the stress associated with her impending delivery. She also helped Rosalind prepare a birth plan that included requesting the support of a doula during her labor and delivery.

Childbirth and Neonatal Assessment

With the doula's support, Rosalind gave birth to a healthy baby girl weighing 8 pounds, 11 ounces. Labor and delivery proceeded without complications, and the therapist visited Rosalind and her baby Sofia at the newborn nursery several hours after delivery.

Sofia was asleep when the therapist arrived, giving the therapist a chance to elicit Rosalind's experience of labor and delivery. With the baby still asleep, the therapist used the NBO System to show Rosalind how capable Sofia was of adapting to her environment and to demonstrate the capacities of a newborn baby. Sofia habituated with ease to both light and sound. When Sofia was uncovered and placed on her back, the therapist helped Rosalind observe the ways Sofia showed physiological reactivity through color changes, tremors, and startle and how to reduce Sofia's reaction by swaddling or tucking in her arms to inhibit their random movement. Together they observed Sofia's strong sucking and rooting responses, her robust crying, and her strong grasp. This pleased Rosalind, who commented how lucky she was to have a "sturdy/robust little girl" and added that she would no longer be scared of hurting her when she handled her.

Postnatal Therapy Sessions

Rosalind resumed regular therapy sessions when Sofia was 4 weeks old, bringing the baby with her. She reported feeling awkward, not knowing when and how to feed Sofia because she wanted to establish a feeding schedule but Sofia sometimes cried hard, became red and sweaty, and had difficulty swallowing her milk. She said, "This baby is impatient like her father. She wants everything right away and gets furious when she does not get it." The clinician had to suppress an impulse to be critical of this negative maternal attribution and say something that was protective of the baby because she knew that this would only alienate Rosalind and make her feel "all alone," a feeling that she reported often during the sessions. Instead, the therapist acknowledged that it took time to establish a feeding routine that worked for both the mother and the baby, and she commented that Rosalind and Sofia were still getting to know each other. The therapist then asked if Sofia gave signals that showed Rosalind that she might be getting hungry before starting to cry so hard. Rosalind said that Sofia started to whimper and move her arms and legs, but often it was soon after her last feeding. It emerged that Rosalind was feeding Sofia every 4 hours, and the therapist wondered aloud whether that might be too long for Sofia. She added, "Do you think that her whimpering may be an effort to tell you that she already digested her last bottle and needs another one because she is hungry?" This possibility came as a surprise to Rosalind, who was cautiously receptive to the idea. The clinician then said, "You know how we enjoy and digest our food better if we are not starving when we start eating? I think you will find that if Sofia starts whimpering and does not calm down if you change her position or hold her, she is telling you that she needs her next bottle and you will have an easier time feeding her before she gets so upset." Rosalind said she would try this. An opportunity to do so emerged later in the session when Sofia started whimpering in the way that her mother had described. The therapist supported Rosalind in noticing Sofia's cues and offering a bottle before Sofia began to cry. Rosalind was pleased that Sofia calmed rapidly and easily swallowed her milk. She also reflected that with Sofia calm, she was able to continue the conversation with the therapist that had been interrupted by Sofia's whimpering.

About 6 weeks after Sofia's birth, Rosalind told the therapist for the first time that when she was 14 she had been raped by her 17-year-old neighbor. Rosalind reported that she had always remembered the rape, but she had been able to put it "out of her mind" until after Sofia's birth, when she began having recurrent nightmares about it. She woke from those nightmares feeling terrified and short of breath and with her heart pounding rapidly. As Rosalind told the therapist about her nightmare and her response to it, her face became flushed; she rubbed her neck, said that her head hurt, and struggled to breathe. The therapist helped Rosalind use the relaxation techniques that she had successfully used to manage other stressors, and Rosalind rapidly regained her sense of calm. Over several weeks, as she explored with the therapist the reasons that the nightmare might have emerged at this particular time, Rosalind was able to make two associations. First, she said that both during the rape and during the delivery of her baby she had felt "tied down" and "unable to run." At both times, she'd experienced pelvic pain. As she made this connection, and continued to use grounding and relaxation to help her manage her nightmares, Rosalind found that both her nightmares and her distress at recalling the rape decreased in intensity. The second association that she made between the rape and her current circumstances was that her husband was pressuring her to resume their sexual relationship. She said tearfully that she did not feel ready and that she was afraid that it would hurt. The therapist gently encouraged her to think about ways to talk to her husband about her experience, something that Rosalind had not done before. The next week, Rosalind reported that she had been able to talk with her husband and that he had been understanding about her fears and agreed to wait a little longer before they resumed sexual activity.

The use of Perinatal CPP with Rosalind and Sofia exemplifies the versatile nature of this intervention. The range of therapeutic modalities deployed had in common an unwavering focus on safety and capacity for reflection. Safety was defined both as external safety in the form of monitoring the risk of violence and taking steps to prevent it and as internal safety in the form of internal regulation and interpersonal attunement. The case of Rosalind and Sofia involved risk of moderate IPV that was decreased by the willing and conscientious participation of Rosalind's husband in a batterers' group and his refraining from physical aggression throughout the time that the therapist met with Rosalind and Sofia. At follow-up 6 months after the termination of treatment, Rosalind reported that things were going well for the family and that Sofia, at 1 year of age, was clearly thriving.

EMPIRICAL FINDINGS OF TREATMENT EFFECTIVENESS

A pilot study without a comparison group showed the preliminary effectiveness of Perinatal CPP for pregnant women exposed to IPV. We examined treatment outcome by comparing maternal scores at intake and at the end of treatment for 41 mothers who completed treatment using one-way within-subjects (repeated measures) analysis of variance. Results revealed that there were significant differences in PTSD between the two times of measurement: $F(1, 40) = 39.91$, $p = .000$, partial $\eta^2 = .499$; depression, $F(1, 41) = 29.05$, $p = .000$, partial $\eta^2 = .415$; and parenting attitudes, $F(1, 39) = 40.94$, $p = .000$, partial $\eta^2 = .512$. Scores for symptoms of PTSD (at intake: $M = 50.78$, $SD = 30.07$; at posttreatment: $M = 19.93$, $SD = 20.17$) and depression (at intake: $M = 26.63$, $SD = 14.62$; at posttreatment: $M = 12.33$, $SD = 9.53$) decreased significantly by the end of treatment. Scores for parenting attitudes improved (at intake: $M = 132.03$, $SD = 19.29$; at posttreatment: $M = 147.33$, $SD = 12.86$)

for the entire sample. On the Mullen Scales of Early Learning, the babies obtained scores in the average range in all domains: gross motor ($M = 53.28$, $SD = 9.41$), visual reception ($M = 55.09$, $SD = 7.29$), fine motor ($M = 51.05$, $SD = 11.92$), receptive language ($M = 46.95$, $SD = 10.89$), expressive language ($M = 49.33$, $SD = 8.65$). By the end of treatment, no child abuse or neglect reports had been filed against any of the mothers, and no incidents of intimate partner violence had occurred, as evidenced by clinical information retrieved from the mothers' charts.

CONCLUSION

Perinatal CPP is emerging as a promising approach to the prevention of the negative consequences of IPV exposure during the perinatal period. The focus on the pregnant woman's physical and emotional safety is used as the vehicle for helping her to prepare for her baby's birth and for the demands of becoming a mother. Although the case illustration of Rosalind and Sofia shows the potential for successful outcome, treatment does not always proceed so smoothly. There are situations of such imminent danger or actual severe violence that the therapist must take drastic action to protect the baby and the mother, including helping to implement their move to a battered women's shelter and making a report to child protective services. One of the features of working with victims of IPV is the relative unpredictability of violent episodes. The therapist must never be lulled into a sense of safety because, once violence has occurred in an intimate relationship, it is always possible that it may happen again.

Attention to and support for the clinician's experience are essential ingredients of treatment. Clinical supervision or consultation that allow for therapist self-reflection and support for the therapist's experience are necessary regardless of levels of experience or expertise because being responsible for many clinical cases in which there is high risk to the safety of mothers and young children drains emotional energy and can easily cloud clinical acumen. Preventing vicarious traumatization through institutionalized sources of supervision and support should be a core element in building an effective treatment delivery system for young children and their parents in situations of IPV and other traumatic stressors.

REFERENCES

Abidin, R. R. (1995). *Parenting Stress Index: Professional manual* (3rd ed.). Odessa, FL: Psychological Assessment Resources.

American Psychiatric Association. (1994). *Diagnostic and statistical manual of mental disorders* (4th ed.). Washington, DC: Author.

Bavolek, S. J., & Keene, R. G. (2001). *Adult-Adolescent Parenting Inventory: Administration and development handbook.* Park City, UT: Family Development Associates.

Child Welfare Information Gateway. (2008). *Child abuse and neglect fatalities: Statistics and interventions.* Retrieved from http://www.childwelfare.gov/pubs/factsheets/fatality.cfm

Cicchetti, D., Rogosch, F. A., & Toth, S. L. (2006). Fostering secure attachment in infants in maltreating families through preventive interventions. *Development and Psychopathology, 18,* 623–649. doi:10.1017/S0954579406060329

Coker, A. L., Sanderson, M., & Dong, B. (2004). Partner violence during pregnancy and risk of adverse pregnancy outcomes. *Paediatric and Perinatal Epidemiology, 18,* 260–269. doi:10.1111/j.1365-3016.2004.00569.x

Davidson, J. R. T., Book, S. W., Colket, J. T., Tupler, L. A., Roth, S., David, D., . . . Feldman, M. E. (1997). Assessment of a new self-rating scale for post-traumatic stress disorder. *Psychological Medicine, 27*(1), 153–160. doi:10.1017/S0033291796004229

Field, T. (2000). Infant massage therapy. In Z. H. Zeanah (Ed.), *Handbook of infant mental health* (pp. 494–500). New York, NY: Guilford Press.

Fraiberg, S. (Ed.). (1980). *Clinical studies in infant mental health: The first year of life.* New York, NY: Basic Books.

Gazmararian, J. A., Lazorick, S., Spitz, A. M., Ballard, T. J., Saltzman, L. E., & Marks, J. S. (1996). Prevalence of violence during pregnancy: A review of the literature. *JAMA, 275,* 1915–1920. doi:10.1001/jama.275.24.1915

Gelles, R. J. (1988). Violence and pregnancy: Are pregnant women at greater risk of abuse? *Journal of Marriage and the Family, 50,* 841–847. doi:10.2307/352652

Golding, J. M. (1999). Intimate partner violence as a risk factor for mental disorders: A meta-analysis. *Journal of Family Violence, 14,* 99–132. doi:10.1023/A:1022079418229

Groves, B. M., Van Horn, P., & Lieberman, A. F. (2007). Deciding on father's involvement in their children's treatment after domestic violence. In J. L. Edleson & O. J. Williams (Eds.), *Parenting by men who batter: New directions for assessment and intervention* (pp. 65–84). New York, NY: Oxford University Press.

Jasinski, J. L. (2004). Pregnancy and domestic violence: A review of the literature. *Trauma, Violence & Abuse, 5,* 47–64. doi:10.1177/1524838003259322

Jones, L., Hughes, M., & Unterstaller, U. (2001). Post-traumatic stress disorder (PTSD) in victims of domestic violence: A review of the research. *Trauma, Violence & Abuse, 2,* 99–119. doi:10.1177/1524838001002002001

Kitzmann, K. M., Gaylord, N. K., Holt, A. R., & Kenny, E. D. (2003). Child witnesses to domestic violence: A meta-analytic review. *Journal of Consulting and Clinical Psychology, 71,* 339–352. doi:10.1037/0022-006X.71.2.339

Lieberman, A. F., Ghosh Ippen, C., & Van Horn, P. (2006). Child–Parent Psychotherapy: 6-month follow-up of a randomized control trial. *Journal of the American Academy of Child and Adolescent Psychiatry, 45,* 913–918. doi:10.1097/01.chi.0000222784.03735.92

Lieberman, A., Padron, E., Van Horn, P., & Harris, W. (2005). Angels in the nursery: The intergenerational transmission of benevolent parental influences. *Infant Mental Health Journal, 26,* 504–520. doi:10.1002/imhj.20071

Lieberman, A. F., & Van Horn, P. J. (2005). *Don't hit my mommy! A manual for child–parent psychotherapy for young witnesses of family violence.* Washington, DC: Zero to Three Press.

Lieberman, A. F., & Van Horn, P. J. (2008). *Psychotherapy with infants and young children: Repairing the effects of stress and trauma on early attachment.* New York, NY: Guilford Press.

Lieberman, A. F., Van Horn, P., & Ghosh Ippen, C. (2005). Toward evidence-based treatment: Child–Parent Psychotherapy with preschoolers exposed to marital violence. *Journal of the American Academy of Child and Adolescent Psychiatry, 44,* 1241–1248. doi:10.1097/01.chi.0000181047.59702.58

Lieberman, A. F., Van Horn, P., & Ozer, E. (2005). The impact of domestic violence on preschoolers: Predictive and mediating factors. *Development and Psychopathology, 17,* 385–396.

Lieberman, A. F., Weston, D. R., & Pawl, J. H. (1991). Preventive intervention and outcome with anxiously attached dyads. *Child Development, 62,* 199–209. doi:10.2307/1130715

McFarlane, J., & Parker, B. (1994). *Abuse during pregnancy: A protocol for prevention and intervention* (pp. 22–23). White Plains, NY: March of Dimes Birth Defects Foundation.

Mullen, E. M. (1995). *Mullen Scales of Early Learning: AGS Edition.* Circle Pines, MN: American Guidance Service.

Nugent, J. K., Keefer, C. H., Minear, S., Johnson, L. C., & Blanchard, Y. (2007). *Understanding newborn behavior & early relationships: The Newborn Behavioral Observations (NBO) system handbook.* Baltimore, MD: Brookes.

Osofsky, J. D. (1999). The impact of violence on children. *The Future of Children, 9*(3), 33–49. doi:10.2307/1602780

Osofsky, J. D. (2003). Prevalence of children's exposure to domestic violence and child maltreatment: Implications for prevention and intervention. *Clinical Child and Family Psychology Review, 6,* 161–170. doi:10.1023/A:1024958332093

Radloff, L. S. (1977). The CES-D Scale: A self-report depression scale for research in the general population. *Applied Psychological Measurement, 1,* 385–401. doi:10.1177/014662167700100306

Riley, D., Shatell, D., Nitzke, S., & Ostergren, C. (2006). *Parenting the first year: Months 1–12.* Madison, WI: Cooperative Extension.

Roberts, D. (2002). *Shattered bonds: The color of child welfare*. New York, NY: Basic Civitas.

Taillieu, T. L., & Brownridge, D. A. (2010). Violence against pregnant women: Prevalence, patterns, risk factors, theories, and directions for future research. *Aggression and Violent Behavior, 15*(1), 14–35. doi:10.1016/j.avb.2009.07.013

Toth, S. L., Maughan, A., Manly, J. T., Spagnola, M., & Cicchetti, D. (2002). The relative efficacy of two interventions in altering maltreated preschool children's representational models: Implications for attachment theory. *Development and Psychopathology, 14*, 877–908. doi:10.1017/S095457940200411X

Toth, S. L., Rogosch, F. A., Manly, J. T., & Cicchetti, D. (2006). The efficacy of toddler–parent psychotherapy to reorganize attachment in young offspring of mothers with major depressive disorder: A randomized preventive trial. *Journal of Consulting and Clinical Psychology, 74*, 1006–1016. doi:10.1037/0022006X.74.6.1006

van der Kolk, B. (1996). The body keeps score: Approaches to the psychobiology of posttraumatic stress disorder. In B. A. van der Kolk & A. C. McFarlane (Eds.), *Traumatic stress: The effects of overwhelming experience on mind, body, and society* (pp. 214–241). New York, NY: Guilford Press.

Wolfe, J. W., Kimerling, R., Brown, P. J., Chrestman, K. R., & Levin, K. (1996). Psychometric review of The Life Stressor Checklist—Revised. In B. H. Stamm (Ed.), *Measurement of stress, trauma, and adaptation* (pp. 198–201). Lutherville, MD: Sidran Press.

4

INFANT–PARENT RELATIONSHIP DISTURBANCE IN THE CONTEXT OF INTIMATE PARTNER VIOLENCE: A CLINICAL CASE STUDY OF JAMES

ALISSA C. HUTH-BOCKS, LAUREN EARLS, AND JESSICA LATACK

Angela, a 26-year-old Caucasian mother, called our community-based outpatient mental health clinic seeking help for her 12-month-old son, James, whom she described as "angry, fussy, and violent" during the initial phone call. Angela was referred to our clinic by the county prosecutor's office because of her substantial financial difficulties and our ability to accept fees as low as $5 per therapy session, after she filed a personal protection order (PPO) against James's father based on a recent incident of intimate partner violence (IPV) in their home. Angela explicitly stated she would like her son to be a "happy, polite, nice little boy again," and she was willing to come to the first available evaluation appointment, which was scheduled for the following week with a female therapist.

THE EVALUATION

At our clinic, the evaluation (or intake) process typically consists of three to four once-weekly sessions lasting 60 to 90 min. In this case, the evaluation process was slightly longer because we were interested in evaluating both the infant (the identified client according to the mother) and the mother, as our approach to working with this family was based largely on attachment theory. Attachment theory maintains that the quality of the caregiver–infant relationship and the caregiver's ability to meet the infant's attachment needs (e.g., protection, care, and proximity) are the foundation of an infant's social-emotional development (Bowlby, 1969/1982). Thus, from our perspective, the identified client was the infant–mother dyad, and the unit of treatment was the relationship; this approach is typical for well-established and empirically supported infant mental health interventions (see Chapter 3, this volume; Lieberman & Van Horn, 2005; Sameroff, McDonough, & Rosenblum, 2004; Slade, Sadler, Miller, & Ueng-McHale, 2009; Zeanah, Larrieu, Heller, & Valliere, 2000). We also suspected that both mother and son were traumatized by their exposure to IPV and were, consequently, affecting each other in significant ways. The therapist explained to Angela that she would be "getting to know" her and her son, James, during the next several weeks, after which she would provide a summary of her impressions to Angela and collaboratively discuss recommendations for treatment. Because of our interest in evaluating both Angela and James, including their respective histories, and their relationship through observations in different settings, we structured the intake process such that the therapist met with Angela alone two times, made a 2-hr home visit to see Angela and meet James for the first time in a more naturalistic environment,[1] met with Angela and James in a playroom at the clinic (a new place for James), and finally met with Angela to discuss the evaluation process. Toward the end of this series of appointments, James was also brought in to the clinic one additional time to complete a 1-hr developmental screening with a different evaluator (while his mother was present in the room).

Identifying Information and Presenting Problems

James's mother, Angela, was employed full time as a waitress. She had a high school education and was born and raised in the same medium-sized suburban town in the Midwest where she resided. Angela had been in a relationship with James's father, Brian, for 4 years before becoming pregnant, although the couple had never married. Per Angela's report, James's father was a 27-year-old Caucasian man who worked as a landscaper inconsistently because of the nature of seasonal work. Until the most recent incident of IPV that prompted initiation of a PPO (which took place approximately 3 months prior to Angela calling the clinic), the couple had lived together and had both contributed to the family's income. At the time of the evaluation, James was 12 months old.

---

[1]Home visits are not typical of our mental health clinic. Although we serve the community, we are a university training center, and exceptions are typically only made when infants are involved in treatment and when appropriate supervision is available.

During his 1st year of life, James was cared for primarily by his mother during the day and his father and maternal grandmother (depending on who was available) in the evening while Angela worked. James had no siblings.

During the evaluation, Angela repeatedly described James as a very difficult infant to care for and described herself as feeling overwhelmed and helpless, although she did so in a relatively flat, "indifferent" manner. She stated that James easily became fussy and irritable and that he had difficulty with transitions, for example, when she needed to drop him off at her mother's house for evening care. During these times, James would reportedly become "hyper," "weird," and cry for intermittent periods of time. Angela stated that she could not understand why this was so, because James was very familiar with his grandmother and her house. Angela also stated that James had "anger problems" and would lash out at her unexpectedly, which she found both enraging and frightening. For example, she noted that he often hit her with hard objects, such as his board books and other toys, after which she would walk away from him to calm down. She also noted that he was very disobedient, had trouble listening to her, and had "many more temper tantrums than a baby should have." She indicated that sometimes his behavior was worse when Brian was in the home, although she did not think that James had a preference for being with his mother over his father. Angela also recalled that James had recently become terrified of the grocery store and riding in the car, for no apparent reason. Angela said that although she was not sure what to expect from therapy, she was glad that she was given the clinic name and number because she felt "desperate" and was hoping that the therapist could help James be a "happy, normal" baby.

Finally, Angela reported that James had significant sleep difficulties. In particular, James reportedly had frequent nighttime wakings, during which he was difficult to soothe and slow to fall back asleep. He did not seem to have a consistent bedtime or wake-up time, sleeping anywhere from 8 to 14 hr during the night, with inconsistent naps as well. Angela stated that she had "tried everything," including ignoring him and letting him cry, holding him, sitting next to his crib, and threatening to take his pacifier away, but nothing seemed to work. Late in the evaluation process, Angela divulged that several nights a week for the previous 4 months, Angela had been picking James up at her mother's house after a waitressing shift around midnight and driving him home, during which he would wake up while being transferred to and from the car seat.

Although Angela made it clear that she was seeking help for James, we felt it was equally important to understand her adjustment following the recent incident of IPV and her history of psychosocial functioning, as attachment and trauma research has repeatedly shown that maternal adjustment following IPV exposure strongly predicts infant adjustment (Levendosky, Leahy, Bogat, Davidson, & von Eye, 2006; Scheeringa & Zeanah, 2001). Therefore, we sought to examine these areas in a less structured manner throughout the evaluation in an effort to understand how we could assist James and Angela and improve their relationship. Similar to the manner in which she spoke about James, Angela appeared somewhat flat and emotionless while describing her experiences. At times, she minimized the impact of her partner abuse, for example, stating once, "I'm sure people have it worse than me," while at other times, she appeared to become visibly tense while talking about difficult experiences. Angela did acknowledge that she had been having sleep problems herself, including nightmares, and had some loss of appetite. She also noted a history of depressive, "low" moods and some trouble being personable at her waitressing job. Through the course of the evaluation, Angela revealed that she felt more "on edge" and "fidgety," had tried unsuccessfully to not think about Brian or his violent behaviors, and felt more impatient and unhappy with James. Angela had never received any form of psychological or mental health treatment.

Objective Test Results

To complement interviews and observations with Angela and James, Angela was asked to complete the Brief Infant-Toddler Social and Emotional Assessment scale (BITSEA; Briggs-Gowan & Carter, 2006), a 42-item questionnaire designed to assess social-emotional and behavior problems in children ages 12 months to 35 months. Responses are scored and summed along several domains, including internalizing and externalizing problems, dysregulation, developmental delays, and competence. Consistent with Angela's report during interviews, her responses on this measure indicated clinically significant concerns about externalizing problems and dysregulation and low levels of competence. For example, she responded "Very true/often" to the following items regarding James: "Is destructive; breaks or ruins things on purpose," "Purposefully tries to hurt you (or other parent)," "Wakes up at night and needs help to fall asleep again," "Cries or has a tantrum until he or she is exhausted," and "Has trouble adjusting to changes." Angela responded "Not true/rarely" to items such as "Looks for you (or other parent) when upset," "Is affectionate with loved ones," and "Plays well with other children."

A different evaluator from the clinic also met with James and his mother for a one-time meeting to complete the Bayley Scales of Infant Development-II (Bayley, 1993), which assesses mental (e.g., language and processing skills) and motor development (e.g., quality of fine and gross motor activities), as well as observed behavior, in children of age 1 month to 42 months. James's performance during this assessment was in the average range across all domains, suggesting no significant concerns with cognitive or motor abilities. His behavior during this assessment was also in the typical range. Consistent with these findings, Angela's responses on the BITSEA indicated no significant concerns with developmental delays.

History of IPV

Although Angela initially focused on the most recent and severe incident of IPV in the home, it quickly became apparent that she had been abused by Brian throughout the couple's relationship history. Early in the relationship, Angela described Brian as a fun-loving and charming guy who also had "a bad temper." He reportedly would occasionally berate Angela, initially only in private, but later in public, calling her names and telling her that she was lucky to be with him; he would also threaten her by saying things such as "Believe me, you don't want to see what I'm capable of." During fights, Brian reportedly would also throw objects around the home, punch holes in the wall, and drive recklessly in the car with Angela. These incidents initially occurred once every few months but increased to once every 1 to 2 weeks over several years. Between such episodes, Angela reported that Brian treated her "pretty well."

During Angela's pregnancy with James, Brian continued to be verbally abusive, making additional disparaging comments about her pregnancy status. For example, it was not unusual for Brian to call her "fat" and "disgusting," and he continued to be physically and verbally threatening. For instance, on several occasions, he threatened to make false reports to Child Protective Services once the baby was born to gain sole legal custody of James if Angela did not comply with his requests. In addition, Brian began to employ more direct physical violence toward Angela, including grabbing her, pulling her hair, and slapping her in the face. Brian often blamed these behaviors on her, saying that she was being "lazy" and "boring" due to being pregnant. Abuse also occurred more frequently and severely if Brian had had a long day at work and/or had been drinking with friends before coming home. The worst incident during pregnancy occurred when Angela was about 8 months along in her pregnancy. Angela explained that she had begun feeling very fatigued toward the end of her pregnancy due to her size and to continuing her waitressing job. Brian came home one evening and she had not felt up to preparing dinner. After a verbal altercation, Brian forcefully struck Angela in the abdomen area and left the home until the following day.

During James's 1st year of life, Brian's violent behavior continued to escalate in frequency and severity. In addition to berating Angela's mothering abilities and her overall contribution to the family's well-being, he continued to be physically aggressive toward her. At various times, Brian reportedly pinned her down, punched her, slapped her, and pushed her onto the ground. These incidents typically also involved verbal yelling and occurred in front of James, as he was usually in close proximity to his mother. Angela stated that while these events were occurring, she was usually "cold and numb," and typically unresponsive out of fear that the violence would escalate. Although she vaguely recalled that James did appear tense and upset during these times, stopping his play to "see what was going on," she stated that he probably did not notice much because he could not understand what was happening. The one exception was the most recent event, which precipitated the couple's separation and the PPO. This event occurred in the early evening after Brian came home from work and on a day that Angela had off from work. The couple began arguing about child care, household responsibilities, and financial concerns, which escalated in a somewhat typical way. However, on this particular evening, Brian became more aggressive, eventually using a large pot from the kitchen to knock Angela down, hitting her repeatedly in the head, shoulders, and chest area. Angela was left with bruises and bleeding lacerations on the kitchen floor with James nearby terrified and huddled in a corner, while Brian left the scene. Neighbors had heard the conflict and called the police, who arrived shortly thereafter to find Angela and James. A PPO was initiated, and Brian was later charged with assault and battery and sent to jail for several months; he had started his sentence at the time of the evaluation.

Notably, Angela appeared to be quite open about these IPV experiences, saying that she had finally reached her "stopping point." She adamantly stated that she did not want to expose James to this type of father figure and could not forgive herself if she allowed it to continue. Angela also stated that whereas Brian was violent toward Angela, he never mistreated James. In addition, Angela denied physically abusing or otherwise maltreating James.

Infant's Developmental and Medical History

According to Angela, her pregnancy with James was unplanned and came as "a total surprise." This was her first and only pregnancy. Angela received prenatal care from month 3 of pregnancy until birth, and she reported a relatively unremarkable pregnancy except for general fatigue in the last trimester and one episode of false labor during month 7 of pregnancy, which was treated with temporary bed rest. She denied smoking, drinking, or using drugs during the pregnancy; she ate well and gained approximately 35 pounds. She reported feeling fairly well physically, but she added that she was under a lot of emotional stress, as described above. She did not reveal this information to her obstetrician. James was born at 41 weeks gestation; weighed 6 pounds, 13 ounces; and was 21 inches long. Angela delivered James vaginally after an 18-hr labor, and James and his mother developed a mild fever late in the delivery, which necessitated a 2-day stay in the hospital for routine monitoring. Subsequently, both were released from the hospital in good health.

James had been bottle-fed with formula since birth and appeared to be growing well physically. He was under regular care with a pediatrician, had received his immunizations, and was eating solid foods by 6 months with relative ease. He was hospitalized once, for pneumonia, for 3 days around age 7 months. Otherwise, Angela reported he had no allergies or major illnesses or injuries, although she did note that he seemed to be accident prone. Overall, Angela described James as being a fussy, difficult baby at birth; although he reportedly slept pretty well during the first 3 months, his sleep difficulties worsened over time. Angela reported that most other people thought he was a "good" baby, but she insisted that this was because they "really didn't know him." James had reportedly recently begun to say just a few words, such as *mama*, *more*, and *no*.

Family History

Angela reported a strained relationship with her mother and father growing up. She reported that her father had an alcohol problem and suffered from other physical ailments; he died when Angela was 23 years old. Angela has a sister (age 29) and a brother (age 30), whom she regards as "acquaintances" and whom she sees only a few times a year. Each of them has their own children. She described her mother as "controlling" and critical; she apparently often criticized Angela throughout childhood regarding how she did in school, what types of friends she chose to socialize with, and her boyfriends. Angela said that she felt she could never please her mother. However, Angela reported that she currently is "close" to her mother and sees her several times a week, though she repeatedly expressed frustration with her because her mother reportedly tells her how difficult James is and tries to tell Angela how to parent him better. As noted earlier, Angela's mother frequently provides care for James in her home when Angela is working and often complains about his fussiness when Angela arrives to pick him up. Angela also reported that her father was both verbally and physically abusive toward her mother during childhood; Angela used to "dread" coming home and would often leave home and stay with friends when her parents' conflicts escalated. She recalled feeling a wish to move out during her teenage years, which she promptly did after graduating from high school.

Angela was 20 years old when she met Brian through a mutual friend. They quickly became romantically involved and often spent their free time socializing with friends at local bars. Angela stated that she did not know much about Brian's family, as he had reportedly been estranged from them since high school. Gradually the couple became more serious; they moved in with each other when Angela was 24 years old and lived together until the most recent incident of IPV. Angela had been romantically involved with several men prior to Brian but was never in a relationship longer than about 6 months. No prior boyfriends had reportedly been abusive toward Angela.

At the time of the evaluation, Angela and James were living alone in a two-bedroom apartment, having moved from the family home after the most recent partner violence. A restraining order was in place, although Brian was currently serving a sentence for assault and battery in the county jail. Brian reportedly had not had contact with either Angela or James since that night and did not know their location.

Maternal Representations and Subjective Experience

In addition to the relatively standard set of questions used for evaluating a new client, in cases where an infant is identified and/or a parent–child relationship disturbance appears to be present, we often assess a caregiver's thoughts and feelings about her child and her relationship with that child. This helps us better understand her subjective experience of the relationship, which provides us with a different framework for understanding presenting problems and a more complete guide to inform treatment planning. We typically use a series of questions from the Working Model of the Child Interview (WMCI; Zeanah & Benoit, 1995), which is a semistructured interview used in both clinical and research settings assessing maternal representations (i.e., thoughts, feelings, and ideas) of the child and her relationship with that child. Through a series of questions, the parent's story of the infant is elicited and explored, and the clinician attends to the content of this story, and importantly, how this story is told by the caregiver (e.g., affective displays, coherence of the story). Prior research has shown that the quality of mothers' responses on this interview predicts both parenting behaviors and infant–mother attachment quality (Dayton, Levendosky, Davidson, & Bogat, 2010; Huth-Bocks, Levendosky, Bogat, & von Eye, 2004), and these maternal representations may be negatively affected by IPV (Huth-Bocks, Levendosky, Theran, & Bogat, 2004).

In this particular case, a number of questions from the WMCI were integrated into the visits with Angela alone at the clinic. The following dialog illustrates how important information was elicited from Angela about her perception of James and her relationship with him that did not, otherwise, come up as striking during other parts of the evaluation.

Interviewer: Pick five words to describe your child's personality.

Angela: Oh! That's hard. . . . Stubborn, difficult, pushy, and playful . . . that's all I can think of.

Interviewer: OK, for each one, what makes you say that?

Angela: Well, stubborn because he always wants his way, doesn't want to make anything easy, ya know? Just wants things right away and only his way, I'm not sure why, but . . . maybe babies are just like that, but he seems more so. Umm . . . difficult for the same reason probably. He doesn't make anything easy for me . . . actually, it's really hard having a baby with work and being a single parent and all . . . I mean, I'm really glad he's around 'cause I love him, but I do worry about him too, ya know, ending up like his dad or something . . .

Interviewer: And pushy?

Angela: Well, that's his dad for sure. Pushing everyone around, trying to intimidate people, ya know . . . who does he think he is? I could only take so much and that was it . . . but anyway, James just gets pushy and angry, and sometimes he seems like he just wants to hurt me, that's all.

Interviewer: Playful?

Angela: Well, he is that too, ya know, he likes to play with his toys, no doubt about that, always trying to get me to play with him too . . .

Interviewer: Who do you think your baby is most like?

Angela: Oh . . . probably his dad, but I hope not. He is sort of bullheaded like his dad and that emotionalness, getting irritated out of nowhere, nothing is ever good enough for him! Sometimes he wants to sit in my lap and just relax and then BAM! He wallops me good for not paying enough attention to him or something. I guess he's most like his dad, that's all. My mom says he's just like me, but I don't know what she's talking about.

Interviewer: How would you describe your relationship now with your baby?

Angela: Pretty good . . . close, you know, we've had to be close and I guess we've bonded over these things with his dad too. Don't get me wrong, we can sure get into it sometimes and he drives me nuts sometimes, but we also look out for each other. You know, check in on each other every now and then. I think we'll be close for a long time too . . . as long as he behaves and all . . . gotta get him back on track with that.

Interviewer: What behavior of James is the most difficult thing for you to handle?

Angela: Umm . . . his crying probably . . . just when he gets real fussy and I can't do anything about it, ya know? It's like he goes on and on and I'm like "c'mon little guy! Mom is trying everything!" and nothing works! Yeah, his crying. . . . Oh, but also his tantrums too, I forgot about that! When he lays on the floor and just kicks his little legs and waves those arms so angry!

Interviewer: Can you give me an example?

Angela: Well, like, the other day, just out of nowhere, I'm sitting there making dinner and he comes in and pulls on my shorts crying and I'm like "what? It'll be ready in one minute, hang on" but he keeps going on and on even though he had his bottle, so I don't know what was wrong. And then he full out starts screaming and pounding on my leg . . . yeah, that's a good example . . . just had to walk away, ya know?

Interviewer: Why is this difficult?

Angela: 'Cause there's really nothing I can do about it, it's just the way he is . . . and it's like "don't hurt me!" for nothing!

Interviewer: What do you feel like doing when he behaves like that?

Angela: Usually I just want to walk away, disappear or something for a minute to calm down and figure things out . . . I usually just end up walking away, take a breather, ya know?

Interviewer: Do you think your child knows you don't like that behavior?

Angela: Umm . . . I have no clue. Probably not, well, maybe . . . not sure about that one . . .

Interviewer: Why do you think he acts like that?

Angela: 'Cause he likes attention I guess. . . . or maybe he's hungry or something. . . . I don't know, he's a tough one to figure out!

Mother–Infant Observational Findings

As noted earlier, part of the evaluation also included two observational visits with Angela and James, the first being a home visit to meet James and the second being a clinic visit in our playroom. The therapist arrived for the first visit at their apartment, which was located on the second floor of a large apartment building in a lower-middle-class neighborhood. Angela answered the door and smiled as she greeted the therapist, directing the therapist to the living room, although her body language made it clear she was quite tense and ill-at-ease. The apartment was small and appeared somewhat disorganized. Angela informed the therapist that Brian was a "neat freak," and that she felt relieved to be living alone. Somewhat to the therapist's surprise, Angela's mother was also present, although she did not speak to the therapist but rather nodded hello with a stern look on her face from the kitchen. She appeared to closely watch the goings-on in the apartment as she sat at the kitchen table, smoking and playing solitaire during most of the visit. Angela informed us that she had been working nights and reminded us that both she and James's sleeping schedules had been quite irregular. She reported that she had just gotten him to take a nap 20 min prior to the visit. About 5 min into the visit, Angela rose to wake him, despite the therapist's offer to finish Angela's portion of the interview first and let him sleep a little while longer.

Angela appeared shortly thereafter with James, who was tired and mildly upset. He cried into her shoulder as she carried him into the living room. Angela appeared frustrated as she made an attempt to soothe James. Her body language was stiff and tense, and she held him away from her body rather than close to her. Finally, she rolled her eyes and appeared to give up. James then squirmed to get down, looked at the therapist in a quizzical and slightly wary manner, and crawled quickly to the far corner of the room where a few toys lay on a basket. The therapist watched as James occupied himself while she continued to make small talk with Angela. A little while later, Angela's mother came into the room and sat near James for a brief period of time saying "What's wrong with you, huh? Are you mad at Momma?" She made a sarcastic comment about Angela's mothering skills, and although Angela laughed, she quickly looked at the therapist in an embarrassed way.

During the remainder of the visit, James sought out his mother's attention a few times and in notably different ways. For example, one time James began to cry with increasing volume with his back toward his mother while playing with toys. Angela, with some exasperation, went over to reposition him and to place a few more toys in front of him. He continued to cry softly for a few minutes but eventually stopped and began wandering around the room. At a different time, James approached Angela with a smile and proceeded to swing a toy somewhat wildly in her direction, which eventually hit his mother's leg with the toy. Angela instantly retracted from him with a frightened look, yelled "ouch!" loudly, and then looked at the examiner, stating "See what I mean?" She reprimanded James by pleading "Can't you just be nice?" and went to get herself a soda and James a bottle. Overall, the mother and child were awkward and tense with each other, and there was a negative affective atmosphere. The therapist had the sense that James was trying to connect with his mother but could not find an effective way to do so, and Angela had a great deal of difficulty reading and responding to James's cues.

The therapist witnessed a similar scene during the second observational visit in the clinic playroom. Angela arrived with James about 15 min past her appointment time and was cursing about having car trouble. She reported that she borrowed her mother's vehicle to make it to the appointment. The first few minutes were spent talking, and then the therapist suggested that the three of them simply play in the playroom to "get to know each other better." Angela winced slightly at this suggestion and asked, "You want me to just . . . play?" When the therapist nodded yes, Angela rolled her eyes somewhat and looked at James in a confused and helpless way. James watched his mother intently as she got up and walked across the room to choose toys from the bin. She returned with a toy monster truck, as well as some Legos. She presented the toys to James and he appeared interested, although he did not use the toys in the way for which they were intended, which seemed to irritate Angela. James banged the truck on the floor a couple of times and Angela quickly grabbed the toy from him, saying "No, you roll it, like this." She then told him, "You're going to break it."

During the session, James did approach the therapist with more ease than during the initial home visit. He appeared to enjoy her company, bringing different toys to her, and sitting next to her while playing with them. He also responded with pleasure when she praised him. Angela freely remarked that she did not have much time to play with James at home because of her work schedule. Once, the therapist picked up a small red ball and rolled it to James, who immediately picked it up and put it in his mouth. Angela took the toy out of his mouth and apologized for getting it "spitty." She continued to sit on the floor with James, but she seemed more inclined to make conversation with the therapist. Her body language was stiff and she made several comments about feeling "silly" playing on the floor like a kid. She continued the rest of the session in this manner, occasionally bouncing the ball for James while she described some of the problems in her personal life and at work. She made almost no eye contact with James throughout the session; she picked him up only when she was preparing to leave.

CONCEPTUALIZATION AND DIAGNOSIS

During the evaluation process, a tremendous amount of information was gleaned about James and Angela, including the quality of their relationship and the ways in which living with IPV had touched their lives. In forming a conceptualization of this clinical case, we considered James's and Angela's functioning individually and their functioning as a dyad, given James's young age and the critical role his mother held for meeting his social-emotional needs. An approach to conceptualizing and diagnosing mental health difficulties in infants and young children that we considered is the Zero to Three Diagnostic and Classification system (Zero to Three National Center for Infants, Toddlers, and Families, 2004), a developmentally appropriate and sensitive scheme for understanding emotional distress in young children (Rosenblum, 2004). Based on the evaluation and history of exposure to IPV, James appeared to easily meet the criteria for posttraumatic stress disorder (PTSD) because of the following presenting symptoms: physiological distress, possible efforts to avoid people or places related to the trauma of witnessing IPV, onset of more problematic sleep difficulties, hyperactivity, increased irritability and outbursts of anger and fussiness, and onset of new fears. According to Axis II of this diagnostic scheme, which assesses the quality of a parent–child relationship, the relationship difficulties between James and his mother appeared to be clinically significant and specific to their relationship (see below for a more detailed discussion), and thus could be thought of as a formal relationship disturbance or possibly a relationship disorder. Based on the information from the evaluation, their score on the Parent-Infant Relationship Global Assessment Scale was determined to be somewhere between 35 and 45 out of 100. Although a formal diagnosis was not made for Angela, available information suggested a history of clinically significant mood disturbance and a strong likelihood of a current mood disorder and/or PTSD, with notable symptoms of distress, reactivity, emotional numbing, persistent avoidance, and increased sleep disturbance and irritability.

Beyond these diagnostic schemes, which are mostly intended for conceptualizing an individual's level of mental functioning, we closely examined the parent–infant relationship from an attachment theory perspective to form a broader and more complete case conceptualization. It became apparent through interviews and observations that this mother and infant had great difficulty relating to one another emotionally. Angela clearly felt helpless in the maternal role, doubting herself constantly and feeling she was never doing "good enough." She both reported this directly to us and provided many examples while interacting with James. These feelings likely originated within her family of origin and continued into her relationship with Brian, and then into her relationship with James. Angela also projected many negative attributions toward James that were, at least in part, distorted to some degree. For example, she had a tendency to misperceive him as malevolent, aggressive, and "just like his father," even though many of James's behaviors were simply an attempt to gain much-needed contact with her when he was emotionally dysregulated (although we did recognize that he was probably more physically active and aggressive than the typical 12-month-old boy). Angela also had trouble recognizing and reading James's cues and his emotional needs, often overlooking them completely, misunderstanding them, and/or feeling confused and uncertain about his feelings and intentions. This resulted in a preponderance of awkward, tense, and disjointed interactions between them. At times, she also did not appear to have knowledge of developmentally appropriate expectations for a 12-month-old.

In turn, James appeared to have difficulty developing and implementing an effective strategy of interacting with Angela to get his needs met. His attempts varied from withdrawing and ignoring her, to increasing his distress signals, and striking out at her. Most likely, he felt helpless in the relationship as well, as he was ultimately unable to rely on his caregiver even though he still needed her protection and care, an "untenable position" for an infant this age (Lieberman, 2004). His response to Angela and the therapist in a variety of settings clearly suggested an insecure attachment relationship, with at least some elements of a disorganized attachment relationship.

Further consideration revealed an intergenerational pattern of harsh, critical, and emotionally distant parenting and an intergenerational exposure to IPV; these experiences were entrenched in this family. In addition, we felt that not only were both individuals traumatized by the IPV in the home (James was traumatized because of the observed and experienced threats to his caregiver, and Angela was traumatized by her abuse from Brian), but their trauma reactions seemed to be exacerbating each other's distress. For example, Angela's symptoms made her less available and effective in caring for James, and James's increased efforts and maladaptive behaviors often triggered a trauma reaction (e.g., when he made rough physical contact with her, she would retract, become fearful, and avoid him). Thus, we found it helpful to view Angela and James's trauma reactions from a relational perspective, consistent with Scheeringa and Zeanah's (2001) concept of relational PTSD. In these cases, there is a co-occurrence and compound effect of posttraumatic symptomatology in a caregiver and a young child. The Withdrawn/Unresponsive/Unavailable pattern, which is characterized by parental withdrawal and avoidance in response to trauma, which then interferes with the ability to respond sensitively to a child's needs, seemed especially relevant to our case. This pattern, along with Angela's helpless frame of mind and occasional frightened response to James, was exacerbating James's emotional and physical dysregulation.

TREATMENT RECOMMENDATIONS

Overall, this infant–parent dyad was in substantial distress at the time of their referral to our clinic, in large part due to their exposure to IPV in the home. While there was an onset of new problems and a worsening of existing problems due to the increasingly frequent and severe violence in the home, this dyad faced other risk factors as well. For example, they recently had experienced other significant stressors, such as losing their home and beloved pet. Angela was financially strained and did not have reliable transportation. The reality was that James's father was also going to be released from the county jail soon and had made it clear he would be seeking some custody rights. In our county, this would likely be possible after some supervised parenting time with a caseworker. We were aware that this might be a potential obstacle, but also something important to work with, for James's well-being. Previous clinical and empirical reports have suggested that young children can have a variety of responses to their violent parent, including intense conflicting emotions, such as a longing for them when they are absent, as well as a fear of them; identification with the violent adult is also possible over time (Lieberman & Van Horn, 1998).

On the other hand, this dyad had many protective factors, which we predicted would aid them in benefiting from therapy and other community social services. For one, Angela had been able to remove herself and James from further abuse, realizing that it was not healthy to raise a child in that environment. She had quickly followed up on the referral to our clinic and made all appointments despite transportation difficulties. Thus, she seemed willing and motivated to participate in the evaluation despite how painful it was to discuss old and new traumas. James also appeared to be in good physical health and was developing well, with no apparent delays despite his emotional stressors. Angela and James also had a fair amount of practical support from Angela's mother, although availability of emotional support was less clear. Finally, it seemed that James had not been maltreated directly by either parent, despite the risk for abuse given his age and the partner violence going on in the home.

At the final evaluation appointment with Angela, dyadic psychotherapy at our clinic was recommended. While parent–infant therapy is often done in the home, we felt that this dyad could participate in this treatment modality at our clinic, and we were prepared to recommend additional home services if needed. As in other well-established and empirically supported infant mental health interventions for trauma-exposed mothers and infants (e.g., Chapter 3, this volume; Lieberman & Van Horn, 2005; Slade et al., 2009), we recommended that the therapist facilitate a safe, supportive, and collaborative therapeutic relationship with Angela and James. In the context of this "holding" environment, we believed that several avenues for intervention would be possible, such as exploring Angela's history, discussing her representations of James and her relationship with James, increasing her ability to consider James's mental states as separate from her own, and assisting with behavioral changes through in vivo parent–infant interactions. Stern (1995) and later others (Lieberman & Van Horn, 2005) have called these avenues for intervention "ports of entry." A port of entry is chosen on the basis of what is most needed at that time, and subsequent changes are expected in the other domains.

Thus, at the onset of treatment with this family, our goals included improving Angela's psychological functioning in order for her to be able to become a more attuned and sensitive caregiver for James. We anticipated that this might include an examination of her negative feelings and expectations about James, as well as her feelings of inefficacy as a mother. Additionally, we hoped to be able to provide guidance about appropriate developmental expectations in a way that did not undermine her role as the primary caregiver. Given that Angela and James would attend together, we anticipated that the therapist might also intervene during interactions to clarify James's feelings and intentions regarding specific behaviors and to highlight effective ways that Angela might respond to James. Thus, the treatment process that was recommended was believed to be ideal in the sense that both individuals would obtain psychological relief and emerge with a much healthier and secure relationship. Importantly, a final goal was to prevent exposure to future IPV for this pair in order to maximize each of their potentials for individual and interpersonal growth.

REFERENCES

Bayley, N. (1993). *Bayley Scales of Infant Development* (2nd ed.). San Antonio, TX: Psychological Corporation.

Bowlby, J. (1969/1982). *Attachment and loss: Attachment* (2nd ed., Vol. 1). New York, NY: Basic Books.

Briggs-Gowan, M. J., & Carter, A. S. (2006). *Brief Infant–Toddler Social and Emotional Assessment manual.* San Antonio, TX: PsychCorp.

Dayton, C. J., Levendosky, A. A., Davidson, W. S., & Bogat, G. A. (2010). The child as held in the mind of the mother: The influence of prenatal maternal representations on parenting behaviors. *Infant Mental Health Journal, 31,* 220–241. doi:10.1002/imhj.20253

Huth-Bocks, A. C., Levendosky, A. A., Bogat, G. A., & von Eye, A. (2004). The impact of maternal characteristics and contextual variables on infant-mother attachment. *Child Development, 75,* 480–496. doi:10.1111/j.1467-8624.2004.00688.x

Huth-Bocks, A. C., Levendosky, A. A., Theran, S. A., & Bogat, G. A. (2004). The impact of domestic violence on mothers' prenatal representations of their infants. *Infant Mental Health Journal, 25,* 79–98. doi:10.1002/imhj.10094

Levendosky, A. A., Leahy, K. L., Bogat, G. A., Davidson, W. S., & von Eye, A. (2006). Domestic violence, maternal parenting, maternal mental health, and infant externalizing behavior. *Journal of Family Psychology, 20,* 544–552. doi:10.1037/0893-3200.20.4.544

Lieberman, A. F. (2004). Traumatic stress and quality of attachment: Reality and internalization in disorders of infant mental health. *Infant Mental Health Journal, 25,* 336–351. doi:10.1002/imhj.20009

Lieberman, A. F., & Van Horn, P. (1998). Attachment, trauma, and domestic violence: Implications for child custody. *Child and Adolescent Psychiatric Clinics of North America, 7*, 423–443.

Lieberman, A. F., & Van Horn, P. (2005). *Don't hit my mommy! A manual for child–parent psychotherapy with young witnesses of family violence.* Washington, DC: Zero to Three Press.

Rosenblum, K. L. (2004). Defining infant mental health: A developmental relational perspective on assessment and diagnosis. In A. J. Sameroff, S. C. McDonough, & K. L. Rosenblum (Eds.), *Treating parent–infant relationship problems: Strategies for intervention* (pp. 43–75). New York, NY: Guilford Press.

Sameroff, A. J., McDonough, S. C., & Rosenblum, K. L. (2004). *Treating parent–infant relationship problems: Strategies for intervention.* New York, NY: Guilford Press.

Scheeringa, M. S., & Zeanah, C. H. (2001). A relational perspective on PTSD in early childhood. *Journal of Traumatic Stress, 14*, 799–815. doi:10.1023/A: 1013002507972

Slade, A., Sadler, L., Miller, M., & Ueng-McHale, J. (2009, April). *Maternal reflective functioning as a moderator of intervention effects in predicting infant attachment.* Paper presented at the 2009 Biennial Conference of the Society for Research in Child Development, Denver, CO.

Stern, D. (1995). *The motherhood constellation: A unified view of parent–infant psychotherapy.* New York, NY: Basic Books

Zeanah, C. H., & Benoit, D. (1995). Clinical applications of a parent perception interview in infant mental health. *Child and Adolescent Psychiatric Clinics of North America, 4*, 539–554.

Zeanah, C. H., Larrieu, J. A., Heller, S. S., & Valliere, J. (2000). Infant–parent relationship assessment. In C. H. Zeanah (Ed.), *Handbook of infant mental health* (2nd ed., pp. 222–235). New York, NY: Guilford Press.

Zero to Three National Center for Infants, Toddlers, and Families (2004). *Diagnostic classification of mental health and developmental disorders of infancy and early childhood* (Rev. ed.). Washington, DC: Zero to Three Press.

II

TODDLER TO EARLY CHILDHOOD

5

THE MULTIPLE IMPACTS OF INTIMATE PARTNER VIOLENCE ON PRESCHOOL CHILDREN

KATHRYN H. HOWELL AND SANDRA A. GRAHAM-BERMANN

In the past decade, significant strides have been made in delineating the impact of intimate partner violence (IPV) on preschool-age children. This chapter is devoted to reviewing the pertinent research studies in this time period with a particular focus on the developmental domains of the preschool years (i.e., the social, cognitive, and emotional challenges, experiences, and functions of children from age 3 to 6). Further, we address the psychological functioning of preschool-age children following IPV exposure, including traumatic stress reactions and problematic internalizing and externalizing behaviors. Thus, the chapter explores cognitive and physical functioning following exposure to interpersonal violence, and the socioemotional consequences to children from ages 3 to 6 who witness violence in the home.

We begin by presenting evidence for the prevalence of preschool-age children's exposure to IPV. Next, we discuss the developmental deficits that can result from prolonged and chronic exposure to stress, including exposure to IPV. We move on to explore resilient coping for those children who, despite witnessing violence in their home, seem to function well. We conclude the chapter by suggesting clinical implications, future research directions, and policy initiatives.

PRESCHOOL-AGE CHILDREN'S EXPOSURE
TO IPV—PREVALENCE

Researchers have shown that children's exposure to IPV does not occur uniformly across the life span, as young children are considered to be at greater risk of exposure than older children (Wolak & Finkelhor, 2001). When compared with census data from five cities, IPV incidents, both single and recurring, occurred disproportionately in households with young children (less than age 5; Fantuzzo & Fusco, 2007). Preschool-age children were also more likely to be exposed to multiple incidents of IPV and were at greater risk of direct exposure to these events than children in older age groups. It appears that preschool-age children are at-risk of greater exposure to IPV than are older children.

A number of questions arise in determining young children's exposure to IPV. First, how often does exposure occur early in the life of the child? How frequent is IPV? How severe and how long does it last? Kilpatrick and Williams (1998) found that most of the children in their study had been exposed to IPV during the first 4 years of life. In another study of school-age children (Graham-Bermann, Lynch, Banyard, DeVoe, & Halabu, 2007), mothers reported that the average length of their abusive relationship was 10 years, while the mean age of their children was 8 years, suggesting that the children witnessed violence throughout their young lives. In different studies comparing the relative effects of the age of first exposure to the effects of lifetime exposure, the majority of children were first exposed to family violence as infants (64%), with only 12% first exposed when of school-age (Graham-Bermann & Perkins, 2010). In this study, both the age of first exposure and amount of lifetime violence were significantly and negatively related to children's greater behavioral problems. Other researchers have also found that younger age at time of exposure to IPV is associated with more deleterious outcomes for the child (Fantuzzo et al., 1991; Holden, Stein, Ritchey, Harris, & Jouriles, 1998). In a meta-analytic review, Kitzmann, Gaylord, Holt, and Kenny (2003) found that children exposed to more severe IPV showed more severe problems in adjustment.

Finally, it is often difficult to discern exactly what children have experienced and what it all means for preschool-age children, as there are a number of different definitions of *exposure to IPV*. Holden (2003) identified differing forms of a child's exposure to IPV, such as witnessing the violence, hearing about it, being hurt during the violence, witnessing the aftermath of a violent event, for example, seeing injuries or medical or police involvement. Reports of severe violence indicate that exposure to IPV varies from family to family but is often an ongoing event in the life of the child. Mothers in an intervention study reported an average of 11 severe violence tactics within the past year (ranging from 0 to 96 tactics), such as being beaten or threatened with or having the assailant use a gun or knife (Graham-Bermann et al., 2007). Several studies indicate that when violence occurs in the home it is frequent and children are eyewitnesses to most of it (Fantuzzo & Fusco, 2007; Graham-Bermann, Kulkarni, & Kanukollu, in press).

DEVELOPMENTALLY SPECIFIC EFFECTS

The effects of IPV are no longer viewed as universal across children of all ages; instead, they vary depending on the intensity, history, and type of violence; the child's vulnerability at certain points in development; and interactions between developmental stage and exposure to violence (Margolin, 2005). IPV is particularly distressing for preschool-age children because they spend a significant proportion of time with parents. In fact, they cannot distance themselves from their circumstances and experience—they cannot leave the scene, seek out refuge in homes of friends, and so forth. They must stay and endure or absorb the violence and/or retreat into hiding, fantasy, or emotional numbing. Preschool-age children rely on parent figures to protect them from dangers and make their environment safe and predictable, functions that can be severely compromised in families with violence (Margolin & Gordis, 2000). These young children may not be able to escape the violence through peer or academic outlets; instead, they likely face the physical and psychological abuse on a regular basis. Exposure to violence during these early years, when children's attachment to parents is strongest, has decidedly severe and long-lasting negative effects (Levendosky, Huth-Bocks, Semel, & Shapiro, 2002).

The extent of child difficulties related to witnessing IPV extends into multiple domains of functioning. Current research shows that preschool-age children, those between the ages of 3 and 6, are especially vulnerable and at risk of developing emotional and behavioral problems (McDonald, Jouriles, Briggs-Gowan, Rosenfield, & Carter, 2007). Preschool-age children's exposure to IPV also has been associated with decrements in optimal development in the areas of cognitive performance and physical health (Rossman, Rea, Graham-Bermann, & Butterfield, 2004). A more thorough understanding of the impact that IPV has in these realms of functioning is necessary for effective prevention and intervention efforts. We begin with a review of neurobiological changes and physiological functioning that can be used to frame an understanding of subsequent forms of dysfunction and maladjustment.

Physiological Self-Regulating Response to Traumatic Stress

Children exposed to IPV vary in their response and degree of distress, depending in part on their level of physiological arousal and on their ability to effectively manage their emotions. These responses are regulated by the autonomic nervous system, which consists of the sympathetic nervous system (SNS) and parasympathetic nervous system (PNS). It is the SNS that is aroused during times of perceived danger and is adaptive and protective in that it prepares the body for the fight or flight response by increasing heart rate, sweating, and blood flow. When the SNS is activated on a frequent basis, however, there is the threat that sustained and prolonged emotional reactivity may result in less response, or underarousal, with ensuing difficulty in regulating behavior and in physical health problems (McEwen, 2002). The PNS serves to slow down the effects of the SNS by reducing heart rate, blood pressure, and rate of breathing. This part of the autonomic nervous system is aroused in states of relaxation and counters the effects of the SNS. Ideally, a balance between SNS and PNS systems allows for homeostasis. The neuroendocrine system controls stress reactions and is called the hypothalamic–pituitary–adrenal (HPA) axis. Simply stated, the HPA system increases the production of cortisol in response to fear that allows the nervous system to act (Margolin & Gordis, 2000). Thus, traumatic early childhood experiences can directly affect the development of the stress response system (DeBellis, 2005). Conversely, positive early childhood relationships can enhance adaptive responses to stressful situations (Nemeroff, 2004).

For children exposed to IPV, evidence of dysregulation can be seen as arousal that does not habituate, does not reduce in intensity, or is inefficient in strength to produce an adaptive response to the stressor. These mechanisms can be used to explain some of the types of dysfunction commonly identified and reported in studies of children exposed to IPV. These are studies of traumatic stress, internalizing and externalizing behavior problems, cognitive impairments, and poor physical health. We begin the review of studies specific to preschool-age children by focusing on traumatic stress and posttraumatic stress disorder (PTSD).

Traumatic Stress Symptoms and Disorder

Exposure to chronic family violence impacts children's arousal capabilities, their startle response, and emotional reactivity—all changes that are linked to traumatic stress symptoms in preschool-age children. Symptoms of traumatic stress using *Diagnostic and Statistical Manual of Mental Disorders* (4th. ed.; *DSM–IV*; American Psychiatric Association, 1994) criteria for adults include involuntarily reexperiencing the traumatic event, emotional numbing or avoidance, and physiological reactivity—symptoms developed and based on studies of men at war and women who had been sexually assaulted. Yet essentially the same diagnostic criteria have been recommended for use in studies with children. To that end, Scheeringa, Zeanah, Drell, and Larieu (1995) created and tested a developmentally appropriate measure that relies on an interview with the mother and consideration by a team of clinicians who decide whether the described behavior meets threshold for a particular symptom of traumatic stress. However, it is only recently that criteria specific to preschool-age children exposed to traumatic events have been adopted.

Although a number of studies of traumatic stress and PTSD have now been undertaken with preschool-age children exposed to IPV, the results vary greatly, depending on the type of measure used, the population studied, and how PTSD is diagnosed. Reported rates of PTSD in preschool-age children range from 3% to 56% (Graham-Bermann, DeVoe, Mattis, Lynch, & Thomas, 2006; Lehmann, 1997; Levendosky et al., 2002). Lower rates are found with more stringent measures, but these rely on outdated diagnostic criteria.

Still, a large number of children who do not meet full criteria for a diagnosis of PTSD may suffer from symptoms of posttraumatic stress (Graham-Bermann & Levendosky, 1998). Researchers have noted developmentally specific symptoms in preschool-age children exposed to IPV, such as intrusive, ruminative thoughts about the trauma, difficulty sleeping, new fears for safety, trauma-specific reenactment, repetitive play, and pessimistic feelings of hopelessness about the future. Regressive symptoms, such as decreased verbalization and bedwetting, are also relevant behaviors seen in preschool-age children exposed to family violence (Margolin & Gordis, 2000).

Graham-Bermann et al. (2008) evaluated the impact of traumatic events, including exposure to IPV, on development in 138 preschool-age children in Head Start. In this group, 93% of mothers reported that their child had experienced at least one potentially traumatic event by age 5. The most common traumatic stress symptoms that followed were increased questions about the event, reenactment of the event, eating and sleep disturbances, and heightened fear responses.

Levendosky et al. (2002) analyzed PTSD in preschool-age children between the ages of 3 and 5 who were exposed to interparental violence. Using questionnaires, various responses to trauma were evaluated, such as playing out the violent event with toys, having frightening dreams about the trauma, displaying fewer feelings since the event, and exhibiting increased irritability since the violent event. Based on this measure, the most frequently reported symptoms were talking about the violent event, an upset reaction in response to memory triggers, hypervigilance, and new separation anxiety (Levendosky et al., 2002). Avoidant and numbing symptoms are particularly uncommon in studies of preschool-age children exposed to IPV. Instead of avoiding feelings and places, young children appear to seek out people and familiar settings in response to trauma. Clearly, the present *DSM–IV* standards do not accurately reflect the kinds of traumatic stress responses exhibited by the young children of abused women as reported in these studies.

Trauma Effects on Cognitive Functioning

Lazarus and Folkman (1984) described coping as contingent on primary appraisals of threat and the assessment of available resources and strategies for responding. Therefore, the ability to successfully regulate one's affect involves attentional processing, choosing among behavioral responses, and exerting enough control over physiological reactions to either escape or avoid an unwanted emotional state (Eisenberg & Spinrad, 2004). Children traumatized by exposure to IPV may be challenged in managing their thoughts and emotions in the face of trauma and stressful events.

Research supports a link between IPV exposure and potentially impaired neurocognitive functioning. Several studies have evaluated the association between IPV and various elements of children's cognitive development. A recent study of attention bias in preschool-age children exposed to IPV used a dot-probe task to ascertain whether attention bias to threat was associated with a diagnosis of PTSD (Swartz, Graham-Bermann, Mogg, Bradley, & Monk, 2009). A bias by preschool-age children toward threatening faces indicates vigilance toward threat cues, which, in turn, has been related to anxiety and affective disorders in adults (Mogg, Bradley, & Williams, 1995). The hypothesis was that children who were traumatized by violence would be more aware of and more focused on angry as opposed to on neutral or happy faces. The results supported this hypothesis, suggesting that being alert to threat may mediate the development of PTSD in children exposed to IPV.

Findings of lower levels of cognitive ability also suggest cognitive deficits in children exposed to IPV. Research on 1,116 twin pairs, age 5, in England showed that children exposed to high levels of violence had IQ's approximately 8 points lower than children who did not witness violence (Koenen, Moffitt, Caspi, Taylor, & Purcell, 2003). A dose–response relationship was found in which preschool-age children exposed to low levels of IPV had IQs 1 point lower than controls, children exposed to medium levels had IQs approximately 5 points lower, and children exposed to severe or high levels of violence had IQs 8 points lower. A second study compared the verbal ability of children ages 4 to 6 exposed to IPV with a national sample of 1,700 same-age children not evaluated for exposure to traumatic events (Graham-Bermann, Howell, Miller, Kwek, & Lilly, 2010). The IPV-exposed children scored significantly lower on verbal ability, as assessed with standardized measures. A third study, by Ybarra, Wilkens, and Lieberman (2007), evaluated the effects of IPV exposure on 3- to 5-year-old children's cognition and behavioral functioning and found that children exposed to family violence had a lower IQ, on average 8.9 points, than controls. Neither maternal psychopathology nor gender influenced these outcomes.

When Jouriles et al. (2008) evaluated the connection between IPV and preschool-age children's (average age of 5) explicit memory functioning, they found that the frequency of IPV negatively correlated with their explicit memory function, after controlling for parent–child aggression and demographic variables related to memory. Preschool-age children's hyperarousal symptoms did not mediate the relationship between IPV and explicit memory functioning. On the other hand, mothers' positive parenting did moderate the relationship. There was a weaker relationship between IPV and preschool-age children's explicit memory in families with higher levels of mothers' positive parenting.

Although much remains to be done, the studies discussed here provide information on the possible neurocognitive consequences of witnessing IPV. These studies, although innovative, were limited by cross-sectional designs and a lack of information on other biological factors, such as stress hormones, that may affect the findings. Additional studies would do well to examine executive functioning across a broad range of abilities, as well as preschool-age children's early academic functioning.

Effects of IPV on Cognitive Schemas

Given the interpersonal nature of IPV, children exposed to such violence are also at risk for developing deleterious paradigms of gender and family roles as well as inappropriate strategies for the resolution of conflicts. Grych, Fincham, Jouriles, and McDonald (2000) used narrative methods to examine 3- to 7-year-old children's maternal, self, and marital representations. They found that the presence of interparental aggression affected all three areas after taking child–parent conflict into account. That is, children exposed to interparental violence had less positive representations of mothers, less positive images of themselves, and less understanding of emotional situations.

When Stover, Van Horn, and Lieberman (2006) used 3- to 6-year-old children's play to evaluate their representations of parents, they found that preschool-age boys from divorced or separated families who witnessed IPV had more negative maternal representations in play, especially if visitation with their father was limited. The authors noted that contact with the father was important for boys in the study, and they tended to blame the mother for the lack visitation. Mother–child relationship functioning did not significantly predict parental representations. Despite a small sample size and the use of a clinic-referred sample that limits generalizability, this study relied on a unique design to elicit children's cognitive schemas of parents following IPV exposure.

Effects of Emotional Reactivity on Emotion Regulation and Prosocial Skills

In this chapter, *reactivity* refers to the emotional response shown by children to environmental stressors; such reactions might include intense emotional outbursts or an inability to match emotional response to the presented situation. Preschool-age children exposed to IPV contend with difficulties around salient developmental tasks, including emotion regulation and prosocial skill development. Initial reactions to family violence may inhibit children from progressing through typical developmental tasks. Specific issues related to arousal and emotion regulation in preschool-age children exposed to violence include the intense separation anxiety and increased aggressiveness that some children exhibit. Young children exposed to IPV may also have difficulty recognizing emotions or understanding complex social roles. They may show deficits in the ability to empathize and accurately attend to social cues (Margolin, 2005). An observational study that compared the social behavior of preschool-age children who were exposed to IPV with a matched sample of similar children not exposed to family violence revealed that the violence-exposed children were less empathic, less adept at expressing emotions, and more aggressive but no less cooperative than their nonexposed peers (Graham-Bermann & Levendosky, 1997).

Physiological Reactivity and Behavioral Problems

There is a substantial literature documenting the effects of preschool-age children's exposure to IPV and their internalizing and externalizing behavior problems (for a review, see Kitzmann et al., 2003). Here, *reactivity* refers to the level of physiological arousal that is regulated by the autonomic nervous system in response to perceived threat. The reactive response can be seen as increases in heart rate, sweating, and blood flow or as intense, unmediated emotional responses. Externalizing behavior was recently explored in a study of preschool-age children in New Zealand (Paterson, Carter, Gao, Cowley-Malcolm, & Iusitini, 2008). The goal was to examine the association between maternal IPV and behavioral problems among 2- and 4-year-olds. The authors found that for 2-year-olds, there was no significance in the relationship between IPV and prevalence rates of behavior problems. However, when evaluating 4-year-olds, the prevalence rates of internalizing, externalizing, and total child behavior problem cases were significantly higher among children whose mothers reported severe IPV. The odds of being in the clinical range for internalizing behavior problems were 2.16 times higher for those preschool-age children who witnessed severe physical violence than for those who did not. For externalizing behavior in the clinical ranges the rate was 2.38 times higher and 2.36 times higher for total problems as compared with young children who did not witness such violence in their home.

Linking Physiological Reactivity to Externalizing Behavior Problems

One significant negative effect associated with exposure to IPV is an increase in aggression, hyperactivity, and externalizing problems among preschool-age children. Children who witness IPV in the home show higher rates of aggression, fighting, and antisocial behavior (Margolin & Gordis, 2000). Exposure to violence can alter children's ability to regulate emotions, leading to more intense, severe aggression.

A unique study by El-Sheikh et al. (2009) tested the hypothesis that physiological reactivity moderates the effects of exposure to marital conflicts on children's externalizing behaviors. Although the study focused on school-age children, its methods and findings have implications for research with younger children. The researchers assessed individual patterns of physiological arousal and regulation in the SNS and PNS and tested their role as vulnerability or protective factors for children exposed to marital conflict. They posited that it is the interplay and interaction of both systems that could account for differences in child outcome. Results indicate that there is an effect of coinhibition of the SNS and PNS that is related to greater externalizing behavior problems for the child, whereas reciprocal activation of the SNS and PNS appeared to have a protective effect and was related to lower externalizing problems. That is, when children in the El-Sheik et al. (2009) study were able to manage their physiological response when exposed to threatening conditions, they were less likely to have high levels of delinquency and aggression.

Linking Physiological Reactivity to Internalizing Behavior Problems

The fear and anger children experience in an abusive home may lead to feelings of helplessness, anxiety, and depression. Young children rely on parents for protection and support; therefore, when trauma occurs in the home, children begin to view life as stressful and lonely, often believing they are not worth respect and comfort. These beliefs contribute to internalizing problems and social withdrawal. Preschool children may exhibit a loss of self-esteem and self-confidence following exposure to family violence (Grych, Jouriles, Swank, McDonald, & Norwood, 2000; Lemmey, McFarlane, Wilson, & Malecha, 2001).

One mega-analysis on family violence found that preschool-age children who witness interparental violence are at similar risk of internalizing problems as children who are direct victims of abuse. Children who are physically abused in the home did not differ on depression scores from children who solely witnessed family violence (Sternberg, Baradaran, Abbott, Lamb, & Guterman, 2006). This mega-analysis divided children exposed to traumatic violence by age; therefore, data on children ages 4 to 6 could be analyzed separately from older children ages 7 to 14. Sternberg et al. (2006) found that type of violence was significantly associated with externalizing and internalizing problems in preschool children. Children who both witnessed and directly experienced abuse in the home were 1.5 times more likely to have externalizing problems and 1.9 times more likely to have internalizing problems than those children who solely witnessed violence or solely personally experienced violence. Compared with grade school children, preschool-age children had a higher likelihood of externalizing problems but a lower likelihood of internalizing problems. In this report, developmental level and age had a direct impact on the experience of violence (Sternberg et al., 2006).

Effects of Physiological Reactivity on Physical Health

Preschool-age children exposed to IPV not only suffer psychological and cognitive complications but also may experience physical health problems. Children's chronic exposure to stress challenges their physiological response systems that can leave them vulnerable to physical illness by adding to the allostatic load. Although less researched, evidence exists for the connection between witnessing violence and child's physical health, as noted in a study by Graham-Bermann and Seng (2005). This study evaluated the functioning of 160 preschool-age children, with a mean age of 4.62. Mothers were interviewed about their child's health, exposure to violence, and the presence of traumatic stress symptoms. The children's teachers also completed questionnaires regarding the child's health and behavioral adjustment. Preschool-age children distressed by violence in the home were 4 times more likely to have asthma, allergies, and gastrointestinal complications. When factors predicting to these health problems were identified, child abuse, IPV, mother's substance use, mother's current health, and child traumatic stress all significantly predicted poorer child health outcomes.

RESILIENT COPING

As research expands on the effects of witnessing violence, we are beginning to recognize that outcomes vary from child to child. For example, while approximately 40% to 50% of preschool-age children exposed to IPV are found to be in the clinical range on internalizing and externalizing behavioral problems, such as anxiety, depression, and aggression (indicating the need for intervention), many children do not show evidence of psychopathology, at least at the time of assessment (Edleson, 2001). Despite the great diversity in the functioning of young children exposed to interparental violence, there is little research on positive outcomes, such as coping or resilience, in this population (Margolin, 2005).

One meta-analytic review of the literature on children exposed to IPV found that 37% of children who witness or personally experience abuse fare as well or better than children who are not exposed to such trauma in the home (Kitzmann et al., 2003). Likewise, while some individuals who experience abuse during childhood eventually become abusers, most do not. In fact, more than 70% of abused children do not become abusive adults. These findings hold across age, gender, and type of trauma (McGloin & Widom, 2001). Therefore, to help children exposed to IPV, future research studies might focus on the factors that lead some young children to show deleterious outcomes and others to appear more resilient. We can take instruction from the work of others who have studied resilience in different groups of at-risk children.

Defining Resilient Functioning

Young children exhibiting resilient functioning have been characterized as surviving adversity (Luthar, Cicchetti, & Becker, 2000), as being successful in achieving developmental tasks and expectations (Masten et al., 1999), and as functioning well across multiple domains, for example, exhibiting both behavioral and emotional competence (Eisenberg et al., 2003). Personal characteristics of the child are particularly relevant to potential resilient outcomes. Research supports the association between more positive outcomes and children's temperamental self-regulation, positive emotionality (Prior, Sanson, Smart, & Oberklaid, 2000), sense of humor, empathy, effective problem-solving and coping skills, social expressiveness (Luthar, Cicchetti, & Becker, 2000), intelligence, internal locus of control (Alvord & Grados, 2005), self-control (Masten & Coatsworth, 1998), self-esteem, self-efficacy, and attractiveness to others in appearance and personality (Osofsky, 1999). Additionally, both social competence and emotion regulation are highly intertwined with positive outcomes. Children with high social competence are often popular with peers and display interpersonal strengths. Such children are able to garner support and protection from individuals outside of the family, often leading to better outcomes following exposure to violence (Alvord & Grados, 2005).

Protective Factors Associated With Resilience

In addition to personal characteristics of the child, environmental and social factors are also highly relevant to the path preschool-age children may follow. Studies show that positive features of families are associated with positive child adaptation, including better autonomic nervous system regulation and control. Familial factors, such as parental social competence, positive family or extrafamilial links, at least one warm, loving parent or surrogate caregiver who provides firm limits and boundaries (Masten & Coatsworth, 1998; Skopp, McDonald, Jouriles, & Rosenfield, 2007), socioeconomic advantage (Osofsky, 1999), and more parental involvement in children's lives (Alvord & Grados, 2005), have all been related to greater resiliency in children exposed to challenging circumstances. Supportive adult figures are especially important for children exposed to traumatic violence in the home. Children who have a strong relationship with another adult seem to fare better than children who lack outside support (Margolin & Gordis, 2000).

Competent Parenting Under Stress as a Protective Factor for Preschool-Age Children

Another consistent finding in the research is that strong parenting provides a protective buffer following exposure to IPV. However, there is great variability in parenting competence in families with violence. Clearly, parents who are abusive or abused (those who are parenting under extreme stress) may be less able to offer warmth and support to their children. Levendosky, Huth-Bocks, Shapiro, and Semel (2003) evaluated the protective role of the mother–child relationship on preschool-age children's functioning in IPV families, with the average child age at 4 years. The authors found that mothers often tried to compensate for interparental violence by becoming more effective parents. Abused women made an effort to pay more attention to their child and be more responsive as a way to compensate for the violence at home. Such a parenting style can lead to stronger mother–child relationships. However, this only held for women who were mentally healthy following abuse. The depressed and traumatized mothers were less able to compensate; therefore, they displayed poorer parenting practices.

The following studies show that poor parenting is associated with higher levels of dysfunction for the child. Katz and Low (2004) examined the relationship between marital violence, coparenting, and family-level processes on child adjustment. These authors hypothesized that family-level and co-parenting processes mediated relations between marital violence and child functioning. The average child age was 5 years. They found that marital violence was related to higher levels of child noncompliance with peers. This is a significant issue because interacting with peers is an important social process for young children. Hostile-withdrawn coparenting mediated the relationship between marital violence and child's anxiety and depression. Family-level and coparenting processes also contributed to predicting children's adjustment after controlling for marital violence and other potential explanatory variables, such as family income. A fragmented family interaction significantly related to peer noncompliance.

Lieberman, Van Horn, and Ozer (2005) also evaluated how maternal stressors, psychological functioning, and the quality of the mother–child relationship contribute to the preschool-age child's behavior following exposure to IPV. In this study, child behavior problems were influenced by multiple family factors, including maternal stress, psychological functioning, and quality of the relationship between mother and child. Additionally, the level and severity of exposure to IPV were significant factors affecting child outcomes. The data supported a significant link between maternal risk factors and child behavior. Mothers who had more risk factors typically had children with higher levels of behavioral problems, but this was mediated by the mother's response to stress on an individual level and in her relationship with the child. The mother's chronic stress was more predictive of child psychological functioning than the amount of violence encountered over the past year.

Johnson and Lieberman (2007) also evaluated internalizing and externalizing behavior problems seen in preschool-age children who witnessed IPV. They focused on the association between the quality of mother–child relations and child behavior reactions to witnessing family violence. Additionally, the impact of mother's posttraumatic stress on the parent–child relationship was examined. Here, family environment related to variations in behavior problems in children exposed to IPV. Externalizing behaviors were associated with the severity of IPV, the quality of the relationship between mother and child, and the attunement of the mother to the child's feelings. The mothers' attunement and adaptive relationship with her child may have helped prevent some externalizing behavior problems. The authors also found that the quality of the relationship between mother and child predicted internalizing behavior; however neither the severity of IPV nor attunement to the child's feelings were linked to internalizing problems.

The effect of father visitation on preschool-age children's externalizing and internalizing behaviors was examined by Stover, Van Horn, Turner, Cooper, and Lieberman (2003). This study observed the relationship between the amount of visitation from the father and behavioral functioning of the child. The authors also examined how the child's behavior might be impacted by the association between severity of violence witnessed and the quality of the mother–child relationship. Results of this study showed that preschool-age children of divorced or separated couples who witnessed IPV evidenced fewer internalizing symptoms if they had weekly visits with their fathers. Loss of contact with the father was more predictive of internalizing symptoms than the severity of violence witnessed. However, the more violent the father, the more externalizing symptoms exhibited by the child, regardless of visitation frequency. Mother–child relationship functioning did not moderate the impact of the father's visitation on child behavior.

These studies gave evidence that parenting practices affect child outcome, but the outcomes were principally negative and focused on psychopathology. The difference between a lack of psychopathology and the presence of strengths is illustrated in the following study.

When Howell, Graham-Bermann, Czyz, and Lilly (2010) examined the parent–child relationship and resilient functioning in preschool-age children exposed to IPV, they conceptualized resilient coping as strengths in emotion regulation and prosocial skills. Coping was evaluated using the Social Competence Scale developed by the Conduct Problems Prevention Research Group (2002). After controlling for relevant demographic factors, findings indicated that better parenting performance, fewer maternal mental health problems, and less severe violence exposure predicted better emotion regulation and prosocial skill scores, which in turn were negatively correlated with maladaptive child behaviors. Such research shows that the pathway to positive or negative functioning following exposure to IPV is influenced by multiple factors, both internal and external to the preschool-age child. Many more studies are needed on the positive qualities and strengths of young children coping with exposure to IPV if we are to understand factors that contribute to their resilience.

TRAJECTORY FOLLOWING IPV EXPOSURE

When so many domains of functioning are challenged as a result of violence exposure, children are often unable to recover. Witnessing IPV at a young age can have long-term consequences, with child witnesses of such violence reporting difficulty with various problems in adulthood, including lower social adjustment, depression and trauma-related symptoms, low self-esteem, and increased risk of perpetrating violence within intimate relationships (Bevan & Higgins, 2002; Ehrensaft et al., 2003).

The preschool years seem like an important time to assess the extent, and hopefully to attenuate the effects, of IPV because young children form much of their worldview and socioemotional response to life during these years. If protective factors and resilience can be promoted, then some of the negative effects associated with violence may be reduced or even mitigated (Margolin, 2005). Thus, to best minimize problems and promote resilience, intervention programs (such as those described in this book's clinical case examples, as well as in the intervention chapters for preschool-age children), should provide affordable services to address some of the mediating variables, including the child's reaction to violence exposure and beliefs concerning violence. Additionally, programs should work to enhance parenting skills and coping. However, most communities do not yet have empirically supported programs for young children exposed to IPV (Graham-Bermann et al., 2007). The lack of effective intervention programs in these communities signals the need for developing collaborative partnerships as a major future challenge for this field of study.

DEVELOPMENTAL AND CLINICAL IMPLICATIONS

This review of the multiple impacts of IPV on preschool-age children has underscored the importance of evaluating such effects from a developmental perspective. By employing a developmental framework, this chapter highlighted the vast differences in prevalence, intensity of exposure, and deleterious outcomes across different age groups. Such negative outcomes for preschool-age children include physiological alterations to the nervous system, a unique presentation of PTSD, and cognitive impairments. Preschool children exposed to IPV also show skewed cognitive representations of the world and important adults; these children hold less positive representations of mothers, less positive images of themselves, and less understanding of emotional situations. Further, preschool-age children who witness IPV exhibit more internalizing and externalizing behavior problems, as well as physical health complications.

Despite such intense, harmful outcomes following exposure to violence, this chapter also highlighted the variations in reaction to witnessing IPV. A substantial subset of preschool-age children do not show evidence of psychopathology and seem to fare as well or better than children who are not exposed to such trauma in the home. The quality of the mother–child relationship substantially contributes to the preschool-age child's functioning following exposure to IPV. Better parenting performance and fewer maternal mental health problems are main contributors to more positive functioning in preschool-age children.

Given such unique differences in response to IPV, a variety of clinical implications are relevant as we focus on factors that lead some young children to show deleterious outcomes and others to appear more resilient. Such findings can be highly influential in clinical work with families exposed to IPV. As opposed to focusing solely on reducing pathology associated with family violence, clinicians could conceptualize treatment from a more positive, empowering perspective and build on the strengths of these families. Clinicians can benefit from knowing that when working with children exposed to family violence, it is important to take an ecological, systemic approach to treatment. This integrated approach will bolster the mother's strengths and help her provide a supportive foundation for her child. In treatment, preschool-age children, in addition to receiving individual care to better cope with the traumatic event of witnessing family violence, can also benefit from their caregiver receiving parent guidance and mental health services. As the mother's health and ability to parent improves, her child's functioning may also grow. While many communities may provide services for women and children exposed to IPV, this research review underscores the importance of employing evidence-based practices proven to be successful with children in this developmental period.

FUTURE DIRECTIONS IN RESEARCH AND POLICY

Using this review as a template, various opportunities for future directions in both research and policy become apparent. Areas of competence should be broadened to look beyond social skills. Clearly, strengths in social functioning and the ability to relate to others help young children sustain during episodes of violence, but more of a focus could be placed on individual competencies. Additionally, risk and resilience should be studied in cultural terms. A young child's cultural background has a significant impact on the way he or she conceptualizes violence and is impacted by violence exposure (Graham-Bermann et al., 2006). Researchers who look to evaluate outcomes in developmentally and culturally appropriate ways can then carry their findings into more sensitive policy initiatives.

The research on the cumulative effects of chronic and early exposure to traumatic violence suggests that we start assessing and intervening early in the life of the child. Yet, as very little is known about the long-term trajectory of preschool-age children exposed to IPV, it is not strictly correct to say that even seemingly resilient children are actually doing well and will not develop problems at a later date. If policy programs and clinical interventions focus only on children suffering immediately following violence, then many individuals who may develop pathology later in childhood are neglected. Researchers whose studies address these longitudinal concerns can provide guidance for future initiatives.

Despite the gaps in current research and policy, it is important to keep in mind that great strides have been made in this field. Until quite recently, many researchers did not recognize the hardships preschool-age children experienced when exposed to IPV. A broader understanding of IPV that incorporates both risk and protective factors may allow children of all ages to receive the assistance they need to experience healthy lives, in spite of exposure to family violence.

REFERENCES

American Psychiatric Association. (1994). *Diagnostic and statistical manual of mental disorders* (4th ed.). Washington, DC: Author.

Alvord, M. K., & Grados, J. J. (2005). Enhancing resilience in children: A proactive approach. *Professional Psychology, Research and Practice, 36,* 238–245. doi:10.1037/0735-7028.36.3.238

Bevan, E., & Higgins, D. J. (2002). Is domestic violence learned? The contribution of five forms of child maltreatment to men's violence and adjustment. *Journal of Family Violence, 17,* 223–245. doi:10.1023/A:1016053228021

Conduct Problems Prevention Research Group. (2002). *Psychometric properties of the Social Competence Scale—teacher and parent ratings* (Fast Track Project Technical Report). Retrieved from http://www.fasttrackproject.org

DeBellis, M. D. (2005). The psychobiology of neglect. *Child Maltreatment, 10,* 150–172.

Edleson, J. L. (2001). Studying the co-occurrence of child maltreatment and domestic violence in families. In S. A. Graham-Bermann & J. L. Edleson (Eds.), *Domestic violence in the lives of children: The future of research, intervention, and social policy* (pp. 91–110). Washington, DC: American Psychological Association. doi:10.1037/10408-005

Ehrensaft, M. K., Cohen, P., Brown, J., Smailes, E. M., Chen, H., & Johnson, J. G. (2003). Intergenerational transmission of partner violence: A 20-year prospective study. *Journal of Consulting and Clinical Psychology, 71,* 741–753. doi:10.1037/0022-006X.71.4.741

Eisenberg, N., & Spinrad, T. L. (2004). Emotion-related regulation: Sharpening the definition. *Child Development, 75,* 334–339.

Eisenberg, N., Valiente, C., Fabes, R. A., Smith, C. L., Reiser, M., Shepard, S. A., Losoya, S. H., . . . Cumberland, A. J. (2003). The relations of effortful control and ego control to children's resiliency and social functioning. *Developmental Psychology, 39,* 761–776. doi:10.1037/0012-1649.39.4.761

El-Sheikh, M., Kouros, C. D., Erath, S., Cummings, E. M., Keller, P., & Staton, L. (2009). Marital conflict and children's externalizing behavior: Interactions between parasympathetic and sympathetic nervous system activity. *Monographs of the Society for Research in Child Development, 74*(1), 1–101.

Fantuzzo, J. W., DePaola, L. M., Lambert, L., Martino, T., Anderson, G., & Sutton, S. (1991). Effects of interparental violence on the psychological adjustment and competencies of young children. *Journal of Consulting and Clinical Psychology, 59,* 258–265. doi:10.1037/0022-006X.59.2.258

Fantuzzo, J. W., & Fusco, R. (2007). Children's direct sensory exposure to substantiated domestic violence crimes. *Violence and Victims*, *22*, 158–171. doi:10.1891/088667007780477375

Graham-Bermann, S. A., DeVoe, E. R., Mattis, J. S., Lynch, S., & Thomas, S. A. (2006). Ecological predictors of traumatic stress symptoms in Caucasian and ethnic minority children exposed to intimate partner violence. *Violence Against Women*, *12*, 662–692. doi:10.1177/1077801206290216

Graham-Bermann, S. A., Howell, K. H., Habarth, J., Krishnan, S., Loree, A., & Bermann, E. A. (2008). Toward assessing traumatic events and stress symptoms in preschool children from low-income families. *American Journal of Orthopsychiatry*, *78*, 220–228.

Graham-Bermann, S. A., Howell, K. H., Miller, L. E., Kwek, J., & Lilly, M. (2010). Traumatic events and maternal education as predictors of verbal ability for preschool children exposed to intimate partner violence (IPV). *Journal of Family Violence*, *25*, 383–392. doi:10.1007/s10896-009-9299-3

Graham-Bermann, S. A., Kulkarni, M., & Kanukollu, S. (in press). Is disclosure therapeutic for children following exposure to traumatic violence? *Journal of Interpersonal Violence*, *26*(5). doi:10.1177/0886260510365855

Graham-Bermann, S. A., & Levendosky, A. A. (1997). The social functioning of preschool-age children whose mothers are emotionally and physically abused. *Journal of Emotional Abuse*, *1*, 59–84. doi:10.1300/J135v01n01_04

Graham-Bermann, S. A., & Levendosky, A. A. (1998). Traumatic stress symptoms of children of battered women. *Journal of Interpersonal Violence*, *13*, 111–128. doi:10.1177/088626098013001007

Graham-Bermann, S. A., Lynch, S., Banyard, V., DeVoe, E., & Halabu, H. (2007). Community-based intervention for children exposed to intimate partner violence. *Journal of Consulting and Clinical Psychology*, *75*, 199–209. doi:10.1037/0022-006X.75.2.199

Graham-Bermann, S. A., & Perkins, S. C. (2010). Contributions of age of first exposure and intimate partner violence (IPV) on child adjustment. *Violence and Victims*, *25*, 427–439.

Graham-Bermann, S. A., & Seng, J. S. (2005). Violence exposure and traumatic stress symptoms as additional predictors of health problems in high-risk children. *Journal of Pediatrics*, *146*, 349–354. doi:10.1016/j.jpeds.2004.10.065

Grych, J. H., Fincham, F. D., Jouriles, E. N., & McDonald, R. (2000). Interparental conflict and child adjustment: Testing the mediational role of appraisals in the cognitive-contextual framework. *Child Development*, *71*, 1648–1661. doi:10.1111/1467-8624.00255

Grych, J. H., Jouriles, E. N., Swank, P. R., McDonald, R., & Norwood, W. D. (2000). Patterns of adjustment among children of battered women. *Journal of Consulting and Clinical Psychology*, *68*, 84–94. doi:10.1037/0022-006X.68.1.84

Holden, G. W. (2003). Children exposed to domestic violence and child abuse: Terminology and taxonomy. *Clinical Child and Family Psychology Review, 6,* 151–160.

Holden, G. W., Stein, J. D., Ritchey, K. L., Harris, S. D., & Jouriles, E. N. (1998). Parenting behaviors and beliefs of battered women. In G. W. Holden (Ed.), *Children exposed to marital violence: Theory, research, and applied issues* (pp. 289–334). Washington, DC: American Psychological Association. doi:10.1037/10257-009

Howell, K. H., Graham-Bermann, S. A., Czyz, E., & Lilly, M. (2010). Assessing resilience in preschool children exposed to intimate partner violence. *Violence and Victims, 25,* 150–164. doi:10.1891/0886-6708.25.2.150

Johnson, V. K., & Lieberman, A. F. (2007). Variations in behavior problems of preschoolers exposed to domestic violence: The role of mothers' attunement to children's emotional experiences. *Journal of Family Violence, 22,* 297–308. doi:10.1007/s10896-007-9083-1

Jouriles, E. N., Brown, A. S., McDonald, R., Rosenfield, D., Leahy, M. M., & Silver, C. (2008). Intimate partner violence and preschoolers' explicit memory functioning. *Journal of Family Psychology, 22,* 420–428. doi:10.1037/0893-3200.22.3.420

Katz, L. F., & Low, S. M. (2004). Marital violence, co-parenting, and family-level processes in relation to children's adjustment. *Journal of Family Psychology, 18,* 372–382. doi:10.1037/0893-3200.18.2.372

Kilpatrick, K. L., & Williams, L. M. (1998). Potential mediators of post-traumatic stress disorder in child witnesses to domestic violence. *Child Abuse and Neglect, 22,* 319–330.

Kitzmann, K. M., Gaylord, N. K., Holt, A. R., & Kenny, E. D. (2003). Child witnesses to domestic violence: A meta-analytic review. *Journal of Consulting and Clinical Psychology, 71,* 339–352. doi:10.1037/0022-006X.71.2.339

Koenen, K. C., Moffitt, T. E., Caspi, A., Taylor, A., & Purcell, S. (2003). Domestic violence is associated with environmental suppression of IQ in young children. *Development and Psychopathology, 15,* 297–311. doi:10.1017/S0954579403000166

Lazarus, R. S., & Folkman, S. (1984). *Stress, appraisal, and coping.* New York, NY: Springer.

Lehmann, P. (1997). The development of posttraumatic stress disorder in a sample of child witnesses to mother assault. *Journal of Family Violence, 12,* 241–257. doi:10.1023/A:1022842920066

Lemmey, D., McFarlane, J., Wilson, P., & Malecha, A. (2001). Intimate partner violence: Mothers' perspectives of effects on their children. *American Journal of Maternal/Child Nursing, 26*(2), 98–103.

Levendosky, A. A., Huth-Bocks, A. C., Semel, M. A., & Shapiro, D. L. (2002). Trauma symptoms in preschool-age children exposed to domestic violence. *Journal of Interpersonal Violence, 17,* 150–164. doi:10.1177/0886260502017002003

Levendosky, A. A., Huth-Bocks, A. C., Shapiro, D. L., & Semel, M. A. (2003). The impact of domestic violence on the maternal-child relationship and preschool-age children's functioning. *Journal of Family Psychology, 17,* 275–287. doi:10.1037/0893-3200.17.3.275

Lieberman, A. F., Van Horn, P., & Ozer, E. J. (2005). Preschooler witnesses of marital violence: Predictors and mediators of child behavior problems. *Development and Psychopathology, 17,* 385–396. doi:10.1017/S0954579405050182

Luthar, S. S., Cicchetti, D., & Becker, B. (2000). The construct of resilience: A critical evaluation and guidelines for future work. *Child Development, 71,* 543–562. doi:10.1111/1467-8624.00164

Margolin, G. (2005). Children's exposure to violence: Exploring developmental pathways to diverse outcomes. *Journal of Interpersonal Violence, 20,* 72–81. doi:10.1177/0886260504268371

Margolin, G., & Gordis, E. B. (2000). The effects of family and community violence on children. *Annual Review of Psychology, 51,* 445–479. doi:10.1146/annurev.psych.51.1.445

Masten, A. S., & Coatsworth, J. D. (1998). The development of competence in favorable and unfavorable environments. *American Psychologist, 53,* 205–220. doi:10.1037/0003-066X.53.2.205

Masten, A. S., Hubbard, J. J., Gest, S. D., Tellegen, A., Garmezy, N., & Ramirez, M. (1999). Competence in the context of adversity: Pathways to resilience and maladaptation from childhood to late adolescence. *Development and Psychopathology, 11,* 143–169. doi:10.1017/S0954579499001996

McDonald, R., Jouriles, E. N., Briggs-Gowan, M. J., Rosenfield, D., & Carter, A. S. (2007). Violence toward a family member, angry adult conflict, and child adjustment difficulties: Relations in families with 1- to 3-year-old children. *Journal of Family Psychology, 21,* 176–184. doi:10.1037/0893-3200.21.2.176

McEwen, B. S. (2003). Mood disorders and allostatic load. *Biological Psychiatry, 54,* 200–207.

McGloin, J. M., & Widom, C. (2001). Resilience among abused and neglected children grown up. *Development and Psychopathology, 13,* 1021–1038. doi:10.1017/S095457940100414X

Mogg, K., Bradley, B. P., & Williams, R. (1995). Attentional bias in anxiety and depression: The role of awareness. *British Journal of Clinical Psychology, 34,* 17–36.

Nemeroff, C. B. (2004). Neurobiological consequences of childhood trauma. *Journal of Clinical Psychiatry, 65,* 18–28.

Osofsky, J. D. (1999). The impact of violence on children. *The Future of Children: Domestic Violence and Children, 9*(3), 33–49.

Paterson, J., Carter, S., Gao, W., Cowley-Malcolm, E., & Iusitini, L. (2008). Maternal intimate partner violence and behavioral problems among Pacific children living in New Zealand. *Journal of Child Psychology and Psychiatry, and Allied Disciplines, 49,* 395–404. doi:10.1111/j.1469-7610.2007.01841.x

Prior, M., Sanson, A., Smart, D., & Oberklaid, F. (2000). *Pathways from infancy to adolescence: Australian temperament project 1983–2000*. Melbourne: Australian Institute of Family Studies.

Rossman, B. B., Rea, J. G., Graham-Bermann, S. A., & Butterfield, P. M. (2004). Young children exposed to interparental violence: Incidence assessment and intervention. In P. G. Jaffe, L. L. Baker, & A. Cunningham (Eds.), *Protecting children from domestic violence* (pp. 30–48). New York, NY: Guilford Press.

Scheeringa, M. S., Zeanah, C. H., Drell, M. J., & Larieu, J. A. (1995). Two approaches to the diagnosis of posttraumatic stress disorder in infancy and early childhood. *Journal of the American Academy of Child and Adolescent Psychiatry, 34*, 191–200. doi:10.1097/00004583-199502000-00014

Skopp, N. A., McDonald, R., Jouriles, E. N., & Rosenfield, D. (2007). Partner aggression and children's externalizing problems: Maternal and partner warmth as protective factors. *Journal of Family Psychology, 21*, 459–467. doi:10.1037/0893-3200.21.3.459

Sternberg, K. J., Baradaran, L. P., Abbott, C. B., Lamb, M. E., & Guterman, E. (2006). Type of violence, age, and gender differences in the effects of family violence on children's behavior problems: A mega-analysis. *Developmental Review, 26*, 89–112. doi:10.1016/j.dr.2005.12.001

Stover, C. S., Van Horn, P., & Lieberman, A. F. (2006). Parental representations in the play of preschool aged witnesses of marital violence. *Journal of Family Violence, 21*, 417–424. doi:10.1007/s10896-006-9038-y

Stover, C. S., Van Horn, P., Turner, R., Cooper, B., & Lieberman, A. F. (2003). The effects of father visitation on preschool-aged witnesses of domestic violence. *Journal of Interpersonal Violence, 18*(10), 1149–1166. doi:10.1177/0886260503255553

Swartz, J. R., Graham-Bermann, S. A., Mogg, K., Bradley, B. P., & Monk, C. S. (2009). *Attention bias to emotional faces in young children exposed to intimate partner violence*. Manuscript submitted for publication.

Wolak, J., & Finkelhor, D. (2001). Children exposed to partner violence. In J. L. Jasinski & L. M. Williams (Eds.), *Partner violence: A comprehensive review of 20 years of research* (pp. 73–112). Thousand Oaks, CA: Sage.

Ybarra, G. J., Wilkens, S. L., & Lieberman, A. F. (2007). The influence of domestic violence on preschooler behavior and functioning. *Journal of Family Violence, 22*, 33–42. doi:10.1007/s10896-006-9054-y

6

INTERVENTIONS FOR YOUNG CHILDREN EXPOSED TO INTIMATE PARTNER VIOLENCE

RENEE McDONALD, ERNEST N. JOURILES, AND LAURA C. MINZE

In any given year, it is estimated that at least 15.5 million children in the United States are exposed to intimate partner violence (IPV; McDonald, Jouriles, Ramisetty-Mikler, Caetano, & Green, 2006), and at least 7 million are exposed to severe IPV. Considerable research has substantiated that such exposure increases children's risk for a variety of adverse mental health outcomes (for reviews, see Evans, Davies, & DiLillo, 2008; Kitzmann, Gaylord, Holt, & Kenny, 2003; Margolin & Gordis, 2000). During the past 25 years, a number of interventions have been developed to address the adjustment problems of children exposed to IPV. However, as Graham-Bermann and colleagues have noted in their reviews of the literature (Graham-Bermann, 2000; Graham-Bermann & Hughes, 2003), the designs of most early intervention studies in this area were limited. As a result, strong conclusions about the effectiveness of these interventions could not really be made from the early studies. Recently, a small handful of interventions have undergone more rigorous evaluation. This chapter picks up where Graham-Bermann's earlier reviews left off; we provide an update on those interventions found earlier to be promising and describe the results of additional interventions that have been evaluated in the interim.

We focus in this chapter on interventions for young children—toddlers through early school age—who have been exposed to IPV. Young children, especially those under age 5, are more likely than older children to be exposed to IPV (Fantuzzo, Boruch, Beriama, & Atkins 1997), and evidence suggests that they are perhaps more likely than older children to have adjustment problems associated with IPV exposure (Levendosky, Huth-Bocks, Shapiro, & Semel, 2003). Although there are similarities in the outcomes of exposure to IPV for children at different developmental levels, their particulars vary. For example, exposure to IPV has been associated with a variety of adjustment problems, including depression, trauma, and conduct disorder. Although such symptoms have been documented in younger and older children alike, their expression and the interventions best suited to alleviate them, are not the same throughout childhood, and adolescence. Furthermore, over the normal course of development, early adjustment problems can translate into continued problems and can mark the beginning of a developmental course in which a range of related problems emerge, and some problems related to young children's IPV exposure (e.g., antisocial behavior) become increasingly refractory to treatment as development unfolds. It is therefore important to identify and provide effective treatments for these problems when they emerge in early childhood.

Knowledge of the natural processes underlying the effects of IPV exposure on children is fundamentally important for identifying potential intervention targets and refining interventions to address them. Fortunately, research on mediators and moderators of the relation between IPV and child outcomes has become increasingly sophisticated, expanding to include consideration of numerous sources of influence on children's adjustment and factors that operate to amplify or modulate that influence. Not incidentally, such knowledge provides a substrate for enhancing and interpreting the findings of intervention research. Hence, in this chapter, we highlight the linkages between theory and empirically supported interventions for young children exposed to IPV, identifying those theoretical propositions that appear to be substantiated and those for which intervention research remains lacking. The interventions reviewed in this chapter are not all solely focused on preschool-age children; for example, some have been evaluated in samples that include preschool- and school-age children. We include those specific to preschool ages and those that have included preschool-age children and older children in their evaluations.

THEORY LINKING EXPOSURE TO IPV WITH CHILD ADJUSTMENT PROBLEMS

The unfolding of mental health problems in children is a complex, multiply determined, and dynamic process. It is transactional in nature, with environmental influences at different levels (individual, family, social, and community) influencing the child, whose behavior, in turn, influences his or her environment. Consistent with this, researchers attempting to understand the processes by which IPV influences children's adjustment have drawn from a diverse array of relevant theories, including social learning, cognitive-contextual, emotional security, family systems, and trauma theory. Below we briefly summarize the major theories behind much of the current research on children exposed to IPV, highlighting in particular those processes and factors that are salient to interventions in this area. Although these theories have been tested among children of varying ages, each is relevant to preschool-age children. It should be noted that none of these theories is held out as a "grand theory" of how IPV influences child development; however, they are each much more complex than the discussion below would suggest. For brevity and emphasis, we focus on those aspects of the theories that have illuminated specific paths leading from IPV to child maladjustment, and that have broadened our knowledge in this area. We also discuss the theoretical relationship between IPV and parenting, as well as additional theoretical considerations.

Social Learning Theory

Social learning theory holds that children learn how to behave and how to think and feel about aggression implicitly, through observation, as well as explicitly, through instruction or incidental learning (e.g., what behaviors parents encourage and discourage in interactions with their children, how parents explain their IPV to the child). Repeated exposure to aggression—especially aggression by individuals who are salient and important to the child—is theorized to facilitate the development of an internal set of beliefs, knowledge structures, expectations, and other internal representations about relationships that increases the likelihood that the child will engage in aggressive behavior (Bandura, 1986, 2001; Fosco, DeBoard, & Grych, 2007; Huesmann, 1988; Riggs & O'Leary, 1989). The sources of learning from exposure to aggression are not limited to direct observation of it (e.g., witnessing IPV) but include implicit learning that follows from interactions, such as discussions with parents about the IPV, or seeing how the consequences of IPV play out (e.g., whether the "winner" achieves some desirable goal). Through repeated exposure to aggression, children thus acquire a rather complex set of cognitions about aggression that operate simultaneously but that may also be incompatible with one another. For example, children may believe that aggression is wrong because they have been told so, but they may also believe that they are unable to control their emotions and that aggression from loss of control is acceptable, particularly in response to provocation. The likelihood of learning such maladaptive interpersonal skills is linked not only to the extent that children are exposed to aggressive conflicts, but also to the extent that they are *not exposed* to alternative, more adaptive means of resolving conflicts by salient others. Social learning theory has contributed more to knowledge on the influence of IPV on children's aggressive and antisocial behaviors than it has for symptoms of depression or PTSD.

Another social learning theory account of the development of aggression and antisocial behavior in young children emphasizes the role of parenting (e.g., Patterson, 1982). By virtue of their interactions with their children, parents are hypothesized to teach (often inadvertently) children to behave in an aggressive manner. Parental aggression toward children is hypothesized to be important in this teaching process. A parent's use of aggression, especially in disciplinary confrontations, might facilitate the development of beliefs and scripts that aggressive behavior is an acceptable method for resolving disagreements and that it can result in positive outcomes. Another dimension of parenting hypothesized to be important in this teaching process involves inconsistent discipline, in which parents sometimes fail to follow through with directives or discipline, particularly when they withdraw directives or discipline in response to oppositional or aggressive child behavior (such inconsistencies are hypothesized to teach children that oppositional or aggressive behavior can pay off). A third dimension of parenting hypothesized to be important is parental supportiveness, in particular, encouragement for prosocial behavior. Poor support for prosocial behavior may result in increased likelihood of oppositional, aggressive behavior. A considerable body of research has documented an association between IPV and these three dimensions of parenting—aggression, inconsistent discipline, and supportiveness (for reviews, see Appel & Holden, 1998; Jouriles, McDonald, Smith Slep, Heyman, & Garrido, 2008). Additionally, these three dimensions have been associated with child aggression in many previous studies (Patterson, 1982).

Consistent with hypotheses derived from social learning theory, children exposed to higher levels of interparental conflict and IPV have been found to be more likely to view aggression as justifiable, and this cognitive set, in turn, is associated with higher levels of aggression toward peers and dating partners (Kinsfogel & Grych, 2004; Lichter & McCloskey, 2004). Experiencing parental aggression also relates to children's beliefs and knowledge about aggression and to subsequent aggressive behavior (e.g., Guerra, Huesmann, & Spindler, 2003). Interventions for child adjustment problems based in social learning theory principles would target changes in the child's salient social-learning environment. These would include important environmental sources of children's social learning, such as parental modeling, positive reinforcement of prosocial child behaviors, nonaggressive parent–child conflict resolution and child discipline strategies, and direct instruction in and appropriate parental communications about acceptable social behavior. Such interventions have been developed and evaluated (e.g., Project Support) and are described in a later section.

Cognitive-Contextual Theory

It is now widely accepted that children's responses to their parents' conflict and IPV are related to their psychological adjustment. Grych and colleagues' cognitive-contextual theory (Grych & Fincham, 1990) articulated how particular cognitive appraisals and emotional responses to interparental conflict might influence children's adjustment. They theorized that children's responses to conflict are based on their appraisals of its meaning and consequences for themselves and their family. In particular, the extent to which the child feels threatened by the conflict (e.g., a parent might be harmed or the family might split up), and holds himself or herself responsible for its occurrence or for ending it were posited to influence their adjustment. Although cognitive-contextual theory acknowledges the importance of affective responses to IPV and recognizes that affective and cognitive processes are inextricably intertwined (Fosco & Grych, 2008), most of the research based on this theory has focused on the cognitive aspects of threat and self-blame appraisals. A substantial body of strong empirical research in community and clinical samples has yielded results that are consistent with the theoretical propositions of the cognitive-contextual framework, indicating that children's threat and self-blame appraisals mediate the relation of IPV to children's adjustment problems (Grych, Jouriles, Swank, McDonald, & Norwood, 2000; McDonald & Grych, 2006). Most of this research has focused on school-age children and young adolescents, but the theorized processes linking IPV with child adjustment are likely to apply as well to younger children, with the caveat that their appraisals are likely to be less complex and more concrete than those of older children.

Cognitive-contextual theory suggests that interventions designed to alter children's interpretation of the meaning of IPV, its causes, and its consequences to themselves have the potential to influence their adjustment. For example, helping children feel safer (i.e., less threatened) and helping them understand that they are not the cause of their parents' IPV would be expected to lead to improved child adjustment. Although interventions for children exposed to IPV often include components to increase children's safety (e.g., Graham-Bermann, Lynch, Banyard, DeVoe, & Halabu, 2007) and to help them develop alternative and more adaptive views of the causes of IPV (e.g., Wilson, Cameron, Jaffe, & Wolfe, 1989), intervention researchers have not explicitly tested the effects of interventions on children's appraisals or examined whether intervening directly on children's threat and self-blame appraisals about IPV enhances their adjustment.

Emotional Security Theory

Cummings and colleagues' emotional security theory (Davies & Cummings, 1994; Cummings & Davies, 1995) highlights children's emotional responses and emotion regulation in the link between IPV exposure and children's adjustment. IPV is theorized to reduce children's sense of emotional security, which is an important contributor to children's well-being. Emotional security theory considers the effects of IPV on the child's internal representation of the parental relationship and the conflict, the child's emotional regulation capacities, and the behaviors that result from efforts to modulate emotion and increase emotional security. Emotions and emotion regulation, cognitive appraisals, and behavior are all recognized as interwoven and reciprocally related; however, affective responses are believed to be the foundation on which children attempt to achieve and sustain emotional security. Not surprisingly, research on the emotional security hypothesis has focused more heavily on the emotional aspects of children's responses to IPV than on the social-cognitive aspects and has contributed a great deal to our understanding of the emotional functioning of children exposed to IPV.

Emotional security theory suggests that interventions designed to alter the extent to which IPV represents a threat to children's emotional security would enhance their adjustment. Intervention strategies that might be useful include those that focus on altering children's emotional reactions and behaviors in response to IPV, perhaps by increasing the child's ability to seek and obtain comfort from the parents, reducing the extent to which the IPV is perceived as threatening, enhancing the child's ability to cope adaptively with the distress caused by IPV, and providing the child with adaptive behavioral strategies for responding to IPV. Some interventions for children exposed to IPV have included components targeting children's emotional responses to IPV (e.g., Huth-Bocks, Schettini, & Shebroe, 2001), but evaluations of those interventions have not tested the effects of the interventions on children's emotional responses, or whether changes in those responses have led to improved child outcomes.

Family Systems Theory

Family systems theory and data link IPV with problematic family functioning in other areas, including family adaptability and cohesion, and the quality of family relatedness (Higgins & McCabe, 2003; Owen, Thompson, Shaffer, Jackson, & Kaslow, 2009). Triangulation is another family process through which IPV is theorized to influence child adjustment. It is manifest in the level of children's involvement and participation in their parents' conflict, including children's feelings of being "caught in the middle" between their parents, pressures to be loyal to one or the other parent that lead to polarized parent–child alliances, and direct involvement or participation in the conflict (Fosco & Grych, 2008; Gagné, Drapeau, Melançon, Saint-Jacques, & Lépine, 2007). Each of these family systems variables has been found to mediate the relation between IPV and children's adjustment (Fosco & Grych, 2008; O'Brien, Margolin, & John, 1995; Owen et al., 2009) and thus might be potentially useful targets of intervention.

In addition to reducing the overall conflict and IPV in the family, family systems interventions for child problems associated with IPV exposure might include strategies to detriangulate the child from the parents' IPV, such as by reducing parental pressures on the child to choose one parent's side over the other, and not allowing children to become involved in the conflict. Improving the quality of the family's relatedness, enhancing the family's flexibility and capabilities in handling conflict, and establishing clear parent–child boundaries are examples of intervention strategies consistent with family systems theory. None of the interventions for young children that have thus far undergone rigorous evaluations have focused on these particular family systems variables. However, most have included components designed to enhance the quality of the parent–child relationship and improve parenting competencies, both of which can be conceived of as family-level variables.

Trauma Theory

Exposure to IPV can be traumatic for a child, and IPV has been associated with symptoms of posttraumatic stress disorder (PTSD; Graham-Bermann & Levendosky, 1998; Kilpatrick & Williams, 1998). Trauma-inducing events, particularly repeated ones (Terr, 1991), have been associated with dysregulation of biological processes that are associated with sensitivity to stress and the ability to react appropriately to stress (Margolin & Gordis, 2000). The biological processes implicated in alterations to children's responses to stress include the functioning of the hypothalamic–pituitary–adrenal (HPA) axis. HPA-axis functioning includes feedback mechanisms that increase or decrease the body's resources for handling stressful situations (e.g., the fight or flight response) as needed. Over time and with chronic stress, these self-regulating mechanisms of the HPA-axis have been theorized to undergo long-term changes that affect the organism's responses to stress. These include changes that lead to increased arousal and hypervigilance for stressors, which are associated with PTSD symptoms, or changes that lead to diminished responsiveness to stress, which is associated with depression.

Present theory on children's responses to interparental conflict and IPV has considered the possible trauma-inducing effects of IPV on children, suggesting that the neurobiological effects of trauma induced by IPV exposure reduce children's ability to regulate their affect in response to stressors, and that this in turn leads to adjustment problems. Empirical research evaluating the links between biology and psychosocial outcomes among children who have experienced traumatic events has revealed a number of biological markers and responses to emotional functioning that characterize these children (for a review, see Margolin & Gordis, 2000). It should be noted that trauma theory is also consistent with emotional security theory, in which emotional security is tied to children's ability to regulate their emotions and to appraise events, and these in turn influence their behavioral responses. Results of empirical research suggest that emotion regulation does indeed mediate the association between interparental conflict and children's adjustment (Davies & Cummings, 1998). Furthermore, consistent with cognitive-contextual theory as well as emotional security theory, emotion regulation and cognitive appraisals have both been found to mediate the association between interparental conflict and IPV when examined simultaneously in mediation analyses. Trauma has also been negatively associated with cognitive functioning (Jouriles, Brown, et al., 2008). Such findings have also emerged for children exposed to IPV (Huth-Bocks, Levendosky, & Semel, 2001; Kitzmann et al., 2003; Ybarra, Wilkens, & Lieberman, 2007) and may be related to alterations and consolidation of the biological processes associated with complex, or multiple, traumatic experiences (Jouriles, Brown, et al., 2008; Minze, McDonald, Rosentraub, & Jouriles, in press; for additional discussion, see Margolin & Gordis, 2000). Interventions developed from the premises of trauma theory include provision of a safe environment in which children can disclose and talk about their traumatic experiences (Groves, 1999; Wilson et al., 1989), with the goals of the interventions including helping children enhance their ability to cope with the emotions aroused by IPV, helping them develop safety skills and strategies that reduce the likelihood of their being overwhelmed by their emotions regarding the IPV, correcting erroneous cognitions that may contribute to their emotional dysregulation, and educating them about their symptoms (Johnston, 2003).

Additional Theoretical Considerations

The interventions reviewed in later sections are also informed by additional theoretical principles or concepts. For example, principles of developmental psychopathology hold that child psychopathology (as well as normal development) unfolds over time as a result of ongoing transactions between the child and his or her environment, with a multitude of potential risk and protective factors specifically operating to influence the child's development and psychosocial adjustment at any point in time. From ecological theory comes the understanding that the risk and protective factors that influence children's development lie within nested levels of the child's environment, from the level of the individual child, to the parents and family, and on through neighborhood, school, community, and broader cultural influences. In addition, it is recognized that the multitude of risk and protective factors may operate within and across these levels of influence. From attachment and psychodynamic theory perspectives has come the recognition that children's internal representations of relationships with others derive directly from their relationships with their primary caregivers, and that the history, nature and quality of those relationships is key to children's psychological and social adjustment.

INTERVENTIONS EVALUATED IN RANDOMIZED CONTROLLED TRIALS WITH FOLLOW-UP DATA

In this section, we first describe our intervention for young children exposed to violence. The intervention has been evaluated using a rigorous experimental design and a multimethod assessment strategy, including assessing the families regularly long after treatment ended to examine whether the treatment effects were maintained over time. We then discuss commonalities between this intervention and two other, similarly supported programs.

Project Support

Project Support is designed to reduce conduct problems among children ages 4 to 9 with clinical levels of externalizing problems living with mothers who recently stayed in a domestic violence shelter (Jouriles et al., 1998, 2009; McDonald, Jouriles, & Skopp, 2006). This population is targeted because conduct problems (a) are the most prevalent problem among children from shelter populations, (b) tend to be stable without intervention, (c) tend to be refractory to treatment in older children, and (d) are strong predictors of antisocial behavior in adolescence and adulthood. The intervention is based on social learning theory on the development of antisocial behavior and evaluation research on interventions for children with conduct problems. It is also consistent with developmental psychopathology and ecological frameworks, which acknowledge various levels of environmental influences on very young children, and which point to parenting and the parent–child relationship as a primary source of influence on young children's development.

Project Support includes two components: the provision of social and instrumental support to the mothers and behavioral parent training to enhance mothers' nurturing and parenting skills. The social and instrumental support component (e.g., assistance obtaining access to community resources, providing home-based intervention services, providing child care during sessions) is designed to reduce women's distress during the transition from a domestic violence shelter back into the community and to facilitate the families' ability to engage in the intervention. The parenting component focuses on parenting as a key vehicle through which to ameliorate the children's conduct problems.

An initial evaluation of Project Support (Jouriles et al., 2001) was conducted with 36 mothers and their children ages 4 to 9 who met diagnostic criteria for oppositional defiant disorder or conduct disorder and who had recently left a domestic violence shelter. Children were randomly assigned to the Project Support condition or a comparison condition that included monthly case management/contact. A multimethod assessment strategy was employed. Families were assessed at pretreatment and four follow-up time points (4 months, 8 months [posttreatment], 12 months, and 16 months). Results at posttreatment indicated that children's conduct problems had improved more rapidly in the Project Support condition than the comparison condition. Among children in the Project Support condition, 84% were in the normal range of conduct problems, compared with 56% of children in the comparison group. Mothers' emotional distress was reduced in both conditions. The quality and effectiveness of mothers' parenting improved for families in the Project Support condition but not those in the comparison condition. Project Support's effects were maintained throughout the follow-up period (McDonald, Jouriles, & Skopp, 2006). Internalizing problems also improved for children in both conditions, with no mean group differences observed. However, 35% of children in the comparison condition continued to experience clinical levels of internalizing problems, but none in the Project Support condition did. It should be noted that all of the children had clinical levels of conduct problems at the outset of the study; thus, it can only be concluded that among this sample of children with clinically elevated conduct problems, the internalizing problems improved over time regardless of the intervention. Project Support's effectiveness for children with internalizing problems, but who do not have accompanying significant conduct problems, is unknown.

A second randomized controlled trial (Jouriles et al., 2009) was conducted with a sample of 66 families, also 4- to 9-year-olds with clinical levels of conduct problems, whose mothers had recently stayed in a domestic violence shelter. A more comprehensive and intensive measurement strategy was used, and formal tests were conducted to examine whether the improvements in mothers' parenting mediated the effects of treatment on the children. Results replicated those of the previous evaluation: At posttreatment, conduct problems of children in the Project Support condition increased more rapidly than those in the comparison condition, and from posttreatment through the end of the 20-month follow-up period, conduct problems of children in the Project

Support condition continued to improve; those in the comparison condition did not. In addition, at posttreatment and follow-up, most of the children in the Project Support condition were in the normal range on measures of externalizing problems (57% at posttreatment and 74% at the final follow-up), as compared with the comparison condition (39% at posttreatment and 48% at the final follow-up). The effect sizes for externalizing problems were $d = .66$ at posttreatment and $d = .63$ at follow-up. Mothers' parenting skills, particularly harsh and inconsistent parenting, and their psychological distress were found to improve in the Project Support condition, but not in the comparison condition. In addition, mothers' parenting—but not their psychological distress— was found to mediate the effect of the intervention on children's conduct problems. Mothers (and thus families) in the Project Support condition were also less likely to experience a recurrence of IPV during the period of participation in the study (McDonald et al., 2006; Jouriles et al., 2009).

Commonalities With Other Effective and Promising Interventions

The Kids' Club Program (Graham-Bermann, 1992) and Child–Parent Psychotherapy (Lieberman, Van Horn, & Ippen, 2005), have also undergone similar evaluations with follow-up data. Together, these three interventions provide a basis for discussion of common components of promising interventions.

Parenting and the Parent–Child Relationship

Each of the studies that have been evaluated in randomized controlled trials includes a component designed to change the quality of the parent–child relationship. Although there is some overlap, the theoretical orientations of each of the interventions also differ from one another, as do the theorized processes underlying the intervention effects. However, the content of the parenting component appears to be more similar than different across the interventions, each focusing on improving parenting skills and competence, enhancing the quality of the parent,–child relationship (in particular, improving maternal warmth and parent–child communication), teaching parents to appreciate and reinforce their children for appropriate behavior, and to discipline effectively and consistently, but without rancor or physical aggression (e.g., Jouriles et al., 2001). Additionally, consistent with research indicating that increased psychological distress is associated with decrements in parenting, each of the interventions also focus on reducing maternal distress by providing emotional and social support and a forum in which mothers can feel safe in talking about their experiences of IPV and about how it may have affected their lives and those of their children (e.g., Graham-Bermann et al., 2007).

Given the centrality of parents to the development of preschool children, this focus on parenting is appropriate, and it may well be that the effects of these interventions are primarily attributable to their influence on parenting. However, a focus on parenting leaves the contribution of the other components of the interventions to improving child adjustment unclear. For example, from Project Support, there is empirical evidence that parenting mediated the effects of treatment on child adjustment, and that reductions in mothers' psychological distress did not. This does not imply that it is not necessary or helpful (or simply morally right) to attend to the emotional distress of mothers who have been victims of IPV. However, it does suggest that doing so is not sufficient for helping the children. Additional research that explicitly tests the theoretical propositions on which these interventions have been developed, especially the processes held to be accountable for the intervention effects, is needed to further advance knowledge and practice in this area. For example, it follows from several theories (e.g., attachment, cognitive-contextual, emotional security, and trauma) that enhancing the child's sense of safety and security in the family should positively influence child mental health; however, the mechanisms responsible for this expected outcome differ across the different theories. Similarly, social learning theory and trauma theory posit different mechanisms to explain how IPV can lead to externalizing problems in children. Testing these mechanisms together in evaluation research will help clarify both theories and can shed light on how interventions based on these theories achieve their effects. Evaluating these theorized mechanisms individually and simultaneously would significantly advance knowledge in this area, and would provide valuable information for intervention developers. Similarly, evaluating directly competing hypotheses would help illuminate the operative mechanisms by which IPV influences child adjustment. Without such research, we have conjecture, but not evidence, for how the interventions work.

Diversity of Children Treated

The interventions noted above were provided to children recruited from a wide variety of community agencies, there was variability in the nature and levels of the children's adjustment problems, and differences in treatment modality (e.g., group vs. dyadic), yet each was found to be effective in helping the children served. Indeed, after intervention, the problems of a sizable number of children were found to have diminished from clinical to normative levels on standard measures of child psychopathology. Thus, although the interventions were tightly focused in concept (i.e., targeting children "exposed to IPV") they were helpful to children with a wide array of problems, and from diverse populations. The length of the interventions (e.g., 10 weeks, 8 months, 1 year) also varied considerably.

INTERVENTIONS EVALUATED IN NONRANDOMIZED DESIGNS

In addition to those interventions with a considerable history of empirical research, there have been a number of recently published evaluations of interventions for children exposed to violence that have not used a randomized controlled design, and some interventions have not included a comparison group of any kind. This immeasurably limits the conclusions that can be drawn about the effectiveness of these interventions. For example, in the absence of a comparison group, it is not clear whether observed improvements may have occurred over time without intervention. For studies with a comparison group but without random assignment to groups, it is not clear whether the results emerged because of differences between the intervention and control groups. Keeping these caveats in mind, we nonetheless summarize these studies because each has novel aspects that raise theoretical and practical questions for the field.

Sibling Play Therapy

Following a controlled trial that demonstrated positive outcomes for individual play therapy with children (Kot & Tyndall-Lind, 2005), a group play therapy intervention was developed that focused on siblings residing in a domestic violence shelter (Tyndall-Lind, Landreth, & Giordano, 2001). The intervention consisted of 12 daily sessions of sibling play therapy ($n = 10$), and three to four sessions focused on psychoeducation and recreation, in which siblings were included with other children as well. Treatment effectiveness was examined in relation to two comparison conditions, one in which children received 12 daily sessions of individual play therapy ($n = 11$), and a wait-list control group ($n = 11$). Data for the two comparison groups were derived from a previously conducted study. The rationale for providing services to all siblings within a family stemmed from the idea that including siblings helps shorten the time needed to develop rapport with the family, and that sibling relationships may act as a buffer against stressful family situations such as extreme conflict between parents. Pre- and postintervention data indicated that siblings in the group and individual play therapy conditions showed greater improvement in self-concept and externalizing behaviors than children in the wait-list control condition. Fewer aggressive as well as anxious and depressed behaviors were also noted in the sibling play therapy group (Kot & Tyndall-Lind, 2005; Tyndall-Lind et al., 2001).

In addition to the design considerations stated earlier, other reasons make it difficult to evaluate the results of this study critically. First, the inclusion criteria for participation were not presented, and thus it is uncertain (a) whether the study included children who were *not* exhibiting adjustment problems, and if so, what effects the intervention would have been expected to yield for them; and (b) whether children who began the intervention with adjustment problems were among those who improved. Second, multiple children from the same family were included in the analyses, and it is not clear whether the corresponding dependencies in their analysis of the data were considered. Thus, it is unknown whether individual children, or all siblings within a family, that account for the results. Third, the magnitude of the intervention effect is indeterminate because mean scores on the outcome measures at pre- and posttesting were not reported. Nonetheless, treating all children in a family simultaneously is novel in this area. If efficacious, such an intervention would be more cost-effective than alternative modalities that focus on individuals, especially in agency settings.

Child FIRST

The Child and Family Interagency Resource, Support, and Training Program (Child FIRST) is an advocacy intervention adapted for use with children exposed to IPV and evaluated as part of the Bridgeport Safe Start Initiative (Crusto et al., 2008). Child FIRST is a "wraparound process" that involves comprehensive assessment followed by the development and implementation of a family plan. Children eligible for the program ranged in age from less than 1 to 6 years, and the sample included children with both clinical and subclinical trauma symptoms. Masters level mental health clinicians assessed each family to determine the needs of the family and develop a plan and then worked together with bachelor's level care coordinators to help the family implement the plan. Services could include coordination of mental health services for the family members, educational advocacy for the child, parenting education, and/or assistance obtaining child care. Analysis of pretreatment and posttreatment data with 82 children were favorable, indicating that at postintervention, children in the intervention condition showed a decrease in exposure to traumatic events as well as a decrease in traumatic stress, and parents reported a decrease in parenting stress. Interpretation of the findings of this program is constrained by the absence of a comparison group and lack of follow-up data. However, providing interventions at community agencies for children exposed to IPV is important for bringing attention to the problem of child exposure to IPV. It is also a treatment model that can help widen the availability of services that are rarely available communitywide. Further evaluation of the intervention, including identifying which components appear to be crucial to improving child adjustment, characteristics of the children and families most likely to benefit from it, and scientifically strong evaluation of treatment effectiveness will be needed in determining the ultimate utility of this approach.

Group Treatment Provided Through Head Start

Another approach to providing services for children exposed to IPV in a community setting is that of a group treatment for 4- and 5-year-old children offered through a Head Start center (Huth-Bocks, Schettini, et al., 2001). The rationale for providing services at a Head Start center was that it would enhance retention and attendance over the course of the program, as dropout and attendance problems are common in other mental health services settings. The intervention consisted of 14 weekly, hour-long group sessions; group size was limited to six, and each group had two leaders. Materials for the sessions—stories, books, dolls—were developmentally appropriate. The group sessions began with a warm-up activity (i.e., making a puppet that expresses how the child feels and then being asked to describe why they chose that particular feeling), followed by a topic of the day and a structured activity around the topic. The last 25 min of the session are devoted to unstructured free play. The content of the intervention appears to be informed by psychodynamic theory. Specifically, through structured activities and through therapist utilization of group process concepts (e.g., reflecting what a given child may be feeling), it was theorized that children would project their feelings and concerns onto the play materials, thus allowing them to discuss and work through their internal conflicts and fears safely. The content and structure of the intervention were designed to focus on (a) helping children learn to identify and express their feelings, (b) teaching children problem-solving and conflict resolution skills, (c) providing them with a safe place to express themselves and to create a positive social experience, (d) correcting misconceptions that they are responsible for the violence/loss they witness, and (e) providing corrective emotional experiences through interactions with the therapists. Anecdotal data from teachers and parents suggested that some children were better able to express feelings and had fewer behavioral problems (Huth-Bocks, Schettini, et al., 2001) after participating in the group. Given the absence of a control group and specific outcome data, lack of clarity about the characteristics of the children included in the sample and about what the outcomes reflect, and reliance on only anecdotal data, these results are not readily interpretable. However, the investigators' approach provides another example of efforts to bring interventions for children exposed to IPV to existing service delivery systems.

Haupoa Family Component Program

This intervention consisted of twelve 90-min psychoeducation and support group sessions for children ages 3 to 17. Groups were formed based on child age, and the study included groups of 3- to 5-year-old children. Group services for parents were provided concurrently with the children's groups; the parent groups also focused on support and education about domestic violence and parenting after domestic violence (Becker, Mathis, Mueller, Issari, & Atta, 2008). This evaluation is unique in that the sample was primarily Asian and Pacific Island Americans. The composition and focus of the intervention were based on recommendations by Peled and Edleson (1992) and drew from trauma theory and social cognitive theory. Children referred to the program had been exposed to frequent and severe violence and were exhibiting adjustment problems. Multiple raters completed measures on child and parent outcomes. Data from 83 children were available for analysis, and measures included counselor ratings of child ($n = 83$) and parent ($n = 71$), domestic violence knowledge and skills, parent reports of domestic violence-related parenting skills ($n = 51$), and parent reports of children's adjustment on the Child Behavior Checklist (CBCL; $n = 47$; Achenbach, 1991). Results indicated improvements at posttreatment on child and parent domestic violence knowledge and skills, and improvements in children's externalizing and internalizing problems. Neither child age nor child sex was associated with treatment outcomes. Although these results appear promising, the study's design limitations preclude drawing clear conclusions about the effectiveness of the intervention. However, the multi-informant assessment strategy, use of a clinical sample, and provision of services through a community agency are commendable. Moreover, the development and deployment of interventions for culturally diverse samples is much needed, and this program presents one such model.

Children's Well-Being Groups

This intervention was based on one originally developed for children whose parents were engaging in custody disputes (Johnston & Roseby, 1997). Adapted for children exposed to violence, the group intervention was developed to increase children's awareness of and alter their internal representations of relationships and their cognitions related to and shaped by their traumatic experiences (Johnston, 2003). Based on aspects of psychodynamic, social-cognitive, and trauma theory, the intervention focused on altering the scripts theorized to underlie children's social relationships and interactions, enhancing children's sense of safety, helping them learn to experience and express their emotions more comfortably and appropriately, and increasing their capacity for empathy. An interesting aspect of this intervention is the authors' recognition that children may not identify IPV exposure as a primary source of their problems; thus the counselors were trained to let intervene from the vantage point of the child's conceptualization of distressing or traumatizing events. Parent groups were offered concurrently with children's groups, but the authors report less than desirable parent attendance. Although exposure to IPV was not a criterion for eligibility, approximately 70% of the sample reported that IPV had occurred during the child's lifetime. The intervention was offered to children ages 5 to 17, with different groups formed according to children's ages. Services were provided through community agencies and schools in ethnically diverse, high-risk neighborhoods, and assessment data were collected from multiple reporters. The intervention was provided as ten 90-min weekly sessions at community agencies, and fifteen 60-min sessions at schools. Baseline and 6-month follow-up data were collected from clinicians ($n = 199$), parents ($n = 106$), and teachers ($n = 123$) on the sample of 223 children (from 193 families). Clinicians and teachers completed the Teachers Rating Scale (Hightower et al., 1986), and parents completed the CBCL (Achenbach, 1991) measures of child adjustment. Results indicated pre-to posttreatment improvements in clinician reports of children's behavior problems and social competence. Results based on parent reports indicate that of the 50 (47%) children who scored in the clinical range of the CBCL Total Behavior Problem Scale at baseline, 27 scored in the clinical range at follow-up (raw scores were reported for the CBCL scores, so clinically meaningful means comparisons are not possible). Teacher ratings on the TRS indicated improvements in children's behavioral problems and social competence, as well, although these results differed across the sites in which the intervention was conducted, with teachers from three of the five participating schools reporting no improvements in either behavioral problems or social competence. These results suggest that it is possible to offer and evaluate a structured, community-based intervention, using a multi-informant measurement strategy and a reasonable follow-up period. However, definitive conclusions about the intervention's effectiveness cannot be made because of previously discussed design constraints.

LOOKING AHEAD

A few additional points warrant consideration in efforts to help children exposed to IPV. First, there are interventions in other areas that have been documented to improve outcomes for children in violent families; indeed, some of the interventions reviewed here were adapted from existing interventions and then tailored to meet the needs of children in families in which IPV had occurred. Parent–child interaction therapy (PCIT) is one example of an intervention developed in a different research area, and there is substantial evidence for its efficacy in alleviating adjustment problems in preschool-age children from varying populations (Hood & Eyberg, 2003). In addition, Eyberg (2005) pointed out issues that should be considered when adapting PCIT for different populations. This is not to suggest that PCIT should be employed with children exposed to IPV, but to illustrate that incorporating knowledge from other areas can facilitate the enhancement of existing interventions, and contribute to efficiencies and advancement in theory and knowledge about children exposed to IPV. In addition to incorporating work from other areas into the area of children exposed to IPV, the field would be well served by research that not only evaluates the efficacy of interventions with this populations but also explicitly tests and extends theory on children exposed to IPV.

Additionally, given the limited community resources available for interventions, it will be important to carefully evaluate "what" and "how much" is sufficient for helping children exposed to IPV and which children are most in need and most likely to benefit from particular aspects of the interventions. For example, some interventions include services designed to address a number of problems, such as trauma, internalizing problems, and externalizing problems; others focus more narrowly on one particular problem, or attempt to effect change in one problem (e.g., externalizing problems) by successfully addressing a co-occurring problem (e.g., trauma). Research to help parse which problems are helped best by which interventions, and by which aspects of the interventions, would considerably advance knowledge in this area.

Finally, by definition, there are at least two adults in children's lives in families in which IPV occurs. Efforts to address the children's problems have been devoted almost solely to providing services for the mothers and children. Yet many of the fathers and father figures (to this date, little is known about the effect of IPV in nonheterosexual populations) in these families continue to play an important role in their children's lives; indeed, many continue to live with their children or have regular contact with them. Despite considerable concern and debate about whether and how to approach this issue, there is growing acknowledgment that the children are not well served by ignoring it. Research on fathering by men who have engaged in IPV has the possibility to help us begin to address important questions, such as the influence on children of particular visitation or custody decisions, or particular aspects of the fathers' parenting, on child outcomes. This nascent area of research entails numerous practical and ethical considerations, but there are equally compelling reasons for pursuing it.

REFERENCES

Achenbach, T. M. (1991). *Manual for the Child Behavior Checklist/4-18 and 1991 Profile*. Burlington: University of Vermont, Department of Psychiatry.

Appel, A. E., & Holden, G. W. (1998). The co-occurrence of spouse and physical child abuse: A review and appraisal. *Journal of Family Psychology, 12*, 578–599. doi:10.1037/0893-3200.12.4.578

Bandura, A. (1986). *Social foundations of thought and action: A social cognitive theory*. Englewood Cliffs, NJ: Prentice-Hall.

Bandura, A. (2001). Social cognitive theory: An agentic perspective. *Annual Review of Psychology, 52,* 1–26. doi:10.1146/annurev.psych.52.1.1

Becker, K. D., Mathis, G., Mueller, C. W., Issari, K., & Atta, S. S. (2008). Community-based treatment outcomes for parents and children exposed to domestic violence. *Journal of Emotional Abuse, 8,* 187–204.

Crusto, C. A., Lowell, D. I., Paulicin, B. P., Reynolds, J. R., Feinn, R., Friedman, S., and Kaufman, J. (2008). Evaluation of a wraparound process for children exposed to family violence. *Best Practice in Mental Health, 4,* 1–18.

Cummings, E. M., & Davies, P. T. (1995). The impact of parents on their children: An emotional security perspective. *Annals of child development: A research annual* (Vol. 10, pp. 167–208). London, England: Jessica Kingsley.

Davies, P. T., & Cummings, E. M. (1994). Marital conflict and child adjustment: An emotional security hypothesis. *Psychological Bulletin, 116,* 387–411. doi:10.1037/0033-2909.116.3.387

Davies, P. T., & Cummings, E. M. (1998). Exploring children's emotional security as a mediator of the link between marital relations and child adjustment. *Child Development, 69,* 124–139.

Evans, S. E., Davies, C., & DiLillo, D. (2008). Exposure to domestic violence: A meta-analysis of child and adolescent outcomes. *Aggression and Violent Behavior, 13,* 131–140. doi:10.1016/j.avb.2008.02.005

Eyberg, S. K. (2005). Tailoring and adapting Parent-Child Interaction therapy to new populations. *Education & Treatment of Children, 28,* 197–201.

Fantuzzo, J., Boruch, R., Beriama, A., & Atkins, M. (1997). Domestic violence and children: Prevalence and risk in five major U.S. cities. *Journal of the American Academy of Child and Adolescent Psychiatry, 36,* 116–122. doi:10.1097/00004583-199701000-00025

Fosco, G. M., DeBoard, R. L., & Grych, J. H. (2007). Making sense of family violence: Implications of children's appraisals of interparental aggression for their short- and long-term functioning. *European Psychologist, 12*(1), 6–16. doi:10.1027/1016-9040.12.1.6

Fosco, G. M., & Grych, J. H. (2008). Emotional, cognitive, and family systems mediators of children's adjustment to interparental conflict. *Journal of Family Psychology, 22,* 843–854. doi:10.1037/a0013809

Gagné, M. H., Drapeau, S., Melançon, C., Saint-Jacques, M. C., & Lépine, R. (2007). Links between parental psychological violence, other family disturbances, and children's adjustment. *Family Process, 46,* 523–542. doi:10.1111/j.1545-5300.2007.00230.x

Graham-Bermann, S. A. (1992). *The Kids' Club: A preventive intervention program for children of battered women.* Ann Arbor: University of Michigan, Department of Psychology.

Graham-Bermann, S. A. (2000). Evaluating interventions for children exposed to family violence. *Journal of Aggression, Maltreatment & Trauma, 4,* 191–215. doi:10.1300/J146v04n01_09

Graham-Bermann, S. A., & Hughes, H. M. (2003). Intervention for children exposed to interparental violence (IPV): Assessment of needs and research priorities. *Clinical Child and Family Psychology Review, 6*, 189–204. doi:10.1023/A:1024962400234

Graham-Bermann, S. A., & Levendosky, A. A. (1998). Traumatic stress symptoms in children of battered women. *Journal of Interpersonal Violence, 13*, 111–128. doi:10.1177/088626098013001007

Graham-Bermann, S. A., Lynch, S., Banyard, V., DeVoe, E., & Halabu, H. (2007). Community-based intervention for children exposed to intimate partner violence: An efficacy trial. *Journal of Consulting and Clinical Psychology, 75*, 199–209. doi:10.1037/0022-006X.75.2.199

Groves, B. M. (1999). Mental health services for children who witness domestic violence. *The Future of Children, 9*, 122–132. doi:10.2307/1602786

Grych, J. H., & Fincham, F. D. (1990). Marital conflict and children's adjustment: A cognitive-contextual framework. *Psychological Bulletin, 108*, 267–290. doi:10.1037/0033-2909.108.2.267

Grych, J. H., Jouriles, E. N., Swank, P., McDonald, R., & Norwood, W. D. (2000). Patterns of adjustment among children of battered women. *Journal of Consulting and Clinical Psychology, 68*, 84–94. doi:10.1037/0022-006X.68.1.84

Guerra, N. G., Huesmann, L. R., & Spindler, A. (2003). Community violence exposure, social cognition, and aggression among urban elementary school children. *Child Development, 74*, 1561–1576. doi:10.1111/1467-8624.00623

Higgins, D. J., & McCabe, M. P. (2003). Maltreatment and family dysfunction in childhood and the subsequent adjustment of children and adults. *Journal of Family Violence, 18*, 107–120. doi:10.1023/A:1022841215113

Hightower, A. D., Work, W. C., Cowen, E. L., Lotyczewski, B. S., Spinell, A. P., Guare, J. C., & Rohrbeck, C. A. (1986). The Teacher–Child Rating Scale: A brief objective measure of elementary children's school problem behaviors and competencies. *School Psychology Review, 15*, 393–409.

Hood, K. K., & Eyberg, S. H. (2003). Outcomes of parent–child interaction therapy: Mothers' reports of maintenance three to six years after treatment. *Journal of Clinical Child & Adolescent Psychology, 32*, 419–429.

Huesmann, L. R. (1988). An information processing model for the development of aggression. *Aggressive Behavior, 14*(1), 13–24. doi:10.1002/1098-2337(1988)14:1<13::AID-AB2480140104>3.0.CO;2-J

Huth-Bocks, A. C., Levendosky, A. A., & Semel, M. A. (2001). The direct and indirect effects of domestic violence on young children's intellectual functioning. *Journal of Family Violence, 16*, 269–290. doi:10.1023/A:1011138332712

Huth-Bocks, A., Schettini, A., & Shebroe, V. (2001). Group play therapy for preschoolers exposed to domestic violence. *Journal of Child and Adolescent Group Therapy, 11*, 19–34. doi:10.1023/A:1016693726180

Johnston, J. R. (2003). Group interventions for children at-risk from family abuse and exposure to violence: A report of a study. *Journal of Emotional Abuse*, *3*, 203–226. doi:10.1300/J135v03n03_03

Johnston, J. R., & Roseby, V. (1997). *In the name of the child: A developmental approach to understanding and helping children of conflicted and violent divorce*. New York, NY: Free Press.

Jouriles, E. N., Brown, A., McDonald, R., Rosenfield, D., Leahy, M. M., & Silver, C. (2008). Intimate partner violence and preschoolers' explicit memory functioning. *Journal of Family Psychology*, *22*, 420–428. doi:10.1037/0893-3200.22.3.420

Jouriles, E. N., McDonald, R., Rosenfield, D., Stephens, N., Corbitt-Shindler, D., & Miller, P. C. (2009). Reducing conduct problems among children exposed to intimate partner violence: A randomized clinical trial examining effects of Project Support. *Journal of Consulting and Clinical Psychology*, *77*, 705–717. doi:10.1037/a0015994

Jouriles, E. N., McDonald, R., Smith Slep, A. M., Heyman, R. E., & Garrido, E. (2008). Child abuse in the context of domestic violence: Prevalence, explanations, and practice implications. *Violence and Victims*, *23*, 221–235. doi:10.1891/0886-6708.23.2.221

Jouriles, E. N., McDonald, R., Spiller, L., Norwood, W. D., Swank, P. R., Stephens, N., . . . Buzy, W. M. (2001). Reducing conduct problems among children of battered women. *Journal of Consulting and Clinical Psychology*, *69*, 774–785. doi:10.1037/0022-006X.69.5.774

Jouriles, E. N., McDonald, R., Stephens, N., Norwood, W. D., Spiller, L. C., & Ware, H. S. (1998). Breaking the cycle of violence: Helping families departing from battered women's shelters. In G. W. Holden, R. G. Geffner, & E. N. Jouriles (Eds.), *Children exposed to marital violence: Theory, research, and applied issues* (pp. 337–369). Washington, DC: American Psychological Association. doi:10.1037/10257-010

Kilpatrick, K. L., & Williams, L. M. (1998). Potential mediators of post-traumatic stress disorder in child witnesses to domestic violence. *Child Abuse & Neglect*, *22*, 319–330. doi:10.1016/S0145-2134(97)00178-6

Kinsfogel, K. M., & Grych, J. H. (2004). Interparental conflict and adolescent dating relationships: Integrating cognitive, emotional, and peer influences. *Journal of Family Psychology*, *18*, 505–515. doi:10.1037/0893-3200.18.3.505

Kitzmann, K. M., Gaylord, N. K., Holt, A. R., & Kenny, E. D. (2003). Child witnesses to domestic violence: A meta-analytic review. *Journal of Consulting and Clinical Psychology*, *71*, 339–352. doi:10.1037/0022-006X.71.2.339

Kot, S., & Tyndall-Lind, A. (2005). Intensive play therapy with child witnesses of domestic violence. In L. A. Reddy, T. M. Files-Hall, & C. E. Schaefer (Eds.), *Empirically based play interventions for children* (pp. 31–49). Washington, DC: American Psychological Association. doi:10.1037/11086-003

Levendosky, A. A., Huth-Bocks, A. C., Shapiro, D. L., & Semel, M. A. (2003). The impact of domestic violence on the maternal-child relationship and preschool-age children's functioning. *Journal of Family Psychology, 17,* 275–287. doi:10.1037/0893-3200.17.3.275

Lichter, E. L., & McCloskey, L. A. (2004). The effects of childhood exposure to marital violence on adolescent gender-role beliefs and dating violence. *Psychology of Women Quarterly, 28,* 344–357. doi:10.1111/j.1471-6402.2004.00151.x

Lieberman, A. F., Van Horn, P., & Ippen, C. G. (2005). Toward evidence-based treatment: Child—Parent Psychotherapy with preschoolers exposed to marital violence. *Journal of the American Academy of Child and Adolescent Psychiatry, 44,* 1241–1248. doi:10.1097/01.chi.0000181047.59702.58

Margolin, G., & Gordis, E. B. (2000). The effects of family and community violence on children. *Annual Review of Psychology, 51,* 445–479. doi:10.1146/annurev.psych.51.1.445

McDonald, R., & Grych, J. H. (2006). Young children's appraisals of interparental conflict: Measurement and links with adjustment problems. *Journal of Family Psychology, 20,* 88–99. doi:10.1037/0893-3200.20.1.88

McDonald, R., Jouriles, E. N., Ramisetty-Mikler, S., Caetano, R., & Green, C. E. (2006). Estimating the number of American children living in partner-violent families. *Journal of Family Psychology, 20,* 137–142. doi:10.1037/0893-3200.20.1.137

McDonald, R., Jouriles, E. N., & Skopp, N. A. (2006). Reducing conduct problems among children brought to women's shelters: Intervention effects 24 months following termination of services. *Journal of Family Psychology, 20,* 127–136. doi:10.1037/0893-3200.20.1.127

Minze, L. C., McDonald, R., Rosentraub, E. L., & Jouriles, E. N. (in press). Making sense of family conflict: Intimate partner violence and preschoolers' externalizing problems. *Journal of Family Psychology.*

O'Brien, M., Margolin, G., & John, R. S. (1995). Relation among marital conflict, child coping, and child adjustment. *Journal of Clinical Child Psychology, 24,* 346–361. doi:10.1207/s15374424jccp2403_12

Owen, A. E., Thompson, M. P., Shaffer, A., Jackson, E. B., & Kaslow, N. J. (2009). Family variables that mediate the relation between intimate partner violence (IPV) and child adjustment. *Journal of Family Violence, 24,* 433–445. doi:10.1007/s10896-009-9239-2

Patterson, G. R. (1982). *Coercive family process.* Eugene, OR: Castalia.

Peled, E., & Edleson, J. L. (1992). Multiple perspectives on groupwork with children of battered women. *Violence and Victims, 7,* 327–346.

Riggs, D., & O'Leary, K. (1989). A theoretical model of courtship aggression. In M. Pirog-Good & J. E. Stets (Eds.), *Violence in dating relationships: Emerging social issues* (pp. 53–71). New York, NY: Praeger.

Terr, L. C. (1991). Childhood traumas: An outline and overview. *American Journal of Psychiatry, 148,* 10–20.

Tyndall-Lind, A., Landreth, G. L., & Giordano, M. A. (2001). Intensive group play therapy with child witnesses of domestic violence. *International Journal of Play Therapy, 10,* 53–83. doi:10.1037/h0089443

Wilson, S. K., Cameron, S., Jaffe, P., & Wolfe, D. (1989). Children exposed to wife abuse: An intervention model. *Social Casework, 70,* 180–184.

Ybarra, G. J., Wilkens, S. L., & Lieberman, A. F. (2007). The Influence of domestic violence on preschooler behavior and functioning. *Journal of Family Violence, 22,* 33–42. doi:10.1007/s10896-006-9054-y

7

A CLINICAL CASE STUDY OF CHRIS: A YOUNG CHILD EXPOSED TO INTIMATE PARTNER VIOLENCE

TOVA B. NEUGUT AND LAURA E. MILLER

The following clinical case study describes a preschool-age child and a mother who participated in the Preschool Kids' Club (Graham-Bermann & Follett, 2000) and Moms' Parenting Empowerment Program (Graham-Bermann & Levendosky, 1994). This case study is based on an amalgamation of real clinical cases and research interviews. The two authors were among the clinical and research staff involved in assessment and treatment. All names and significant identifying information have been altered to protect individuals' confidentiality.

Sharon, a 39-year-old African American mother, called the Preschool Kids' Club and Moms' Parenting Empowerment Program offices after noticing a flyer at a local supermarket. She said that when she saw the flyer, announcing the availability of services for young children who have been exposed to violence in their homes, it immediately struck her as something that could bene-fit her family. Sharon said that she had long ago resigned herself to the violence that she experienced within her marriage, but she was just beginning to recognize that her children were suffering as a result of their exposure to violence between their parents. In particular, Sharon observed that her 5-year-old son, Chris, was becoming unusually withdrawn for a child of his age, and she felt sure that this was largely due to his fear of his father, Kevin. Sharon worried a lot about Chris reenacting his father's violent acts, which she had seen him do: Chris was occasionally extremely violent with his younger sister and imitated exact behaviors that he had seen his father direct toward his mother. Additionally, Chris had picked up on his father's patterns of verbal abuse and attempted to order his mother around in a similar fashion. Sharon knew she wanted to help Chris but did not know how.

PROGRAM FRAMEWORK

The Preschool Kids' Club and Moms' Parenting Empowerment Program is based on intimate partner violence (IPV) and developmental research. Studies that show childhood exposure to IPV can lead to serious developmental difficulties, including emotional and behavioral problems, posttraumatic stress disorder (PTSD), and academic difficulties (Bogat, DeJonghe, Levendosky, Davidson, & von Eye, 2006; Carlson, 2000; Fantuzzo, Brouch, Beriama, & Atkins, 1997; Skopp, McDonald, Jouriles, & Rosenfield, 2007; Turner, Finkelhor, & Ormrod, 2006). Children may become dysregulated when they repeatedly experience high levels of stress and subsequently may have difficulty managing and expressing their feelings (Graham-Bermann, Kulkarni, & Kanukollu, in press). Emotional and behavioral disturbances in early childhood, if severe and sustained, may be associated with the emergence of clinical disorders that can become entrenched if not effectively addressed, making intervention for children who have witnessed IPV important for fostering their long-term mental health (Sameroff & Emde, 1989; Scheeringa & Gaensbauer, 2000; Scheeringa, Zeanah, Myers, & Putnam, 2005).

Research has also shown that child exposure to IPV is most effectively addressed through an intervention that includes both children who have been exposed to IPV and their mothers in treatment (Graham-Bermann, Lynch, Banyard, DeVoe, & Halabu, 2007), incorporating a focus on strengthening the parent–child relationship with efforts to restore the child to a positive developmental trajectory. Because parents are both behavioral models and emotional anchors for their children, their coping is essential to their children's well-being, and in families recovering from IPV, addressing the mother's parenting needs is one vital avenue for addressing the needs of the child (Graham-Bermann et al., 2007; Levendosky & Graham-Bermann, 2001).

In addition to the above research findings, several theories form the basis of the Preschool Kids' Club and Moms' Parenting Empowerment Program: social learning theory (Patterson, 1982), in which parents are thought to model and reinforce central elements of social relationships; emotional security and cognitive theories (Davies & Cummings, 1994; Grych & Fincham, 1993), which describe how children try to make sense of the violence they have seen; and trauma theory (Graham-Bermann & Levendosky, 1998), which has been used to explain symptoms of distress that often accompany children's difficulties in modulating emotions and processing traumatic events.

INITIAL ASSESSMENT

When mothers contact the Preschool Kids' Club and Moms' Parenting Empowerment Program to indicate their interest in the intervention, they participate in an intake interview to ensure that they and their child meet criteria for participation. The child should be between age 4 and 6, the mother must have experienced severe violence in the past 2 years, and the child must have been exposed to this violence. If these criteria are met, an initial evaluation is immediately scheduled to assess the types of violence that the mother has experienced, the nature of her parenting practices, her experience of depression and/or trauma symptoms, and her ways of coping. The child is assessed for symptoms of PTSD and other emotional and behavioral problems. Each mother may choose whether the evaluation will be conducted at the site of the intervention program or at her home if she is no longer living with a violent partner. In Sharon's case, mother and child were assessed individually by two highly trained interviewers with the mother's evaluation lasting about 80 min and the child's evaluation lasting about 30 min.

IDENTIFYING INFORMATION AND PRESENTING PROBLEMS

Chris was a 5-year-old African American boy who was very energetic. At the start of the evaluation session, he was bashful and crouched on the floor, looking coyly up at the therapist. He seemed genuinely excited to meet everyone. He was a very attractive child, of average height, although perhaps a bit slight for his age. He was well-dressed but had not received a haircut in a while. After his mother introduced him, Chris began talking about his brand new tennis shoes and how much he loved them. He then pulled out several pairs of tennis shoes and showed each one in turn to the therapist, pointing out their different colors and designs.

According to Sharon, Chris had a history of problems at school. His teacher had mentioned that Chris was frequently inattentive and had suggested that he might qualify for a diagnosis of attention-deficit/hyperactivity disorder. Sharon, however, did not see any symptoms of unusual hyperactivity or inattentiveness at home and believed that Chris's inattention at school was primarily due to distraction by their problems at home.

It was apparent to the therapist that Chris's energy was in part due to some anxiety. Throughout the first interview, he frequently squatted down on the floor and threw his arms across it, dragging his fingernails through the carpet as he righted himself. His responses during the intake interview were erratic; sometimes Chris did not answer at all, and other times he shouted a harried "Yes" or "No!" Chris also demonstrated a habit of trying to "scare" adults. At the intake session and throughout treatment, Chris leaped out from behind doors and tables waving his arms in the air, not relenting until he had gotten a reaction of "fear" from the adults he was working with that day.

Six months prior to his evaluation, Chris witnessed a violent episode between his mother and father. As described by Sharon, much of the abuse she had experienced was sexual in nature and had taken place behind closed doors, but Chris still witnessed several violent episodes that were precursors to consequent sexual violence. In the episode identified by Sharon as particularly distressing to Chris, after Sharon refused Kevin's sexual advances, he slammed her up against a wall. Chris entered the room when his mother was pinned against the wall and saw his father punch his mother repeatedly in the face. At the time of the event, Sharon reported that Chris was crying and shaking and refused to leave her side. Fortunately, Kevin soon after was offered a professional promotion that required him to move out of state. He accepted the promotion and, by the time of the intake interview, had not been present in the home for several months.

This was the last physically violent event that Chris witnessed. Though Kevin had left the home several months prior to intake, he had subsequently made frequent visits and phone calls to the home. Kevin was verbally abusive when he spoke with Sharon on the phone. When he visited home, he and Sharon got in many fights, which typically culminated with Kevin being verbally abusive toward Sharon, Chris, and Chris's sister. According to his mother, Chris avoided his father as much as possible. When his father called and asked to speak to him, Chris said that he was busy playing, and when his father visited the home, Chris shut himself in his bedroom.

Despite Chris's attempts to avoid his father, he still had some interaction with him. Kevin spent time playing with Chris, but the play was rough in nature, and Chris expressed frequently that he got hurt when his father played with him. When Chris screamed for his mother's help, his father began to taunt him, telling him that "boys need to learn to toughen up." Sharon believed that Kevin had always been too hard on Chris. She said that Kevin would taunt Chris until he cried and then would say, "What are you gonna do, crybaby? Go run to your mommy?" She described her role with her husband and son as "referee" and said she could not understand how a grown man could be so competitive and cruel in his interactions with a 5-year-old. Sharon said that Kevin's relationship with Chris was markedly different than his relationship with

Chris's younger sister, Brianna. Kevin spoiled Brianna and treated her relatively kindly—a sharp contrast to his interactions with Chris. Sharon was worried about this dynamic because she was afraid that it would reinforce negative behaviors in both of her children.

OBJECTIVE TEST RESULTS AT BASELINE

Child's Mental Health, Coping, and Diagnosis

Appropriate measures were selected in order to assess whether Chris had problems in adjustment and his level of traumatic stress. Sharon's responses on empirically validated measures designed to screen for presence of PTSD and other emotional and behavioral problems (Achenbach, 1991; Scheeringa & Zeanah, 1994) in children establish that, at the time of the initial evaluation, Chris qualified for a PTSD diagnosis. Sharon reported that Chris routinely displayed several symptoms in each of the three diagnostic categories: reexperiencing, avoidance, and hyperarousal (see Figure 7.1). Sharon reported that Chris made repeated statements about the traumatic event and spaced out in a daze when they begin to talk about his father. He had become socially withdrawn at school since the event and did not play with other children his age. When he got frustrated, he became depressed and told his mother, "I'm a failure!" He also showed many symptoms of hyperarousal, including an intensification of crying and screaming since witnessing the violent episode between his parents, and jumping whenever the front door opened or closed. Chris also developed a greater attachment to his mother and yelled for her to stop at red

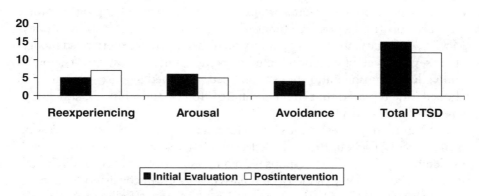

Figure 7.1. Chris's posttraumatic stress disorder (PTSD) symptoms pre- and postintervention (Posttraumatic Stress Disorder Semi-Structured Interview and Observational Record for Infants and Young Children).

TABLE 7.1
Chris's Behavioral Adjustment Problems Scores
Pre- and Postintervention (Child Behavior Checklist)

Adjustment problem	Preintervention	Postintervention
Withdrawal	0	3
Somatic complaints	0	0
Anxiety/depression	20	8
Social problems	10	4
Thought problems	5	6
Attention problems	5	2
Delinquency	1	1
Aggression	18	6
Total internalizing problems	20	11
Total externalizing problems	19	9

lights, telling her, "Stop! Don't get hurt because I need you!" Chris's aggression toward his peers had also grown continually worse since witnessing the traumatic event 6 months prior.

During his concurrent evaluation session, Chris indicated clinical levels of anxiety, depression, and thought problems. He was assessed as borderline clinical range for aggressive behavior, but for behavior problems in general, Chris also exceeded clinical cutoffs typical for his age group. Chris did not show any significant attention problems (see Table 7.1).

Mother's Experience of Violence, Mental Health, and Coping

Sharon completed a series of measures chosen to assess the types of violence she had experienced, the nature of her parenting practices, her experience of depression and trauma symptoms, and her ways of coping. Sharon's responses on the Revised Conflict Tactics Scale (Straus, Hamby, Boney-McCoy, & Sugarman, 1996) demonstrated that she had experienced moderate to severe levels of violence, including being insulted and sworn at, shouted and yelled at, pushed and shoved, grabbed, slammed against the wall, and choked. She reported that she had suffered from sprains, bruises, and cuts as a result of fights with Kevin.

Sharon's responses on the Center for Epidemiological Studies Depression Scale (CES-D; Radloff, 1977) yielded a cumulative score of 23, consistent with moderate depression. Her responses on a measure of PTSD (Foa, Cashman, Jaycox, & Perry, 1997) yielded a cumulative score of 24, consistent with moderate to severe PTSD. On the Ways of Coping Measure (Folkman & Lazarus, 1988), Sharon indicated that she most often used emotion-focused coping strategies. She had particular strengths in the areas of positive reappraisal, planful problem-solving, and self-control. Sharon struggled most with accepting responsibility and seeking social support.

Relationship Between Mother and Child

To assess the extent to which there were problems in the realm of parenting, Sharon also was asked to complete the Alabama Parenting Questionnaire (Frick, 1991), and she received high scores for positive interactions with Chris. She endorsed such affirmative statements as, "I often have a friendly talk with my child"; "I always ask about his day at school"; "I always help with homework"; and "I often play games with my child, or engage in other fun, shared activities." Clinical observations also supported a strong rapport between Chris and Sharon. At the time of the assessment, the therapist observed that Chris continuously sought attention and approval from his mother, and Sharon responded with affection, although she became impatient when he interrupted multiple times as she was being interviewed.

Mother's Family History

To better understand this mother and her background, and to go beyond the information provided by standardized measures, an intake interview was undertaken to explore Sharon's family history. At the time of intake, Sharon was 39 years old. She and her husband Kevin, both African American, were parents to two children: 5-year-old Chris and 2-year-old Brianna. Sharon was a full-time homemaker and Kevin worked as an engineer; as noted previously, he had been living and working out of state for the past several months. Sharon and the children remained in the home where the family has lived since the children were born, with Kevin returning periodically to visit. In the interim, he sent Sharon small and unpredictable sums of money to cover household expenses. Sharon was continuously anxious about when the next check would arrive, and if it would be sufficient to cover the bills that were piling up.

Sharon was raised in a small Midwestern town. She grew up in a home that included both parents and two older sisters. She described her parents as distant and disengaged. Specifically, she described her father as "a workaholic" and her mother as "always unavailable." Sharon recalled that her parents drank heavily and fought often. Her childhood was characterized by feelings of anxiety and instability; she never knew if it would be a "good" day or a "bad" day. When her parents fought, Sharon and her sisters would cluster together in their room to wait out the storm. She said, "We all knew better than to go downstairs when they were fighting; anything could happen." From the relative safety of their bedroom, they heard the sounds of violence: shouted threats, breaking glass, and occasionally cries of pain.

Beginning at age 11, Sharon encountered a new source of terror. She was sexually abused by an uncle for the first time, in her own room, while her parents were out of the house. The abuse continued sporadically over a period of years, with Sharon never feeling safe enough to report what was happening to her parents. Their volatile temperaments did not allow her to trust that she could rely on them to believe her and protect her, and her uncle threatened her with various punishments if she were to tell. Most terrifying to Sharon, her uncle threatened that he would harm her sisters if she reported the abuse. Years later, Sharon told her parents, and it turned out that they had known her uncle was a sex offender but had not limited his access to their home. They appeared neither surprised nor upset by Sharon's story, which caused her to be extremely angry with her parents.

As an adult, Sharon had chosen to limit contact with her parents. She had also become gradually estranged from her sisters. As she described it, she wanted "to get as far away as possible from where I grew up." Sharon moved to a Midwestern city and attended college, successfully completing a bachelor of arts degree. After college, she described herself as being a successful professional until choosing to marry and devote herself full-time to raising a family. She envisioned eventually returning to work when her children are older and when both attend school for a full day.

History of Intimate Partner Violence

Sharon's initial impression of her husband was that he was "charismatic" and "confident"; only much later did she begin to see the same behaviors that had originally impressed her as "dominant" and "controlling." Sharon and Kevin married after a whirlwind courtship, and she found out that she was pregnant with her first child within a few months of their marriage. Initially charming, over time Kevin became increasingly verbally and emotionally abusive, and eventually he became physically and sexually abusive as well. Sharon first considered leaving Kevin while she was pregnant with Chris. During her pregnancy, Kevin taunted her for being "fat" and undesirable, and he criticized her for laziness at times when she would say she needed to sit down to rest her back or to relieve her swollen ankles. However, she wanted her baby to have a father and she said that this motivated her to continue hoping and striving to appease her husband and strengthen their marriage.

After Chris was born, the abuse continued. Sharon regularly dreamed of leaving her husband, but she could not begin to imagine how it would be possible. She had no access to financial resources and no relatives or friends to whom she could turn for assistance. Not only was she estranged from her family, but she had also lost contact with her college friends after her marriage. At the start of their relationship, she found it flattering that Kevin told her he did not want her to spend time with male friends, saying that she had no idea how appealing she was. Gradually, he stopped disguising his hostility toward her friends in flattery. He became critical of all her friends, including her female friends, whom he described as "sluts." He suspected every man who came near of being her lover. Once, after a day at the beach with Chris, a friend, and her friend's child, Sharon brought home a picture of the foursome at the beach. There was a group of lifeguards in the distant background of the photo, and Kevin demanded to know which one she was sleeping with. When she maintained that she was not sleeping with any of the lifeguards, did not even know any of the lifeguards, Kevin grabbed her by the throat and said that he would continue to choke her until she confessed. Eventually, gasping for air, she "confessed" to sleeping with a man she had never met. Kevin then insisted that Sharon make up for her "infidelity" by having sex with him. Still recovering from being choked, Sharon had no desire for sex but feared the consequences of resisting. Sharon said that was the moment she first felt sure that her husband would eventually kill her.

Kevin told Sharon repeatedly that he would kill her if she left him, and she believed him. She gave up thinking of leaving with the children because she did not think there was anywhere they could go where he would not find them and follow through on his threat. She described it as her "salvation" that her husband was reassigned to a job out of state and did not want to take his family with him.

Present Family Circumstances

At the point of the evaluation, Sharon's living situation was precarious, with Kevin contributing to household expenses only sporadically and being vague about his intention to return (or not). He called home daily at unpredictable times, and if she was not home when he called, he was accusatory when he eventually got her on the phone. Kevin accused Sharon of sleeping with other men and neglecting "his" children, and he threatened to withhold money, saying he was not going to support her so she could run around sleeping with other men.

TREATMENT RECOMMENDATIONS

Based on the initial evaluation, including the results of the standardized assessments and clinical interview with Sharon and Chris, the clinical team decided to recommend the Preschool Kids' Club and Moms' Parenting Empowerment Program as a course of treatment for mother and son. This treatment plan was recommended for several reasons. First, because Sharon and

Chris were both suffering and their relationship was harmed due to the violence in their lives, it seemed most appropriate to recommend joint treatment rather than treatment for mother or child separately. Second, because Sharon's husband had been consistently critical of her girlfriends and suspicious of her male friends, Sharon had become increasingly socially isolated. Her strained relationship with her parents was an additional limitation on social support available for the family. This lack of social support was concerning, as research indicates that greater levels of social support is related to better well-being for women (Beeble, Bybee, Sullivan, & Adams, 2009). Thus, the clinicians believed that group therapy would be of particular significance to Sharon and Chris, who might benefit from greater levels of social support in addition to the concrete strategies on coping and parenting that the program offers.

The Preschool Kids' Club and Moms' Parenting Empowerment Program is an intervention that includes mothers who have experienced IPV and their young children in treatment (Graham-Bermann, 1992; Graham-Bermann, Lynch, Banyard, DeVoe, & Halabu, 2007). The 10-session, manualized intervention targets children's emotional adjustment by addressing attitudes and beliefs about families and violence, helping children to identify and process feelings associated with their experiences of violence, and enhancing children's coping behaviors. Chris was deemed in need of support in identifying and expressing his feelings and thoughts in relation to the violence that he had witnessed. Groups include boys and girls ages 4 to 6. The program provides an environment for children to discover that they are not alone in their exposure to violence, to share their experiences, and to learn new strategies for coping with violence exposure. Activities designed to identify family strengths are incorporated, and only after relationships among group participants and leaders are well established do children's group leaders allow for discussion of violence in the family.

Concurrent with each children's group, mothers meet in a separate group to share their experiences, concerns, and support related to parenting. Graham-Bermann and Levendosky (1994) described the Moms' Parenting Empowerment program as a 10-session intervention based on goals of enhancing mothers' social and emotional adjustment and improving mothers' repertoire of parenting and disciplinary skills, and thereby reducing the behavioral and adjustment difficulties of their children.

THE COURSE OF TREATMENT: SEEING CHANGE OVER TIME

Chris's Participation in the Preschool Kids' Club

Sessions 1 and 2 of the Preschool Kids' Club Program were designed to orient children to the group. To familiarize children with the building, group leaders, and each other, a tour of the facilities was given and a number of ice-breakers and games were played. The children were informed that they were all there because there had been fighting in their family, but the first two sessions focused primarily on building a positive and safe group through the children's participation in choosing a group name (e.g., The Cool Hawks Club) and making a list of rules pertaining to in-session behavior. The children were encouraged to come up with whatever rules they wanted, but group leaders ensured that privacy and a pass rule (i.e., being able to opt out of participation) were included. Chris was quiet when he first arrived at the group, but he quickly warmed up to the other children and expressed his desire to make friends. During the first session he made three rules, all pertaining to violence: "no hitting, no smacking, and no punching." For the first sessions, Chris was friendly but reserved. He enjoyed the opportunity to talk with the other children and did not balk from talking about family problems, frequently making comments about his father without any prompting. He clung to the group leaders throughout each session and briefly engaged the other children one at a time.

Session 3 was designed to help children accurately identify the emotions they were having and to learn that many kids feel the same way that they do. Chris was particularly interested in learning about emotions, and he participated in this session with great relish. Although he was excited about talking about emotions, when the group leaders asked everyone to name emotions, Chris was only able to name negative emotions, naming "sad," "angry," and "upset." One of the early activities for these sessions involved learning emotions through displacement. The group leaders and other children decided to draw pictures of farm animals that were feeling different things. Chris said that he was interested in drawing a sad chicken, and he asked the group leader to draw it for him while he colored. While the leader and Chris were working together, Chris abruptly said, "My dad is mean to me." The leader responded that sometimes kids feel sad when parents are mean to them and asked if that was how Chris was feeling. He said yes, that was how he felt. Chris requested to draw an angry monster, but halfway through this he became very anxious and walked away from the project.

Session 4 focused on identifying emotions that children have when there is fighting in the family. Though this session was done completely in displacement (e.g., role plays with a family of dogs who fight), children nonetheless frequently commented on the violence in their own lives. During this session, Chris got up and showed the group leaders and children how his dad punched his mom and commented, "I get scared when my mom and dad punch each other." Leaders affirmed that this was indeed a scary event and that many kids are scared when parents fight. Chris continued to say, "I was sad when my dad hit my mom and I had to call the police and my dad got arrested." Leaders again affirmed this feeling and other children also talked about how they were scared and sad after their parents had a fight. After this discussion, the group moved back toward a more displaced activity to help the children prepare to leave. Each of the children had the opportunity to make a puppet. Chris drew a puppet that had a sad face, and then acted out his puppet crying. Chris ran around the room for several minutes with his crying puppet and when group leaders tried to settle him down and help make his puppet happy, Chris told them, "Nothing will make me happy."

Session 5 was designed to both review previous sessions on emotion and teach children appropriate ways of handling these emotions. In this session, Chris was able to list a variety of emotions, and unlike before, he was able to name positive as well as negative emotions. Group leaders led Chris and the other children through various role-plays and discussed appropriate ways to handle anger (e.g., counting to 10 to cool down, talking to someone instead of hitting). Additionally, one of the intersession themes for the Preschool Kids' Club was introduced: "It's never the kids' fault when the parents fight." Chris was attentive and interested as this was introduced; it was clearly a new idea to him. He had a very hard time repeating the phrase after the leaders, even after all of the other children had memorized it. Chris was also clearly agitated by this topic, and screamed, "I don't like fighting!" and ran to the wall and began pounding his fists against it. The group leaders redirected Chris to a coloring activity, which seemed to help him settle down, and Chris worked on coloring a poster that said "It's never the kids' fault when the parents fight." After the session, the leader asked if Chris would like to show his mother the poster. He nodded, and the leader and Chris brought Sharon into the room. Sharon read the poster aloud and was very positive and affirmed that it was never Chris's fault when she and his father fought. Though Chris did not directly reply to his mother, he seemed pleased with her response and stared at his poster proudly.

Chris and Sharon consistently reviewed the content of their group discussions at home throughout the treatment. At the following session (Session 6), Chris was able to clearly say, "It's never the kids' fault when the parents fight," undoubtedly due to his mother's support and review of the topic between sessions. His anxiety around the topic had clearly decreased, and he began shouting the phrase loudly with a smile on his face. The other kids joined in, and they took turns running up to a podium at the front of the room and yelling, "It's never the kids' fault when the parents fight!" During this session, children also discussed their fears and worries, including fighting in the family, and group leaders helped them to come up with coping strategies through activities about what kids like.

Session 7 was arguably one of the most important sessions for the children. The session focused on safety planning. Group leaders discussed situations where kids might need to call for help, including fires, crimes, and fighting in the family. Group leaders taught the children what constituted an emergency (e.g., a dog getting out vs. a serious injury) and then helped the children practice dialing 911 on a toy phone. Chris did not have a clear idea of what constituted an emergency at first, and he would call 911 to tell them that he had lost a book. Once the group leaders gave an example of a fire, Chris practiced repeatedly, though he had a difficult time remembering how to answer all of the questions.

To close the program on a positive note, Sessions 8 and 9 focused on practicing the skills previously learned and discussing what is good about families. Chris continued to appear comfortable in the group, and he became much more animated with both the group leaders and the other children. He was clearly proud of being able to recite "It's never the kids' fault when the parents fight" and requested to practice calling 911 frequently. However, he still showed more withdrawal than was typical for his age, engaging the group leaders mostly and the other children only occasionally. When the group leaders began to talk about the program ending, Chris did not demonstrate any reaction.

In the final session (Session 10), the children received an individualized booklet including all of the information covered in order to commemorate their participation in the program. The children then invited the mothers to come to their closing ceremonies, where group leaders spoke to each child's strengths and presented him or her with a diploma. Children had the opportunity to show their mothers their projects from previous sessions, and then they all shared a meal together in celebration. Though Chris clearly enjoyed this final session, he did not seem to feel sentimental about leaving Preschool Kids' Club, as many other children did. Rather, he left after a perfunctory goodbye to the group leaders.

At the Close of Treatment: Final Impressions of Chris

After completing the intervention, a follow-up interview was conducted with Chris and Sharon to assess his symptom levels on the same empirically validated scales used during the intake. Though Chris was still showing symptoms of reexperiencing (spacing out when reminded of the violence, repeated statements about the violence) and hyperarousal (being jumpy, having temper tantrums), according to his mother Chris no longer exhibited avoidance symptoms and thus no longer qualified for a PTSD diagnosis. His mother also reported that although he still had some problems, they were interfering with his life much less than they used to. Additionally, Chris showed a marked drop in anxiety and depression symptoms, dropping to below clinical cutoff marks. His aggression and behavior problems showed a slight decrease, but he still had similar levels of thought problems.

Sharon's Participation in the Moms' Parenting Empowerment Program

The first session of the Moms' Parenting Empowerment program aimed to establish the purpose of the group as a support group with a focus on parenting and to have the women introduce themselves, tell their stories, and describe their children. At the first meeting of the Moms' Parenting Empowerment Group, the group leaders observed that Sharon seemed to try to separate herself from the group. She took on the role of helper and advice giver, but she did not share any of her own experiences. She gave the impression of needing to be in control, speaking in a hasty and directive manner.

Most notably, Sharon did not acknowledge any commonalities between her experiences and those of other group members. Though all the mothers present had experienced abuse in intimate partner relationships, and all expressed concern about the impact of exposure to violence on their 3- to 5-year-old children, Sharon maintained, "I think my situation is pretty different than everyone else here. I mean, I'm educated and I understand all this."

Over the course of participating in twice-weekly group meetings for a period of 5 weeks, Sharon gradually demonstrated a reduced sense of separation from the group. Listening to the other mothers share their experiences and concerns related to parenting, Sharon began to make connections between her son's behaviors and the behaviors he had been exposed to at home. At the third group meeting she stated,

> I'm starting to see that some of the behaviors I worry about in Chris are a lot like the behaviors he's seen from his father. . . . He uses bad language that he's heard from his father, and he talks down to me like he's heard his father do. . . . He's controlling toward his sister like his father is to me.

In the second session, which focused on parents' fears, worries, feelings, and stresses, Sharon began to share her personal story with the group. She continued to do so in subsequent sessions centered on mothers' experiences in their family of origin, communicating with children and helping them to regulate emotion, child development, empathy, discipline, stress management, and having fun with one's children. As Sharon received support from the group, she was able to be supportive of others in a less directive way, which allowed others to feel genuinely supported and established a sense of community and reciprocity within the group.

Sharon spoke in the group of feeling proud of her ability to be supportive of others as well as strengthened by the support that she herself received. She stated that she looked forward to group meetings as an opportunity to exchange support with mothers who could understand her specific worries about protecting her son from his father and helping him to grow up to be a better man. Sharon was an active and avid participant in sessions designed to enhance each mother's repertoire of parenting and disciplinary skills. Her initial focus on reducing Chris's behavior problems and supporting his growth and healing gave rise to a dawning interest in identifying her own needs and promoting her growth and healing. Sharon gradually realized that "anything I can do to build myself up will help Chris and Brianna."

By Session 10, Sharon had come a long way from her initial attempts to draw boundaries between herself and the other mothers. She said, "It's amazing. I listen to the other women tell their stories and you could be telling my story." Group leaders observed her listening empathically to other group members and forging strong connections; in fact, Sharon had extended friendships with group members to outside of the group, scheduling mother–child playground play-dates.

As Sharon shared more of her personal experiences and feelings with the group, she came to recognize patterns in the behaviors and relationships she had witnessed, experienced, and engaged in across her life span. For example, she spoke to the group about the abuse she experienced as a child and noted a parallel between her quiet resignation at that time and her later quiet resignation as Kevin became increasingly abusive. She observed, "Standing up for myself is something I've been needing to do for a very long time." However, Sharon expressed lingering uncertainty about if, when, and how she would do so. Other group members responded by reminding her of the steps she had already taken over the previous 5 weeks. Sharon had begun to focus on providing her children with greater consistency, had become more of an advocate for her son at school, and had become more confident with setting and holding limits at home. Sharon had begun thinking about starting to work outside the home again and had begun a search to find suitable, long-term housing. She had also scheduled a first appointment to consult with a lawyer about divorce. At the last group meeting, Sharon told the group that she was still unsure about proceeding with divorce, but she was leaning in the direction of moving forward, and she planned to consult with local advocates about safety planning in case her husband reacted with violence if and when she filed for divorce.

At the Close of Treatment: Final Impressions of Sharon

Sharon demonstrated significant improvements in multiple domains by the end of the 10-session intervention. She reported a reduction in feelings of isolation, increased hopefulness for her future, and increased belief that through her actions she could achieve her desired future for herself and her children. She believed that through her participation in the Moms' Parenting Empowerment Group she had improved her parenting skills, and she stated with conviction that her participation in the moms' group along with Chris's participation in Preschool Kids' Club had been helpful for Chris and for their relationship.

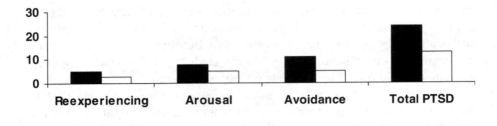

Figure 7.2. Sharon's posttraumatic stress disorder (PTSD) symptoms pre- and postintervention (Posttraumatic Diagnostic Scale).

Postintervention screening demonstrated that Sharon experienced a significant decrease in both depression and trauma symptoms from preintervention to postintervention. Her score on the CES-D changed from 23 (moderate depression) preintervention to 15 (mild depression) postintervention, and her score for overall PTSD symptoms changed from 24 (moderate to severe PTSD) preintervention to 13 (mild to moderate PTSD) postintervention (see Figure 7.2).

CLINICAL IMPLICATIONS

The Preschool Kids' Club and Moms' Parenting Empowerment Program offered several advantages for families who experienced IPV. First, the group structure offered social support and facilitated the recognition among mothers and children that they were not alone in their experience of violence. Receiving services within a community context allowed families to see that others share their history and have face similar challenges, encouraging those who might otherwise be disinclined to seek help to come forward. Sharon's participation in the Moms' Parenting Empowerment Program demonstrated that initial reserve could dissolve to reveal a great capacity for reaching out and connecting with others. Further, empathizing with others could be a gateway for recognizing painful elements of one's own experience.

In addition to creating social support networks among families that experienced IPV, the Preschool Kids' Club and Moms' Parenting Empowerment Program were uniquely structured to enhance support and communication within the family. Prior to treatment many mothers believed that their children did not really comprehend the valence or import of the IPV in their homes. They may have seen that their children were struggling with behavioral and emotional problems but not associated these problems with the presence of IPV in the home. Through participation in the intervention, mothers became aware of the ways in which exposure to IPV could affect a child's developmental trajectory. As mothers and children learned a developmentally appropriate language for discussing the traumatic violence that they had experienced or witnessed, they were able to communicate more effectively about the underlying emotions that may have given rise to adjustment problems. Consistent with research showing a moderating effect of parenting stress on children's adjustment following exposure to IPV (Levendosky & Graham-Bermann, 1998), Sharon's stress in parenting Chris was reduced by what she learned and by the parenting support provided by the program. Sharon's and Chris's participation in the Preschool Kids' Club and Moms' Parenting Empowerment Program demonstrated that teaching preschoolers and their parents how to recognize and understand their emotional responses to situations could help alleviate some adjustment difficulties by opening up lines of communication about sensitive situations.

Sharon and Chris both expressed appreciation for the skills learned and support gained from their participation in the Preschool Kids' Club and Moms' Parenting Empowerment groups, and they chose to participate in a second cycle of the intervention program. Their experience illustrated the individual benefits for both mother and preschool-age child, as well as the cumulative benefits to the family, of joint participation in intervention.

Though the intervention program was of great benefit to Sharon and Chris, there were some important next steps to consider. Completing the program did not result in the elimination of all symptoms, and it was therefore important to realize that Sharon and Chris would likely need continuing support. Sharon and Chris chose to participate in the program a second time, but other families may not have the time or means to do so. Recognizing that early exposure to violence had both short-term and long-term effects on development, the clinicians were equipped to recommend additional resources to families for support beyond the 5 weeks of treatment. Participants are typically given a take-home packet of ideas and information that have been developed throughout the 10 sessions at the end of the intervention program, while having a booklet of information throughout the program might be more useful. Future research studies could ascertain what resources mothers find most useful and what program aspects might be applicable for at-home work.

REFERENCES

Achenbach, T. M. (1991). *Integrative guide to the 1991 CBCL/4-18, YSR, and TRF Profiles*. Burlington: University of Vermont, Department of Psychology.

Beeble, M. L., Bybee, D., Sullivan, C. M., & Adams, A. E. (2009). Main, mediating, and moderating effects of social support on the well-being of survivors of intimate partner violence across 2 years. *Journal of Consulting and Clinical Psychology, 77*, 718–729. doi:10.1037/a0016140

Bogat, G. A., DeJonghe, E., Levendosky, A. A., Davidson, W. S., & von Eye, A. (2006). Trauma symptoms among infants exposed to intimate partner violence. *Child Abuse & Neglect, 30*, 109–125. doi:10.1016/j.chiabu.2005.09.002

Carlson, B. E. (2000). Children exposed to intimate partner violence: Research findings and implications for intervention. *Trauma, Violence, and Abuse, 1*, 321–340.

Davies, P. T., & Cummings, E. M. (1994). Marital conflict and child adjustment: An emotional security hypothesis. *Psychological Bulletin, 116*, 387–411.

Fantuzzo, J. W., Brouch, R., Beriama, A., & Atkins, M. (1997). Domestic violence and children: Prevalence and risk in five major U.S. cities. *Journal of the American Academy of Child and Adolescent Psychiatry, 36*, 116–122. doi:10.1097/00004583-199701000-00025

Foa, E. B., Cashman, L., Jaycox, L., & Perry, K. (1997). The validation of a self-report measure of posttraumatic stress disorder: The Posttraumatic Diagnostic Scale. *Psychological Assessment, 9*, 445–451. doi:10.1037/1040-3590.9.4.445

Folkman, S., & Lazarus, R. S. (1988). *The Ways of Coping Questionnaire*. Palo Alto, CA: Consulting Psychologists Press.

Frick, P. J. (1991). *The Alabama Parenting Questionnaire* [Unpublished rating scale]. Tuscaloosa: University of Alabama.

Graham-Bermann, S. A. (1992). *The Kids' Club: A preventive intervention program for children of battered women*. Ann Arbor: Department of Psychology, University of Michigan.

Graham-Bermann, S. A., & Follett, C. (2000). *Fostering resilience in young children exposed to violence*. Ann Arbor: Department of Psychology, University of Michigan.

Graham-Bermann, S. A., Kulkarni, M., & Kanukollu, S. (in press). Is disclosure therapeutic for children following exposure to traumatic violence? *Journal of Interpersonal Violence, 26*(5).

Graham-Bermann, S. A., & Levendosky, A. A. (1994). *The Moms' Group: A parenting support and intervention program for battered women who are mothers*. Ann Arbor: University of Michigan, Department of Psychology.

Graham-Bermann, S. A., & Levendosky, A. A. (1998). Traumatic stress symptoms of children of battered women. *Journal of Interpersonal Violence, 13*, 111–128. doi:10.1177/088626098013001007

Graham-Bermann, S. A., Lynch, S., Banyard, V., DeVoe, E., & Halabu, H. (2007). Community based intervention for children exposed to intimate partner violence: An efficacy trial. *Journal of Consulting and Clinical Psychology, 75*, 199–209. doi:10.1037/0022-006X.75.2.199

Grych, J. H., & Fincham, F. (1993). Children's appraisals of marital conflict: Initial investigations of the cognitive-contextual framework. *Child Development, 64,* 215–230. doi:10.2307/1131447

Levendosky, A. A., & Graham-Bermann, S. A. (1998). The moderating effects of parenting stress on children's adjustment in woman-abusing families. *Journal of Interpersonal Violence, 13,* 383–397. doi:10.1177/088626098013003005

Levendosky, A. A., & Graham-Bermann, S. A. (2001). Parenting in battered women: The effects of domestic violence on women and children. *Journal of Family Violence, 16,* 171–192. doi:10.1023/A:1011111003373

Patterson, G. R. (1982). *Coercive family process.* Eugene, OR: Castalia.

Radloff, L. S. (1977). The CES-D Scale: A self-report depression scale for research in the general population. *Applied Psychological Measurement, 1,* 385–401.

Sameroff, A. J., & Emde, R. N. (1989). *Relationship disturbances in early childhood: A developmental approach.* New York, NY: Basic Books.

Scheeringa, M. S., & Gaensbauer, T. J. (2000). Posttraumatic stress disorder. In C. H. Zeanah Jr. (Ed.), *Handbook of infant mental health* (2nd ed., pp. 369–381). New York, NY: Guilford Press.

Scheeringa, M., & Zeanah, C. (1994). *Posttraumatic Stress Disorder Semi-Structured Interview and Observational Record for infants and young children.* New Orleans, LA: Tulane University.

Scheeringa, M. S., Zeanah, C. H., Myers, L., & Putnam, F. W. (2005). Predictive validity in a prospective follow-up of PTSD in preschool children. *Journal of the American Academy of Child and Adolescent Psychiatry, 44,* 899–906. doi:10.1097/01.chi.0000169013.81536.71

Skopp, N. A., McDonald, R., Jouriles, E. N., & Rosenfield, D. (2007). Partner aggression and children's externalizing problems: Maternal and partner warmth as protective factors. *Journal of Family Psychology, 21,* 459–467. doi:10.1037/0893-3200.21.3.459

Straus, M. A., Hamby, S. L., Boney-McCoy, S., Sugarman, D. B. (1996). The revised Conflict Tactics Scales (CTS2): Development and preliminary psychometric data. *Journal of Family Issues, 17,* 283–316. doi:10.1177/019251396017003001

Turner, H. A., Finkelhor, D., & Ormrod, R. (2006). The effect of lifetime victimization on the mental health of children and adolescents. *Social Science & Medicine, 62*(1), 13–27. doi:10.1016/j.socscimed.2005.05.030

III

SCHOOL-AGE CHILDREN

8

THE EFFECTS OF INTIMATE PARTNER VIOLENCE ON SCHOOL-AGE CHILDREN

RENEE L. DeBOARD-LUCAS AND JOHN H. GRYCH

Much of the empirical research examining the effects of intimate partner violence (IPV) on children has focused on middle childhood. The reasons for this are largely practical in nature: Studies seeking to assess children's perspectives on the violence they have witnessed or their psychological functioning are limited to youths who can report reliably on their experiences, which typically means children over age 7 or 8. Children older than age 12 or 13 often are not represented in studies using samples from battered women's shelters because many shelters do not accept adolescents, especially boys. Consequently, a large literature documenting the nature of adjustment problems in school-age children from violent homes has been generated over the past 3 decades.

In this chapter, we review this literature, focusing on two meta-analyses and a "mega-analysis" that combined data from 15 empirical studies, and we discuss the contributions and limitations of the existing work for understanding the effects of IPV. We then discuss critical directions for future research in this area, focusing on the need for more developmentally informed research, the role of children's perceptions and understanding of violence, the value of studying violence within a broader family context, and the importance of examining sources of resilience in children exposed to violence.

RESEARCH ON THE ADJUSTMENT OF SCHOOL-AGE CHILDREN FROM VIOLENT FAMILIES

Empirical work on the adjustment of children living in violent homes has progressed from studies that used brief and unstandardized measures of violence in small samples of women and children residing in domestic violence shelters to large, methodologically sophisticated investigations that draw on samples from clinical, legal, and community settings. This literature has been the subject of several reviews, and in the next section we focus on three quantitative analyses that summarized findings from more than 20 years of research on IPV and child adjustment.

Results of Meta- and Mega-Analyses

Kitzmann, Gaylord, Holt, and Kenny (2003) conducted a meta-analysis of 118 studies published between 1978 and 2000 that included both a measure of child functioning and a measure of physical aggression between two adults or parent figures in a family. This analysis incorporated findings from 84 peer-reviewed articles, five book chapters, and 29 theses or dissertations, and a range of child outcomes, including symptoms of maladjustment, social and academic competence, and children's responses to interparental conflict (either real or simulated). The latter studies were included to examine the hypothesis that exposure to IPV affects how children perceive and respond to more normative levels of conflict. In most of these studies, IPV was assessed with a self-report questionnaire, usually the Conflict Tactics Scale (CTS; Straus, 1979), and child adjustment through maternal reports on a questionnaire such as the Child Behavior Checklist (CBCL; Achenbach, 1991a) or children's rating on the Youth Self-Report (YSR; Achenbach, 1991b). In some cases, children's exposure to violence was measured directly, by obtaining reports from children or mothers, whereas in others it was assumed that children were aware of the violence occurring in the home. Although the latter group of studies provides a less accurate estimate of children's experiences, Kitzmann et al. (2003) found that effect sizes for the relation between IPV and child adjustment did not differ significantly between studies that directly measured versus assumed children's exposure to violence.

More than half of the studies included in the meta-analysis reported correlations between measures of IPV and child adjustment, with the remainder comparing the adjustment of children who witnessed violence to one of four other groups: children not exposed to violence, children exposed to verbal but not physical interparental aggression, victims of physical child abuse, or children who had both witnessed violence and experienced maltreatment. The average correlation between IPV and child adjustment was $r = .29$, but effect sizes in the group comparisons depended on the nature of the comparison group. Whereas children who witnessed violence exhibited more symptoms of maladjustment than children not exposed to violence ($d = .40$) or children exposed only to verbal aggression ($d = .28$), witnesses did not differ significantly from either victims of physical abuse ($d = .15$) or children who had experienced both IPV and maltreatment ($d = .13$). Effect sizes did not differ significantly for boys and girls or for children in different developmental periods (classified as preschool-age, school-age, or adolescent). Effect sizes also were consistent across the general classes of adjustment problems assessed (internalizing, externalizing, social, academic, and "other" psychological problems). However, within the domain of externalizing problems, the average effect size for studies assessing aggression ($d = .14$) was smaller than studies assessing other types of externalizing problems (e.g., disruptive or rule-breaking behavior; $d = .35$). Within the domain of internalizing problems, studies assessing posttraumatic stress disorder (PTSD) symptomatology showed a larger effect size ($d = .51$) than studies examining other types of internalizing problems ($d = .33$), though the comparison was based on only 12 studies and only tended toward significance ($p < .06$).

A second, more narrowly focused meta-analysis was published in 2003 by Wolfe, Crooks, Lee, McIntyre-Smith, and Jaffe. This analysis was based on 41 studies, all but seven of which also were represented in Kitzmann et al.'s (2003) meta-analysis; six of the seven were published in 2000 or later. Wolfe et al. included only studies published in peer-reviewed journals that assessed symptoms of both internalizing and externalizing problems, and they excluded studies if the group of children compared to witnesses of violence also had been exposed to some form of abuse or maltreatment (e.g., children who had been abused and witnessed IPV) or if results were presented in a form other than group comparisons or correlations (e.g., multiple regression analyses). IPV was defined as the occurrence of at least one act of physical aggression in the past year and generally was measured with the CTS. Half of the studies used community samples, one third drew on shelter samples, and the remainder recruited from clinical settings. As in the Kitzmann et al. meta-analysis, children's exposure was directly assessed in some cases and assumed in others. Child adjustment was assessed via self-report questionnaires, most often the CBCL or YSR.

Wolfe et al. (2003) calculated effect sizes in terms of correlation coefficients that were then transformed to Z values using Fisher's r to z transformation. They reported an effect size of $Z = .28$ across all studies and adjustment symptoms, nearly identical to the average *r* of .29 that Kitzmann et al. (2003) found in correlational studies. Neither child gender nor age was related to effect sizes once studies producing effects that included extreme outliers were removed from the analysis. Effect sizes were similar for internalizing and externalizing problems; PTSD symptoms were coded for analysis but the three studies that assessed PTSD did not also include a measure of externalizing problems and so were excluded from the meta analysis. Wolfe et al. also examined the effect sizes from four studies that compared witnesses of violence to children who had experienced both IPV and child abuse (all of which were included in Kitzmann's analysis). Children exposed to both types of aggression exhibited somewhat greater symptomatology, but because the number of studies including this comparison was so small, Wolfe et al. did not test whether differences between effect sizes were significantly different.

One limitation of these meta-analyses is that the sample size for group comparisons is determined by the number of studies that examined a particular question, and some of the group comparisons are based on very small samples. For example, in the Kitzmann et al. (2003) meta-analysis, comparisons between witnesses and physically abused witnesses were based on between two and seven studies, depending on the outcome assessed. Thus, the power to detect significant differences between effect sizes is low, and the magnitude of effect sizes can be unduly influenced by individual studies, raising questions about their validity.

To address these limitations, Sternberg, Baradaran, Abbott, Lamb, and Guterman (2006) adopted a different approach to aggregating data across studies. They conducted a mega-analysis in which they obtained the raw data from 15 published studies of IPV and conducted new analyses on the combined sample of 1,870 children and their mothers. These analyses thus have more power and sensitivity to detect effects than group comparisons based on a handful of studies. The disadvantage to this approach is that only studies that included the same measures of IPV and child adjustment could be included. The 15 studies that provided data for the mega-analysis had used the CBCL to assess child adjustment problems and either the CTS or records from Child Protective Services (CPS) to assess IPV. The names of 13 researchers who shared their raw data are provided in the article but not the references for the studies themselves, and consequently it is not clear from which studies the data are drawn. However, all of the researchers are represented in the list of studies on which the Kitzmann et al. (2003) meta-analysis was conducted, and so there is likely considerable overlap with the data included in the meta-analyses.

Sternberg et al. (2006) classified children into a "witness" group if their parent reported one or more acts of mild or more severe aggression on the CTS (69% of witnesses) or on the basis of reports to CPS (31%). Children were considered "victims" if there had been at least one act of parent–child aggression reported on the CTS or in CPS records, and "abused witnesses" if they had experienced at least one act of both types of violence. Effect sizes were presented as odds ratios derived from logistic regression analyses that describe the increased probability that children in each of the three groups demonstrated adjustment problems relative to the nonviolent comparison group. After controlling for source of information about children's violence status (CTS vs. CPS records), Sternberg et al. found that youths exposed to IPV were 2.40 times more likely to exhibit clinically significant levels of externalizing problems than children from nonviolent families and 2.03 times more likely to exhibit severe internalizing problems. Although children who had experienced both IPV and child maltreatment were more likely to exhibit each type of problem than witnesses of violence, the difference between the groups was not statistically significant. Child gender did not moderate the relation between exposure to violence and either type of maladjustment, but age moderated the association between type of violence and externalizing problems. For children ages 7 to 14, all three violence groups differed significantly from the nonviolent comparison groups in the probability of exhibiting externalizing problems, but for children ages 4 to 6, only the abused-witness group exhibited elevated risk for externalizing problems.

Person-Centered Studies

Together, these quantitative reviews indicate that children exposed to IPV exhibit elevated levels of a range of adjustment problems. All of the studies included in the reviews, and nearly all published since then, have been variable centered; that is, the analyses examined associations between exposure to IPV and particular kinds of adjustment problems across all children in the sample. Consequently, it is not clear whether the findings indicate that children from violent homes typically demonstrate a wide range of symptoms or whether some children exhibit certain types of problems but not others. The research also does not address whether there are resilient children who do not develop adjustment problems despite exposure to highly stressful events. Identifying groups of children who demonstrate qualitatively different patterns of adjustment is a step toward developing a more refined understanding of the factors that shape the functioning of children living in violent homes (Bogat, Levendosky, & von Eye, 2005). There have been three studies that conducted person-centered analyses in an effort to determine whether homogeneous subgroups characterized by reliably different profiles of adjustment problems could be identified within the population of children exposed to violence.

Grych, Jouriles, Swank, McDonald, and Norwood (2000) assessed the adjustment of two hundred twenty-eight 8- to 14-year-old children who were living with their mothers in domestic violence shelters. Mothers completed the CTS to assess interparental violence and the Externalizing scale of the CBCL. Children reported on symptoms of depression and anxiety, which were standardized and combined into a general measure of internalizing symptoms, and completed a measure of self-esteem. Cluster analysis of a randomly selected half of the sample produced five distinct patterns of adjustment, and this cluster solution was cross-validated with the other half of the sample. Four of the clusters described children with varying levels of internalizing and external-izing problems: children in the externalizing group (21% of the sample) exhibited high levels of externalizing problems on the CBCL (89% of this group were above the cutoff for clinically significant symptoms) but were below the sample average on internalizing problems and above average in self-esteem; the multiproblem-externalizing group (19% of the sample) also showed high levels of externalizing problems (86% were above the clinical threshold), along with above average but largely subclinical levels of inter-nalizing problems (9% exceeded the clinical cutoff); those in the mild distress group (18% of the sample) had slightly elevated scores on the internalizing scale (5% above the clinical threshold) and below average scores on the externalizing scale; the multiproblem-internalizing group (11% of the sam-ple) reported high levels of internalizing problems (65% exceeded the clini-cal cutoff) and above average but subclinical levels of externalizing problems; and the final and largest group (31% of the sample), the no problems reported group, exhibited below-average levels of maladjustment (with no children exceeding threshold) and the highest levels of self-esteem. The composition of these five groups is similar to that identified in Hughes and Luke's (1998) cluster analysis of a small sample of children residing in domestic violence shelters.

Grych et al. (2000) also examined whether children in the five clusters could be distinguished based on mothers' or children's reports of violence in the family. Mothers' scores on the CTS did not differ across the groups, but children in the two multiproblem groups described higher levels of father–mother aggression than those in the other three clusters, who did not differ from each other. Children's appraisals of interparental conflict and aggression also were assessed, and those in the no problems reported and externalizing clusters reported less perceived threat in response to interparental conflict than the other three groups, whereas the multiproblem–internalizing group reported the highest levels of self-blame.

More recently, Graham-Bermann, Gruber, Howell, and Girz (2009) examined patterns of adjustment in 219 children ages 6 to 12 who were exposed to violence in the prior year but were not residing in a shelter, and the study included more indices of positive functioning in order to better assess resilience in these children. Cluster analysis revealed one group (24%

of the sample) reporting elevated levels of all types of adjustment problems and moderate levels of social competence and global self-worth, and one group (11% of the sample) characterized by high levels of depression. A third group was termed *struggling* (45% of the sample) because they did not exhibit significant adjustment problems but had low scores on the positive adjustment measures. Finally, one group was deemed *resilient* (20% of the sample) because they had high levels of self-worth and social competence and low scores on the maladjustment measures. Children in the resilient group were distinguished from other three by better maternal mental health and parenting skills.

These studies support the findings of variable-centered research in showing that many children from violent families exhibit elevated levels of maladjustment. However, they also indicate that different patterns of adjustment can be reliably identified, and that a significant proportion of children appear to be functioning well despite witnessing IPV. Further work is needed to determine whether the patterns of symptoms identified in these studies replicate across samples and over time, and to identify whether they can be distinguished on the basis of unique sets of risk and protective factors. Moreover, a more comprehensive understanding of the pathways between exposure to IPV and children's development requires longitudinal research. Unfortunately, nearly all of the research on school-age children from violent homes is cross-sectional, and consequently little is known about the developmental trajectories of these children.

Longitudinal Research

The few longitudinal studies that have been conducted with school-age children followed samples of children and their mothers after leaving shelters for victims of domestic violence (Graham-Bermann, Lynch, Banyard, DeVoe, & Halabu, 2007; McDonald, Jouriles, & Skopp, 2006; Ware et al., 2001). These studies indicate that children's functioning over time is closely tied to their mothers' mental health and parenting. Graham-Bermann et al. (2007) conducted a treatment efficacy study that compared three conditions: child-only treatment, child-plus-mother-treatment, and a wait-list comparison group. Treatment for children targeted their knowledge and attitudes/ beliefs about IPV, emotional adjustment, and social behavior. Mothers learned effective parenting and disciplinary skills, discussed parenting issues, and were empowered to talk to their children about IPV and to address their concerns (Graham-Bermann et al., 2007). Results of this study suggest that the child-plus-mother condition was more effective than child-only treatment in reducing and maintaining changes in children's externalizing problems and attitudes about IPV at an 8-month follow-up. In contrast, children in the child-only condition expressed increasingly accepting attitudes toward IPV.

McDonald et al. (2006) also found that mothers' involvement in treatment during their residence in the shelter was associated with a decrease in clinically significant child conduct problems, but Ware et al. (2001) reported that children's externalizing behavior problems did not improve even though mothers reported decreasing levels of maternal distress over time. Unfortunately, neither study assessed whether changes in IPV were related to either mothers' or children's functioning, and consequently it is not clear if children's adjustment problems at follow-up were a product of their earlier exposure or concurrent experiences in the family.

There is a critical need to conduct longitudinal research to understand the developmental sequelae of witnessing aggression between caregivers, but the studies following women and their children after they leave shelter demonstrate both the difficulty of distinguishing the effects of violence exposure from continued stressors in the lives of the families and the practical problems involved with tracking this population. For example, McDonald et al. (2006) reported that 68% of their sample of 30 families moved at least three times in the 32 months following their departure from the shelter. Because residential changes often involve changing peer groups, schools, and churches, mothers and their children often experience disruptions in social support during a time of high stress. Community families with more stable living situations likely will prove easier to follow over time, but researchers will need to thoroughly assess covarying risk factors if the unique effects of violence are to be identified.

SUMMARY AND CRITIQUE

The quantitative reviews of the extensive literature on children's adjustment in violent homes clearly establish that exposure to IPV is a risk factor for the development of psychopathology. Children who witness family violence consistently exhibit greater externalizing, internalizing, social, and academic problems than those who do not, and a small number of studies suggest that children exposed to IPV may be at particularly high risk for PTSD. Person-centered analyses offer additional insight into variability in the patterns of symptoms exhibited by children from violent homes. They indicate that some children exhibit high levels of both internalizing and externalizing problems, whereas other groups are characterized by predominantly internalizing or predominantly externalizing symptoms; notably, there is a significant minority of children who do not display adjustment problems, at least at the time of assessment. However, the factors that may lead to one symptom pattern versus another are not known. Although gender differences in child adjustment have been reported in some studies, the meta- and mega-analyses found that the effects of IPV are similar for boys and girls. Similarly, although the findings pertaining to age are not entirely consistent across the three quantitative reviews, they indicate that children of all ages are at increased risk for maladjustment. The meta- and mega-analyses are based on a similar set of studies and so their results are not independent, but the fact that differences in inclusion and exclusion criteria do not substantively change the conclusions, suggest that the findings are robust.

However, a number of methodological and conceptual issues make it difficult to draw more precise or nuanced conclusions about the impact of IPV on children. Nearly all of the research in this area has been cross-sectional, and consequently little is known about the effects of violence over time, whether the timing of children's exposure has differential effects on development, or how changes in exposure to violence may affect child functioning. In the next section, we discuss several critical factors that limit understanding of the impact of violence on children.

Conceptualization of Violence in Close Relationships

Different terminology has been used to describe violence between romantic partners, including *domestic violence, intimate partner violence, family violence, interparental violence, spousal abuse,* and *woman abuse* (see Holden, 2003), and studies using the same term have varied in how they conceptualize what constitutes violence. In particular, whereas some investigations defined violence specifically in terms of acts of physical aggression, other studies included a broader range of behaviors, including verbal, sexual, and emotional abuse. Consequently, studies ostensibly examining the same construct may actually be assessing different phenomena, and some studies using different terms may be assessing the same construct.

Differences in defining the parameters of the construct reflect a broader disagreement in the field regarding the unilateral versus reciprocal nature of IPV. Some theorists conceptualize IPV as a systematic effort by men to exert power over their female partners through the use of physical force, threats, coercion, sexual assault, and control of their access to friends and financial resources. Studies that label one partner the *perpetrator* (nearly always male in heterosexual couples) and the other the *victim* (nearly always female in heterosexual couples) reflect this view. Others conceptualize IPV as the product of a dyadic process in which each individual contributes to an escalation of hostility and engages in aggression; in this case, there is no clear-cut perpetrator and victim, though women are more likely to be hurt by physical aggression because men generally are larger and stronger.

Johnson (e.g., 2006) attempted to resolve this discrepancy by proposing that there are qualitatively different types of IPV. Johnson used the term *intimate terrorism* for the gendered pattern of abuse and control described above and argued that this is the form of violence most often seen in women who use domestic violence shelters. The term *common couple violence* was used to describe the reciprocal pattern of escalating aggression in which men and women contribute roughly equally and is proposed to be the type of violence most prevalent in community samples. Although this distinction is widely cited and has received some empirical support (see Johnson, 2006), existing data do not clearly indicate whether violence in close relationships is best understood in terms of a typology versus a continuum that ranges from no violence to frequent and severe aggression (e.g., Capaldi & Kim, 2007). For example, the proposition that intimate terrorism involves more frequent and severe aggression in addition to a broader pattern of control has not always been supported (Capaldi & Kim, 2007). To determine whether variation in IPV reflects qualitatively different types or a continuum of severity, studies need to include large samples of couples reporting a wide range of aggressive and violent behavior in order to represent adequately the hypothesized subtypes; thus, studies that sample only from shelters or only from largely well-functioning community couples are unlikely to resolve this issue. Further, it is essential to assess both partners' behavior, rather than assuming that one partner is the perpetrator and the other the victim, and to examine the interactional context in which violence arises. However, limitations in the measurement of IPV contribute to a lack of clarity in its conceptualization.

Measurement of IPV

Most of the research assessing the impact of IPV on children has employed the CTS (Straus, 1979). The CTS is a well-validated self-report measure that assesses the frequency of specific behaviors reflecting verbal and physical aggression. In response to concerns that the measure was too limited in the scope of behaviors assessed and failed to assess the effects of aggressive behaviors, the CTS was revised in 1996 (Straus, Hamby, Boney-McCoy, & Sugarman, 1996). The CTS-2 includes a broader range of abusive behaviors, including sexual aggression, and inquires about the extent of injury resulting from the behaviors. The revised version thus is more comprehensive than the original and represents a considerable improvement over self-report measures and interviews used in early studies that were brief, vague, or unvalidated. By adding an injury subscale, it also addresses the criticism that assessing a behavior without assessing its impact on the recipient underestimates the differential effects of male versus female physical aggression. However, it also has a number of limitations for understanding the nature of violence occurring in the family.

First, although the CTS asks respondents to report on their behavior and the behavior of their partner, it does not assess the sequence in which the behavior occurs. Consequently, it is not clear if similar levels of aggression reflect a reciprocal interaction in which both individuals contribute to escalation, or a pattern in which one person consistently initiates aggression and the other fights back in self-defense (a third form in Johnson's typology). Thus, the CTS provides little insight into the context in which violence occurs. Second, the assessment of attempts to control and dominate the partner that do not involve overt threats or physical aggression remains fairly minimal. Thus, it is difficult to test the hypothesis that physical violence represents the most salient manifestation of a more pervasive pattern of control. Although other questionnaires have been developed that more thoroughly assess controlling behavior, they are not widely used; including both types of measures would enable researchers to examine a broader array of abusive behavior.

Other problems in measuring IPV lie not with the CTS itself but with how it is used. Rather than using the full range of scores on the CTS, some studies divide respondents into violent versus nonviolent groups; most often, a single incident of physical aggression is sufficient to categorize an individual (or couple) as violent. This approach reflects the assumption that there are types of couples rather than a continuum of violence, but the choice of cut-off point is rarely based on either theory or empirical data. Although it could be argued that a couple in which one partner has pushed, grabbed, shoved, or hit the other partner is different from one in which conflict and hostility have never been expressed physically, there is little empirical basis for concluding that a couple who has engaged in physical aggression one or two times is more similar to couples engaging in chronic and severe violence than to couples whose conflicts remain verbal. Further, the statistical consequences of dichotomizing a continuous variable when the construct is not truly categorical are well known. This approach results in a loss of information and less sensitive measurement and thus limits the potential for a study to detect significant relations between violence and other constructs.

Assessing Children's Exposure to Violence

As described previously, studies vary in whether and how children's exposure to IPV is assessed. Some studies directly assess children's exposure by having them report on their experiences, whereas others rely on mothers to indicate how much violence their children have witnessed, and still others do not assess children's exposure but assume that they were exposed to it to some degree. Research examining how much violence occurs in the presence of children suggests that the assumption that children are aware of violence is well founded. Further, as noted earlier, the meta-analysis of Kitzmann and her colleagues (2003) showed that effect sizes do not differ significantly when children's exposure is assessed versus assumed. However, if we are to develop a deeper understanding of how children's experience with violence in the family affect their adjustment, it is important to accurately measure their exposure.

Holden (2003) recommended use of a *taxonomy of exposure* to describe children's experiences with IPV. At one end of the continuum, children may be directly involved in the violence, either by intervening, being personally assaulted, or participating in the assault. Other types of exposure include observing a violent interaction; overhearing but not observing it; or hearing about it from a parent, sibling, or someone else. In addition, children may see some of the consequences of violence in the form of bruises, police presence in the home, or emergency room visits. The term *exposure* could even be applied to children whose mothers are abused while pregnant, which can have adverse effects on the developing fetus. Children may certainly be exposed to IPV in more than one way, and future research would benefit from assessing different types of exposure and describing children's experiences in greater detail.

Specificity of IPV as a Risk Factor

One important difficulty in interpreting research on IPV is that it occurs within a broader constellation of risk factors, and the unique and combined effects of violence on child adjustment are not well understood. For example, families in which IPV occurs tend to have higher levels of stress, parental substance abuse, and child maltreatment, and are more likely to live in violent neighborhoods. Group comparisons that classify families on the basis of the occurrence of IPV may inaccurately ascribe any differences to violence between parents rather than other potential causes. This is particularly problematic when women and children residing in shelters are compared to families recruited from the community. In addition to being exposed to violence severe enough to precipitate their mother to seek shelter, these children often face additional stressors that may include emergency room visits, seeing a parent get arrested, and being displaced from the family home (Holden, 2003). Women who use shelters for victims of domestic violence also are more likely to be economically disadvantaged than women who experience violence but do not seek shelter. These factors may explain why children who were residing in a domestic violence shelter exhibited poorer social competence and higher levels of internalizing problems than same-age peers living in the community whose mothers reported similar levels of verbal and physical aggression (Fantuzzo et al., 1991).

Kitzmann et al. (2003) attempted to disentangle the effects of IPV from co-occurring risk factors in their meta-analysis. First, they examined effect sizes in studies that accounted for other predictors of maladjustment (e.g., general stress, economic deprivation, frequent moves, parental substance use). Relatively few studies had controlled for these factors, and effect sizes were only slightly smaller for studies controlling for only one ($d = .37$) or two stressors ($d = .38$) than for studies controlling for none of these factors ($d = .46$); however, effect sizes were smaller for the nine studies that statistically accounted for three stressors ($d = .20$). Second, they compared studies that had drawn the witness and comparison groups from either similar or different populations (community, at-risk, clinical, or shelter) and found that the source of the samples did not moderate effect sizes. Finally, the researchers examined the strength of the correlation between IPV and child adjustment within different types of samples, and they found a significant association in community, at-risk, and clinical samples. This association was not significant in studies using shelter samples, perhaps because of limited range on one or both variables. Thus, even though other stressors likely exacerbate adjustment problems seen in children exposed to IPV, they do not appear to fully account for the association between violence and child maladjustment.

Lack of Theoretical Development

Most of the research on the adjustment of children from violent homes is descriptive in nature. Although some studies have been guided by theory, few have investigated mechanisms proposed to explain how exposure to violence leads to adjustment problems. Consequently, the processes that mediate and moderate the impact of violence on children's functioning are not well understood. Social learning theory is often evoked as a model for explaining how exposure to violence gives rise to externalizing problems, but it is difficult to determine whether the aggressive and antisocial behavior seen in children from violent families is the result of modeling or reinforcement. Rather, research guided by social learning theory has focused on the idea that exposure to violence affects children's beliefs about the justifiability or normativeness of aggression in close relationships. It is hypothesized that children from violent families may learn that it is acceptable to use aggression, at least under certain conditions, for example, if one is provoked, to win an argument, or to assert power over others. There is substantial empirical evidence that youths exposed to high levels of interparental conflict and aggression report more accepting attitudes toward the use of aggression, and that these attitudes mediate the association between interparental aggression and aggression toward peers (e.g., Marcus, Lindahl, & Malik, 2001) and dating partners (Kinsfogel & Grych, 2004; Riggs & O'Leary, 1989).

Children's subjective perceptions of aggressive behavior also are highlighted in the cognitive-contextual framework (Grych & Fincham, 1990), which proposes that children's appraisals guide their immediate response to interparental conflict and have implications for their adjustment more broadly. Although developed to understand conflict rather than violence, studies with violent samples have produced results similar to those reported with non-violent families; specifically, appraisals of threat and self-blame mediated the association between children's exposure to interparental aggression and adjustment problems (Grych et al., 2000; Jouriles, Spiller, Stephens, McDonald, & Swank, 2000). Fosco, DeBoard, and Grych (2007) discussed the extension of the cognitive-contextual framework to understanding the impact of IPV on children. They argued that in addition to guiding children's immediate response to interparental aggression, the meaning that children take away from these interactions is likely to shape their beliefs and expectations about aggression and about close relationships more generally, which in turn influence interactions with peers, romantic partners, and others. We discuss this issue in more detail below.

Conceptual models developed to understand the impact of traumatic events also have been applied to child witnesses of IPV. One mechanism by which trauma is proposed to lead to maladjustment is by altering the functioning of neurobiological stress response systems, leaving children less able to regulate their arousal, affect, and behavior when stressful events occur (e.g., De Bellis, 2001). Saltzman, Holden, and Holahan (2005) investigated this hypothesis by assessing markers of the hypothalamic–pituitary–adrenal axis and sympathetic nervous system in children exposed to interparental violence. They compared a group of children from families in which there were police-substantiated incidents of IPV with a group of children recruited from a community mental health center, and found that children from violent families exhibited higher heart rates and salivary cortisol levels both prior to and after participating in an interview about the violence. The groups did not differ on two other indices (blood pressure, heart rate in response to a physical stressor) or on the degree of change in heart rate, blood pressure, or salivary cortisol over the course of the interview. This study thus provides initial support for the proposition that exposure to IPV can lead to maladjustment by affecting children's capacity to respond adaptively to stress.

Finally, ecological models that incorporate multiple contexts and levels of analysis also have been applied to understanding how violence affects their adjustment. For example, Levendosky and Graham-Bermann (2001) integrated ecological and trauma theory to examine the impact of IPV on children's adjustment. With a sample of 120 women and their 7- to 12-year-old children, Levendosky and Graham-Bermann (2001) tested a model in which IPV was proposed to affect parenting though effects on maternal psychological functioning. In turn, these contextual variables were proposed to negatively affect children's adjustment. Results of this study showed that the adverse effects of IPV on parenting were mediated by contextual variables such as maternal psychological functioning and marital satisfaction. This ecological model accounted for a substantial amount of the variance in child adjustment (40%), which suggests that taking contextual factors into account paints a more complete picture of how IPV affects parents and children.

FUTURE DIRECTIONS

The limitations discussed to this point have implications for guiding future investigations into the effects of IPV on children, but in the final section of the chapter, we offer four additional recommendations that we believe are important for advancing understanding of the impact of witnessing IPV on children.

Thinking Developmentally

As the literature review shows, most studies of children exposed to IPV have assessed symptoms of psychopathology as outcome measures. Documenting associations with adjustment problems has been essential for establishing the nature of the clinical risk and highlighting the public health significance of family violence, but it provides a limited perspective on its potential impact on children's development. Witnessing violence between their caregivers may have more subtle effects on children that do not represent symptoms of psychopathology but have implications for healthy development. For example, it may interfere with children's ability to form close relationships with peers and, later, romantic partners. The limited work examining social and academic competence suggests that broadening the assessment of child adjustment will provide a more complete picture of the sequelae of witnessing IPV.

One useful approach to understanding adaptive functioning focuses on the mastery of stage-salient tasks (e.g., Masten & Coatsworth, 1998). This perspective holds that there are normative challenges that occur across development and that successful mastery of these challenges promotes healthy adaptation, whereas failure to master a task makes children more vulnerable to developing serious problems in functioning later. Masten and Coatsworth (1998) described the developmental tasks in middle childhood in relation to functioning in four interrelated domains: school adjustment, academic achievement, peer relationships, and rule-governed conduct. Emphasizing mastery of developmental tasks highlights two issues pertinent to understanding the effects of violence. First, it directs attention from documenting the presence of adjustment problems to understanding their functional impact on children's short- and long-term development. For example, disruptive, aggressive behavior is likely to interfere with the development of peer relationships, and problems with anxiety or depression may undermine learning and academic achievement, each of which has important implications for healthy development in adolescence and beyond. Second, focusing on developmental tasks leads to questions regarding the effects of violence on the basic social, emotional, and cognitive processes that foster successful mastery of these tasks. Although different theoretical perspectives emphasize different basic processes, the capacities to regulate emotions, exert self-control over behavior, and establish relationships generally are considered central for healthy adaptation in middle childhood. Investigating these processes is likely to provide a deeper understanding of why exposure to violence appears to have such pervasive effects on child functioning.

Finally, thinking developmentally raises issues pertaining to the timing and chronicity of children's exposure to violence (i.e., when and for how long violence occurred). Cross-sectional research can only document concurrent associations between violence and maladjustment, and consequently little is known about how experiences with violence at different time points and varying duration influence child functioning. Longitudinal studies that track children's exposure and adjustment over time are needed to determine whether there are lasting effects of violence, and whether there are developmental periods when exposure to violence has particularly adverse effects on children.

Understanding Children's Understanding of Violence

One of the most salient developmental changes over the span of middle childhood involves children's growing capacity to think about and make meaning of their experiences. Children actively try to make sense of salient events in their lives, and as their cognitive processing become increasingly sophisticated, the nature of their thinking about why aggression occurs between their caregivers, whether it is justified, and their role in stopping or preventing violent interactions changes. Their perceptions and interpretations of IPV have been proposed to influence both their immediate responses and the development of beliefs about close relationships (see Fosco et al., 2007). For example, if children believe that they had a role in causing conflict between their parents they may feel responsible for stopping or intervening in the interaction, which can place them in physical danger, and they may feel guilty, sad, or helpless for not preventing violence from occurring. In support of this idea, Grych et al. (2000) found that appraisals of self-blame mediated the association between exposure to interparental aggression and adjustment problems in a sample of children recruited from domestic violence shelters.

Children's efforts to understand why IPV occurred also may have implications for their developing beliefs about whether or when aggression may be justified. Witnessing violence between their caregivers is distressing for most children, and their explanations for why one parent would hurt another could be influenced by a variety of sources. They may draw on their experiences being punished by their parents for some wrongdoing, and they may infer that one parent must have done something to incur the wrath of the other. Graham-Bermann and Brescoll's (2000) finding that severity of IPV predicted stronger endorsement by ethnic minority children that violence is a parent's prerogative is consistent with this idea, as are the results of a study of moral reasoning conducted by Astor (1994). He compared children's attributions about provoked and unprovoked interparental violence in a sample of violent and nonviolent 8- to 12-year-olds and found that violent children were significantly more likely to approve of interparental violence when they perceived that the perpetrator was provoked.

Parents may also shape children's understanding of why IPV occurs in the way they talk to them about violent events. Even after a stressful event has ended, children may continue to reappraise the event and their response to it (Grych & Fincham, 1990; Pynoos, Steinberg, & Aronson, 1997), and parents who discuss the violence with them can help shape their understanding of it. According to Vygotsky (1978), parents scaffold children's understanding of events by prompting and cueing them in the course of conversation, and consequently the aspects of the events that parents emphasize teach children which components are important and thus facilitate their independent interpretation of events. Parents who justify or excuse violent behavior therefore may be implicitly endorsing violence as an acceptable way to deal with interpersonal conflicts, whereas those who focus more on the physical and psychological pain that violence causes send the message that violence is wrong. Examining how children come to understand violence in their family may provide an important link with research on violence in romantic relationships.

Assessing the Family Context

Because IPV often co-occurs with other types of family dysfunction, its impact on children may well depend on the constellation of risk and protective factors in the family as a whole. For example, children whose parents engage in violence in the context of heavy drinking or drug use live in an unpredictable and threatening environment that may have particularly pernicious effects on their developing ability to regulate affect and behavior. However, there has been little research examining the unique and joint effects of interparental aggression and other dimensions of family functioning. Developing conceptual models that propose mechanisms by which different kinds of adverse family processes affect children's functioning is an important next step for research on IPV.

The one family factor that has been investigated in relation to violence is parenting, or more accurately, mothers' parenting. This research has produced mixed findings. Some studies have shown that IPV is associated with increased parenting stress, less sensitivity to children's emotional needs, and less warm and effective parenting (Levendosky & Graham-Bermann, 1998, 2001). However, other studies have indicated that mothers experiencing violence can maintain good parenting (Levendosky, Huth-Bocks, Shapiro, & Semel, 2003; Sullivan, Juras, Bybee, Nguyen, & Allen, 2000), perhaps by compensating for the negative impact of the violence on the home environment, and that maternal warmth can serve as a protective factor that buffers the adverse effect of violence on children (Skopp, McDonald, Jouriles, & Rosenfield, 2007).

In contrast to the work on mother–child relationships, there has been little attention to fathers in violent families. Fathers are rarely included as research participants, and assessment of their behavior typically is limited to maternal reports of their aggression toward their partners and/or their children. It is understandable that studies of shelter samples do not include fathers in order to protect the safety and confidentiality of mothers, but in higher functioning community samples in which safety issues are less prominent, the absence of fathers restricts knowledge of their role in their children's development. Investigating children's relationships with and perceptions of both their mothers and their fathers could provide important insights into their attitudes about aggression as well as their behavior toward others. For example, children with close relationships with a violent parent may perceive parent's aggression in a more favorable light and be more likely to act aggressively themselves. If fathers are not included along with mothers in research, then potentially important elements of the family context are omitted from both theory and intervention focused on this problem.

Focusing on Resilience

The emphasis on documenting the nature of adjustment problems in children from violent homes has drawn attention away from data indicating that many of these children do not appear to be maladjusted. As noted previously, Graham-Bermann and colleagues (2009) found that 20% of children exposed to IPV exhibited high levels of self-esteem and social competence; although it is possible that some of these youths had problems that were not assessed in the study or developed problems later, these findings suggest that a substantial number of children living in violent homes demonstrate resilience. Luthar, Cicchetti, and Becker (2000) identified resilience as a process of adapting positively in the face of adversity, or functioning at a level that is substantially better than what would be expected following their particular risk exposure. Little is known about how some children continue to function well despite exposure to violence, but work on resilience in other contexts (e.g., socioeconomic disadvantage, parental mental illness) has identified three types of factors that contribute to positive adaptation: personal attributes, such as good intellectual functioning and high self-esteem; characteristics of the family, such as supportive relationships; and effective parenting and connections to people and institutions in the community, such as supportive adults, prosocial organizations and effective schools (DuBois, Felner, Brand, Adan, & Evans, 1992; Luthar et al., 2000; Masten et al., 1999). The limited research on resilience in children exposed to intimate partner supports the protective function of two of these factors: parenting (Graham-Bermann et al., 2009; Hughes & Luke, 1998), and supportive peer relationships (Kolbo, 1996).

Future work on resilience in this context will be most valuable if it moves beyond identifying correlates of competent functioning to investigating the processes that lead to positive adaptation. It also is important to determine whether children exhibiting better functioning have been exposed to similar levels of violence as poorer functioning children. For example, in their cluster analysis of children residing in shelter, Grych et al. (2000) found that children who exhibited no adjustment problems reported lower levels of interparental and parent–child aggression than children in groups marked by elevations in symptoms. Because these children were exposed to less violence, it is not clear whether they demonstrate resilience or if they simply experienced lower levels of the stressor, thus highlighting the importance of evaluating violence severity when assessing its impact on children. Further, it is essential to directly assess indicators of competence (e.g., school achievement, formation of supportive peer relationships) rather than treating the absence of psychopathology as evidence of resilience. The lack of adjustment problems in itself does not indicate that children are functioning well, except in situations where pathology is the expected outcome for most children.

CONCLUSION

Two decades of research have thoroughly documented the risk of maladjustment that children exposed to IPV face. For the field to move forward, attention now needs to turn to understanding how exposure to violence affects children and what makes children more or less vulnerable to these adverse effects. This goal requires the development and testing of conceptually guided models that specify the emotional, cognitive, physiological, and interpersonal processes that lead to both adaptive and maladaptive trajectories. Expanding the assessment of child outcomes to include stage-salient developmental tasks and basic psychological processes and placing IPV in a broader family context will enrich the next decade of research and speed the development of theoretically grounded prevention and intervention efforts.

REFERENCES

Achenbach, T. M. (1991a). *Manual for the Child Behavior Checklist/4-18 and 1991 Profile*. Burlington: Department of Psychiatry, University of Vermont.

Achenbach, T. M. (1991b). *Manual for the Youth Self-Report and 1991 Profile*. Burlington: Department of Psychiatry, University of Vermont.

Astor, R. A. (1994). Children's moral reasoning about family and peer violence: The role of provocation and retribution. *Child Development, 65*, 1054–1067. doi:10.2307/1131304

Bogat, G. A., Levendosky, A. A., & von Eye, A. (2005). The future of research on intimate partner violence: Person-oriented and variable-oriented perspectives. *American Journal of Community Psychology, 36*, 49–70. doi:10.1007/s10464-005-6232-7

Capaldi, D. M., & Kim, H. K. (2007). Typological approaches to violence in couples: A critique and alternative conceptual approach. *Clinical Psychology Review, 27*, 253–265. doi:10.1016/j.cpr.2006.09.001

De Bellis, M. D. (2001). Developmental traumatology: The psychobiological development of maltreated children and its implications for research, treatment, and policy. *Development and Psychopathology, 13*, 539–564. doi:10.1017/S0954579401003078

DuBois, D. L., Felner, R. D., Brand, S., Adan, A. M., & Evans, E. G. (1992). A prospective study of life stress, social support, and adaptation in early adolescence. *Child Development, 63*, 542–557. doi:10.2307/1131345

Fantuzzo, J. W., DePaola, L. M., Lambert, L., Martino, T., Anderson, G., & Sutton, S. (1991). Effects of interparental violence on the psychological adjustment and competencies of young children. *Journal of Consulting and Clinical Psychology, 59*, 258–265. doi:10.1037/0022-006X.59.2.258

Fosco, G. M., DeBoard, R. L., & Grych, J. H. (2007). Making sense of family violence: Implications of children's appraisals of interparental aggression for their short- and long-term functioning. *European Psychologist, 12*, 6–16. doi:10.1027/1016-9040.12.1.6

Graham-Bermann, S. A., & Brescoll, V. (2000). Gender, power, and violence: Assessing the family stereotypes of the children of batterers. *Journal of Family Psychology, 14*, 600–612. doi:10.1037/0893-3200.14.4.600

Graham-Bermann, S. A., Gruber, G., Howell, K. H., & Girz, L. (2009). Factors discriminating among profiles of resilience and psychopathology in children exposed to intimate partner violence (IPV). *Child Abuse & Neglect, 33*, 648–660. doi:10.1016/j.chiabu.2009.01.002

Graham-Bermann, S. A., Lynch, S., Banyard, V., DeVoe, E. R., & Halabu, H. (2007). Community-based intervention for children exposed to intimate partner violence: An efficacy trial. *Journal of Consulting and Clinical Psychology, 75,* 199–209. doi:10.1037/0022-006X.75.2.199

Grych, J. H., & Fincham, F. D. (1990). Marital conflict and children's adjustment: A cognitive-contextual framework. *Psychological Bulletin, 108,* 267–290. doi:10.1037/0033-2909.108.2.267

Grych, J. H., Jouriles, E. N., Swank, P. R., McDonald, R., & Norwood, W. D. (2000). Patterns of adjustment among children of battered women. *Journal of Consulting and Clinical Psychology, 68,* 84–94. doi:10.1037/0022-006X.68.1.84

Holden, G. W. (2003). Children exposed to domestic violence and child abuse: Terminology and taxonomy. *Clinical Child and Family Psychology Review, 6,* 151–160. doi:10.1023/A:1024906315255

Hughes, H. M., & Luke, D. A. (1998). Heterogeneity in adjustment among children of battered women. In G. W. Holden, R. Geffner, & E. N. Jouriles (Eds.), *Children exposed to family violence: Theory, research, and applied issues* (pp. 185–221). Washington, DC: American Psychological Association. doi:10.1037/10257-006

Johnson, M. P. (2006). Violence and abuse in personal relationships: Conflict, terror, and resistance in intimate partnerships. In A. L. Vangelisti & D. Perlman (Eds.), *The Cambridge handbook of personal relationships* (pp. 557–576). New York, NY: Cambridge University Press. doi:10.1017/CBO9780511606632.031

Jouriles, E. N., Spiller, L. C., Stephens, N., McDonald, R., & Swank, P. (2000). Variability in adjustment of children of battered women: The role of child appraisals of interparent conflict. *Cognitive Therapy and Research, 24,* 233–249. doi:10.1023/A:1005402310180

Kinsfogel, K. M., & Grych, J. H. (2004). Interparental conflict and adolescent dating relationships: Integrating cognitive, emotional, and peer influences. *Journal of Family Psychology, 18,* 505–515. doi:10.1037/0893-3200.18.3.505

Kitzmann, K. M., Gaylord, N. K., Holt, A. R., & Kenny, E. D. (2003). Child witnesses to domestic violence: A meta-analytic review. *Journal of Consulting and Clinical Psychology, 71,* 339–352. doi:10.1037/0022-006X.71.2.339

Kolbo, J. R. (1996). Risk and resilience among children exposed to family violence. *Violence and Victims, 11,* 113–128.

Levendosky, A. A., & Graham-Bermann, S. A. (1998). The moderating effects of parenting stress on children's adjustment in woman-abusing families. *Journal of Interpersonal Violence, 13,* 383–397. doi:10.1177/088626098013003005

Levendosky, A. A., & Graham-Bermann, S. A. (2001). Parenting in battered women: The effects of domestic violence on women and their children. *Journal of Family Violence, 16,* 171–192. doi:10.1023/A:1011111003373

Levendosky, A. A., Huth-Bocks, A. C., Shapiro, D. L., & Semel, M. A. (2003). The impact of domestic violence on the maternal-child relationship and preschool-age children's functioning. *Journal of Family Psychology, 17,* 275–287. doi:10.1037/ 0893-3200.17.3.275

Luthar, S. S., Cicchetti, D., & Becker, B. (2000). Research on resilience: Response to commentaries. *Child Development, 71,* 573–575. doi:10.1111/1467-8624.00168

Marcus, N. E., Lindahl, K. M., & Malik, N. M. (2001). Interparental conflict, children's social cognitions, and child aggression: A test of a meditational model. *Journal of Family Psychology, 15,* 315–333. doi:10.1037/0893-3200.15.2.315

Masten, A. S., & Coatsworth, J. D. (1998). The development of competence in favorable and unfavorable environments: Lessons from research on successful children. *American Psychologist, 53,* 205–220. doi:10.1037/0003-066X.53.2.205

Masten, A. S., Hubbard, J. J., Gest, S. D., Tellegen, A., Garmezy, N., & Ramirez, M. (1999). Competence in the context of adversity: Pathways to resilience and maladaptation from childhood to late adolescence. *Development and Psychopathology, 11,* 143–169. doi:10.1017/S0954579499001996

McDonald, R., Jouriles, E. N., & Skopp, N. A. (2006). Reducing conduct problems among children brought to women's shelters: Intervention effects 24 months following termination of services. *Journal of Family Psychology, 20,* 127–136. doi:10.1037/0893-3200.20.1.127

Pynoos, R. S., Steinberg, A. M., & Aronson, L. (1997). Traumatic experiences: The early organization of memory in school-age children and adolescents. In P. S. Applebaum, L. A. Uyehara, & M. R. Elin (Eds.), *Trauma and memory: Clinical and legal controversies* (pp. 272–289). New York, NY: Oxford University Press.

Riggs, D. S., & O'Leary, K. D. (1989). A theoretical model of courtship aggression. In M. A. Pirog-Good & J. E. Stets (Eds.), *Violence in dating relationships: Emerging social issues* (pp. 53–71). New York, NY: Praeger.

Saltzman, K. M., Holden, G. W., & Holahan, C. J. (2005). The psychobiology of children exposed to marital violence. *Journal of Clinical Child and Adolescent Psychology, 34,* 129–139. doi:10.1207/s15374424jccp3401_12

Skopp, N. A., McDonald, R., Jouriles, E. N., & Rosenfield, D. (2007). Partner aggression and children's externalizing problems: Maternal and partner warmth as protective factors. *Journal of Family Psychology, 21,* 459–467. doi:10.1037/ 0893-3200.21.3.459

Sternberg, K. J., Baradaran, L. P., Abbott, C. B., Lamb, M. E., & Guterman, E. (2006). Type of violence, age, and gender differences in the effects of family violence on children's behavior problems: A mega-analysis. *Developmental Review, 26,* 89–112. doi:10.1016/j.dr.2005.12.001

Straus, M. A. (1979). Measuring intrafamily conflict and violence: The Conflict Tactics (CT) Scales. *Journal of Marriage and the Family, 41,* 75–88. doi:10.2307/ 351733

Straus, M. A., Hamby, S. L., Boney-McCoy, S., & Sugarman, D. B. (1996). The revised conflict tactics scale (CTS2): Development and preliminary psychometric data. *Journal of Family Issues, 17,* 283–316. doi:10.1177/019251396017003001

Sullivan, C. M., Juras, J., Bybee, D., Nguyen, H., & Allen, N. (2000). How children's adjustment is affected by their relationships to their mothers' abusers. *Journal of Interpersonal Violence, 15*, 587–602. doi:10.1177/088626000015006003

Vygotsky, L. S. (1978). *Mind in society: The development of higher psychological processes* (M. Cole, V. John-Steiner, S. Scribner, & E. Souberman, Eds. & Trans.). Cambridge, MA: Harvard University Press.

Ware, H. S., Jouriles, E. N., Spiller, L. C., McDonald, R., Swank, P. R., & Norwood, W. D. (2001). Conduct problems among children at battered women's shelters: Prevalence and stability of maternal reports. *Journal of Family Violence, 16*, 291–307. doi:10.1023/A:1011190316783

Wolfe, D. A., Crooks, C. V., Lee, V., McIntyre-Smith, A., & Jaffe, P. G. (2003). The effects of children's exposure to domestic violence: A meta-analysis and critique. *Clinical Child and Family Psychology Review, 6*, 171–187. doi:10.1023/A:1024910416164

9

EVIDENCE-BASED PRACTICES FOR SCHOOL-AGE CHILDREN EXPOSED TO INTIMATE PARTNER VIOLENCE AND EVALUATION OF THE KIDS' CLUB PROGRAM

SANDRA A. GRAHAM-BERMANN

All women and children exposed to family violence are considered to be in need of intervention and support services, just as much to prevent additional problems from developing as to treat those in evidence at the time of assessment (Graham-Bermann & Hughes, 2003). While most shelters have some services for the women that they serve, few shelters and communities offer services to school-age children who have been exposed to intimate partner violence (IPV). Given the vast numbers of children exposed to IPV each year, it is not surprising that the majority receive no assistance in their efforts to cope with the violence. Unfortunately, many communities, agencies, and shelters that offer services have no way of knowing whether their services are helpful, ineffective, or even harmful. Further, most settings do not have the staff or expertise available to evaluate programs fully, and few use programs proven to be effective for children of specific ages or children with particular problems. But this situation is changing. This chapter reviews existing programs and focuses on the evaluation of one particular program, the Kids' Club, designed to assist school-age children and their mothers following exposure to IPV (Graham-Bermann, 1992).

Although the research on the efficacy of intervention programs for school-age children is slight, it is evolving. Still, in many cases evaluation studies are inadequately or poorly done. To help children to heal following exposure to IPV, in addition to other traumatic events, it is essential that evidenced-based treatment services—those proven to be effective using rigorous methods with a specific population—be used (Weisz, Jensen-Doss, & Hawley, 2006; Weisz, Sandler, Durlak, & Anton, 2005). Those rigorous methods can be derived in part from the Consort Standards (available at http://www.consort-statement.org/consort-statement) developed for use in medical clinical trials and in part from standards set for research that takes place in community settings (Wandersman, Kloos, Linney, & Shinn, 2005). The Consort Standards recommend using valid samples, having a large enough sample to adequately assess effects, having at least one group for purposes of comparison to the treatment group, using random or systematic assignment to groups, using manualized programs with some way of accounting for fidelity, relying on multiple standardized measures to assess outcomes, reporting attrition, and the independence of those who provide the intervention from those who assess it. Still, research that takes place in community settings is often more complex, with multiple stakeholders, frequently changing personnel, and agency policies that sometimes require adaptations that are both practical and ethical to provide and to evaluate services (Sarason, 2003). This chapter describes each of the standards and the issues that are raised when trying to apply Consort Standards to community interventions, and then it illustrates these in terms of the evaluation that was done for the Kids' Club intervention program.

DESIGNING AND SELECTING THE INTERVENTION PROGRAM FOR EVALUATION

How Valid Is the Sample?

Many intervention programs for school-age children take a one-size-fits-all approach. That is, these programs serve all of the children needing services in a given setting, regardless of the degree of IPV exposure or the presence or lack of specific symptoms. Some programs include children from a broad range of ages and use a group format, whereas others serve children individually and may or may not include the parent, usually the mother, in the intervention. However, most programs rely on treating mothers and their school-age children separately in the small group format.

The earliest programs were developed for use by children residing in shelters for abused women in Fayetteville, Arkansas (Hughes, 1982); London, Ontario, Canada (Jaffe, Wolfe, & Wilson, 1990); and Minneapolis, Minnesota (Peled & Davis, 1995; Peled & Edleson, 1992). These group intervention programs employed a 10-week psychoeducational format that offered (but did not require) intervention services for the mothers as well. Hughes (1982) was the first to develop a child-plus-mother program for children in shelters for abused women. She assessed the shelter-based program and found that compared with scores at the start of the program, children had lower anxiety following intervention (Hughes & Barard, 1983). Only a few of their mothers attended a support group that was also provided. Peled and Davis (1995) designed a program to assist children in telling their story, in reducing self-blame for the violence and enhancing their coping. Group activities helped children to create safety plans, and to gain knowledge about family violence. When Wagar and Rodway (1995) evaluated this program they found that it reduced children's anger and self-blame but did not improve their coping. The Jaffe and Wolfe program also relied on groups for children in crisis, living in shelters for battered women, and successfully assessed change in their attitudes toward violence (Jaffe, Wilson, & Wolfe, 1986; Wilson, Cameron, Jaffe, & Wolfe, 1989).

Still, only a small percentage of abused women and their children ever reside in shelters, thus calling into question the generalizability of results of intervention studies done with these shelter populations. These populations may not be replicable in the broader population of abused women and their children. Further, women and children in shelters can be considered a convenience sample, as they are easier to locate than abused women in the community and may be more available to participate in studies. Attrition may be lower, as the lack of transportation is a common barrier to participation for poor families in community settings. While more challenging in some ways, evaluating interventions provided for children in the larger community can produce results that are applicable to a broader range of children. Still, community research is rife with challenges. While these evaluations may be more representative, it is often difficult to work with community agencies whose mission is not solely directed to abused women (e.g., mental health clinics). In addition, such community connections can take months to develop and may change as personnel change.

Who Is the Target of Intervention?

Helping the Mother to Help the Child

A number of programs are aimed primarily at supporting the abused woman to help her school-age child. For example, Ducharme, Atkinson, and Poulton's (2000) program focused only on work with individual mothers who were given "errorless compliance training" to help her oppositional child to respond better and to cooperate more. The specific aim was to reduce oppositional behavior in the child. It was theorized that abused women may rely on harsh and ineffective discipline strategies and are in need of training in this area. Change for the individual mother was measured over time, and the program was found to be effective.

Other programs work simultaneously with the mother and the child. One program includes groups of mothers and their children in the same group with a therapist (Rabenstein & Lehmann, 2000). A different stance was taken by Sullivan (Sullivan & Bybee, 1999), who also created a community-based program for mothers and children that takes place in the home. Services include support and advocacy for the mother and practical help with the children, such as babysitting and doing homework with the child, in order to reduce the stress of parenting children exposed to IPV. This is a strengths-building, rather than a psychopathology-treating, approach to assisting women exposed to IPV. The program is designed to provide extensive support in terms of both time and scope. There is an advocate who assists the mother for 16 weeks and provides assistance in helping to finding a job, arranging adequate transportation, obtaining information about educational opportunities, and assisting in interaction with the school system. The program was evaluated and found to be effective in supporting mothers and in reducing harsh parenting for the child (Sullivan, Nguyen, Allen, Bybee, & Juran, 2000). The program evaluation study reported a low rate of attrition, suggesting that when women receive instrumental help they are more likely to remain in treatment.

Children in Groups

The most common strategy for working with school-age children of abused mothers is the small group format. Here the child participates in the intervention in a small group with similar-age children. These groups can be either ongoing or with the same children meeting over a set period of time. The group format is especially conducive to helping children normalize their experiences and feel validated, in part through the relationships they establish with other children their age in the group. For school-age children, intervention that takes neurological development into account when helping children heal from traumatic experiences may include interactive activities (Perry, 2005). Children's groups can also reduce the child's sense of physical and emotional vulnerability, a common reaction to witnessing IPV. Finally, the small group therapy format is more affordable than individual therapy sessions, as well as developmentally and culturally appropriate.

Is There an Adequate Sample Size to Show Effects?

When evaluating whether a particular program is effective, power analyses should be calculated that indicate the sample size needed to produce findings within a specific range of effect sizes. The strength of the findings in efficacy studies is dependent on a number of design variables, including adequate sample size. Results of early studies were reported with as few as 12 and 13 participants (Hughes & Barard, 1983), while other early outcome evaluations used samples as large as 30 or 40 (Hughes, 1982; Peled & Edleson, 1995). Still, studies with 40 or fewer children are simply insufficient to the task of finding adequate effects or testing models that include a number of risk and protective factors that could contribute to outcomes. However, other intervention studies with large sample sizes often take years to complete and require significant funding. This severely limits the number of studies that are done and the extent of their follow-up.

Use of Independent Comparison Groups

To determine whether change was the result of intervention or simply the passage of time, it is essential that independent groups of similar children and their parents be used for purposes of comparison. A number of studies, some based on the Kids' Club Program, either did not use comparison groups or used the dropout families for purposes of comparison (Basu, Malone, Levendosky, & Dubay, 2009; Becker, Mathis, Mueller, Issari, & Atta, 2008; Carter, Kay, George, & King, 2003; Johnson, 2003; Ragg, Sultana, & Miller, 1998). Without a comparison group, it is unclear whether results are due to the intervention program, to time, or to some other unspecified variable. The use of those who have received partial services for purposes of comparison—for example, those who dropped out of the program—is also problematic because they are not an entirely independent group (Graham-Bermann, 2000). Such evaluation designs would clearly disqualify studies in medical clinical trials because they would seriously limit confidence in the results.

Still, it is difficult to conduct a rigorous clinical study that asks people at high risk and in need of services to become part of a wait-list treatment as usual (often this means no services) or a comparison group. In some instances the wait-list is a natural phenomenon, such that some agencies often cannot offer services to all who need them at the same time or only offer services on a set schedule. At other times, in clinical trials, families are assigned to an experimental (treatment) or control (no treatment) group. While this would be the most rigorous process in designing the evaluation study, some community agencies may find such a random assignment procedure to be unacceptable or untenable. The ethical issue related to delaying services to conduct a rigorous clinical trial is the appropriateness of weighing the balance between risk to individuals against the ultimate contribution to the larger group of women and children exposed to IPV. Once the researcher is convinced of the value of delaying treatment that has to be explained next to the community advocates and service providers who may not share this view.

Use of Treatment Manuals

A treatment manual guides the implementation of the intervention program. Manuals, such as that developed for the Kids' Club Program (Graham-Bermann, 1992), include protocols and instructions for each session, activities and educational materials designed for specific purposes, and possibly examples of treatment sessions and process notes. Programs that have an underlying theory of effects and theory of change and those that have clearly spelled out directions and expectations for each session—in other words, those with a clear blueprint—will be more consistently applied, thus increasing the chances that the same effects and results will be found when used by others. Once programs have been found to have efficacy (positive results in the controlled clinical trial), they can be used in other settings, often with an additional effectiveness study to test whether the program works in the same way when not conducted by the original author.

Treatment Fidelity

Treatment fidelity is the extent to which an intervention is implemented as planned and is at the core of evidence-based practice (Fraser, Richman, Galinsky, & Day, 2009). The treatment manual helps to assure that the program will be uniformly applied. Initial training in implementing the program, ongoing supervision of service providers, and checking process notes against the manual are ways of enhancing treatment fidelity. Unfortunately, many early programs (and most programs today) did not use manualized procedures and did not rigorously evaluate either program process or individual outcomes. The gold standard for assessing treatment fidelity is to videotape each session and have the supervisor able to determine whether the program was implemented exactly as described. However, especially in community settings, these fidelity procedures are not only potentially highly intrusive, they are also often close to impossible to implement.

The next section describes the challenges, rewards, and ethical issues pertaining to evaluating one community-based program. The dilemmas and eventual decisions are described that were made along the way when trying to adopt the highest standards of evaluation to provide evidence for the practices of the Kids' Club Program.

THE PROCESS OF EVALUATING THE KIDS' CLUB PROGRAM

The Kids' Club Program was developed and manualized in 1992 and evaluated in 1994 with a grant from the Centers for Disease Control and Prevention. The program was initially begun at the SafeHouse Center in Ann

Arbor, MI, a setting that serves women and their children who either reside in their shelter or who live in the surrounding communities and participate in educational and therapeutic serves at the center. Since then, the program has been adopted for use by agencies in 26 states and adapted for use in other countries, specifically, Canada, Australia, Sweden, Mexico, and Israel.

Program Background

The Kids' Club Program has run continuously at SafeHouse Center in Ann Arbor, Michigan, for 19 years and at Catholic Social Services and the Aware Shelter, in Jackson, Michigan, for 10 years, for both sheltered and non-sheltered families. The program is also being conducted in Windsor, Canada, at the Children's Aid Society. The program was recognized by the governor of the State of Michigan and the Department of Social Services with two awards for "Prevention of Domestic Violence" in 1993 and 1994. The program was also identified as one of three "exemplary" programs for children exposed to IPV by experts at a nationally convened workshop sponsored by the U.S. Department of Health and Human Services, National Institute of Child Health and Human Development, and the National Institutes of Health (National Advisory Mental Health Council Workgroup on Child and Adolescent Mental Health Intervention and Deployment 2001). Similarly, a group sponsored by the National Crime Prevention Center of the Department of Justice in Ottawa, Canada, included this program as a model of "best evidence for children exposed to family violence" (Cunningham & Baker, 2004). The program was featured on PBS's *Bill Moyers' Journal* (Moyers, 1995) in a documentary titled *Violence in the Family, School and Community*. A preschool version of the program was created and manualized with support from the Better Homes Fund's National Center on Family Homelessness in 2001 and is currently being evaluated with support from the Blue Cross and Blue Shield of Michigan Foundation.

Program Design: The Small Group Format

The group format was specifically chosen for the Kids' Club Program (Graham-Bermann, 1992) to take advantage of the process of relationships that occur for each child across the 10-week sessions. Relationships are formed with both the group leaders and others in the group, and both types of relationships are thought to be helpful, especially for children undergoing this type of trauma. In addition to providing information to the children about how to deal with IPV in their families, the group leaders have the role of providing support and empowerment to the children. At the time of joining a support group for women with IPV, many of the mothers are in the process of separating from their abusive partners. This is a time of substantial worry and concern for all members of the family. The group leaders serve to value each child and to clarify that children are not responsible for the violence between the adults around them. Further, children feel more empowered about their reactions to the violence—both in how to appropriately express their own feelings and in identifying ambivalent feelings toward their parents as reasonable and common responses to this violence. Relationships with peers in the group are equally important in that there is a special quality of relief and comfort in being with other children who share the "secret" of IPV in their own families. This atmosphere allows children to feel less stigmatized and less alone in their distress, to exchange information and impressions, and to validate their feelings of outrage and sadness. Groups are age-graded (6–8 years, 9–12 years) and gender mixed. Each intervention group consists of five to seven children and two group leaders of ethnicity similar to the children in the group, when possible.

Theory and Goals of the Kids' Club Program Treatment Manual and Sessions

Theoretical Bases and Aims of the Program

The Kids' Club Program (Graham-Bermann, 1992) is based on a number of theories that account for the diverse types of problems in adjustment expressed by children exposed to IPV. The theories are defined here, and their implementation is illustrated in the section on session goals. Social learning theory (Bandura, 1986; Patterson, 1982) can be used to explain why some children have heightened levels of aggression in interpersonal interaction, for example, children learn aggressive responses to conflict situations that are reinforced through modeling or directly through parenting, and they subsequently develop internal paradigms over time that lead them to respond in particular ways. The Kids' Club Program aims to teach children a broader range of conflict resolution skills along with the understanding that physical aggression is not an acceptable method of coping with conflict. Emotional security theory (Davies & Cummings, 1994) and cognitive-contextual theory (Grych & Fincham, 1993) are useful in explaining the ways in which the development of emotion regulation can be disrupted following violence exposure. When children are unable to regulate their emotions, they feel less secure and their coping is reduced. Further, what a child thinks following a violent episode can be damaging to adjustment and self-esteem—for example, a child may interpret that he or she is at fault or blamed for the violence in the family.

Trauma theory can also be used to account for symptoms and behaviors expressed by children in IPV families (Graham-Bermann & Levendosky, 1998). Exposure to traumatic events can leave children with a sense of numbing or avoidance of emotions, as well as with physical reactions, such as increased heart rate, irritability, and hypervigilance. Many of these symptoms are related to emotion regulation, which are both psychological and physical processes that allow children to manage and modulate emotional experiences, their expression, and their responses (Gross, 2001). Problems in emotion regulation have been associated with the development of posttraumatic stress disorder (PTSD) in both adults and children (Frewen & Lanius, 2006; Kring & Werner, 2004) and with problems in social relationships with peers (Shields, Ryan, & Cicchetti, 2001). For example, Tull, Jakupcak, McFadden, and Roemer (2007) linked intense negative affect and fear of emotions to PTSD symptoms in children exposed to IPV. An emerging body of research on facial recognition also indicates that children exposed to family violence have heightened awareness of angry and hostile emotions (Masten et al., 2008; Swartz, Monk, Castor, & Graham-Bermann, 2009). While most children experience traumatic events and show elevated levels of trauma symptoms, it should be noted that the majority of children exposed to IPV typically do not have a diagnosis of PTSD (Graham-Bermann et al., 2008). Interventions based on trauma theory would emphasize the need to tell the story and to break through the silence imposed on children by either isolation or direct threats not to tell or talk about abuse to the mother.

The Kids' Club Program aims to help children understand that the violence between their parents is not their fault. It also aims to help children identify a range of feelings about violence and to express them to be able to talk about the violence and improve their coping ability. Specific coping skills are also taught to reduce the negative effects of exposure to IPV (e.g., safety planning) and to promote healing. The psychoeducational component of the program provides factual and practical information concerning IPV and how most children react to it. Thus, this program addresses the cognitive, social, and emotional needs of children exposed to violence.

Session Goals

The program is phase-based, such that early sessions are designed to enhance the child's sense of safety, to develop the therapeutic alliance, and to create a common vocabulary of emotions for making sense of violence experiences. Later sessions address the traumatic aspects of the violence and responsibility for it, managing conflict and its resolution, and reframing traumagenic family and gender paradigms, thereby reducing the self-blame and shame that often accompany violence exposure. The following examples of program sessions and the research that supports their goals are used to illustrate how the program works.

Creating a Sense of Safety and Ownership. Several of the program's features are specifically designed to promote the child's sense of safety and to give the child a sense of control when joining and helping to create the group during the first session. That is, the intervention program seeks to provide a supportive arena for a group of children to share their experiences, to learn that they are not alone in their trauma, and to feel comfortable right from the beginning. Specific goals of the first session are to introduce the group leaders (therapists) to group members and group members to one another. This is accomplished through a number of introductory games and activities. Leaders mention that everyone is present because there has been fighting in the family, although this topic is not discussed at this time because the therapeutic relationships have not yet been developed. Rather, activities that aim to give the child comfort and a sense of ownership of the group are begun. Specific activities tailored to the ages and gender of the group members are arranged by the individual group leaders and discussed and approved during clinical supervision that takes place before each group. Activities typically include creating a group poster, participants introducing themselves, setting up rules for the group, and perhaps even voting on and giving the group a name. For example, in one group, children introduced themselves to one another by showing, through drawing pictures or cutting pictures from magazines, some of the things and activities they like, as well as depicting negative images, those which are unlike them or things that they do not like.

The groups allow for discussion of the specifics of violence in the family only after relationships between the group leaders and other participants are well established. Recent research has supported the notion that spontaneous disclosure (e.g., disclosure that is not initiated by the therapist) is related to improvements in anxiety and/or depression and changes in attitudes for children exposed to IPV (Graham-Bermann, Kulkarni, & Kanukollu, in press). Most activities address family violence through displacement, that is, by using stories, films, drawings, puppets, and so on. This method is comfortable for most children because it allows them to react openly to the issues without the pressure to discuss their particular family. Unlike other therapeutic modalities, such as cognitive behavior therapy, at no time is a child specifically asked to report what happened in his or her family, although most children do so spontaneously at some point in the program.

Identifying and Expressing Emotions. There are sessions devoted to identifying and naming feelings, and then specifically, to discussing feelings associated with violence in the family to enhance emotion regulation. The goals are for children to develop a vocabulary of emotions, to identify their feelings about the violence in their family, and to express these feelings in an appropriate manner. Most children exposed to IPV have conflicting emotions about the adults in their lives, and many have learned about the extreme expression or suppression of emotions that can leave them with difficulty in managing their own feelings (Maughan & Cicchetti, 2002). They may have a parent who becomes enraged and/or a parent who avoids expressing feelings. Nevertheless, the family is the main context for the development of emotion regulation (Morris, Silk, Steinberg, Myers, & Robinson, 2007). Children in families exposed to IPV often suppress their feelings during violent episodes because it may not be safe to express them. Thus, they may not have the opportunity to sort out and work through their feelings following these often-traumatic events at home.

Researchers have shown that cognitive reappraisal, or changing how one thinks about a situation, can alter the emotional impact of the event, whereas suppressing emotions does little to diminish the emotional experience and attendant physiological reactivity associated with highly emotional events (Gross, 2001). It has been theorized that identifying and working through feelings associated with the violence helps to reduce the effects of their often traumatic exposure to violence. The cathartic experience of expressing emotions is postulated to relieve the child of the burden, as well as to reconnect appropriate emotions to events, and to reduce the need for post-traumatic play (e.g., attempting to master an overwhelming experience through repetitive play or perseverative attempts at working through the problem). In the Kids' Club Program, a number of activities are designed to help children to identify a range of feelings, and then, in a subsequent session, to apply feelings to the issue of violence in the family using displacement. Activities designed to elicit feelings are having the group list as many different feelings as they can, then demonstrate feelings through a variety of methods. These can include making feelings posters, feelings masks, playing games, and showing feelings though songs, dances or skits. Children can then let group leaders know which feelings they associate with exposure to family violence. These exercises normalize the child's response to traumatic events while giving support for and voice to the appropriate expression of hard-to-grasp feeling states.

Guilt and Responsibility for Violence. Two of the most difficult emotions that are the hallmark for children exposed to IPV are guilt and shame. Children feel ashamed and isolated in their knowledge that something terrible is happening in their family. They know that it is wrong, but they feel powerless to do anything about it. Children also tend to blame themselves for what is happening in their family, even though it is never their fault.

Several research studies have shown that children exposed to IPV may experience a heightened sense of guilt and self-blame, as well as a sense of vulnerability and hopelessness following the violence (Grych & Fincham, 1993; Jaffe, Poisson, & Cunningham, 2001). Children develop a sense of right and wrong from their parents, as well as an idea of what is expected of them by other people in the world. They incorporate a system of justice and conscience. Children raised in families with IPV may have witnessed extreme forms of violence and punishment to their mothers and to themselves. As a result, they are often overly harsh and self-critical, leading to lower self-esteem and lower self-competence when compared with nonexposed peers, as a number of researchers have documented (Graham-Bermann, Gruber, Girz, & Howell, 2009).

The activities of the Kids' Club Program are designed to provide a normative and empathic response by the group leaders concerning violence exposure that may differ from what the child has experienced in the past, for example, being blamed or feeling shamed. By having an avenue for discussing IPV and related feelings, children are given the chance to make sense of what has happened without the overlay of self-blame. The program provides ways for children to understand that the violence between their parents was not the fault of the children, while establishing a clear sense of who is responsible for the violence. Myths about family violence are explored, for example, children need to learn that individuals are responsible for their own behavior and that their mother's safety is a community concern, not a young child's responsibility.

Activities designed to establish who is responsible for violence include showing videotaped vignettes about conflict and asking the group to describe what happened, why, what led up to it, who did what and why, and who was to blame. Other vignettes start out with simple problem-solving situations, such as mild conflict between friends, and move toward the issues of family violence. The vignettes are culled from existing movies, cartoons, or can be made to order with scenes enacted by volunteer students. The discussion of family violence is often a highly emotional one for children. Thus, to reduce stress and to finish the session on a more positive note, a final comical situation might be chosen and presented for discussion.

Naming Fears and Worries. Fear and anxiety are hypothesized to occur when the child is newly unable to accurately and effectively appraise and respond to events, feels unprotected, and feels highly vulnerable and endangered (Terr, 1983). Children exposed to family violence feel exposed to both the reminders of the assaults or worried about and anticipate renewed fighting between their parents (Graham-Bermann, 1996; Graham-Bermann & Levendosky, 1998).

In response to hearing their concerns while working with children exposed to IPV for many years, a study was created to compare the fears and worries about family members for children exposed to IPV with those in a matched sample of similar children not exposed to IPV (Graham-Bermann, 1996). In order to do this, a new measure of Family Fears and Worries was created. Results showed that children raised in families with IPV were significantly more afraid and worried about family members in two broad areas: vulnerability and violence. They were more worried about the vulnerability of their mothers and siblings than were children in nonviolent families. That is, they carried concern that physical violence would happen to their mother and/or that she would become incapacitated in various ways. In addition, children raised in violent families were more afraid and worried about their father perpetrating violence, getting arrested, or behaving inappropriately than were children in nonviolent families. Both fears and worries associated with vulnerability and those associated with violence perpetration were associated with the child's increased anxiety, depression, and aggression. Other researchers have now made the link between problems in emotion regulation and chronic worry and anxiety disorders (Salters-Pedneault, Roemer, Tull, Rucker, & Mennin, 2006; Tull et al., 2007). Here children may avoid intense negative emotions, such as those associated with IPV, which leaves them feeling threatened and with heightened concern that violence may continue.

Although it is particularly difficult for children to talk about things of which they are frightened, several sessions of the Kids' Club Program are devoted to fears and worries. By creating a format for children to express their fears and worries—first about general fears and concerns that children typically have—we set the stage for the discussion of fears and worries that children have in families when there is IPV. The goal is to normalize children's fears and worries in general and then to legitimize their fears and worries when exposed to IPV. In doing so we help children to feel empowered by letting them see that they are not alone and that they can identify fears, create safety plans, and hopefully reduce their fears and worries.

Additional Session Topics and Goals. Children raised in families with violence also may have learned deleterious paradigms for conflict resolution (Graham-Bermann & Brescoll, 2000). The Kids' Club Program attempts to provide children with a broader range of conflict resolution skills along with the understanding that physical aggression is not an acceptable method of coping with conflict. Additional goals are to discuss conflict and its resolution, and to learn new strategies for problem solving. Gender stereotypes are discussed through activities designed to elicit children's impressions of the roles of men and women in the family and to imagine the possibilities for themselves as men and women in the future. One session is devoted to family strengths. The activities of previous sessions are reviewed at the start of subsequent sessions, and the program concludes with a discussion of termination as well as a brief ceremony that honors the children with their mothers.

Theory and Goals of the Moms' Parenting Empowerment Program

Parenting effectiveness is a recently identified protective factor for behavioral adjustment problems in children exposed to IPV. In general, decrements in parenting and poor handling of parenting stress have been associated with greater internalizing problems and depression in children. For example, Katz and Low (2004) found that while positive parenting did not buffer children from the effects of violence, hostile and/or aggressive coparenting may increase the risk of depression in violence-exposed children. Similarly, Morrel, Dubowitz, Kerr, and Black (2003) found that verbally aggressive parenting mediated the relationship between maternal victimization and children's internalizing symptoms. Conversely, the ability to parent well in the face of stressful family circumstances has been identified as both a mediator and a moderator of outcomes for children exposed to domestic abuse. Boney-McCoy and Finkelhor (1995) reported that strong parent–child relationships mitigated the effects of victimization on children but did not eliminate them. Levendosky and Graham-Bermann (2001) found that greater parenting effectiveness reduced the negative effects of violence on children's internalizing and externalizing behavior problems. In contrast, McCloskey, Figueredo, and Koss (1995) did not find that familial warmth buffered the effects of IPV on children's mental health.

The results of these studies suggest that effective parenting, even in the face of deleterious family circumstances, may serve to reduce the negative effects of violence exposure on children's adjustment problems and depression. Parenting that is aggressive and hostile, however, may increase the allostatic stress load for children in ways that detrimentally affect them. Rice, Harold, Shelton, and Thapar (2006) concluded that "intervention programs that incorporate one or more family systems may be of benefit in alleviating the adverse effect of negative family factors on children" (p. 841).

The Moms' Parenting Empowerment Program (MPEP; Graham-Bermann & Levendosky, 1994) runs concurrent with the Kids' Club Program and was designed to empower mothers to discuss the impact of the violence on various areas of their children's development, to support parenting competence, to provide a safe place to discuss parenting fears and worries, and to build connections and support for the mother in the context of a supportive group. Given the traumatic experiences of abused women, the early sessions of the program are designed to build the therapeutic alliance, as well as a sense of trust and safety within the group—factors necessary to set the stage for healing. This usually means that mothers share their experiences about what happened to them with others in the group. More often than not, mothers note how similar their experiences of abuse have been. The group also provides a place for mothers to discuss their worries and concerns about their children following violence exposure, and to consider ways of talking with their children about the violence that has occurred and answering children's trauma-related questions in a supportive way. To address children's externalizing behavior problems, sessions are devoted to empowering and supporting parenting practices. Mothers create a parenting plan that focuses on problem areas and report back to the group each week. Mothers share their suggestions on parenting practices, and group leaders give positive reinforcement as well as reading material, when appropriate.

Parents in the MPEP receive information about the ongoing support group for children when interviewed for their participation in a women's group. Written permission is obtained just before the first meeting. A brief meeting with the parents is held before the start of the first children's support group session. The intent is to give the mothers more information about the groups and an opportunity to ask questions. Here parents are told that some children may ask questions the parents may not have encountered before as a result of their participation in the group. The parents are given a handout of this information at this time. A final, brief meeting with parents is also held after the last group session, with the intent of providing some feedback and entertaining the parents' questions, comments, and ideas. To ensure privacy for those involved, parents are told that they will be informed of the group's activities but not of individual responses by particular group members. Feedback to group leaders from these and similar children's groups indicates that most children and their families find the support group to be a highly positive, beneficial experience. Both group leaders are also available to talk with parents about issues raised in conjunction with the children's support group, if needed.

As with the children's program, the group leaders for the mothers' program are similar in ethnicity to the majority of mothers in a group. The MPEP has been developed over the years to include ethnically appropriate resources and materials (e.g., resources on social and community support, spirituality, and child management), as well as culturally appropriate measures for assessing progress in treatment (e.g., the African-American Women's Stress Scale; Watts-Jones, 1990). We believe that it is the relationships that the women develop with the group leader and with one another that promote healing and change, and provide support and relief. The process of this change is ongoing. There is no set of goals for every woman to accomplish in each group. Instead, we seek to support each woman wherever her point of entry into the change process.

EVALUATING THE KIDS' CLUB INTERVENTION PROGRAM

Choosing the Efficacy Trial Evaluation Design and Outcome Measures

The Kids' Club Program was evaluated with a semirandomized control design (Graham-Bermann, 2000; Graham-Bermann, Lynch, Banyard, DeVoe, & Halabu, 2007). Following institutional review board approval from the University of Michigan, flyers were posted in local venues such as laundromats, grocery stores, low income housing units, doctor's offices, emergency rooms, and social services offices in communities in southeast Michigan advertising the study and the support groups for woman and children. Specifically, the flyers stated that women who had physical conflict with an intimate partner within the past year and who had children between ages 6 and 12 were invited to call the program office for more information or to participate in the survey and support programs. A toll-free number was provided.

The evaluation compared three groups or conditions to which study participants were sequentially and randomly assigned. That is, the first seven children were assigned to the child only group, while the next seven children were assigned to the child-plus-mother intervention group, and the next seven children were assigned to the wait-list comparison group. This method was chosen to facilitate creating groups for services in community settings where children were recruited into the study. If the study had relied on a completely random assignment to group, it would have taken a much longer time to build enough children in a group to provide services in these community settings and attrition might have been higher.

There were approximately 60 children in each group—those in the child only (CO) condition participated in the Kids' Club Program, but their mothers did not receive services; those in the child + mother (C+M) condition had mothers who also received services and in the comparison, or delayed treatment, condition neither the mother nor the child received services for 10 weeks. To compare results for three groups a power analysis was used to determined that approximately 60 children in each group was needed to find a moderate effect (Graham-Bermann et al., 2007). It took 4 years to locate, treat, and evaluate the 221 families that were part of this evaluation.

In this study all mothers and children in the comparison group were offered the opportunity to participate in the intervention after 10 weeks. Few agreed to do so. While this policy constricted the information that was available for the third wave of data collection, where it was only possible to compare those in the CO to the C+M groups, providing services to the comparison families was deemed to be ethically appropriate in this study.

Managing Attrition

Strikingly, attrition was low for those in either intervention group—only 5.7% dropped out from posttreatment to follow-up. The comparison group was oversampled, as we discovered that people who did not receive services were more likely to drop out of the evaluation study. It was important to consider whether the 40 families who dropped out of the study were unique in some way. When tested, no significant differences were found in terms of child age, gender, ethnicity, mother's age, income, education, marital status, or the amount of violence to which the child had been exposed, for those who did and did not receive services.

Outcome Measures

The expected child-related outcomes were change in behavioral problems and improved attitudes and beliefs about the acceptability of violence in the family. The outcomes were measured with the Child Behavior Checklist (Achenbach, 1991a), completed by the child's mother; the Teacher Report Form (Achenbach, 1991b), completed by the child's teacher; and the Attitudes About Family Violence Scale, completed by the child (Graham-Bermann, 1994a). Exposure to IPV was measured with the Straus (1979) Conflict Tactics Scale, the Severity of Violence Against Women Scale (SVAWS; Marshall, 1992), and the Family of Origin Violence scale (FOOV; Graham-Bermann, 1994b).

Data were collected at three time intervals. All of the children, all of the mothers, and all of the children's teachers were interviewed before the intervention began. Ten weeks following the initiation of the intervention, all children and all mothers were interviewed for a second time. A third interview for mothers, children, and the children's teacher was conducted approximately 6 months following the 110-week intervention program for those in the two treatment groups. Mothers were paid $20 for each interview, and children received a gift worth approximately $5. It is important to note that those who provided the intervention program were not the same people as those who interviewed the mothers and the children before and after the program. Evaluators should be blind to the assignment of participants to groups in order to have a truly independent evaluation. In other words, the clinicians and therapists should not be the ones doing the assessments.

Participant Characteristics

Children ranged in age from 6 to 13 ($M = 8.49$, $SD = 2.16$) with gender evenly split. They were from diverse ethnic groups: 52% were Caucasian, 34% African American, 9.5% biracial, 1.4% Latino/a, 1.8% Native American, and 1.3% other minority. Their mothers were age 33, on average ($SD = 5.29$), and reported their race/ethnicity as Caucasian (57%), African American (34%), biracial (1%), Latina (3.2%), Native American (2.3%), and 2.5% other minority.

More than half of the mothers were working at least part time outside of the home (52%). The average number of hours worked each week was 16.89 ($SD = 18.76$). Monthly income varied considerably, with the average income being $1,366 ($SD = $1,315$). Many of the mothers were single and separated, but about 20% were married, and most had been married at some point in their lives.

Exposure to Violence

Mothers in this study had a mean of 1.7 violent partners in their lifetime ($SD = 1.23$, range $= 0–10$). At the time of the study 18% were living with a violent partner, but 69% still had contact with their violent partner. Contact with the violent partner ranged considerably, from none to every day ($M = 158$ days per year, $SD = 141$ days). Violence was a regular part of the lives of the children in this study, as the length of the mother's relationship with the most recent violent partner was reported as 125 months or approximately 10.41 years. Family of origin violence was reported by 64% of the women. Approximately one third (31%) stated that their mother had been subjected to mild physical violence and severe physical violence (30%). Of mothers, 24% had been physically abused and 14% sexually abused as a child.

Statistics on exposure to various types of violence tactics reported by the mother as having happened to her by a partner in the past year are shown in Table 9.1. The most frequent type of maltreatment in her relationship was control tactics, followed by physical threats and sexual assaults. When violence did occur, severe violence took place approximately once per month. Children were eyewitness to 73% of severe violence events in the home in the past year. Most of the mothers (69%) and some of the children (12.3%) in the study had been injured by the violent partner in the past year (69%), whereas few of the partners received injuries (0.5%). Questions concerning the nature of the mother's injuries revealed that one third were mild, one third moderate, and one third severe with permanent damage.

TABLE 9.1
Range and Frequency of Domestic Violence Tactics
(Conflict Tactics Scale and Psychological Maltreatment Scales)
per Year Used Against the Woman and Relationship Characteristics

Measure	M	SD	Minimum	Maximum
M Control Tactics	95.46	79.01	.00	320.88
M Physical Threats	45.72	48.13	.00	221.09
M Sexual Coercion	37.38	59.72	.00	273.75
CTS Mild Physical Violence	18.89	30.86	.00	202.27
CTS Severe Physical Violence	11.13	19.08	1.00	94.06

Note. M = Marshall's Violence Against Women Scales (1992); CTS = Straus' Conflict Tactics Scale (1979).

Data Analysis and Results for the Total Sample

The three groups were compared using two-level hierarchical linear modeling to assess whether there were group differences over time in outcomes, comparing baseline scores to those 10 weeks later. Analyses revealed that in comparison to the wait-list group, the children's program significantly reduced child externalizing behavior symptoms and improved negative attitudes and beliefs about violence (Graham-Bermann, 2000; Graham-Bermann et al., 2007). Moreover, children whose mothers also participated in the parenting program showed the most positive effects, with reductions in both externalizing behavior problems and change in attitudes about violence. The effect size for short-term change in externalizing behavior problems for the child plus mother group was $d = 0.23$ and change in attitudes was $d = 0.41$. These results indicate small to medium short-term effects.

Longer term change was evaluated for two groups (CO and C+M) over time, controlling for baseline score, again using hierarchical linear modeling. The third assessment took place approximately 8 months following the end of treatment or the end of the second interview. Here the changes were much greater—the effect size for change in externalizing behavior problems for children in the C+M group was $d = 0.65$. Individual children in the C+M group also had significantly less deleterious attitudes toward violence over time ($d = 1.07$). These are large effects that indicate that treating the child as well as supporting and empowering the mother was the best way to reduce externalizing behavior problems for the child following exposure to IPV.

Data Analysis and Results for the Clinical Range Sample

While there were no significant results on change in internalizing behavior problems when comparing the three groups and using the whole sample, an analysis of those in the clinical range on internalizing behavior problems was undertaken. In this fashion there were 65% fewer children in the clinical range immediately following treatment when their mothers also participated in treatment, compared with 35% fewer with the child only treatment in contrast to the comparison group. At follow-up the figures were an additional 48% fewer in the clinical range on internalizing behavior problems comparing C+M with no treatment and 28% fewer than no treatment when only the child participated in treatment. Once again, treating the child and the mother appears to have the greatest effect.

Mediators and Moderators of Change

Because little is known about factors that may contribute to change for children who participated in the intervention, an analysis was undertaken to discern for which children the program was most effective (Graham-Bermann, Howell, Lilly, & DeVoe, in press). To assist in refining and further developing the program, both fixed and modifiable risk factors were identified and used to predict change in children's adjustment after the intervention. Stepwise regressions were used to show that there was a significant relationship between the extent of exposure to IPV, gender, change in mothers' mental health, and the outcome of change in child adjustment. Among fixed factors (e.g., child age, gender, ethnicity, years of violence exposure) it was the length of exposure to violence that moderated the relationship between the amount of the child's and mother's participation in the intervention and program efficacy—here, change in child internalizing behavioral problems. The second group of variables used as predictors were those modified by the intervention program. Among these modifiable risk factors, reduced symptoms of mothers' posttraumatic stress mediated the relationship between the amount of intervention participation and change in child adjustment.

Limitations

As in any evaluation, there are a number of limitations to this study. The first concerns the sample participants. This was a study of people who lived in five different communities in Michigan and so may not be representative of those exposed to IPV in other locales. Similarly, not all ethnicities were included in the sample, and those that were included may not have been statistically representative of the population of abused women as a whole. The findings may also differ if the programs are implemented with other cultural or language groups. The program included only children of a specific age range, thus limiting the utility of the results for children of different ages.

When recruiting women and children for a study such as this, the sample is limited by self-selection. That is, only those who may feel the need for help and only those who are willing to subject themselves to interviews and join a support group come forward. In this way, other abused women, particularly those who were not ready to get help for themselves or their children, were not included. While mothers and their children attended an average of seven of the 10 intervention sessions, there were absences and attrition for those who joined the intervention groups. As in other intervention evaluation studies, attrition for those who did not participate in the intervention was considerable.

CONCLUSIONS AND CHALLENGES

All children deserve a safe and supportive family environment in which to grow and develop. School-age children need stability, nurturing parents, and reasonable family rules. They also need the opportunity to make mistakes, and to learn from these, without being punished or held to unreasonable standards. Further, no child should be subjected to violence or have to witness the battering of his or her mother. When children suffer from the deleterious actions of family members they deserve support, understanding and the chance to make sense of these painful and difficult events in their lives. This is particularly true of children who witness IPV. School-age children of IPV are often cut off from peers since children in high conflict families may try to hide their experience of violence from others. Thus, these children may not only be highly anxious about when the next violent incident at home will occur, but they may also be afraid to let other children get to know too much about them, lest the terrible family secret be revealed. The Kids' Club and Moms' Parenting Empowerment Programs were designed to help children exposed to IPV. The results of the efficacy trial suggest that these programs do serve the needs of school-age children exposed to IPV and that the greatest effects are found when both the mother and the child participate in the intervention program. While the program was most effective in changing the behavior and attitudes of children in the clinical range, children with lower level problems were also assisted in their recovery and coping with the violence in their lives. This suggests a possible preventive function of programs for children exposed to IPV, such as the one described here. While most existing programs are targeted at children with diagnosable problems (e.g., conduct disorder, delinquency), it can be argued that all children exposed to violence are at risk of developing problems in the future and so might benefit from services. One of the strengths of the Kids' Club Program is its focus on families currently residing in the community rather than the exclusive selection of those in battered women's shelters. Of course, the challenge is in finding ways to implement such programs in other community settings, those that are not part of evaluation studies.

The work described in this chapter has begun to provide useful information on the role of intervention in reducing the effects of IPV on children and in the transmission of deleterious relationship paradigms. The results of this project have implications for theory and practice in the identification, evaluation, and treatment of children living with IPV with psychological problems. The evaluation showed that children's behaviors were changed and attitudes improved with this program that focused on the cognitive, social, and emotional needs of children exposed to IPV. The mothers' participation in the parenting program was associated with change in the child's externalizing problems, lending support to the social learning theory in that mothers learned to communicate better with their child, to use more appropriate and effective methods of discipline, and to be consistent (all goals of the MPEP), and children showed fewer problems in aggression. Trauma theory was also supported in that spontaneous disclosure by children was related to change in their internalizing behaviors and attitudes and beliefs (Graham-Bermann et al., in press). The need to have a secure place to talk about what happened and to express and reframe traumatic experiences was satisfied for mothers as well, and when mothers' posttraumatic stress was reduced there was greater change in their child's adjustment. When both children and mothers become more emotionally secure, it appears that they are better able to manage emotions and subsequently, their behavior, be that parenting or in social interaction with others. It remains to be seen whether programs that specifically target only trauma symptoms or only treat those with diagnosable trauma are more effective than interventions that offer services to all children exposed to IPV, regardless of their condition.

Overall, studies such as these are rarely undertaken due to the high cost of implementing and carrying out this research. Yet without significant further funding it is unlikely that we will be able to answer important research questions, such as for whom a particular program is most effective, how much treatment and what sort of intervention is required, whether effects last beyond the typically 1-year follow-up period, and how best to disseminate evaluated studies to communities that need them. While challenging, the efficacy trial described in this chapter adhered to a number of best practices, while amending others, as needed, to carry out the evaluation research in community settings. It is hoped that continued interest in the problem of children's exposure to IPV by national and state governmental agencies, as well as local communities, will stimulate the support necessary for undertaking these critical studies and that they will conform to the highest standards in the field.

REFERENCES

Achenbach, T. M. (1991a). *Manual for the Child Behavior Checklist: 4–18 and 1991 profile*. Burlington: University of Vermont, Department of Psychiatry.

Achenbach, T. M. (1991b). *Manual for the Teacher's Report Form and 1991 profile*. Burlington: University of Vermont, Department of Psychiatry.

Bandura, A. (1986). *Social foundations of thought and action: A social cognitive theory*. Englewood Cliffs, NJ: Prentice-Hall.

Basu, A., Malone, J., Levendosky, A., & Dubay, S. (2009). Longitudinal treatment effectiveness outcomes of a group Intervention for women and children exposed to domestic violence. *Journal of Child & Adolescent Trauma, 2*, 90–105. doi:10.1080/19361520902880715

Becker, K. D., Mathis, G., Mueller, C. W., Issari, K., & Atta, S. S. (2008). Community-based treatment outcomes for parents and children exposed to domestic violence. *Journal of Emotional Abuse, 8*, 187–204. doi:10.1080/10926790801986122

Boney-McCoy, S., & Finkelhor, D. (1995). Psychosocial sequelae of violent victimization in a national youth sample. *Journal of Consulting and Clinical Psychology, 63*, 726–736. doi:10.1037/0022-006X.63.5.726

Carter, L., Kay, S. J., George, J. L., & King, P. (2003). Treating children exposed to domestic violence. *Journal of Emotional Abuse, 3*, 183–202. doi:10.1300/J135v03n03_02

Cunningham, A., & Baker, L. (2004). *What about me! Seeking to understand the child's view of violence in the family*. London, Ontario, Canada: Centre for Children & Families in the Justice System.

Davies, P. T., & Cummings, E. M. (1998). Exploring children's emotional security as a mediator of the link between marital relations and child adjustment. *Child Development, 69*, 124–139.

Ducharme, J., Atkinson, L., & Poulton, L. (2000). Success-based, noncoercive treatment for oppositional behaviour in children from violent homes. *Journal of the American Academy of Child and Adolescent Psychiatry, 39*, 995–1004. doi:10.1097/00004583-200008000-00014

Fraser, M., Richman, J. M., Galinsky, M. J., & Day, S. H. (2009). *Intervention research: Developing social programs*. New York, NY: Oxford University Press.

Frewen, P. A., & Lanius, R. A. (2006). Toward a psychobiology of posttraumatic self-dysregulation: Reexperiencing, hyperarousal, dissociation, and emotional numbing. In R. Yehuda (Ed.), *Psychobiology of posttraumatic stress disorders: A decade of progress* (pp. 110–124). Malden, MA: Blackwell.

Graham-Bermann, S. A. (1992). *The Kids' Club: A preventive intervention program for children of battered women*. Ann Arbor: University of Michigan, Department of Psychology.

Graham-Bermann, S. A. (1994a). *Attitudes About Family Violence Scale*. Ann Arbor: University of Michigan, Department of Psychology.

Graham-Bermann, S. A. (1994b). *Family of Origin Violence Scale (FOOV)*. Ann Arbor: University of Michigan, Department of Psychology.

Graham-Bermann, S. A. (1996). Family worries: The assessment of interpersonal anxiety in children from violent and nonviolent families. *Journal of Clinical Child Psychology, 25*, 280–287. doi:10.1207/s15374424jccp2503_4

Graham-Bermann, S. A. (2000). Evaluating interventions for children exposed to family violence. *Journal of Aggression, Maltreatment & Trauma, 4*, 191–215. doi:10.1300/J146v04n01_09

Graham-Bermann, S. A., & Brescoll, V. (2000). Gender, power, and violence: Assessing the family stereotypes of the children of batterers. *Journal of Family Psychology, 14*, 600–612. doi:10.1037/0893-3200.14.4.600

Graham-Bermann, S. A., Gruber, G., Girz, L., & Howell, K. H. (2009). Factors discriminating among profiles of resilient coping and psychopathology in children exposed to domestic violence. *Child Abuse & Neglect, 33*, 648–660.

Graham-Bermann, S. A., Howell, K. H., Habarth, J., Krishnan, S., Loree, A., & Bermann, E. A. (2008). Toward assessing traumatic events and stress symptoms in preschool children from low-income families. *American Journal of Orthopsychiatry, 78*, 220–228. doi:10.1037/a0013977

Graham-Bermann, S. A., Howell, K. H., Lilly, M. M., & DeVoe, E. (in press). Mediators and moderators of change in adjustment following intervention for children exposed to intimate partner violence (IPV). *Journal of Interpersonal Violence*.

Graham-Bermann, S. A., & Hughes, H. M. (2003). Intervention for children exposed to interparental violence: Assessing needs and research priorities. *Clinical Child and Family Psychology Review, 6*, 189–204. doi:10.1023/A:1024962400234

Graham-Bermann, S. A., Kulkarni, M., & Kanukollu, S. (in press). Is disclosure therapeutic for children following exposure to traumatic violence? *Journal of Interpersonal Violence*.

Graham-Bermann, S. A., & Levendosky, A. A. (1994). *The Moms' Group: A parenting support and intervention program for battered women who are mothers*. Ann Arbor: University of Michigan, Department of Psychology.

Graham-Bermann, S. A., & Levendosky, A. A. (1998). Traumatic stress symptoms of children of battered women. *Journal of Interpersonal Violence, 13*(1), 111–128. doi:10.1177/088626098013001007

Graham-Bermann, S. A., Lynch, S., Banyard, V., DeVoe, E., & Halabu, H. (2007). Community based intervention for children exposed to intimate partner violence: An efficacy trial. *Journal of Consulting and Clinical Psychology, 75*, 199–209. doi:10.1037/0022-006X.75.2.199

Gross, J. J. (2001). Emotion regulation in adulthood: Timing is everything. *Current Directions in Psychological Science, 10*, 214–219. doi:10.1111/1467-8721.00152

Grych, J. H., & Fincham, F. (1993). Children's appraisals of marital conflict: Initial investigations of the cognitive-contextual framework. *Child Development, 64*, 215–230. doi:10.2307/1131447

Hughes, H. (1982). Brief interventions with children in a battered women's shelter: A model preventive program. *Family Relations, 31,* 495–502. doi:10.2307/583924

Hughes, H., & Barard, S. (1983). Psychological functioning of children in a battered women's shelter: A preliminary investigation. *American Journal of Orthopsychiatry, 53,* 525–531.

Jaffe, P. G., Poisson, S. E., & Cunningham, A. (2001). Domestic violence and high conflict divorce: Developing a new generation of research for children. In S. A. Graham-Bermann & J. L. Edleson (Eds.), *Domestic violence in the lives of children: The future of research, intervention, and social policy* (pp. 189–202). Washington, DC: American Psychological Association.

Jaffe, P. G., Wilson, S. K., & Wolfe, D. A. (1986). Promoting changes in attitudes and understanding of conflict resolution among child witnesses of family violence. *Canadian Journal of Behavioral Sciences, 18,* 356–366.

Jaffe, P. G., Wolfe, D. A., & Wilson, S. K. (1990). *Children of battered women.* Newbury Park, CA: Sage.

Johnston, J. R. (2003). Group interventions for children at-risk from family abuse and exposure to violence: A report of a study. *Journal of Emotional Abuse, 3,* 203–226. doi:10.1300/J135v03n03_03

Katz, L. F., & Low, S. M. (2004). Marital violence, co-parenting, and family-level processes in relation to children's adjustment. *Journal of Family Psychology, 18,* 372–382. doi:10.1037/0893-3200.18.2.372

Kring, A. M., & Werner, K. H. (2004). Emotion regulation and psychopathology. In P. Philippot & R. S. Feldman (Eds.), *The regulation of emotion* (pp. 359–385). Mahwah, NJ: Erlbaum.

Levendosky, A. A., & Graham-Bermann, S. A. (2001). Parenting in battered women: The effects of domestic violence on women and children. *Journal of Family Violence, 16,* 171–192. doi:10.1023/A:1011111003373

Marshall, L. L. (1992). Development of the severity of violence against women scales. *Journal of Family Violence, 7,* 103–121. doi:10.1007/BF00978700

Masten, C. L., Guyer, A. E., Hodgdon, H. B., McClure, E. B., Charney, D. S., Ernst, M., . . . Monk, C. S. (2008). Recognition of facial emotions among maltreated children with high rates of post-traumatic stress disorder. *Child Abuse & Neglect, 32*(1), 139–153.

Maughan, A., & Cicchetti, D. (2002). Impact of child maltreatment and interadult violence on children's emotion regulation abilities and socioemotional adjustment. *Child Development, 73,* 1525–1542. doi:10.1111/1467-8624.00488

McCloskey, L. A., Figueredo, A. J., & Koss, M. P. (1995). The effects of systemic family violence on children's mental health. *Child Development, 66,* 1239–1261. doi:10.2307/1131645

Morrel, T. M., Dubowitz, H., Kerr, M. A., & Black, M. M. (2003). The effect of maternal victimization on children: A cross-informant study. *Journal of Family Violence, 18*(1), 29–41. doi:10.1023/A:1021401414414

Morris, A. S., Silk, J. S., Steinberg, L., Myers, S. S., & Robinson, L. R. (2007). The role of the family context in the development of emotion regulation. *Social Development, 16,* 361–388. doi:10.1111/j.1467-9507.2007.00389.x

Moyers, B. (1995). Violence in the family, school and community [Television series episode]. In *Bill Moyer's Journal.* Arlington, VA: Public Broadcasting Service.

National Advisory Mental Health Council Workgroup on Child and Adolescent Mental Health Intervention and Deployment. (2001). *Blue-print for change: Research on child and adolescent mental health.* Rockville, MD: U.S. Department of Health and Human Services, Public Health Service, National Institutes of Health.

Patterson, G. R. (1982). *Coercive family process.* Eugene, OR: Castalia.

Peled, E., & Davis, D. (1995). *Groupwork with children of battered women.* Thousand Oaks, CA: Sage.

Peled, E., & Edleson, J. L. (1992). Multiple perspectives on groupwork with children of battered women. *Violence and Victims, 7,* 327–346.

Perry, B. D. (2005). Applying principles of neurodevelopment to clinical work with maltreated and traumatized children. The neurosequential model of therapeutics. In N. B. Webb (Ed.), *Working with traumatized youth in child welfare* (pp. 27–52). New York, NY: Guilford Press.

Rabenstein, S., & Lehmann, P. (2000). Mothers and children together: A family group treatment approach. *Journal of Aggression, Maltreatment & Trauma, 3,* 185–205. doi:10.1300/J146v03n01_12

Ragg, D. M., Sultana, M., & Miller, D. (1998, July). *Decreasing aggression in child witnesses of domestic violence.* Presentation at Program Evaluation and Family Violence Research Conference, University of New Hampshire, Durham.

Rice, F., Harold, G. T., Shelton, K. H., & Thapar, A. (2006). Family conflict interacts with genetic liability in predicting childhood and adolescent depression. *Journal of the American Academy of Child and Adolescent Psychiatry, 45,* 841–848. doi:10.1097/01.chi.0000219834.08602.44

Salters-Pedneault, K., Roemer, L., Tull, M. T., Rucker, L., & Mennin, D. S. (2006). Evidence of broad deficits in emotion regulation associated with chronic worry and generalized anxiety disorder. *Cognitive Therapy and Research, 30,* 469–480. doi:10.1007/s10608-006-9055-4

Sarason, S. B. (2003). The obligations of the moral-scientific stance. *American Journal of Community Psychology, 31,* 209–211. doi:10.1023/A:1023946301430

Shields, A., Ryan, R. M., & Cicchetti, D. (2001). Narrative representations of caregivers and emotion dysregulation as predictors of maltreated children's rejection by peers. *Developmental Psychology, 37,* 321–337. doi:10.1037/0012-1649.37.3.321

Straus, M. A. (1979). Measuring intrafamily conflict and violence: The conflict tactics (CT) scales. *Journal of Marriage and the Family, 41*(1), 75–88. doi:10.2307/351733

Sullivan, C. M., & Bybee, D. L. (1999). Reducing violence using community-based advocacy for women with abusive partners. *Journal of Consulting and Clinical Psychology, 67,* 43–53. doi:10.1037/0022-006X.67.1.43

Sullivan, C. M., Nguyen, H., Allen, N., Bybee, D., & Juran, J. (2000). Beyond searching for deficits: Evidence that bettered women are nurturing parents. *Journal of Interpersonal Violence, 15,* 583–598.

Swartz, J. E., Monk, C. S., Castor, L. E., & Graham-Bermann, S. A. (2009, August). *The attention to facial expressions in children exposed to domestic violence.* Paper presented at the 117th Annual Convention of the American Psychological Association, Toronto, Ontario, Canada.

Terr, L. C. (1983). Chowchilla revisited: The effects of psychic trauma four years after a school bus kidnapping. *American Journal of Psychiatry, 140,* 1543–1550.

Tull, M. T., Jakupcak, M., McFadden, M. E., & Roemer, L. (2007). The role of negative affect intensity and the fear of emotions in posttraumatic stress symptom severity among victims of childhood interpersonal violence. *Journal of Nervous and Mental Disease, 195,* 580–587. doi:10.1097/NMD.0b013e318093ed5f

Wagar, J., & Rodway, M. (1995). Evaluation of a group treatment approach for children who have witnessed wife abuse. *Journal of Family Violence, 10,* 295–306. doi:10.1007/BF02110994

Watts-Jones, D. (1990). Toward a stress scale for African-American women. *Psychology of Women Quarterly, 14,* 271–275.

Wandersman, A., Kloos, B., Linney, J. A., & Shinn, M. (2005). Science and community psychology: Enhancing the vitality of community research and action. *American Journal of Community Psychology, 35,* 105–106. doi:10.1007/s10464-005-3387-1

Weisz, J. R., Jensen-Doss, A., & Hawley, K. M. (2006). Evidence based youth psychotherapies versus usual clinical care: A meta-analysis of direct comparisons. *American Psychologist, 61,* 671–689. doi:10.1037/0003-066X.61.7.671

Weisz, J. R., Sandler, I. N., Durlak, J. A., & Anton, B. S. (2005). Promoting and protecting youth mental health through evidence-based prevention and treatment. *American Psychologist, 60,* 628–648. doi:10.1037/0003-066X.60.6.628

Wilson, S., Cameron, S., Jaffe, P., & Wolfe, D. (1989). Children exposed to wife abuse: An intervention model. *Social Casework, 70,* 180–184.

10

INTIMATE PARTNER VIOLENCE IN THE SCHOOL-AGE YEARS: A CASE STUDY OF THE EVALUATION OF ALIA, A MULTIPLY ABUSED GIRL

ALYTIA A. LEVENDOSKY AND SANDRA A. GRAHAM-BERMANN

As demonstrated by the research described in this book, intimate partner violence (IPV) may have particular effects depending on the age of the child when the exposure occurs. Children who are school-age (approximately ages 6–12) show great variability in their responses to IPV, including profiles that reflect adjustment that is primarily internalizing, externalizing, multiproblem, or resilient (e.g., Grych, Jouriles, Swank, McDonald, & Norwood, 2000). Their variability in response may be in part due to the variability in exposure, including type of IPV, severity of IPV, and chronicity of IPV. For example, some of these children have been exposed chronically since their time in utero, whereas others may be exposed only in middle childhood while their mother is in a new relationship. An additional issue is that children exposed to IPV are often the victims of other kinds of violence in their families (Edleson, 2001). A number of studies have reported concomitant violence in the form of severe emotional abuse, sexual abuse, sibling violence, and physical abuse in as many as 40% of IPV families (Appel & Holden, 1998). Treatment of school-age children must take into account both the variability of response as well as the variability in exposure. The current chapter presents a case study of a child, Alia, age 9, who was evaluated due to exposure to IPV. Similar to many other children exposed to IPV, Alia also experienced other traumas and stressors, including sexual abuse by her older brother and an ongoing legal battle over the divorce and custody arrangements between her parents.

Alia was first seen in a group treatment program for children exposed to IPV. During one of her first sessions with that group, Alia told her group leaders that she was upset and frightened when her father came to pick the children up for a scheduled visitation. Her parents had recently separated and filed for divorce. In this group session, Alia reported that her parents had argued earlier that week and that the father had slammed the mother's arm in the car door while she was holding Alia's younger brother, Billy, age 3, in her arms. Upstairs, Alia and the older siblings called the police. Following the reporting of this incident, the two group therapists discussed these events, Alia's reactions to the events, and the need for Alia to receive an evaluation for individual therapy.

The mother, Justine, agreed to the consultation and reported that Alia had been having behavior problems in school. Further, Justine reported that she had recently walked in on Alia with her oldest brother, Tom, age 13. They were dancing in their underwear, and Alia appeared to be touching her brother's genitals. The group therapist made a referral to a psychological clinic that included a summary of Alia's behavior in the group setting. She noted that, compared with others of her age in the group, Alia was easily upset, quarreled with other children in the group, swore and called them names, and seemed sexualized in her interactions and style of dressing. That is, Alia often wore clothes that she pulled over one shoulder, and she "vamped" the little boys in the group. In another example, when asked to draw a picture of what she might like to be in the future, Alia elected to draw herself as a lounge singer with a sexy red dress and bright lights shining on her. The group therapist consulted with protective services and was told that the evaluation for treatment should include the question of whether the child had been sexually abused.

THE EVALUATION

At the clinic, the evaluation process with children and families typically takes about four to five once-weekly sessions, which last 45 min. For this particular evaluation, the therapist met with Justine first to clarify the presenting problems, family history, and Alia's developmental history. The therapist explained that she would be meeting with both Justine and Alia in separate sessions over the next few weeks to get to know them and would then meet with Justine to give her feedback about treatment recommendations. In addition, Justine gave permission to the therapist to contact the teacher. The therapist interviewed the teacher over the phone to evaluate Alia's behavioral and academic functioning. Justine explained her financial situation and requested a reduced fee for the evaluation sessions. She was currently living in the home that she and her husband had purchased. However, she was unable to make the mortgage payments with the money given to her monthly by her husband, so she would soon be moving. Her recent separation from her husband left her with seriously reduced means. Justine revealed that she had never worked during their marriage, and although her husband had a large income, he was currently disputing the financial and custody arrangements and had decided not to pay child support until that was resolved. She was given a reduced fee of $10 per evaluation session.

Theoretical and Empirical Bases for Assessment and Intervention

Alia's presenting problems were viewed in light of an attachment and trauma theory framework (e.g., Bowlby, 1988; Busch & Lieberman, 2007; Gil, 2002; Lieberman & Van Horn, 2008). She had experienced betrayal at the hands of trusted intimate others—namely, her father and her brother. Thus, there were likely to be disruptions of her internal working models of self and other as she struggled to integrate the betrayals into her schemas of relationships (e.g., Cicchetti & Toth, 1995; Egeland & Sroufe, 1981). In addition, the trauma itself would likely be related to disruptions in Alia's emotional, behavioral, and cognitive functioning (van der Kolk, 2005). Thus, the evaluation proceeded according to an attachment-trauma framework, assessing both Alia's internal working models and her trauma symptoms. A child-centered approach was used to evaluate Alia, relying not only on interviews with the mother but also on play interviews with Alia to assess her functioning in a setting natural for a child (Greenspan, 1991). Psychologists have long understood play to be the medium through which children are comfortable and able to express their inner worlds, that is, their concerns, worries, fears, joys, and pleasures (e.g., Axline, 1969; Greenspan, 1991). The play interview format allowed for assessment of Alia's capacity to function in a new relationship, thus revealing important information about her internal working models of self and others. Justine was interviewed with a clinical interview—the Schedule for Affective Disorders and Schizophrenia for School-Age Children-Present and Lifetime version (K-SADS-PL; Kaufman et al., 1997)—to assess Alia's symptoms in a diagnostic framework, focusing in particular on her traumatic symptoms. Justine and Alia's teacher were both asked to complete the appropriate versions of the Child Behavior Checklist and Teacher's Report Form (Achenbach & Edelbrock, 1993) to obtain situation-specific information regarding the severity and extent of her behavioral problems.

Identifying Information

Justine was a 38-year-old Caucasian woman who had been a homemaker for the 15 years of her marriage. Alia was the second youngest of four children, with an older brother, Tom, age 13; older sister, Karen, age 11; and younger brother, Billy, age 3. Justine had experienced intermittent IPV from her husband, John, that took the form of cruel, sadistic, emotional, and controlling behaviors that began during her first pregnancy. Although the incidents of physical violence were rare, the emotional control extended to the entire family. Justine described various events, including her husband bringing their older son into their bedroom and opening Justine's shirt while she was dressing to "show him what a woman looks like," and herding the family into the living room while threatening to detonate a home-made bomb that was placed just outside the sliding door but in everyone's plain sight. The incident at the car that Alia had described was part of this similar pattern of terror and shaming. Clearly, Justine, and perhaps her children as well, was convinced that John would carry out his threats one day and that they would die.

Justine reported that Alia was struggling emotionally, socially, and academically. She described Alia as seemingly the most vulnerable child in the family to the IPV exposure. The mother reported that, compared with her siblings, Alia responded in the most labile ways to the IPV and appeared the most consistently distressed. Justine was also concerned about her new knowledge of the sexually tinged play behavior between Alia and Tom.

Evaluation Sessions

The therapist met with Alia three times during the evaluation period and with Justine twice and then met with Justine and Alia together to provide feedback and treatment recommendations. Consistent with a child-centered approach within an attachment-trauma framework, the individual assessment sessions with Alia allowed the therapist to evaluate Alia's capacity to form a new relationship and to observe the themes of her play.

In the first session, Alia came with Billy and her mother, as well as her new kittens in a large basket. She showed the kittens to the therapist in the waiting room and then eagerly bounded up the stairs ahead of her. She was thrilled with the large dollhouse and began to play with the dolls immediately. She seemed to focus mostly on a blonde girl doll, who she said was the owner of the home. She developed the following story in this session (paraphrased):

> The girl is a star—a lounge singer—and has so much money that she bought this house for her family. However, they do not know that she is a singer because she is afraid that they won't like her music. Actually, they love her music, they just don't know that it is her that is singing on

TV all the time because she is dressed up in such fancy clothes that they don't recognize her. She has a boyfriend who adores her. She was going to go meet the governor for lunch, but then it turned out to be only her grandfather, and she felt like she had been tricked because she thought it was going to be the governor, who wanted to meet her because he loved her singing so much.

After playing out this story, it was time to clean up. She did not want to leave, and she resisted cleaning up and walking out of the room. As she was leaving, she requested some turquoise satin fabric so she could make a beautiful dress for the doll.

In the second evaluation session, Alia squealed with excitement and said, "You *are* here, you *are* here!" when the therapist walked into the waiting room to get her. Her delight in seeing the therapist suggested both her desire to form attachment relationships and her concern that she could not trust others who appear trustworthy, consistent with findings about abused children in relationships (see Cicchetti & Toth, 1995). They went directly to the same room as the prior week, and Alia was very excited to see the turquoise satin. She immediately sat down and began to cut out a dress for the blonde girl doll in the dollhouse. The therapist asked her how things were going at home, and Alia replied that her older brother and sister were "bitches"—that they teased her and were mean to her. She reported that her sister told her that Alia wanted her brother Tom to do bad things to her. She said, "But I didn't, he made me." When the therapist asked about the bad things, she said, "He sexually abused me and my little brother made me do the same thing, and my grandfather sexually abused my mother and my uncle sexually abused my aunt." The therapist commented on how awful it is when girls and women are not safe from boys and men. She told the therapist about her mother finding Tom and her dancing in their underwear, and she said that she had been scared because she knew it was wrong. Alia told her that she hoped it would not happen again. The therapist reassured her about her mother's protection. When the therapist then wondered aloud what kind of sexual abuse had happened to her from her brother, Alia did not respond and went into play. The following story was narrated to the therapist as she moved the dollhouse figures around:

> The same blonde girl is the main character. She is the best person in the home, all the others are bitches, especially her brothers. Her brothers liked to see her naked and so when she had a slumber party, they sneaked in and watched all the girls get undressed and inspected each of them. She was mad, so she was going to do the same thing to them.

The therapist commented on how a kid could want to do the same thing back to someone who hurt her. The therapist then asked whether the brothers had done anything else to her blonde girl. Alia gave no response to that question but then said that this girl was going out to sing and do a show and so she dressed her in the new turquoise satin dress she had made. She again resisted cleaning up and leaving the room.

For the third and final evaluation session Alia ran ahead of the therapist up the stairs and into the room. She pulled out the blonde girl doll and announced that her name was Melissa. Finding a wrestler doll, she said that he was Melissa's boyfriend. Alia seemed very excited about this and started making clothes for him from the turquoise satin fabric. Then she said that he was not Melissa's boyfriend, only that Melissa had a big crush on him and wanted to introduce herself to him. Alia began speaking as Melissa in the play. Melissa hoped that if she made the wrestler a beautiful blue satin cape that he would want her to be his girlfriend. Alia pulled out the two boy dolls she had played with last week, naming them Mark and Markus and telling the therapist that they were Melissa's brothers. She added that Melissa said to Mark that she was very excited to see him back from the hospital and so made a blue coat for Mark. Alia then pulled off Mark and Markus's clothes to see if they were really boys. She seemed disappointed with the lack of male genitalia and said, "I guess they don't put that on there?" When the therapist asked what she was looking for, she responded, "I don't know." The therapist said that she wondered if Alia was looking for their penises, and she said, "Yes, but I just hate that word. I hate it." The therapist commented that she could understand why she would hate that word given her experiences with her brother. Alia then became frustrated with the coat that she was trying to make for Mark, and when the therapist tried to help her, she became angry at her and would not look at what the therapist was doing.

The therapist mentioned that the next week's session would be a feedback session with Alia and her mother to figure out the best plan for working together. Alia said that if her father found out about her coming she would die. The therapist asked why she would die and she said, "Because I would not get to come and see you anymore." The therapist responded that it would be very upsetting if they could not see each other anymore, but that perhaps she (the therapist) could work something out with her father. Alia replied, "I don't think so. He hates therapists."

The development of Alia's play themes across the three sessions was interpreted in light of an attachment-trauma framework. She showed elements of posttraumatic play in that the themes of the play were related to the trauma she had experienced and the traumatic reactions, including confusion around sexuality and womanhood. In addition, the play involved very confusing attachment relationships for a young girl, that is, the absence of parents and sexualized relationships with brothers. Alia's internal working models involve a lack of trust in caregivers as well as confusion about herself and her role in significant relationships.

The therapist also met with the mother twice to learn about Alia's developmental history, family circumstances, presenting problems, and clinical symptoms. In addition, this was an opportunity to assess Justine's views of her own parenting and her relationship with Alia—an important view of the attachment relationship. Justine began by describing Alia as the scapegoat. Justine reported that her siblings blame Alia for the divorce because her parents often fought over her behavior, and her older sister blames her for the sexual abuse from her brother. She also noted that the two older siblings call Alia "Mommy's girl" because Alia always defends her to them. She said that Tom makes Alia feel that she is a bad person and unlovable. She then described walking in on Tom and Alia dancing naked, with Alia holding Tom's penis. When Justine spoke with Tom, he denied forcing or even asking Alia to touch his penis. Justine said she forgave him but wanted to know if anyone ever did this to him—and he refused to respond.

Justine told the therapist that the night she was served with divorce papers her husband told the children that she (Justine) was crazy and having a mental breakdown because her father had sexually abused her. John is currently in a batterer's program, where he was sent after his arrest for the car door incident. She said that the group therapist called yesterday to tell her that John is making wonderful progress and that they are aware from what he has said that Justine was psychologically abusive to him, and they recommended that she get treatment for this. She said that John is suing for joint physical custody, which she opposes. She said that John has been physically and psychologically abusive to all of the children, but mostly to Tom. She thinks that this may be why Tom is so physically and verbally abusive to his younger siblings and to her. She fears for Tom and specifically worries that he will become depressed and suicidal. The therapist asked her what protection she could provide for Alia, and she just said that she knows Alia can tell her if it happens again. Regarding the bedroom arrangement, the therapist suggested that Tom have the bedroom next to Justine's (at the time it was on a different floor and was next to Alia's). She agreed to switch rooms and to not leave Alia alone with Tom. Meanwhile she also informed the therapist that the trial for custody, visitation, and financial support was happening in 2 months. Her lawyer told her that the children may be subpoenaed by John to talk about their desires for custody arrangements. She said that John currently has a "nanny" living with him but noted that the children told her that it is obvious that she is his girlfriend. Finally, she is afraid that John will act out sexually with the "nanny" in front of their children. Following this session with the mother, the therapist called protective services to report the suspected abuse of the child, even though the two children involved were less than 5 years apart in age. When she explained that this was an ongoing evaluation the protective services worker advised her to report back with additional information should the situation change or the family drop out of treatment.

In the second session, the therapist asked about the family history of abuse and Alia's developmental history, and conducted the structured clinical interview (i.e., K-SADS) about Alia's symptoms. Justine described the abuse from her husband as escalating during her pregnancy with Alia. She reported the following: The family was in a car and she was settling Tom into his car seat when John became furious with her and hit her hard with his arm across her face. At the same time John called Tom a shithead and bozo. The next day the family car was hit by a truck on a highway and John and Justine each suffered serious injuries. Justine was 11 weeks pregnant with Alia at the time. She had a broken back and lacerated abdomen and spent the next few months in a brace. As soon as she was home from her 7-week hospital stay, John wanted her to resume all normal duties immediately, which did not leave her any time to get continued treatment for the back injury. He only "allowed" her to stay for 24 hr in the hospital when she gave birth to Alia because he wanted her to cook and take care of the older siblings. Alia had a normal birth and was 6 pounds, 4 ounces. Although Alia was smaller than her other children, Justine attributed it to her spending much of the pregnancy in a brace. Alia's baby teeth came in with a brown mark on her front teeth, which is still there. The doctor said this was likely due to the car accident and the injuries sustained by Justine.

The mother informed the therapist that Alia had had academic trouble in school since the beginning. She was in a special program to help children with reading and math and spent the summer in a special education program. However, she had been tested and has a high average IQ and no learning disabilities. Still, the mother said that Alia describes herself as "very stupid" and compares herself with her older siblings, both of whom are academic stars. John was adamantly opposed to her being in a special program, and the two of them fought about this a lot when they were living together. John also charged Justine with child abuse, saying her discipline of hitting the children with a wooden spoon was physical abuse. He would call them names and humiliate them, instead. She said that John was rarely around when the children were little, and when he was, she never did anything right enough or good enough, and neither did the children. At age 4, Alia once refused to take her medication for an illness, and John put her outside without clothes on in the cold winter night air to punish her. Finally, Justine reported that, again unlike her older siblings, Alia had difficulty making friends and had struggled with friends since early childhood. Currently, Justine feels that she alienates many children by her almost constant use of swear words.

The K-SADS interview with Justine clarified for both the therapist and Justine the types of symptoms that Alia was presenting, as well as their severity and frequency.

SUMMARY OF PRESENTING PROBLEMS
BASED ON EVALUATION

The following summary of Alia's presenting problems is based on the interviews with Justine, play sessions with Alia, and a telephone interview with the teacher.

Social Behavior

Alia was quite manipulative, which manifested in her relationships with her siblings and her mother. The therapist was also aware of this aspect of her personality from her behavior in the evaluation sessions, as described later. This manipulative behavior was similar to that exhibited by her father and brother and may have been her attempt to identify with her aggressors. Alia also had difficulty both relating to and cooperating with other children her age. In school, she cursed at her peers when they did not follow her instructions or did not want to play with her. The teacher reported that she was bossy, gave lots of commands, and that other children found her unpleasant and avoided her. Consequently, she was a lonely child who did not understand why other children did not like her. Her attempts to engage others by force or coercion left her rejected and angry. In the play interview sessions with the therapist, Alia could not name any child who was her friend.

Academic Assessment

Justine and Alia's teacher both reported that Alia had had trouble with her academic work since the first grade, where she seemed to have trouble reading and following directions on assignments. Her reading trouble was identified in the second grade, and she had been placed in a special reading remediation program during the past summer. Intellectual testing by the school yielded a full-scale IQ of 113 with both performance and verbal IQ within 5 points of each other. Her achievement tests indicated that she was able to read and compute at age-appropriate levels and thus did not indicate a learning disability. Her teacher reported some issues with attention and concentration but did not report attention or hyperactive problems in the clinical range on a measure of adjustment problems—the Child Behavior Checklist (Achenbach & Edelbrock, 1993).

Affective Regulation

The therapist noted that Alia showed many affective features consistent with a trauma history, including anger, fear, and terror. She was frightened of visitation with her father and feared her older brother. She reported night-mares about the sexual abuse and her father's physical assault on her mother. She had difficulty feeling loving and happy feelings and seemed restricted to the angry and frightened spectrum of feelings. Alia was easily aroused and star-tled at noises and movement behind her. When Alia was talking about upset-ting events, she spoke in a high-pitched voice, very rapidly, and her heart rate accelerated. She needed help in calming down, as she would easily become dysregulated with little ability to self-regulate. These traumatic reactions are likely to be related to her difficulties in social and academic functioning.

Physical Health

Alia appeared to be in good physical health. However, she dressed and wore her hair in a somewhat disheveled manner that contrasted strongly with the rest of her family, who were always well dressed and neat in their appearance.

Family History and Functioning

Interparental violence was not new for the mother in this family. Justine reported that in her family of origin, her father physically abused her mother, as well as Justine and her siblings. Justine was the oldest of eight children. In public, her father was a prominent attorney, but at home he ruled the family with violence and sexual aggression. Her father sexually abused her and her next oldest sibling, a brother. This brother, in turn, sexually abused his younger siblings. Her family lived across the country and was not a source of support or understanding. Justine graduated from college with a degree in history. She married shortly after graduation but had not been employed outside the home at any point in her life.

John was one of two siblings whose father died early in his life. His mother moved to another state. In essence, Alia did not have any grandpar-ents in her life. John was a highly successful businessman who owned a large clothing store, two antique automobiles, and an airplane. He worked long hours. Neither John nor Justine drank or smoked.

Justine mentioned that Alia appeared afraid of her father and had a dis-tant relationship with him. She was overly connected to her mother and identified with her. Given that the father favored the two older children, those who did well in school and seemed the brightest to him, Alia keenly felt rejected by her father. She aspired to be one of his favorites but could not find a way to get his approval.

Approval seeking was part of her relationship with her older brother. She was jealous of her older sister, who got along well with Tom. The older sister, Karen, was pretty, very bright, and popular in school—the very things that Alia was not but desperately wanted to be. Alia's closest relationship of all of her siblings was with Billy, spending the most time with him. They played games and watched television together. Tom had a history of lashing out at the younger two siblings, often hitting them or threatening them with a belt. When Tom tried to hurt Billy, Alia would come to his defense.

Given that this family was cut off from Justine's family and distant from John's mother and much younger brother, the children effectively had no contact with relatives outside the immediate family. Like many abusive families, there were few friends invited to the house, and the older children preferred to spend time with friends away from home. Consequently, Alia spent a considerable amount of time with her mother and Billy.

Risk and Protective Factors for Alia

The risk factors for Alia are fairly evident from the evaluation, including an abusive father and depleted, depressed, and severely traumatized mother, neither of whom was able to parent well under stress, to foresee dangerous events, or to actively protect their children. In addition, Alia's experience of her father was that he appeared to be uninvolved and uninterested. She also experienced her older brother as a sexual predator and her sister as indifferent or annoyed at her presence. Finally, she reported having no friends.

In addition to these risk factors, some additional contextual risk factors were currently affecting Alia. Although her father had financial resources, he refused to pay child support. John could afford expensive legal counsel in his custody battle over the children, whereas in contrast Justine was relying on legal aid and went through several attorneys who quickly tired of her case and the many motions filed against her. The children were about to lose their childhood home, and the family car had recently had been repossessed when the father stopped payments on it.

However, some protective factors for Alia also became apparent during the evaluation. Despite reports of her academic difficulties, it was clear that Alia was quite intelligent and very articulate when she was not distressed and angry. These competencies boded well for her ability to participate in treatment and to work through her traumatic experiences. She was a physically attractive child, although she did not recognize this in herself. In addition, over the three sessions, the therapist gained another view of Alia, distinct from that of her mother, siblings, and peers—Alia could be an engaging child with the ability to be appealing to others, even though she was at times very difficult. She laughed frequently and could enjoy activities and getting the attention of adults. She was able to form a meaningful relationship with the therapist, demonstrating an important protective capacity to form attachment bonds.

In addition to these personal protective factors, there were also some important resources that the family brought to the treatment. The mother understood the value of bringing the children to therapy and had called the group intervention program in the first place to receive services for herself and her children. In addition, the family was in a neighborhood with access to good schools and mental health services. Justine was well-educated and appreciated and understood the value of education and mental health treatment for herself and her children.

DSM DIAGNOSIS AND FORMULATIONS

Alia was diagnosed with posttraumatic stress disorder (PTSD) because she displayed symptoms of reexperiencing (i.e. nightmares), avoidance (i.e., restriction of feelings) and arousal (i.e., startle response, and hyperarousal). She was also given a rule-out diagnosis of oppositional defiant disorder (ODD). Alia fit *Diagnostic and Statistical Manual of Mental Disorders* (4th ed.; American Psychiatric Association, 1994) criteria for ODD based on her mother's reports of frequent temper tantrums, frequent deliberate attempts to annoy others, blaming others for her mistakes, being mean and swearing profusely at others when upset. However, the ODD diagnosis was conceptualized to be symptoms related to her experience of multiple severe traumatic experiences and exposure to psychological manipulation and abuse. It was included as a rule-out diagnosis because once the trauma was treated it would become clearer as to whether or not Alia had ODD and/or an anxiety disorder.

Alia was a child suffering from multiple forms of interpersonal trauma. She was unhappy, angry, and frightened in response to these events. She had also been thrust into the position of the family scapegoat and was quite lonely there. Her distress was evident in her (a) poor performance at school, (b) angry use of swear words to describe her family members and peers, (c) provocative behavior at home that helped to maintain her position as scapegoat, (d) sullen demeanor, and (e) low sense of self-worth.

In an attempt to control her painful feelings, Alia frequently demonstrated externalization, that is, blaming and hating all of those around her. Her emotionally and verbally aggressive behavior was interpreted as identification with the aggressor (both her father and brother) in an attempt to control her own feelings and others' behaviors toward her. Alia also blamed herself for the sexual abuse and the divorce, feelings that were reinforced by her siblings. The scapegoating may have begun even before birth, as she may literally have been the "marked" child due to the terrible car accident and her "marked" teeth at the beginning of the serious abusive behavior by John toward Justine.

Although Justine had the capacity for emotional connection and warmth, her ability to be present for Alia appeared inconsistent. She was suffering from her own traumatic response to her husband's years of abuse and the ongoing difficulty of the legal battles with him. She was frequently overwhelmed, absorbed by the ongoing crisis, and was unable to be emotionally engaged with her challenging and distressed daughter, whom she found quite difficult.

Thus, from an attachment-trauma perspective, Alia's problems can be conceptualized as arising from a combination of her experiences of trauma including witnessing IPV and experiencing sexual abuse with trusted intimate others as the perpetrators, along with the emotional neglect she experienced with her mother and father. She had no warm and consistent caregivers who were responsive to her needs for caregiving or to her particular needs, concerns, and fears in light of the traumatic events in her family. Thus, she developed a lack of trust in others and struggled to manage her emotions triggered in relationships and thus acted out with peers, teachers, and at home.

TREATMENT RECOMMENDATIONS

Multiple recommendations were given to Justine and Alia during the feedback session. First, the group intervention program, in which they continued to be involved, was emphasized for both the mother and the child because of its psychoeducational component and therapeutic support elements. In that program, children learn that others share their experiences with IPV and that the violence is not their fault. They also learn how to cope with and make sense of these difficult experiences (see Chapter 9, this volume). In groups for the women, mothers receive support and learn what is appropriate behavior for children at different ages and how to help children cope with IPV. In Alia's case, however, the overlay of sexual abuse trauma in the face of IPV and emotional abuse created a special situation such that these issues may not have been as freely discussed in the group format. Alia needed a separate place to discuss the events in her life and her feelings about them. Further, the other children in the group may be traumatized by hearing stories of sexual assaults from a child as young as Alia.

Thus, in addition to maintaining involvement in the groups, individual play therapy and parent guidance were recommended based on the attachment-trauma framework. Individual play therapy affords the therapist the opportunity to work closely and individually with the child in building an emotionally secure environment for the child through the attachment relationship with the therapist in order to process the traumatic experiences and to develop healing and mastery of them (e.g., Gil, 2002). Two prior meta-analyses have shown the effectiveness of play therapy (Bratton, Ray, Rhine, & Jones, 2005;

Leblanc & Ritchie, 2001). In addition, a recent review of studies of therapy with traumatized children suggests that play therapy is an effective intervention (Wethington et al., 2008). The therapist also proposed working with the mother in parent guidance such that particular and specific issues that need to be addressed to ensure the safety of Alia and to help her to heal emotionally would be a regular part of the conversation. While the group treatment was believed helpful for Justine, it was not the place for developing individual therapeutic relationships to the extent needed for intensively processing the emotional damage done to her child, Alia.

Further, ongoing monitoring and coaching of Justine's parenting was deemed essential in this case. An individual evaluation also was recommended for Tom to pursue the allegations of sexual abuse and treatment for his sexual, physical, and verbal abuse directed at his family members. The reasons for a follow-up call to protective services were explained to the mother. Justine and Alia agreed to all of the recommendations and proceeded with them immediately. Protective services was then informed of these treatment plans and wished to be kept apprised of the case.

TREATMENT OUTCOMES

Alia was treated in once-weekly play therapy for about 1 year. Her mother attended parent guidance sessions for the same time period. At the end of the treatment, Alia's symptoms of PTSD had diminished significantly such that she no longer fit criteria for the diagnosis. In addition, she had made a couple of friends at school and had frequent play dates with them, indicating improvement in her capacity to get along with her peers and likely reflecting changes in her internal working models of self and others. Her relationships with her siblings improved but still remained an ongoing challenge for her and her mother to manage. Justine had made significant progress in her parenting strategies, and Alia was now safe at home. Tom received individual treatment and had responded well to a behavioral plan for his physical violence toward his mother and siblings. Ongoing challenges for the family remained in the father's continued pursuit of gaining full physical custody of the children so that a court battle was continuing as the family terminated their work with the therapist.

REFERENCES

Achenbach, T., & Edelbrock, C. (1993). *Manual for the Child Behavior Checklist and Revised Child Behavior Profile*. Burlington: University of Vermont, Department of Psychiatry.

American Psychiatric Association. (1994). *Diagnostic and statistical manual of mental disorders* (4th ed.). Washington, DC: Author.

Appel, A. E., & Holden, G. W. (1998). The co-occurrence of spouse and physical child abuse: A review and appraisal. *Journal of Family Psychology, 12*, 578–599. doi:10.1037/0893-3200.12.4.578

Axline, V. M. (1969). *Play therapy*. New York, NY: Ballantine Books.

Bowlby, J. (1988). *A secure base: Clinical applications of attachment theory*. London, England: Routledge.

Bratton, S. C., Ray, D., Rhine, T., & Jones, L. (2005). The efficacy of play therapy with children: A meta-analytic review of treatment outcomes. *Professional Psychology, Research and Practice, 36*, 376–390. doi:10.1037/0735-7028.36.4.376

Busch, A. L., & Lieberman, A. F. (2007). Attachment and trauma: An integrated approach to treating young children exposed to family violence. In D. Oppenheim & D. F. Goldsmith (Eds.), *Attachment theory in clinical work with children: Bridging the gap between research and practice* (pp. 139–171). New York, NY: Guilford Press.

Cicchetti, D., & Toth, S. L. (1995). Child maltreatment and attachment organization: Implications for intervention. In S. Goldberg, R. Muir, & J. Kerr (Eds.), *Attachment theory: Social, developmental, and clinical perspectives* (pp. 279–308). Hillsdale, NJ: Analytic Press.

Edleson, J. L. (2001). Studying the co-occurrence of child maltreatment and domestic violence in families. In S. A. Graham-Bermann & J. L. Edleson (Eds.), *Domestic violence in the lives of children: The future of research, intervention, and social policy* (pp. 91–110). Washington, DC: American Psychological Association. doi:10.1037/10408-005

Egeland, B., & Sroufe, L. A. (1981). Attachment and early maltreatment. *Child Development, 52*, 44–52. doi:10.2307/1129213

Gil, E. (2002). Play therapy with abused children. In F. W. Kaslow (Ed.), *Comprehensive handbook of psychotherapy: Interpersonal/humanistic/existential* (Vol. 3, pp. 59–82). Hoboken, NJ: Wiley.

Greenspan, S. I. (1991). *The clinical interview of the child* (2nd ed.). Washington, DC: American Psychiatric Association.

Grych, J. H., Jouriles, E. N., Swank, P. R., McDonald, R., & Norwood, W. D. (2000). Patterns of adjustment among children of battered women. *Journal of Consulting and Clinical Psychology, 68*, 84–94. doi:10.1037/0022-006X.68.1.84

Kaufman, J., Birmaher, B., Brent, D., Rao, U., Flynn, C., Moreci, . . . Ryan, N. (1997). Schedule for Affective Disorders and Schizophrenia for School-Age Children-Present and Lifetime version (K-SADS-PL): Initial reliability and validity data. *Journal of the American Academy of Child and Adolescent Psychiatry, 36*, 980–988. doi:10.1097/00004583-199707000-00021

Leblanc, M., & Ritchie, M. (2001). A meta-analysis of play therapy outcomes. *Counselling Psychology Quarterly, 14*, 149–163. doi:10.1080/09515070110059142

Lieberman, A. & Van Horn, P. (2008). *Psychotherapy with infants and young children: Repairing the effects of stress and trauma on early attachment.* New York, NY: Guilford Press.

van der Kolk, B. A. (2005). Developmental Trauma Disorder: Toward a rational diagnosis for children with complex trauma histories. *Psychiatric Annals, 35,* 401–408.

Wethington, H. R., Hahn, R. A., Fuqua-Whitley, D. S., Sipe, T. A., Crosby, A. E., Johnson, . . . Chattopadhyay, S. K. (2008). The effectiveness of interventions to reduce psychological harm from traumatic events among children and adolescents: A systematic review. *American Journal of Preventive Medicine, 35,* 287–313. doi:10.1016/j.amepre.2008.06.024

IV

ADOLESCENTS

11

THE IMPACT OF INTIMATE PARTNER VIOLENCE ON ADOLESCENTS

LAURA ANN McCLOSKEY

Researchers have amassed a strong set of findings describing how young and school-age children respond to intimate partner violence (IPV). Yet a parallel program of research on IPV exposed adolescents is missing. In this chapter, findings from disparate sources are reviewed to better understand the rate of exposure and the impact on youth entering their 2nd decade. Are teenagers less likely to experience IPV than younger children? Do they resist the same psychological symptoms? Are they entering a cycle of violence as they start their own sexual relationships? I believe that the evidence compiled here shows that we have made a mistake in omitting adolescents, however hard they are to recruit or how challenging they are to "measure." Although the present review is by no means exhaustive, it represents a first step toward expanding the developmental landscape in the study of IPV. It also offers a nudge to researchers, scholars, and clinicians to explore the fascinating population of adolescents and young adults with histories of IPV exposure.

Adolescence marks a transition point during which youth may express new or magnified problems. There are many normative challenges that are unique to adolescence and that can be exacerbated by stressful family circumstances. Adolescence is a pivotal period for the formation of character and the consolidation of moral values expressed through interpersonal relationships (Smetana, Campione-Barr, & Metzger, 2006). Steinberg and Cauffman (1996) pointed out that certain benchmarks of moral development are critical during adolescence: responsibility, temperance, and perspective. If such characteristics fail to develop, long-term adjustment difficulties arise in work and relationships. According to Arnett (2000), a similar palette of traits marks entry into adulthood that includes accepting responsibility, independent decision making and financial independence. Arnett (2000) and others have identified the period of development in the United States between about age 18 and age 25 as *emerging adulthood*—distinct from the dependency and parental monitoring of adolescence and lacking the breadth of responsibilities and identity characteristics of adulthood. He observed that there is a paucity of studies on emerging adulthood of non-college-bound young adults. In other words, most of the theory of emergent adulthood has derived from the analysis of college students, which weakens the application to youth exposed to IPV, many of whom are not college-bound. The line between adolescence and adulthood, therefore, is thin in American culture. Therefore, for the purposes of this chapter, we include some studies of young adults under age 21 as falling within the developmental period of adolescence or emergent adulthood.

Adolescence often marks the beginning of adultlike behavior problems and mood disorders. Adolescents with a history of childhood exposure to family violence, even when such violence ends by their teen years, may be at special risk for such problems. Should the violence be continuous with their past or introduced during their teenage years, adolescents may channel their anger and frustration from their family lives into social and school milieus—getting into fights, abandoning interest in school, running away. Although there are many empirical reports describing the impact of IPV on children under the age of 12, there are relatively few studies of affected adolescents. The omission of adolescents in most studies may be in part due to the difficulty of recruiting them into research, even when their mothers are the key informants. The studies that are available have relied on varied sampling approaches including population-based cohort studies (e.g., Fergusson & Horwood, 1998), community outreach and engagement with youth-oriented agencies (Levendosky, Huth-Bocks, & Semel, 2002), longitudinal studies retaining the adolescents from childhood (e.g., Lichter & McCloskey 2004; McCloskey & Lichter, 2003), and retrospective studies of late adolescents and young adults (e.g., Zinzow et al., 2009).

The chapter addresses several themes related to the impact of IPV on adolescents, including risk factors, prevalence, mental health effects, the cycle of violence, and gender differences.

RISK FACTORS ASSOCIATED WITH IPV
FROM CHILDHOOD TO ADOLESCENCE

Several meta-analyses pooling dozens of studies have yielded small to moderate effect sizes of witnessing IPV on children and adolescents after other forms of abuse are measured and controlled (Kitzmann, Gaylord, Holt, & Kenny, 2003; Wilson, Stover, & Berkowitz, 2009; Wolfe, Crooks, Lee, McIntyre-Smith, & Jaffe, 2003). Such studies indicate that youth exposed to IPV display heterogeneous outcomes across the course of childhood (see Margolin & Gordis, 2000). In addition to general psychopathology and adjustment, other studies focus exclusively on aggressive outcomes from delinquency to dating violence. Youth from violent households may conform to a family "cycle of violence," with aggressive behavior transferring to the next generation. Youth may be aggressive across a spectrum of relationships, including those with peers, dating partners, parents, other family members and even pets. There are additional areas of risk emanating from violence and resulting in psychopathology that fans out to major life decisions. Such decisions, from substance use to dropping out of school, may permanently shape an adolescent's future.

IPV is often associated with risk factors inside and outside the family (Margolin et al., 2009). The co-occurrence of IPV with child abuse, poverty, unemployment, paternal alcoholism, maternal depression, and many other risk factors creates a challenge for tying any outcome uniquely to violence alone. One approach to such a challenge is to pool the different sources of stress, including violence exposure and maltreatment. Indeed, medical researchers in California, in a series of analyses of large-scale studies, have measured a panoply of childhood risk factors to arrive at a single adversity index that is strongly tied to adult health (Fellitti et al., 1998). Findings from the Adverse Childhood Experiences Study surveying more than 8,000 adult HMO members in California revealed that different adverse experiences are highly interrelated, with the odds of having more experiences increasing with the number (Dong et al., 2004). Patients were surveyed about various forms of abuse including exposure to IPV. Only 5% of patients reporting IPV exposure recounted no other form of abuse or adversity, and the adjusted odds ratio (OR) that physical abuse co-occurred was 4.7:1. It is often the case that different risk markers signify overlapping populations: that is, studies of child abuse implicitly include families with IPV even if unmeasured, and studies of IPV implicitly include parents with substance use problems—which sometimes is measured and sometimes not (see Dong et al., 2004).

The most commonly studied risk factor in households marked by IPV is child-directed aggression or abuse. Men who perpetrate IPV are often abusive or poor parents (McCloskey, 2001; Salisbury, Henning, & Holdford, 2009).

Indeed, nearly half of men arrested for IPV met the clinical level for child abuse potential (Salisbury et al., 2009). Some research shows that abused women may also be rejecting of their teenage children, using tactics of humiliation and excessive criticism more often than mothers without abusive partners (Stuewig & McCloskey, 2005).

PREVALENCE OF ADOLESCENT EXPOSURE TO IPV

Some estimates of rates of child exposure to IPV are as high as 30% for those who reside with two parents (McDonald, Jouriles, Ramisetty-Mikler, Caetano, & Green, 2006). When children and adolescents are in such households, fully 90% actually witness the violence or, worse, become physically involved in violent episodes (Fusco & Fantuzzo, 2009).

Initial estimates of the number of U.S. adolescents exposed to IPV derived from a national survey asking young adult respondents to recollect whether they witnessed parental violence as teenagers (Straus, 1992). Respondents were asked "whether, *during [their] teenage years* [italics added], [their] father had hit their mother and how often" plus another item about their mothers hitting fathers. About one in eight (12.6%) reported witnessing some form of marital violence as teens, and for many there were recurrent instances, with the mean number being 8.9 episodes. Extrapolating from this report to the general U.S. population of adolescents in the early 1990s Murray Straus (1992) proposed that approximately 10 million Americans were exposed to marital violence *as adolescents* as a prevalence (not incidence) estimate. Subsequent epidemiologic studies have confirmed high rates of adolescent exposure to marital violence. Kilpatrick, Ruggiero, Acierno, and Saunders (2003), in a national survey, estimated that approximately 9 million U.S. adolescents witness IPV during any given year. This incidence figure suggests even higher rates than those advanced by Straus, since new cases would be added cumulatively throughout the teenage years. Another recent epidemiological survey of adolescents revealed that 9% recounted childhood scenes of IPV and 38% witnessed community violence (Zinzow et al., 2009). If one includes in prevalence estimates the youth who experienced IPV as younger children, the number of adolescents affected would climb further.

One question is whether adolescents are exposed to IPV or other forms of abuse more than younger children. A partial answer is offered through a national epidemiological survey of more than 1,000 children ages 2 to 17 with which researchers traced the age differences in exposure to various forms of victimization and witnessing, within and mostly outside of the family (Finkelhor, Ormrod, & Turner, 2009). The authors found, consistent with

Zinzow et al.'s (2009) findings, that violent threats outside the home are more frequent than within. More adolescents are exposed to community violence than very young children, with the mean number of different forms of violence at 1.7 for 2- to 5-year-olds and 3.4 for teens (ages 14–17), signifying what the authors label *polyvictimization*. Girls' victimization increases with age due to sexual abuse both within and outside of the family. On the other hand, exposure to marital violence in the home remains constant, with about 5% of children from any age group exposed to marital violence across the spectrum.

MENTAL HEALTH EFFECTS OF IPV ON YOUTH

Young children are vulnerable to the trauma of IPV, although one might expect adolescents to be more resilient given their greater maturity, autonomy, and even their ability to temporarily escape violent situations at home (which may also expose them to new risks). In a recent meta-analysis on the impact of community violence on internalizing and externalizing problems, the authors found evidence for higher vulnerability among teens than among young children for both externalizing and internalizing symptoms (Fowler, Tompsett, Braciszewski, Jacques-Tiura, & Baltes, 2009). But different age-related findings emerged from a meta-analysis of studies examining the effects of exclusively IPV exposure on children of different ages. Wolfe et al. (2003) found that the effect size was greater for school-age children ($Z = .23$) than adolescents ($Z = .11$). A meta-analysis including 118 studies on the impact of IPV showed that levels of psychopathology were elevated for children from violent households but did not vary by age (Kitzmann et al., 2003). The relative effect size (Cohen's $d = .34$) for preschool-age children, for instance, was not significantly higher than for adolescents (Cohen's $d = .25$). The authors concluded that between 50% and 63% of children of any age develop clinically significant problems in the aftermath of IPV. A subsequent meta-analysis along similar lines comparing three age categories (ages 0–5; 6–12; 13–18) found no age differences in the relative impact of IPV on any index of mental health (Cohen's $d = .47$; Evans, Davies, & DiLillo, 2008).

It appears that adolescents respond to IPV in many of the same ways as younger children (Kilpatrick, Ruggiero, Acierno, & Saunders, 2003). Further information is needed to discern exactly how youth are responding at different ages and how they are interpreting the violence. In many of the cases relating to adolescents, the violence may have been ongoing for many years, and the longer duration might compound the effect. Psychological symptoms such as anxiety or depression may also recede when the stressors are removed. Yet if children are exposed for a long duration or at a sensitive juncture in their development, such symptoms may prevail, shaping future vulnerability to stress (Hammen, Brennan, & Shih, 2004). Hammen et al.'s (2004) theory of adolescent vulnerability has yet to be applied to some of the findings linking IPV exposure to mental health problems, but her work offers a theoretical framework by which teenagers in particular face unique challenges, primed by early destabilizing family dynamics.

Attachment Relations

The vicissitudes of family life marked by IPV can result in attachment problems, especially if the dysfunction has early roots. In a study of adolescents (ages 14–16), researchers investigated whether exposure to IPV and to child abuse results in insecure attachment, abusive peer relationships, or mental health symptoms (Levendosky et al., 2002), adopting an attachment theory framework to interpret their results. The study was based on a convenience sample ($N = 111$), although adolescents were recruited both from shelters or programs and from the community at large (with flyers) that is an improvement over sampling exclusively from a shelter. Child abuse accounted for 23% of the variance in secure attachment style. Attachment was related to social relationships and mental health, although by far the strongest direct influence on depression and posttraumatic stress symptoms was a history of child abuse. IPV, when entered into the same models, contributed a negligible amount of variance in explaining adolescent mental health. Levendosky et al. (2002) concluded that exposure to IPV in childhood has fewer ramifications for adolescents than it does for younger children and that abuse has a lasting effect for both. There are some methodological issues, however, which could account for the age differences. In most studies of young children the mother is the respondent both for the IPV and for children's symptoms; therefore, due to single-respondent method variance the effect sizes for younger children may be inflated. IPV has a background role in the mental health of adolescents, but an insidious one insofar as it relates to two strong direct influences on psychopathology: child abuse history and maternal mental health. Although child abuse trumped IPV in predicting adolescent adjustment in this study, the story may be complex because the authors also found that maternal mental health predicted child mental health, consistent with other findings on children exposed to abuse (Davies & Windle, 1997). IPV is related to depression in abused women. Therefore, IPV may exert influence on adolescents—but through its impact on mothers.

Depression

Researchers examining the role of severe family stress have found that teenagers whose mothers are depressed and who are subject to high levels of family stress are much more likely to show enduring depression (Hammen, Brennan, & Shih, 2004). Marital violence was not explicitly measured in Hammen et al.'s (2004) study, though it would qualify as a notable family stressor. Therefore, adolescents exposed to marital violence and whose mothers, perhaps as a result, are depressed are at high risk of persistent depression. Depression is a particularly widespread diagnosis of teenagers in the United States, with as many as 20% experiencing clinical depression at some point during their adolescent years. Although most youth do not develop lifelong problems, youth exposed to IPV with the compounded risk of maternal depression and paternal psychopathology are at high risk of later depression.

Posttraumatic Stress

Posttraumatic stress symptoms have been observed in IPV-exposed children as early as the preschool years (Graham-Bermann & Levendosky, 1998; McCloskey & Walker, 2000), and posttraumatic stress symptoms appear to be nearly as likely in teenagers who witness violence in the home. A 1995 survey of 3,735 high school students (ages 14–19) revealed that among those who witnessed IPV between their parents a substantial number had elevated scores on Briere and Runtz's (1989) Trauma Symptom Checklist (TSC; Singer, Anglin, Song, & Lunghofer, 1995). In another college survey of freshmen (mean age = 18 years), more than one in three reported some exposure to partner violence in their family of origin, and women displayed more symptoms of traumatic stress on the TSC than did men (Silvern et al., 1995). The women's entire abuse history was more complex and traumatic than that of the young men because nearly 7% of girls who witnessed parental violence were also incest survivors. Nevertheless, even controlling for past history of sexual abuse and physical child abuse, exposure to marital violence accounted for a significant portion of the variance in trauma-related symptoms, depression, and self-esteem.

In assessing the relationship of IPV and abuse to posttraumatic stress, researchers have acknowledged that such experiences fall under the rubric of a *complex trauma*, with extensive, repeat occurrences over a long duration (Margolin & Vickerman, 2007). In addition to the psychological suffering linked to posttraumatic stress disorder (PTSD), new research shows that it also takes a physiological toll on health. In a remarkable case-control medical records study of more than 1,000 youth (ages 9–17) diagnosed with PTSD, the authors identified a wide variety of associated health problems (Seng, Graham-Bermann, Clark, McCarthy, & Ronis, 2005). The authors coded whether "violence victimization" was recorded in the medical charts, and a positive indication of victimization was highly related to PTSD. However, it was not determined what sort of violence accounted for their victimization.

The connection between PTSD and poor health was stronger in adolescents than in young children, similar to the link that has been reported for adults. In summary, the consequences of PTSD that may result from IPV relate to many areas of functioning.

The "Double Whammy" Effect of Child Abuse and Exposure to IPV

All of the handful of studies focusing exclusively on adolescents exposed to marital violence report higher overall psychopathology among exposed compared with nonexposed youth. Carlson (1990) developed a 12-point scale of well-being that includes several indicators of depression and mental health for 101 youth (age 13–18) already in residential treatment or a runaway shelter. Youth subjected to two forms of abuse (child-directed and marital violence) had worse scores on well-being than youth reporting either form alone, consistent with reports that younger children are more disturbed in the face of a "double whammy" of abuse and IPV (Hughes, Parkinson, & Vargo, 1989). While the youth in Carlson's study were distressed, they were not more likely to act aggressively. This last finding can be explained by a likely ceiling effect in the measurement of aggression because the youth were drawn from programs to treat antisocial and aggressive behavior. The study was also limited by the absence of a control or comparison group without abuse exposure. Nevertheless, the finding that even in this high risk sample two forms of abuse together are more harmful than single exposure lends support for the important role IPV may have over and above the correlation with direct child abuse.

Another study of at-risk youth (mean age = 15.4 years) recruited through the New York State Department of Social Services with confirmed abuse and IPV histories (Pelcovitz, Kaplan, DeRose, Mandel, & Salzinger, 2000) used an improved study design that included a nonabused comparison sample derived from random-digit dialing. The research team included extensive psychiatric assessments with standardized measures and also used clinical diagnoses from psychiatrists on the team (e.g., Schedule for Affective Disorders and Schizophrenia for School-Age Children-Epidemiological Version; Structured Clinical Interview for the DSM). They had an adequate sample ($N = 185$) for such extensive clinical assessments. The investigators' aim was to determine whether double exposure (both IPV and abuse) affected adolescent mental health more than a single form of exposure. The authors found strong evidence for an additive or even multiplicative effect when two forms rather than one form of violence exposure (interparental or child abuse) were documented. For instance, among the "double-exposed," 19% had PTSD in contrast to only 2% with a single exposure; 16% with double exposure were diagnosed with dysthymia in contrast to only 4% with a single exposure. Youth were 27 times more likely to report drug abuse with an abuse history of any sort than control group youth. Such findings lend further support to claims that children exposed to IPV often experience a double whammy where interparental violence combines with an increased risk of child-directed abuse to exert pronounced psychological injury (Hughes et al., 1989). While Pelcovitz and colleagues' (2000) research shows that the double whammy of abuse and IPV has a long reach into adolescence, new research in Taiwan illustrates the same effect across cultural boundaries (Shen, 2009). A survey of nearly 2,000 Taiwanese college students reporting on their childhood exposure to abuse and interparental violence affirmed that students' self-esteem was lowest when both forms of exposure occur. The effect was strongest for young men, although both men and women with dual exposure were lower in self-esteem than their counterparts. This finding is notable because, like many of the studies of adolescents and young adults, the research hinges on memories for rather distant events; that violence recollected years later still influences self-esteem or shapes other outcomes testifies to the power of childhood family adversity. Depression and low self-esteem are also observed in youth exposed to marital violence. In our longitudinal study of about 300 youth exposed to marital violence in childhood, we found that they were significantly more likely to have elevated depression scores than comparison youth drawn from similar communities but without IPV (McCloskey & Lichter, 2003). Depression was found to mediate aggressive behavior with peers. IPV exposure seems to exert similar effects on youth internationally, as demonstrated by a recent study of nearly 2,000 college students in Taiwan (Shen, 2009). Youths' recollection of IPV exposure resulted in lower self-esteem scores for both boys and girls, although if they had witnessed violence and were targets of abuse they had even lower self-esteem, lending further evidence to the double whammy hypothesis.

There appears, therefore, to be extensive support for the double whammy hypothesis, but few have advanced a theoretical interpretation of this pattern of findings. There are several potential explanations. One is that more of anything painful is worse, expressed in the theory put forth by Sameroff and his colleagues over the years (see Barocas, Seifer, & Sameroff, 1985). These authors showed that the more stressors in childhood, the worse the child's ultimate outcome. The double whammy in the IPV literature may reflect another version of the cumulative risk model. On the other hand, it is possible that in the case of studies measuring both child abuse and IPV there is special toxicity added to the child's welfare if abuse occurs; if IPV occurs on top it may be an indicator actually of the severity of family dysfunction, parental substance abuse, and heightened violence—which spills over against the children despite perhaps not being measured.

One major concern surrounding violence exposure is the risk that youth will repeat the antisocial violence they have witnessed. Such a "transfer" of risk for aggression (see Serbin & Karp, 2003) has been observed in adolescents and adults with abuse histories, especially in the realm of delinquency (Smith & Thornberry, 1995). In addition to delinquency, there is the risk of peer aggression, dating violence, and even assaults against parents and family members. Because of the overlap between IPV and child abuse, and the many similarities in ecosocial risk between households with both problems, similar outcomes may be seen in both populations.

Peer Aggression

By far the most common expression of aggression in childhood and adolescence is peer aggression, which may be either physical or relational. For purposes of this chapter, we include only findings relating to IPV and physical aggression, which have been measured in several studies. In my own longitudinal follow-up of youth exposed to IPV in childhood, we found that, controlling for self-reported child abuse victimization, IPV increased the likelihood that either boys or girls would be physically aggressive toward peers (McCloskey & Lichter, 2003). Adolescents with childhood exposure to IPV were more likely than comparisons to get into physical fights with peers, to hit a dating partner, and to attack a parent.

Social learning theory provides another framework for interpreting the connection between exposure to violence and subsequent aggressive behavior. In Bandura's (1973) classic studies on observational learning of aggression, children were more likely to model the aggression of a same-sex adult. A similar pattern was observed in youth with histories of IPV. Moretti, Obsuth, Odgers, and Reebye (2006) studied youth (ages 13–18) who were referred to a residential treatment setting for severe aggressive behavior to determine whether witnessing their same-sex parent as a perpetrator of IPV was an added risk factor for aggression. The researchers found that girls who witnessed their mothers as perpetrators were more likely to be physically aggressive against both peers and dating partners. Boys were more likely to report dating violence if they witnessed their fathers as perpetrators. Such findings lend support to the notion that youth are "processing" the violence against a backdrop of gender and relationship dynamics, and perhaps, as Bandura has suggested, are active agents in the creation of their own cognitive frameworks for aggression.

Although modeling may be one route by which aggression is transferred across generations, psychopathology and poor emotion regulation also play a role. Among the youth in Moretti's study, those who developed PTSD as a result of witnessing violence, and especially violence against their mothers with fathers as perpetrators, were more prone to aggression in intimate and peer relationships. Therefore, witnessing resulted in heightened PTSD symptoms that in turn related to aggressive behavior, but only among the girls. In our follow-up study of youth exposed to IPV and comparison youth, we found that high scores on depression raised the risk of several forms of youth aggression (peer, dating, and parent-directed; McCloskey & Lichter, 2003). The role of psychopathology in adolescent aggression is further confirmed in David Wolfe's research (as described in Wolfe, Crooks, Chiodo, & Jaffe, 2009). Their results showed that the symptoms of traumatic stress resulting from child maltreatment accounted for the high dating violence prevalence in teenagers. One mechanism they offer to further explain the results is a failure of emotion regulation to suppress violent behavior. These findings, therefore, support the view that psychopathology is one channel to increased aggression with teens, echoing findings reported on abused preschoolers who are both more withdrawn and at the same time more likely to lash out aggressively (Rogosch & Cicchetti, 1994). Studies of youth who commit violent crimes also show comorbid rates of depression (Ge, Best, Conger, & Simons, 1996).

Delinquency

Various researchers have documented increased peer aggression among school-age children, but to what degree does such aggression persist or even transform into criminal behavior in adolescence among youth exposed to IPV? It is well established that youth with histories of physical child abuse are at increased risk of aggression (see Smith & Thornberry, 1995, for review), but we know less about the unique contribution marital violence might make to adolescent aggression or delinquency (see Kruttschnitt & Dornfeld, 1993). Youth exposed to IPV are more likely to be arrested for property crimes (e.g., theft, vandalism; Fergusson & Horwood, 1998) and assault (Miller, Guo, Flannery, Frierson, & Slovak, 1999). In one of the few prospective study of its kind examining the effects of childhood exposure to marital violence on adolescent delinquency, Herrera and McCloskey (2001) reported that youth from maritally violent homes were twice as likely to be arrested as youth from nonviolent but mostly low-income households, and marital violence was a greater predictor of an arrest than childhood physical abuse.

There are expressions of antisocial behavior outside the normative delinquent acts (i.e., theft, vandalism) that often raise particular concern for the potential of escalating youth aggression. Fire setting and animal cruelty are sometimes cited as behaviors that precede serious crimes of arson and even homicide. In our follow-up of nearly 300 adolescents, half of whom were exposed to marital violence during childhood, we found a heightened risk for both forms of antisocial aggression that was compounded if the youth were also the recipients of paternal abuse (Becker, Stuewig, Herrera, & McCloskey, 2004). Such findings suggest that youth in violent households, in which the adults fail to respect personal boundaries and in which relationship norms are violated, eventually grow up to push boundaries themselves. Although sadistic impulses may explain the increased rates of animal cruelty and fire setting among these youth, another unique element of such behaviors lies in their willingness to go to extremes to draw attention to their activities and desires.

Adolescent Aggression Against Parents

One area of potential risk is when adolescents become strong enough to engage in physical conflicts with their parents or even to abuse their mothers. One study of delinquency found a high rate of IPV arrests for the teenagers, which nearly always pertained to a physical altercation with a parent and usually the mother (Herrera & McCloskey, 2001). Girls more than boys were arrested for assaulting their mothers if they had been physically abused themselves and exposed to marital violence in childhood or early adolescence. Similar gender-related patterns were recently confirmed in a large cross-sectional study of nearly 1,500 seventh-graders in which the researchers found that early physical abuse (before age 10) predicted girls' criminality more than boys (Logan, Leeb, & Barker, 2009). In the same study, however, physical fights and violence were higher among boys from abusive backgrounds than comparisons. In addition, researchers investigating the determinants of adolescent assaults against parents have discovered a strong association of such behavior with childhood and adolescent exposure to both child-directed physical abuse and IPV (Boxer, Gullan, & Mahoney, 2009). Youth from families with a history of marital violence were three times more likely to attack one of their parents (OR = 2.98; Boxer et al., 2009). Furthermore, there is evidence of a double whammy, with youth who experienced both abuse and marital violence 6 times more likely to assault a parent—twice as likely as if they experienced any one form alone. These findings were obtained with a clinical sample of families with particularly high rates of youth to parent physical aggression (about half of the youth). Even within a clinical sample, with potential ceiling effects and few controls, a strong association was uncovered for abuse and adolescent aggression toward parents; such a finding should be even stronger in a more representative sample with wider variability in risk and outcome variables.

In addition to patterns of relationship violence extending into the next generation, exposure to IPV elevates the risk that those youth will have an abusive predisposition as parents, as measured with Milner's Child Abuse Potential inventory (CAP; Miller, Handal, Gilner, & Cross, 1991). Indeed, those adolescents with histories of both physical abuse and witnessing parental violence showed greater potential for child abuse (according to the CAP score) than youth exposed to only one form of abuse.

Dating Aggression

Dating violence among adolescents in some form is relatively common in the United States, with estimates ranging from 15% to 40% (Foshee, Linder, MacDougall, & Bangdiwala, 2001). Estimates of serious dating violence with the potential for injury run as high as 15% (for a review, see Foshee, Ennet, Bauman, Benefield, & Suchindran, 2005). Exposure to parental violence may create the risk of imitation of aggressive behavior in peer relationships and eventually in close sexual relationships (Ellis, Crooks, & Wolfe, 2009). Indeed, it is possible that youth acquire "scripts" of intimacy that are recreated years later in their dating and sexual relationships. Researchers have found many correlates of dating violence: having friends who are perpetrators and parents who fail to supervise (Foshee et al., 2001; Leadbeater, Banister, Ellis, & Yeung, 2008); using alcohol or reporting many dating partners (O'Keefe, 1997); holding traditional and patriarchal beliefs, especially among boys (Lichter & McCloskey, 2004). Any of these and additional contextual variables may derive from living in violent families. Yet it remains contested how much of a direct role IPV exposure plays in launching violent dating relationships.

In their in-depth study of about 1,300 high school students, Wolfe, Wekerle, Scott, Straatman, and Grasley (2004) found that child abuse predicted dating aggression, but only indirectly, through the production of trauma symptoms. Trauma symptoms resulting from an abuse history were correlated with relationship violence and emotional abuse in dating relationships.

If adolescents exposed to IPV were more likely to express dating violence in contrast to other forms of aggression there would be reason to believe that a type-specific intergenerational transmission occurred (Kim, 2009). Some research has shown that parents with histories of either physical abuse or neglect in their own childhoods tend to replicate the form to which they were exposed (Kim, 2009). There is also research indicating that girls in particular show an elevated risk of relationship violence in adolescence as either perpetrator or victim. Some researchers find that exposure to IPV adds little variance to parent–child abuse in predicting dating aggression (O'Keefe, 1997), and others find evidence for the unique role of IPV especially in shaping traditional sex role beliefs in boys (Lichter & McCloskey, 2004). Although there may not be consistent evidence that exposure to IPV translates directly into dating violence, at least some findings support such a trend. Research following adolescents beyond their teenage years may be more informative in the future about a "cycle of violence" in intimate relationships.

Although there is some indication that IPV generates a risk of aggression and an apparent cycle of violence, it is uncertain whether exposure to marital violence per se accounts for this risk. IPV is nearly always accompanied by other sources of risk for children within the family spanning parental substance use, criminal or antisocial history, arrests, psychopathology, and frequent moves or itinerant homelessness. Ecosocial forces outside of the family include dangerous neighborhoods (Molnar, Browne, Cerda, & Buka, 2005) and other adverse influences concentrated in poor communities. All such risks may contribute to aggressive behavior across multiple relationships during adolescence.

GENDER DIFFERENCES IN RESPONSE TO IPV EXPOSURE

There is some evidence that exposure to parental violence during adolescence leaves an especially protracted mark on daughters. In the Dunedin longitudinal study of New Zealand, the authors found that exposure to parental conflict and potential physical abuse and altercations as measured by the Moos family relations inventory were most associated with adult self-reports of marital or relationship violence (as either a perpetrator or victim) if the abuse occurred during the adolescent years (Magdol, Moffitt, Caspi, & Silva, 1998). In trying to understand or predict the risk for adult cycles of relationship violence, it appears that while childhood exposure to family and parental physical abuse as an impact if it occurs during childhood, it is robust if it happens during adolescence. A broken adolescent relationship with one's mother, which is often a byproduct of family violence, is especially damaging to girls (Magdol et al., 1998). Three fourths of the adolescent characteristics significantly correlated with adult self-reports of relationship violence as either a perpetrator or victim in contrast to weaker and fewer correlations between adult behavior and childhood (Magdol et al., 1998).

Gender differences emerge in the ways IPV affect aggressive behavior and especially dating violence (Molidor, Tolman, & Kober, 2000). Girls more than boys are likely to be arrested for IPV themselves if they come from a violent household (Herrera & McCloskey, 2001), and girls show different and more escalated forms of violent behavior compared with boys from the same kind of family background. Various researchers have found gender differences in how IPV affects the risk of dating violence: Marital violence affects boys' beliefs, which in turn generates the risk that they will be perpetrators; beliefs are unrelated to dating violence for girls (Lichter & McCloskey, 2004).

Whether exposure to IPV affects boys or girls differently remains unclear and depends on the types of exposure, what dependent outcomes are measured, and the age at which children are assessed. Patterns shift with age and teenage girls from abusive families show marked increases in antisocial behavior (Herrera & McCloskey, 2001). Young adult women exposed to IPV report many more symptoms of depression and anxiety than similarly exposed men (Silvern et al., 1995).

CONCLUSION

There is evidence for continuous effects of childhood exposure to IPV into adolescence in virtually every expected domain. Adolescents exposed to IPV are more likely to show psychological adjustment problems and behavior problems, especially aggression. Although we can be relatively confident of an association, there remain large and important questions in the study of adolescents exposed to marital violence. First, because marital violence is so often accompanied by other risk factors it is important to make efforts to discover what is unique about exposure to marital violence in the trajectory of adolescent risk. Being the target of physical abuse in the home is certainly a closely associated risk that is a widely acknowledged precursor to antisocial behavior. Second, we know relatively little of the mechanisms that account for teenage problems in the aftermath of IPV exposure. In the case of later symptoms of depression or trauma, is it because youth from such homes are continually exposed to risk through perhaps low parental monitoring and shallow support networks? In the case of the intergenerational transfer of aggression, are there ecosocial determinants unique to such families that further augment their risk? Such questions are important to answer to address the social ecology of adolescent development and to be able to shape interventions accordingly. Finally, although we have reviewed nuanced findings of gender differences in the response to partner violence, no researchers to date have made vigorous efforts to analyze the broader social context of gender for adolescents and how that might influence their outcomes. Researchers often neglect the broader context that sometimes is only accessible through qualitative methods. Lending meaning to the various standardized scores, however, is crucial if we are going to generate a knowledge base that grabs the next generation of researchers and provides a foundation for useful prevention and intervention programs.

What are some of the most productive research approaches to address these areas? Although most of the studies in this area, and certainly the current preferred research designs, are large population-based correlational data sets, it is worth revisiting careful scientifically controlled subject selection to rule out other sources of covarying risk. If the key variables—which we are well aware of now and therefore can measure and designate—are held constant in subject selection, sample size could be smaller and there might be more clarity in the findings. One meta-analytic review of studies examining the effect of marital violence on a wide spectrum of child problems (e.g., internalizing, externalizing, academic problems) presented a comparison of effect sizes (d-prime) for studies that were correlational and studies with a between-group design (Kitzmann, Gaylord, Holt, & Kenny, 2003). The effect sizes were significantly larger for the between-group designs even though the sample sizes were typically smaller.

IPV exposure does not occur in a vacuum, and influences compound during adolescence. Youth have more freedom to interact with the outside world, which presents new areas of risk and heightened challenges from childhood. Researchers are calling for new and integrated ways to examine stressors—away from a single-variable model to a cumulative one. The cumulative impact of many stressors harms children and adolescents alike with the sheer number of stressors threatening adjustment (Sameroff, Peck, & Eccles, 2004). IPV may precipitate a cascade of stressors emanating from even a single violence incident in the home: police are called; one or both parents are arrested; mother and children are forced to vacate, leaving possessions and pets behind, potentially leading to homelessness and subsequent maternal depression. If the number rather than the kind of stressors is as central as Sameroff et al. (2004) argued, youth from households with IPV have more than their share. Few researchers focusing on adolescents' response to marital violence have adopted Sameroff's contextual approach, and it is a worthwhile goal but also difficult because of the varying time frames for different stressors across a youth's life course.

In at least one review of the many studies that have been performed examining IPV and children's adjustment findings across studies findings were inconsistent vis-à-vis age and gender (Onyskiw, 2003). Some researchers report that younger children show more symptoms than older, consistent with a view that they may be more vulnerable at an early age (O'Keefe, 1997) and a few researchers found that older children showed more elevated symptoms (see Hughes et al., 1989). Few studies even included youth above age 12, and the questions of whether teenagers show more symptoms than younger children, what sorts of adverse outcomes they display—and especially what kinds might be new to their stage in maturity and how adolescents process the violence they have observed during their childhood—are all intriguing questions that the studies reviewed here partly address but that need further exploration. Adolescence is often the gateway into new areas of risk that hold serious concern for researchers and policymakers, and there has been much concern on the damaging effects of violent communities and neighborhoods, poor schools, and extrafamilial sources of risk. Expanding research protocols to include both community and family violence indicators would offer a richer portrait of adolescent adjustment.

REFERENCES

Arnett, J. J. (2000). Emerging adulthood: A theory of development from the late teens through the twenties. *American Psychologist, 55,* 469–480. doi:10.1037/0003-066X.55.5.469

Bandura, A. (1973). *Aggression: Social learning analysis.* Englewood Cliffs, NJ: Prentice-Hall.

Barocas, R., Seifer, R., & Sameroff, A. J. (1985). Defining environmental risk: Multiple dimensions of psychological vulnerability. *American Journal of Community Psychology, 13,* 433–447. doi:10.1007/BF00911218

Becker, K. D., Stuewig, J., Herrera, V. M., & McCloskey, L. A. (2004). A study of firesetting and animal cruelty in children: Family influence and adolescent outcomes. *Journal of the American Academy of Child and Adolescent Psychiatry, 43,* 905–912. doi:10.1097/01.chi.0000128786.70992.9b

Boxer, P., Gullan, R. L., & Mahoney, A. (2009). Adolescents' physical aggression toward parents in a clinic-referred sample. *Journal of Clinical Child and Adolescent Psychology, 38,* 106–116. doi:10.1080/15374410802575396

Briere, J., & Runtz, M. (1989). The trauma symptom checklist (TSC-33): Early data on a new scale. *Journal of Interpersonal Violence, 4,* 151–163. doi:10.1177/088626089004002002

Carlson, B. (1990). Adolescent observers of marital violence. *Journal of Family Violence, 5,* 285–299. doi:10.1007/BF00979065

Davies, P. T., & Windle, M. (1997). Gender-specific pathways between maternal depressive symptoms, family discord, and adolescent adjustment. *Developmental Psychology, 33,* 657–668. doi:10.1037/0012-1649.33.4.657

Dong, M., Anda, R. F., Felitti, V. J., Dube, S. R., Williamson, D. F., Thompson, . . . Giles, W. H. (2004). The interrelatedness of multiple forms of childhood abuse, neglect and household dysfunction. *Child Abuse & Neglect, 28,* 771–784. doi:10.1016/j.chiabu.2004.01.008

Ellis, W. E., Crooks, C. V., & Wolfe, D. A. (2009). Relational aggression in peer and dating relationships: Links to psychological and behavioral adjustment. *Social Development, 18,* 253–269. doi:10.1111/j.1467-9507.2008.00468.x

Evans, S. E., Davies, C., & DiLillo, D. (2008). Exposure to domestic violence: A meta-analysis of child and adolescent outcomes. *Aggression and Violent Behavior, 13,* 131–140. doi:10.1016/j.avb.2008.02.005

Felitti, V. J., Anda, R. F., Nordenberg, D., Williamson, D. F., Spitz, A. M., Edwards, . . . Marks, J. S. (1998). Relationship of childhood abuse and household dysfunction to many of the leading causes of death in adults. *American Journal of Preventive Medicine, 14*, 245–258. doi:10.1016/S0749-3797(98)00017-8

Fergusson, D. M., & Horwood, L. J. (1998). Exposure to interparental violence in childhood and psychosocial adjustment in young adulthood. *Child Abuse & Neglect, 22*, 339–357. doi:10.1016/S0145-2134(98)00004-0

Finkelhor, D., Ormrod, R. K., & Turner, H. A. (2009). The developmental epidemiology of childhood victimization. *Journal of Interpersonal Violence, 24*, 711–731. doi:10.1177/0886260508317185

Foshee, V. A., Ennett, S. T., Bauman, K. E., Benefield, T., & Suchindran, C. (2005). The association between family violence and adolescent dating violence onset. Does it vary by race, socioeconomic status, and family structure? *Journal of Early Adolescence, 25*, 317–344.

Foshee, V. A., Linder, MacDougall, & Bangdiwala, S. (2001). Gender differences in the longitudinal predictors of adolescent dating violence. *Preventive Medicine, 32*, 128–141. doi:10.1006/pmed.2000.0793

Fowler, P. J., Tompsett, C. J., Braciszewski, J. M., Jacques-Tiura, A. J., & Baltes, B. B. (2009). Community violence: A meta-analysis on the effect of exposure and mental health outcomes of children and adolescents. *Development and Psychopathology, 21*, 227–259. doi:10.1017/S0954579409000145

Fusco, R. A., & Fantuzzo, J. W. (2009). Domestic violence crimes and children: A population-based investigation of direct sensory exposure and the nature of involvement. *Children and Youth Services Review, 31*, 249–256. doi:10.1016/j.childyouth.2008.07.017

Ge, X. J., Best, K. M., Conger, R. D., & Simons, R. (1996). Parenting behaviors and the occurrence and co-occurrence of adolescent depressive symptoms and conduct problems *Developmental Psychology, 32*, 717–731.

Graham-Bermann, S. A., & Levendosky, A. A. (1998). Traumatic stress symptoms in children of battered women. *Journal of Interpersonal Violence, 13*, 111–128. doi:10.1177/088626098013001007

Hammen, C., Brennan, P. A., & Shih, J. H. (2004). Family discord and stress predictors of depression and other disorders in adolescent children of depressed and nondepressed women. *Journal of the American Academy of Child and Adolescent Psychiatry, 43*, 994–1002. doi:10.1097/01.chi.0000127588.57468.f6

Herrera, V. M., & McCloskey, L. A. (2001). Gender differences in the risk for delinquency among youth exposed to family violence. *Child Abuse & Neglect, 25*, 1037–1051. doi:10.1016/S0145-2134(01)00255-1

Hughes, H. M., Parkinson, D. L., & Vargo, M. C. (1989). Witnessing spouse abuse and experiencing physical abuse: A "double whammy"? *Journal of Family Violence, 4*, 197–209. doi:10.1007/BF01006629

Kilpatrick, D. G., Ruggiero, K. J., Acierno, R., & Saunders, D. G. (2003). Violence and risk of PTSD, major depression, substance abuse/dependence, and comorbidity: Results from the national survey of adolescents. *Journal of Consulting and Clinical Psychology, 71*, 692–700. doi:10.1037/0022-006X.71.4.692

Kim, J. (2009). Type-specific intergenerational transmission of neglectful and physically abusive parenting behaviors among young parents. *Children and Youth Services Review, 31*, 761–767. doi:10.1016/j.childyouth.2009.02.002

Kitzmann, K. M., Gaylord, N. K., Holt, A. R., & Kenny, E. D. (2003). Child witnesses to domestic violence: A meta-analytic review. *Journal of Consulting and Clinical Psychology, 71*, 339–352. doi:10.1037/0022-006X.71.2.339

Kruttschnitt, C., & Dornfeld, M. (1993). Exposure to family violence: A partial explanation for initial and subsequent levels of delinquency. *Criminal Behaviour and Mental Health, 3*, 61–75.

Leadbeater, B. J., Banister, E. M., Ellis, W. E., & Yeung, R. (2008). Victimization and relational aggression in adolescent romantic relationships: The influence of parental and peer behaviors, and individual adjustment. *Journal of Youth and Adolescence, 37*, 359–372. doi:10.1007/s10964-007-9269-0

Levendosky, A. A., Huth-Bocks, A., & Semel, M. A. (2002). Adolescent peer relationships and mental health functioning in families with domestic violence. *Journal of Clinical Child Psychology, 31*, 206–218.

Lichter, E. L., & McCloskey, L. A. (2004). The effects of childhood exposure to marital violence on adolescent gender-role beliefs and dating violence. *Psychology of Women Quarterly, 28*, 344–357. doi:10.1111/j.1471-6402.2004.00151.x

Logan, J. E., Leeb, R. T., & Barker, L. E. (2009). Gender-specific mental and behavioral outcomes among physically abused high-risk seventh-grade youths. *Public Health Reports, 124*, 234–245.

Magdol, L., Moffitt, T. E., Caspi, A., & Silva, P. A. (1998). Developmental antecedents of partner abuse: A prospective longitudinal study. *Journal of Abnormal Psychology, 107*, 375–389. doi:10.1037/0021-843X.107.3.375

Margolin, G., & Gordis, E. B. (2000). The effects of family and community violence on children. *Annual Review of Psychology, 51*, 445–479. doi:10.1146/annurev.psych.51.1.445

Margolin, G., & Vickerman, K. A. (2007). Posttraumatic stress in children and adolescents exposed to family violence: I. Overview and issues. *Professional Psychology, Research and Practice, 38*, 613–619. doi:10.1037/0735-7028.38.6.613

Margolin, G., Vickerman, K. A., Ramos, M. C., Serrano, S. D., Gordis, E. B., Iturralde, E., . . . Spies, L. A. (2009). Youth exposed to violence: Stability, co-occurrence, and context. *Clinical Child and Family Psychology Review, 12*, 39–54. doi:10.1007/s10567-009-0040-9

McCloskey, L. A. (2001). The Medea complex among men: The instrumental abuse of children to injure wives. *Violence and Victims, 16*, 19–37.

McCloskey, L. A., Figueredo, A. J., & Koss, M. P. (1995). The effects of systemic family violence on children's mental health. *Child Development, 66*, 1239–1261. doi:10.2307/1131645

McCloskey, L. A., & Lichter, E. L. (2003). The contribution of marital violence to adolescents aggression across different relationships. *Journal of Interpersonal Violence, 18,* 390–412. doi:10.1177/0886260503251179

McCloskey, L. A., & Walker, M. (2000). Posttraumatic stress in children exposed to family violence and single-event trauma. *Journal of the Academy of Child and Adolescent Psychiatry, 39,* 108–115. doi:10.1097/00004583-200001000-00023

McDonald, R., Jouriles, E. N., Ramisetty-Mikler, S., Caetano, R., & Green, C. E. (2006). Estimating the number of children living in partner-violent families. *Journal of Family Psychology, 20,* 137–142.

Miller, D. B., Guo, S. Y., Flannery, D. J., Frierson, T., & Slovak, K. (1999). Contributors to violent behavior among elementary and middle school children. *Pediatrics, 104,* 878–884.

Miller, T. R., Handal, P. J., Gilner, F. H., & Cross, J. F. (1991). The relationship of abuse and witnessing violence on the child-abuse potential inventory with Black adolescents. *Journal of Family Violence, 6,* 351–363.

Molidor, C., Tolman, R. M., & Kober, J. (2000). Gender and contextual factors in adolescent dating violence. *Prevention Researcher, 7*(1), 1–4.

Molnar, B. E., Browne, A., Cerda, M., & Buka, S. (2005). Violent behavior by girls reporting violent victimization. *Archives of Pediatrics & Adolescent Medicine, 159,* 731–739. doi:10.1001/archpedi.159.8.731

Moretti, M. M., Obsuth, I., Odgers, C. L., & Reebye, P. (2006). Exposure to maternal vs. paternal partner violence, PTSD, and aggression adolescent girls and boys. *Aggressive Behavior, 32,* 385–395. doi:10.1002/ab.20137

O'Keefe, M. (1997). Predictors of dating violence among high school students. *Journal of Interpersonal Violence, 12,* 546–568. doi:10.1177/088626097012004005

Onyskiw, J. E. (2002). Health and use of health services of children exposed to violence in their families. *Canadian Journal of Public Health, 93,* 416–420.

Pelcovitz, D., Kaplan, S. J., DeRose, R. R., Mandel, F. S., & Salzinger, S. (2000). Psychiatric disorders in adolescents exposed to domestic violence and physical abuse. *American Journal of Orthopsychiatry, 70,* 360–369. doi:10.1037/h0087668

Rogosch, F., & Cicchetti, D. (1994) Illustrating the interface of family and peer relations through the study of child maltreatment. *Social Development, 3,* 291–308.

Salisbury, E. J., Henning, K., & Holdford, R. (2009). Fathering by partner-abusive men: Attitudes on children's exposure to interparental conflict and risk factors for child abuse. *Child Maltreatment, 14,* 232–242.

Sameroff, A. J., Peck, S. C., & Eccles, J. S. (2004). Changing ecological determinants of conduct problems from early adolescence to early adulthood. *Development and Psychopathology, 16,* 873–896. doi:10.1017/S0954579404040052

Seng, J. S., Graham-Bermann, S. A., Clark, M. K., McCarthy, A. M., & Ronis, D. L. (2005). Posttraumatic stress disorder and physical co-morbidity among female children and adolescents: Results from service-use data. *Pediatrics, 116,* e767–e776. doi:10.1542/peds.2005-0608

Serbin, L., & Karp, J. (2003). Intergenerational studies of parenting and the transfer of risk from parent to child. *Current Directions in Psychological Science, 12,* 138–142.

Shen, A. C. (2009). Self-esteem of young adults experiencing interparental violence and child physical maltreatment: Parental and peer relationships as mediators. *Journal of Interpersonal Violence, 24,* 770–794. doi:10.1177/0886260508317188

Silvern, L., Karyl, J., Waelde, L., Hodges, W. F., Starek, J., Heidt, E., & Min, K. (1995). Retrospective reports of parental partner abuse: Relationships to depression, trauma symptoms and self-esteem among college students. *Journal of Family Violence, 10,* 177–202. doi:10.1007/BF02110599

Singer, M. I., Anglin, T. M., Song, L. Y., & Lunghofer, L. (1995). Adolescents' exposure to violence and associated symptoms of psychological trauma. *JAMA, 273,* 477–482.

Smetana, J. G., Campione-Barr, N., & Metzger, A. (2006). Adolescent development in interpersonal and societal contexts. *Annual Review of Psychology, 57,* 255–284. doi:10.1146/annurev.psych.57.102904.190124

Smith, C., & Thornberry, T. (1995). The relationship between childhood maltreatment and adolescent involvement in delinquency. *Criminology, 33,* 451–481. doi:10.1111/j.1745-9125.1995.tb01186.x

Steinberg, L., & Cauffman, E. (1996). The maturity of judgment in adolescence: Psychosocial factors in adolescent decision-making. *Law and Human Behavior, 20,* 249–272. doi:10.1007/BF01499023

Straus, M. A. (1992). *Children as witnesses to marital violence: A risk factor for lifelong problems among a nationally representative sample of American men and women. Report of the Twenty-Third Ross Roundtable.* Columbus, OH: Ross Laboratories.

Stuewig, J., & McCloskey, L. A. (2005). The relation of child maltreatment to shame and guilt among adolescents: Psychological routes to depression and delinquency. *Child Maltreatment, 10,* 324–336. doi:10.1177/1077559505279308

Wilson, H. W., Stover, C. M., & Berkowitz, S. J. (2009). The relationships between childhood violence exposure and juvenile antisocial behavior: A meta-analytic review. *Journal of Child Psychology and Psychiatry, and Allied Disciplines, 50,* 769–779. doi:10.1111/j.1469-7610.2008.01974.x

Wolfe, D. A., Crooks, C. V., Lee, V., McIntyre-Smith, A., & Jaffe, P. (2003). The effects of children's exposure to domestic violence: A meta-analysis and critique. *Clinical Child and Family Psychology Review, 6,* 171–187. doi:10.1023/A:1024910416164

Wolfe, D. A., Wekerle, C., Scott, K., Straatman, A., & Grasley, C. (2004). Predicting abuse in adolescent dating relationships over one year: The role of child maltreatment and trauma. *Journal of Abnormal Psychology, 113,* 406–415. doi:10.1037/0021-843X.113.3.406

Wolfe, D. A., Crooks, C. C., Chiodo, D., & Jaffe, P. (2009). Child maltreatment, bullying, gender-based harassment, and adolescent dating violence: Making the connections. *Psychology of Women Quarterly, 33,* 21–24. doi:10.1111/j.1471-6402.2008.01469.x

Zinzow, H. M., Ruggiero, K. J., Resnick, H., Hanson, R., Smith, D., Saunders, B., & Kilpatrick, D. (2009). Prevalence and mental health correlates of witnessed parental and community violence in a national sample of adolescents. *Journal of Child Psychology and Psychiatry, and Allied Disciplines, 50,* 441–450. doi:10.1111/j.1469-7610.2008.02004.x

12

THE ADOLESCENT'S EXPERIENCE OF INTIMATE PARTNER VIOLENCE AND IMPLICATIONS FOR INTERVENTION

ALISON CUNNINGHAM AND LINDA L. BAKER

Of the 52.7 million children in the United States (ages 0–17) living with two parents, an estimated 10.7 million live in homes where male-to-female intimate partner violence (IPV) between adults has occurred in the previous year. For 2.3 million of them, that violence was severe (McDonald, Jouriles, Ramisetty-Mikler, Caetano, & Green, 2007). How many are teenagers? Some data suggest that adolescents are underrepresented in violent homes relative to their prevalence in the general population, at least in homes that come to official attention because of IPV. For example, young people ages 12 to 17 made up only 17% of the children known by police to be in the home during domestically violent incidents in one Rhode Island jurisdiction (Gjelsvik, Verhoek-Oftedahl, & Pearlman, 2003). In Canadian shelters for abused women in 2006, only 33% of child residents were ages 10 or over (Vaillancourt & Taylor-Butts, 2007). In a study of men in court-ordered evaluation after conviction for intimate assault, 17% of their children were ages 13 to 17 (Salisbury, Henning, & Holdford, 2009).

The fact that adolescents are underrepresented in cross-sectional samples of exposed youth suggests four hypotheses. First, some abused mothers manage to extricate themselves from violent relationships before their children reach adolescence. Second, some teenagers absent themselves from the home, perhaps by leaving home early or moving to live with relatives. Exposure to violence in general is statistically associated with a higher probability of leaving home as a teenager (Haynie, Petts, Maimon, & Piquero, 2008). Third, it is possible that some teenagers were excluded from the home by being "kicked out" or sent to live elsewhere. Fourth, mandated agencies may have prevented some young people from continuing to live at home, perhaps through a child welfare intervention or by assigning custody to a biological father if a mother's abusive partner is acting as stepparent. Some violence-exposed youth will be living in juvenile correctional facilities or other care settings for a portion of their teenage years (Baker & Jaffe, 2003).

In a national sample of 12- to 17-year-olds, 8.9% reported observing IPV in their lifetime so far, estimated to represent 2.3 million of the 25.4 million American teenagers (Zinzow et al., 2009). Some of these teenagers were exposed to IPV only while they were small, some only when they were teenagers, and some during most or all of their childhoods. Few data are available to help us understand these temporal patterns but it seems that adolescent onset of IPV exposure is the exception rather than the rule. In a longitudinal study of a New Zealand birth cohort questioned at age 26 about incidents of IPV witnessed, overheard, or about which they were told when children, 9% reported one to four incidents, and 10% reported five or more such incidents. Most of them (62%) described male-to-female violence only, whereas 25% described bidirectional violence. The mean age of respondents at the first (or only) incident was 7.5 years. For 20%, the first (or only) incident occurred when they were 11 years or older (Martin, Langley, & Millichamp, 2006). In an Australian general population survey of adolescents, 16.6% of 12-year-olds reported having seen male-to-female physical violence between parents (in their lifetime thus far), while the same figure for 17-year-olds was 28.7%, suggesting that less than half of them had first been exposed during adolescence (Crime Research Centre, 2001).

Goldblatt (2003) noted that adolescents who currently live with IPV differ from younger peers and siblings: They are more active outside the home, can view problems from multiple perspectives, are aware of wider social values against violence, and are better able to express their opinions. Because they are larger and stronger, they can intervene physically in altercations and may be emotionally able to confront the abuser. Indeed, data collected by Gewirtz and Medhanie (2008) about 911 calls suggest that older children are more likely to be directly involved in IPV incidents as opposed to witnessing or being indirectly exposed. A teenager's interpretations of cause and consequence of IPV are growing more sophisticated, and they manifest an expanding repertoire of coping reactions that can include healthy choices, such as seeking peer support; more concerning options, such as physical avoidance by leaving home; or emotional disengagement, such as drug use (Baker & Cunningham, 2004).

This chapter uses the knowledge about how IPV affects adolescents to focus on implications for developmentally appropriate interventions with adolescents. We make three assumptions here, grounded in clinical work with children and young people and also with consideration of empirical studies. First, even siblings living in the same home can have dramatically different recollections and understanding of shared events, so individual assessment and case planning are crucial. Some teens are coping well, and some are having enormous problems. Accordingly, there is no "one-size-fits-all" approach appropriate for all youth in terms of either understanding or intervention. Second, IPV rarely occurs in isolation of other family adversities, such as direct child maltreatment or poverty, which also challenge normal child development. Exposure to violence in the home is often correlated with other types of direct and indirect victimization (e.g., Finkelhor, Turner, Ormrod, Hamby, & Kracke, 2009). Case planning and referrals are most profitably undertaken with consideration of all co-occurring adversities and the assumption that some may be more pressing at this minute than others. Third, how children process, understand and remember IPV depends to a great extent on the age when they were exposed. Developmentally sensitive interventions will take into account the current age of a young person and also the age at the time of exposure. Thus, this chapter uses a developmental framework to understand the needs of adolescents exposed to IPV and the kinds of services that may help them.

ADOLESCENT DEVELOPMENT AND INTIMATE PARTNER VIOLENCE

In the last incident resulting in her father's arrest, Malika, age 12, for the first time joined her older siblings in verbally and physically intervening to protect her mother: "We got on him and tried to pull him off her while my brother went to a neighbour's [home] to call the police" (Cunningham & Baker, 2004, p. 90). Malika's increased age and maturity combined with her father's escalating violence caused her to intervene directly.

Teenagers are moving rapidly from self-identifying as a "child" toward but not quite reaching the phase of "young adulthood." Key aspects of this developmental stage are an increased sense of self and autonomy from the family, dramatic physical and mood changes brought on by puberty, increased peer group influence and desire for acceptance, and the possible onset of dating, raising issues of sexuality, intimacy, and the need for relationship skills. Young people are individuating from their parents, negotiating a new type of relationship with the adults in their lives, gaining greater self-reliance, trying new challenges, and adopting more decision-making autonomy. Ideally, parents guide young people through these dramatic changes, providing a solid and reassuring presence against which to rebel and test boundaries in a safe way. Important aspects of this process are clear and age-appropriate rules and consequences, supervision and monitoring, and open communication.

While adolescence is an important period of transition, teenagers living with IPV may not experience the stability and guidance required for optimal development (Goldblatt, 2003). Table 12.1 summarizes how exposure to IPV can affect adolescents' development.

POTENTIAL IMPACT OF EXPOSURE TO INTIMATE PARTNER VIOLENCE ON ADOLESCENT DEVELOPMENT

When a home is characterized by IPV, one child may be pushed or pulled into pseudoadult roles, such as caretaking of younger siblings, as discussed later in the section about family roles. An onset or deepening of parent/child conflict may be seen, and some teens will opt to leave home or be forced to do so. Physically intervening in incidents or defending the victimized parent will lead to criminal assault charges for some. When academic success is compromised by factors such as lack of sleep, teens are old enough to opt out of school attendance. Overall, the IPV and conflict generated can prematurely end conventional teenage roles if it precipitates precocious transition to independent living, parenthood, school dropout, or even imprisonment. At the same time, abused parents, usually a mother, may be unable to function as the parents they want to be or can be (Baker & Cunningham, 2004).

Peers become an enormously important influence, and teens desire greatly to be accepted. Where IPV is present, teens may feel shame and embarrassment about their families and life at home. Some will make poor choices about risky behaviors in efforts to impress others or fit in. As discussed later, coping choices may be worrisome to the adults who care about them. Some will seek sexual intimacy as comfort, or control. Adolescents may engage in problematic coping strategies discussed later, such as drug use or emotional numbing. In contrast to younger children, gender differences in perceptions and reactions to violence at home become evident at this age (McGee, Wolfe, & Wilson, 1997). Adolescents are developing a sense of body image and self-worth that can be grossly distorted, as was the case for this teenager who lived with severe IPV:

> [My stepfather would] always comment about my breasts and make me dance in front of his friends. I hated it but never said no 'cause I was so scared. I got implants but it didn't help, now I hate my stomach. To this day I have to change my clothes three to five times before I go out 'cause I feel so bad about myself. My boyfriend for two years [now] always says I'm beautiful but it goes in one ear and out the other 'cause of all those years. (Cunningham & Baker, 2004, p. 94)

TABLE 12.1
Potential Impact of Exposure to Intimate Partner Violence on Adolescent Development

Key aspects of development	Potential impact
Increased sense of self and autonomy from family	Accelerated responsibility and autonomy may position youth in care-taking roles and/or premature independence; family skills for respectful communication and negotiation may be poorly developed, so transition to adolescence may be more difficult and result in such challenges as increased parent–child conflict, early home leaving, or school drop-out
Physical changes brought on by puberty	May try physically to stop violence; may use increased size to impose will with physical intimidation or aggression
Increased peer group influence and desire for acceptance	Possibly more embarrassed by family resulting in shame, secrecy, insecurity; may be susceptible to high risk behaviors to impress peers (e.g., theft, drugs); may try to escape by increasing time away from home; may engage in maladaptive defensive (e.g., drugs) and offensive (e.g., aggression towards batterer) strategies to avoid or cope with violence and its stigma
Self-worth more strongly linked to view of physical attractiveness	View of self may be distorted by batterer's degradation of mother and/or the co-occurrence of child maltreatment; may experience eating disorder and use of image management activities (e.g., body piercing, tattoos)
Dating raises issues of sexuality, intimacy, and relationship skills	May have difficulty establishing healthy relationships; may fear being abused or being abusive in intimate relationships, especially when conflict arises; may avoid intimacy or may prematurely seek intimacy and child bearing as means of escape and creating own support system
Increased capacity for abstract reasoning and broader worldview	"All or nothing" interpretations of experiences may be learned and compete with greater capacity to see "shades of grey" (e.g., everyone is a victim or a perpetrator); this style of processing information may be intensified by experiences of child maltreatment; may be predisposed toward attitudes and values associated with violence and/or victimization
Increased influence by media	May be more influenced by negative media messages regarding violent behavior, gender role stereotypes

Note. From *Helping Children Thrive: Supporting Woman Abuse Survivors as Mothers* (p. 49), by L. Baker and A. Cunningham, 2004, London, Ontario, Canada: Centre for Children & Families in the Justice System. Copyright 2004 by the Centre for Children & Families in the Justice System. Reprinted with permission.

Teenagers continue to need adult input and supervision but may not readily recognize or accept that reality. Intervention is crucial, yet they may be difficult to engage.

MECHANISMS OF INFLUENCE
AND IMPLICATIONS FOR INTERVENTION

As Cunningham and Baker (2007) observed, children who live in homes with violence are often isolated from helpful support by shame and secrecy. They may experience compromised parenting and are exposed to poor male role models. Children living with abuse can learn to see the world as a negative and unsafe place, and they often experience family stresses and negative influences statistically correlated with family violence such as parental substance abuse, poverty, and residential instability. In consequence, these children can develop ways of coping and surviving that may limit them in later life, such as substance abuse, emotional numbing, school dropout, sexual exploitation by others, or early exit from the family home. Cognitive distortions supporting violence (e.g., being angry or being drunk is a good reason to hit someone) may increase the likelihood violence is used outside the home or used or accepted in dating relationships (Cunningham & Baker, 2007).

When we see correlational evidence of a link between IPV and poor child outcomes, we need to ask: What are the dynamics at play? Why are different children affected in different ways by living with the same experiences? Much work has been done to raise awareness in both the helping professions and the general public about the deleterious effects of living with IPV on children and teens. It is now axiomatic that a home with IPV, and its adverse but common correlates such as child maltreatment, is not a healthy environment for growing children. Less work has focused on how to ameliorate that impact (Cunningham & Baker, 2004), beyond the obvious imperative of reducing or eliminating children's exposure to IPV. As Cunningham and Baker (2007) observed, a child who lives with violence is forever changed but not forever "damaged." These authors suggested that understanding the linkages between IPV and child outcomes help define intervention approaches, and they posited 10 ways in which children and teenagers may be shaped by living with IPV. As summarized in Table 12.2, each mechanism has at least one implication for intervention that can include correcting distorted ideas such as rationalizations for IPV, encouraging helpful coping strategies, building skills such as problem solving, and helping with the management of intense emotions. Six of these mechanisms are discussed here: exposure to abusive male role models, erosion of the mother–child bond, isolation from helpful supports, evolution of unhealthy family roles, presence of co-occurring adversities, and recourse to problematic coping.

TABLE 12.2

Ten Ways Living With Intimate Partner Violence (IPV) Can Shape
Children and Related Implications for Intervention With Teenagers

Potential mechanisms of impact of IPV on teenagers	Implications for intervention with teens
1. Exposure to abusive role models for men and fathers	• Use psychoeducational group or individual counseling to learn about abusive vs. healthy relationships • Expose youth to healthy male role models and mentors • Use skills training for effective communication and problem solving
2. Damaged mother–child bond	• Use therapeutic work to heal the bond, reestablish trust, and increase mutual understanding and/or improve parent–teen communication • Help mothers regain (or gain) parental authority and develop adolescent-appropriate parenting skills
3. Negative core beliefs of self	• Explore core beliefs and reframe negative self-image if present • Support school success and identify areas of strength to help teenagers feel competent and confident • Encourage mother to reinforce (e.g., through positive feedback) healthy self-image of teen
4. Isolation from helpful supports	• Use psychoeducational group counseling to meet other youth in same situation • Use websites, chat groups, and hot-lines to communicate with other teens • Recommend books designed for this age group
5. Unhealthy family roles	• Identify roles and current dynamics that may be causing tension and conflict in family • Help teenagers identify roles, reframe any distorted thinking, and provide support to adopt a healthier or more balanced role
6. View of world as unsafe	• Encourage mastery of safety skills and safety self-efficacy
7. Probability of co-occurring adversities	• Conduct thorough intake assessment and information gathering to compile complete picture of adversities and family functioning • Assist family to find safe/stable housing and income support if needed • Assist mother to address any personal challenges compromising her parenting
8. Adoption of problematic coping styles	• Assess coping methods and encourage healthy coping • Provide emotion coaching to teach identification, expression, and regulation of emotions and to read the emotions of others • Help mothers to identify their teen's coping style and encourage helpful coping
9. Adoption of rationalizations for violence within intimate relationships	• Provide education on dynamics of power and control and healthy relationships • If required, hold youthful perpetrators accountable using prosecution
10. Adoption of victimization myths	• Provide education on dynamics of power and control and healthy relationships • If appropriate, maintain victim safety through prosecution of youthful perpetrators of intimate violence

Abusive Role Models

Men who are abusive to female partners are poor models for children about what men and fathers should be. By definition, their abusive behavior toward their female partners fosters disrespect for women in general, reflects an antisocial value system, and teaches poor problem-solving and conflict-resolution skills. As parents, abusive men can be rigid, authoritarian, manipulative, and uninvolved (Bancroft & Silverman, 2002). Abusive men can underestimate the degree of impact the IPV has on their children (Salisbury, Henning, & Holdford, 2009) or believe it will have no long-term impact (Rothman, Mandel, & Silverman, 2007). Arguing against such "sweeping generalizations," Perel and Peled (2008) cautioned that much of our understanding of abusive men as parents comes solely from partner reports and is grounded in a deficit paradigm. However, there is much good evidence to show that a man who is abusive to his partner may also abuse his children (e.g., McDonald, Jouriles, Tart, & Minze, 2009).

Several studies have identified a correlation between exposure to IPV in childhood and later use of violence in intimate relationships or victimization by a partner (e.g., Kwong, Bartholomew, Henderson, & Trinke, 2003; Stith et al., 2000; Whitfield, Anda, Dube, & Felitti, 2003), although the statistical association may be partly explained by psychosocial covariates within the family context, such as child abuse, low maternal age, parenting style, and socioeconomic disadvantage (Fergusson, Boden, & Horwood, 2006), or other family dynamics, such as attachment or discipline strategies (Schwartz, Hage, Bush, & Burns, 2006). While by no means the only one (Schwartz et al., 2006), social learning theory is arguably the most common orientation used to explain the apparent intergenerational transmission of the propensity for intimate violence from one generation to the next (Indermaur, Atkinson, & Blagg, 2001). Simply put, the abusive parent—typically the father—models the use of abuse and violence as ways to solve his problems, suppress conflict, and get his needs met. If no negative consequences follow, violence appears to be a successful strategy and one that at least some of his children may adopt as they grow older. Even parental attitudes on aggression and violence can have powerful impacts on teenagers (Solomon, Bradshaw, Wright, & Cheng, 2008), but the influence of peers must also be considered (Arriaga & Foshee, 2004).

The direct implications for intervention are that children's exposure to abusive role models should be diminished and their exposure to positive role models encouraged. One way to accomplish this end is to help abusive men understand that their behavior is unacceptable and to cultivate new interpersonal skills. Many IPV services and policies take this approach. Policies promoting arrest and prosecution serve as a tangible statement that use of violence is not socially acceptable and can involve severe penalties, including perhaps imprisonment. Batterer intervention programs now exist in most areas of the United States and Canada.

Increasingly, programs are aimed at the parenting of abusive men (Edleson & Williams, 2007; Mathews, 1995), including the Fathering After Violence initiative of the Family Violence Prevention Fund. These efforts are important because a good proportion of men continue to have contact with their children—including teenagers—even after the spousal relationship ends (Salisbury, Henning, & Holdford, 2009). Also, helping men understand how IPV impacts their children can be used as a motivating factor in batterer interventions (e.g., Fox, Sayers, & Bruce, 2001), and at least some fathers yearn for a healthier relationship with their children (Perel & Peled, 2008). Some children want very much to continue the relationship (Peled, 2000). Due attention to child safety must, of course, be considered (Groves, Van Horn, & Lieberman, 2007).

Another type of intervention is targeted at so-called high-risk groups, such as young men who lived with IPV or young males who use violence or control in dating relationships. In adolescent boys, exposure to IPV has been linked to the elevated probability of perpetration of dating violence, which in turn is linked to the elevated probability of IPV in adulthood, the so-called cycle of violence or intergenerational transmission of violence. Some adolescent programs modeled on adult batterer treatment have been developed in recent years. It can be argued that programs designed for adult men may not be the best fit with adolescent boys, so developmentally sensitive modification is wise. The Young Men's Program of the Domestic Abuse Project in Minnesota (Davis, 2004) is one example, as is the Turning Point adolescent program of the Emerge agency near Boston.

Another implication is the use of universal programs to convey and reinforce prosocial values and critique common rationalizations of violence against women. An Australian review concluded that universal instruction of this type should coexist with efforts focused on at-risk subpopulations of youth, especially if using the whole-school approach (Indermaur, Atkinson, & Blagg, 2001). A key problem with universal, school-based programs is that the principal target group may have absented themselves from the education system. In an Australian survey of young people both in school and who had left school, 25% of the respondents who supported the use of violence in relationships were no longer in school (Crime Research Centre, 2001).

Erosion of the Mother–Child Bond

Parents are ideally the secure base on whom a child can rely for comfort during times of distress (Bowlby, 1988). However, abused women are rarely able to be the mothers they can be and want to be. The dynamics of power and control permeate every aspect of daily life at home. Women eventually change how they think, feel, and act as they react to or try to prevent abuse and its recurrence (Baker & Cunningham 2008). Inevitably, this dynamic affects women as mothers. The effects of abuse dynamics on a woman's parenting include eroding her confidence as a parent, lowering her self-esteem and feelings of self-efficacy, overwhelming her capacity to manage daily tasks, believing (and potentially reinforcing with the children) an abuser's rationalizations for violence, or developing an overly permissive or authoritarian parenting style in response to his parenting style (Baker & Cunningham, 2004).

An abusive man can foster disrespect of children toward their mother and undermine her parenting authority through direct or indirect interference in the mother–child relationship, including overriding her decisions, ridiculing her in front of the children, portraying himself as the only legitimate parenting authority, and encouraging or tolerating their mistreatment of her (Bancroft & Silverman, 2002). Over time, a woman may lose the respect of some or all children. Where IPV is present, adolescents may feel low affinity for their parents, who may in turn create a rigid view of people as either victims or perpetrators (Winstock & Eisikovits, 2003).

It is a paradox, but children may blame the abused mother more than the abusive father for abuse and its consequences (Cunningham & Baker, 2007). In the New Zealand birth cohort study (Martin, Langley, & Millichamp, 2006), among respondents reporting male-to-female violence between parents, 61% considered the father as solely or mostly to blame, meaning that 39% felt the mother was to blame or the parents were jointly responsible. When the mother was reported as threatening or hitting the father, whether or not he was violent as well, the proportion holding the father more responsible fell to 27%. Children may be angry with a mother for failing to protect them and confused about why she cannot protect herself. As children enter adolescence, they may resent a mother for ignoring their needs, expecting them to take care of younger siblings, or continuing a relationship with an abusive man.

In earlier developmental stages, the site of intervention is necessarily focused on the child's environment and key people in it. For example, with babies and toddlers, supporting their mothers as parents is an important strategy (Baker & Cunningham, 2004). The early childhood educator will play a role in supporting preschool-age children who live or have lived with IPV by, for example, creating a safe and calm classroom environment (Baker & Cunningham, 2009). As children mature, interventions can turn toward healing the mother–child bond that has been damaged by the previously described dynamics. Intervening with school-age children and their mothers as a dyad can be followed by improvements in the child's emotional and behavioral functioning and greater improvements than working with the child alone (Graham-Bermann, Lynch, Banyard, DeVoe, & Halabu, 2007). At least one intervention program is designed to strengthen the mother–child bond, the Australian PARKAS program (Bunston, 2001). Compromised attachment to a mother can strengthen over time once abuse ends (Sternberg, Lamb, Guterman, Abbott, & Dawud-Noursi, 2005).

The parenting of women who live with violent partners usually improves after the relationship ends (Casanueva, Martin, Runyan, Barth, & Bradley, 2008), so efforts to promote the safety of a mother will, by extension, increase the exposure of children to more effective parenting. Self-care and healing are also important for a caregiver parent after violence exposure (Ziegler & Weidner, 2006). Mothers can learn their teenager's perspective on family events and apply adolescent-specific parenting strategies that correlate with how IPV affects children and teens (Baker & Cunningham, 2004; Bilinkoff, 1995). In working with women, helping them believe they can avoid a future violent partner is also an important strategy. When children are exposed to more than one abusive father-figure over the course of their childhood, the negative effect can accumulate (Israel & Stover, 2009). Bancroft (2002) provided practical guidance on the warning signs of abuse observable early in a relationship.

Isolation From Helpful Supports

Children who live with IPV know, or are warned, that bad things will happen if the world learns the family secrets. They may learn to pass as "normal" because fitting in and being accepted is important. This combination of shame and secrecy cuts them off from people who could listen and help or people who could recognize the problem.

A variety of approaches that may be termed *self-help* can come into play here, such as websites, books, hot-lines, online forums and chats, peer-support groups, and the like. Compared with their younger siblings, teenagers are better able to reach out to seek assistance and answer pressing questions. Is my life normal? Is anyone else going through this? What can I do to help my mom? How can I feel better or get away from this? Opportunities for teenagers to learn online and interact with others who share the same story could well be the mode of intervention preferred by most adolescents. Indeed, the first person to whom they turn is not likely to be an adult (Safe Start Center, 2009).

Adolescents are peer oriented, and most need to present the image of being just like the others. Some will reject the idea of conventional sources of counseling, such as school guidance staff or therapists, because of how attendance appears to others. Confidentiality, while desirable among younger children, is crucially important for teens. The *Dr. Phil* show and other television programs periodically address this issue and may have links to important resources on their websites. Chat rooms and other forms of electronic and anonymous communication would also be welcomed by some teens as a way to work through thoughts and feelings. Some books are designed for this age group (e.g., Finn, 2002), as are some educational videos (e.g., National Film Board of Canada, 1988). At this age, youth can draw parallels between media depictions of family violence and what is happening in their homes. Many Hollywood and other movies portray the various issues associated with IPV and child abuse and can be used to stimulate discussions in individual or group interventions (Lenahan, 2009).

The Internet can reach directly into the lives of young people to help them put labels on what is happening at home and how they feel about it. Such information helps them know they are not alone and gives direction to sources of support. Some websites address adult IPV specifically, such as http://www.notyourfault.org from the United Kingdom, and some address related legal issues, such as http://www.familyviolencehurts.gc.ca from Canada. From Australia, http://www.burstingthebubble.com helps teenagers define what they see and experience at home as abuse. Site content provides steps for "working it out," answers frequently asked questions, gives guidance to help a friend, provides a template for formulating a personalized safety action plan, and lists the legal and practical contingencies of leaving home as a teenager. It uses quizzes, checklists, and true stories from youth and celebrities who describe their childhood experiences. Feedback from 87 website users who acknowledged living with family violence, almost all of whom were female, reported that visiting the site increased their knowledge of support services, gave them advice they could apply at home, and helped them to feel less alone (Shrimpton & McKenzie, 2005).

Many websites address the issue of dating violence and provide an opportunity for teens to learn about red flags of abusive relationships and characteristics of healthy ones, such as http://www.loveisnotabuse.com, http://www.seeitandstopit.org, http://www.knowtheredflags.com, and http://www.thesafespace.org. Much of the material is oriented toward how to help a friend whom you believe to be in an abusive relationship. The site http://www.thatsnotcool.com addresses specifically how digital communication such as texting can be used as surveillance and control of a dating partner. Most of these sites are present on Facebook and MySpace in addition to their Internet presence and post public service announcements to the YouTube site (http://www.youtube.com). At YouTube, teens can surf through a variety of educational material on IPV, including clips from afternoon talk shows, public service announcements, commentaries, music videos, movie clips, high school video projects, and the postings of other young people. Most countries have national help lines with toll-free numbers and some of these services offer web-based counseling opportunities.

Unhealthy Family Roles

In one orientation to therapeutic work, the family is seen as a system in which each member is assigned or adopts roles that govern interactions within that system. Examples of family roles are the golden child who can do no wrong, the responsible one on whom everyone relies, or the misfit who is expected to disappoint the others. Roles developed or assigned in families characterized by severe IPV reflect the unique ways each person adapts to and copes with their secret, confusing, and sometimes dangerous worlds. Each child who is old enough may characteristically play a role during violent incidents, perhaps as referee, rescuer, deflector or distracter, the protector of younger siblings, the one who needs protection, or the reliable seeker of outside help (e.g., calling 911). Goldblatt and Eisikovits (2005) identified the roles of pacifier and protector during violent incidents, roles that were at once burdensome, empowering, and exhausting.

After and between violent incidents, children may also play roles, including the caretaker, the rebel, or the entertainer (see Table 12.3). The caretaker role is arguably one of the most common child roles in families characterized by IPV, and it is also seen in families strained by other (or co-occurring) adversities, such as parental substance abuse (ICF International, 2009). When adults are preoccupied with interpersonal conflict, Goldblatt and Eisikovits (2005) argued, adolescents especially can precociously fill the vacuum of abandoned parental roles, such as nurturer, guide, and controller. The caretaker might be an only child or the oldest child. Both boys and girls can be caretakers, but familial and social expectations for females may combine to create an expectation for the oldest daughter to adopt a caretaker role when someone is needed to take care of younger siblings. Indeed, the full role reversal of parentification is more commonly seen in female children (Mayseless & Scharf, 2009). Because any one child can adopt or be assigned more than one role, some caretakers are also "perfect children," while some caretakers are rebels or even scapegoats.

FAMILY ROLES THAT MAY DEVELOP IN HOMES CHARACTERIZED BY INTIMATE PARTNER VIOLENCE

The caretaker may coparent with the mother or, in the extreme, parent the mother. They may oversee routines and household responsibilities, such as feeding younger children, bathing them, and putting them to bed. During violent episodes, caretakers shepherd the little ones to a safe location and provide emotional support, such as reassurance. They may comfort a

TABLE 12.3
Family Roles That May Develop in Homes Characterized by Intimate Partner Violence

Role	Characteristics
Caretaker	This child, often the eldest or the eldest girl, is given or assumes the role of practical and/or emotional overseeing of younger siblings and perhaps also the abused parent. This child is sometimes labeled as *parentified*.
Perfect child	By excelling in school and through other desirable behaviors, this child seeks control over his or her life by working hard to avoid conflict. Perfect children seek to avoid or suppress the perceived triggers of conflict by never arguing, rebelling, misbehaving, or needing help with problems.
Prince or princess	This child is assigned by the abuser (and perhaps the abused parent as well) a special role, is considered perfect, and is treated better than the others. In some cultures, the eldest son is granted this role vis-à-vis the others, or the boys in general have special status vis-à-vis the girls. Or this child may be the biological child of a man who now plays the stepfather role to his partner's older children or may be the "baby" of the family. A prince or princess will not be mistreated and gets other types of preferential treatment. This child will sorely grieve the loss of a parent whom the others are glad to see go.
Referee/peacekeeper	This child acts as a mediator to avoid likely triggers of conflict, suppress the escalation of brewing conflict, and perhaps even intervene physically when arguments turn violent. A referee becomes superattuned to signs perceived as early indication of conflict, such as tone of voice or subject matter of conversations that lead to arguments. A referee may lie or avoid mentioning issues known to trigger arguments or criticism of the mother (e.g., receiving a bad report card or school suspension) and use distraction when sensing growing tension in the home.
Scapegoat	This child is identified as the cause of family problems and tensions. Scapegoat children may have special needs or be a stepchild to the abusive parent. The unspoken (or sometimes spoken) belief is that family life would be peaceful if not for the behavior or needs of this child. Hence, this child is often used by an abusive parent to justify or excuse angry outbursts and conflict. After a parental separation, scapegoat children may blame themselves for the breakup, and others in the family may do the same.

TABLE 12.3
Family Roles That May Develop in Homes Characterized by Intimate Partner Violence *(Continued)*

Role	Characteristics
Mother's confidant/ best friend	This child is privy to the mother's feelings, concerns, and plans. This child may be asked by the mother to serve as witness to events in the home as a "reality check" if the abusive parent later minimizes or lies about those events or if others doubt her description. The mother and child may appear to be like peers and share decision making and social activities.
Abuser's confederate/ confidant	This child is co-opted to listen to the abuser rationalize his behavior and perhaps stand in for him. This child may be asked to monitor the family when the abuser is not home, take the lead in speaking for the children if questioned by child protective services, preempt any attempt by a sibling to disclose a family secret to outsiders, defend the actions of the abusive parent to other family members, and, in the extreme, abuse the mother verbally or physically. This child may get preferential treatment and be made to feel superior to the other children. This child is not always a boy. A daughter can be co-opted to play the role of replacement "partner" to an abusive parent, to be a listening ear, and to be his defender. If the abusive partner is no longer with the family, this child may worry about him being lonely or maligned, and some will move to live with him.
Rebel	This child labels the situation at home as untenable and unacceptable. Efforts to manage the public image of the family as "normal" are viewed by the rebel as hypocrisy. The rebel's reactions to life at home may be viewed as oppositional defiance to parental authority or conduct problems. The rebel may be the first to leave home and may end up in conflict with the law.
Entertainer or smiler	This child is an entertainer who jokes, sings, or dances to calm a distraught mother or cheer up a sad one. Their beaming smile elicits a responsive smile from the mother. Young children believe that a smiling mother is no longer upset or worried. So their efforts are rewarded by an end to the upsetting episode and resumption of normal life. Humor may also act as a safety valve to reduce tension or distract an abusive parent to protect others in the family. When this tactic is successful, the child feels empowered and the use of humor is reinforced. This smiling or wisecracking behavior can be generalized to other contexts such as school. A teacher's efforts to ask about troubles at home are redoubled when a child responds with silence or tears. A child who smiles and jokes in response to an expression of concern can dissuade an adult from further inquiries.

mother after violent episodes or tidy up if the home is in disarray. Ivy lived with a violent stepfather from age 10 until she left home at age 15. She has two younger sisters:

> I tried to protect my little sisters. I would try to keep them with me. I would bring them into my bed when the abuse was happening. Other times I'd try to get them out of the house. I used to get angry 'cause I had so much responsibility. Once I actually hit my sister and then I felt so, so bad. I wanted to think it was ok 'cause I got it [hit] but I knew it wasn't [okay]. But I'd let them sleep with me and take them places to keep them safe. I feel like I've already had my kids and been a Mom. I'm not sure I want to do it again. (Cunningham & Baker, 2004, p. 92)

Older children or teens, such as Ivy, may seem mature beyond their age. Especially when they compare their lives with those of peers, resentment can bubble to the surface, but there is also a sense of resignation because failure to pitch in and help out puts strain on their mother. Again in the extreme cases, a child may see the mother as incapable of parenting or too fragile to parent, or the child may be afraid of the mother's angry reaction if the child refuses to help her.

Examining family roles helps us understand how different children in the same family can have dramatically different understandings and memories of what happened in their homes. It is also a framework for viewing the tension that can occur between siblings or in the mother–child relationship. A child's role may reflect an attempt to exercise a degree of control over an unwanted situation that seems completely out of their control. Accordingly, a role can be seen as a coping strategy for some young people. Referees and perfect children, for example, work hard to prevent conflict by avoiding and suppressing factors perceived as potential triggers. They are skilled observers but may be poor interpreters and may see any eruption of violence as a failure on their parts rather than a choice of the abusive parent.

Understanding family roles also helps us interpret the variable ways children perceive the absence of an abusive parent, specifically if they grieve his absence or dread his return. Assessing family roles also helps shed light on the sources of any conflict and tension in the remaining family unit. When an abusive parent leaves the family system, members of the newly reconstituted family may retain their roles in interactions with each other or have difficulty adjusting to new expectations. The "abuser's confederate" may take up the role of abuser once he is gone. The "scapegoat" child's isolation within the family may be intensified by feelings of responsibility for the marital breakup. The "princess" may be isolated with her private hopes for family reconciliation. The "perfect child" may be impatient with and blaming toward siblings who misbehaved or otherwise triggered an unwanted change, such as a marital separation or the father's arrest.

When children use their roles as strategies for coping at home, that strategy may not be turned off overnight once the abuse stops or the abuser is gone. For example, children who adopt pseudoadult roles such as the caretaker may have difficulty adjusting if expected to reassume the role of child, as with this young woman who had been the primary caretaker to her younger siblings before their stepfather left:

> When I get angry, I say things to Mom I shouldn't. I wouldn't talk to her 'cause I didn't want to hurt her. But when I'm angry it just comes out. She's trying to be a good Mom but I don't think she's doing the right thing. It's like there's two Moms now and sometimes we don't agree. (Cunningham & Baker, 2004, p. 94)

We can see reflections or vestiges of these roles in the intimate relationships and parenting styles of adults exposed to IPV as children. Having adopted the role of pseudoparent as a child, for example, can manifest in a woman's current coping through caretaking (Earley & Cushway, 2002) and denial of her own needs and wants (Cunningham & Baker, 2008). Goldblatt and Eisikovits (2005) also believed that the different roles adopted or given to children may help explain differential outcomes, especially the apparent resilience of children who do well in school and have good interpersonal skills.

These roles probably evolve in late childhood and solidify in adolescence, so intervention with teenagers is timely. The use of family systems theory to guide counseling in domestically violent couples is fraught with controversies (Murray, 2006). However, there are many intervention strategies suggested by an examination of family roles in teenagers and how these youngsters interpreted and coped with IPV. Teenagers are old enough to recognize family dynamics and can be helped to assign labels to their current role(s) and their desired role. In addition, it is important to normalize and reinforce any desire to be "just a kid" if they have adopted or been given pseudoadult roles. With the appropriate support, they can reframe distortions, such as when they blame themselves for not preventing violent incidents or not being able to avoid or deescalate conflict. Few scapegoat children will be able to resist a negative self-image and feelings of inadequacy and guilt. They especially need help to attribute responsibility to adults for adult choices such as violence. As with healing the mother–child bond, helping a mother restore her parental authority is an important support for her and her children for all ages. She can come to understand how her teenaged children are thinking and feeling about the past and the future, adopt positive discipline techniques, learn to negotiate limits and expectations with teenagers, and create boundaries around information that is best shared only with adults (Baker & Cunningham, 2004).

Co-occurring Adversities

It is a rare family in which IPV is the only factor with potentially negative influence on the healthy development of children and teens. Put another way, where IPV is found in a family, there is likely to be other adverse events or circumstances. For example, severe male violence toward a female partner only rarely occurs in isolation from direct child maltreatment and other forms of family violence, and the cumulative effect will be reflected in child adjustment (McDonald, Jouriles, Tart, & Minze, 2009). The Christchurch Health and Development Study in New Zealand has also been helpful in describing the psychosocial context in which IPV is found, including socioeconomic disadvantage (Fergusson, Boden, & Horwood, 2006). Children who live with violence at home may also be exposed to violence in the community and experience other forms of criminal victimization (Finkelhor et al., 2009).

The Adverse Childhood Experiences (ACE) Study helps us understand how often childhood adverse events cluster together in some families and work in a staged and cumulative fashion to increase the probability of adverse health outcomes (e.g., Dong, Anda, Felitti, Dube, Williamson, et al., 2004). Male violence against one's mother is one of the 10 ACEs measured (Dube, Anda, Felitti, Edwards, & Williamson, 2002). Family adversities such as drug use and violence exposure have been intercorrelated in a national representative sample of adolescents (Hanson et al., 2006). In an Australian general population survey of adolescents, 14% reported that a father or father figure "gets drunk a lot," and this was true for 6% in relationship to a mother or maternal figure. Among youth who reported male-to-female IPV, the same figures were 55% and 56%, respectively (Indermaur, 2001).

It is desirable to assess for the full range of adversities and abusive experiences to design an intervention that is responsive to family and individual needs. When grappling with multiple issues and adversities, teenagers may appreciate assistance with some and scorn help with others. For example, teenagers may have a hierarchy of impact when exposed to multiple adverse experiences, viewing experiences of direct victimization as more negative than the victimizations they witnessed (Lipschitz, Winegar, Hartnick, Foote, & Southwick, 1999).

Feeling Better Through Problematic Coping

Adolescents may not select coping strategies that are the healthy for them or even very effective. The following is a list of tactics used to manage situations that were reported by adolescents in families with IPV:

> I ran away from home. I hung out with friends . . . dropped out of school . . . spent lots of time with boyfriends. I drank everyday, did drugs and had lots of sex partners. I tried to take my life on many occasions. I wanted to

escape my life. I got a criminal record . . . I went to holding cells 'cause of a boyfriend—he'd just leave me and [the] cops would come and I'd be with stuff [drugs]. I didn't want to be at home—but I felt like I couldn't be alone. I still get really lonely. (Cunningham & Baker, p. 94)

Goldblatt (2003) defined coping strategies as "those perceptions, interactions, and behaviors that the youths define as modes of dealing or struggling with their exposure and understanding of inter-parental violence" (pp. 532–533). Methods of coping change as young people mature. Ornduff and Monahan (1999), after reviewing counseling files at a shelter, noted that preschool-age children cannot use problem-focused or action-oriented strategies for coping. Instead, they rely on mental and behavioral disengagement, such as turning up the television volume or covering their heads with a pillow. These youngsters can also use magical thinking, perhaps believing Superman will rescue them.

COPING STRATEGIES OBSERVED IN ADOLESCENTS WHO LIVE WITH INTIMATE PARTNER VIOLENCE

If exposure to IPV and similar adversities continues, the strategies evolve as the children mature. By adolescence, a range of both engagement and disengagement options is available, concomitant with their increased independence from the home, physical size and opportunities to interact with others outside the home (see Table 12.4). Some of these coping options are helpful and some are troubling, but all help teenagers cope in the moment. Teens may leave home, involve the police, or use drugs to dampen troubling thoughts and feelings (Cunningham & Baker, 2007). Some will still engage in emotional disengagement such as thought blocking and numbing, strategies that may be augmented through alcohol or substance use.

> Nintendo was perfect for blocking out. I'd get [my sister] and we'd play Nintendo first thing every morning. I tried to block out as much as I could. I blocked out everything. That way I could just be happy. I'm sort of a professional at blocking it out. Only problem is I sometimes block out stuff I need to remember. Like I'll block out calling my welfare worker, walking the dog, taking out the garbage. . . . People say "your memory is gone" but it's not, it's just I block so much out. If you asked about my childhood, I'd tell you about [going to an amusement park]. Yeah, I can just remember the good times, like—I had a phone. So, it's like I have two lives. (Cunningham & Baker, 2004, p. 97)

Some teens will engage in revenge fantasies, such as this young woman interviewed by Cunningham and Baker (2004):

> I called the police all the time. He'd be arrested, in jail, or there'd be a restraining order and it'd happen all over again, and again and again. I

TABLE 12.4
Coping Strategies Observed in Adolescents
Who Live With Intimate Partner Violence

Type of behavior	Specific strategy
	Engagement coping strategies
Physical avoidance	• Going into another room, leaving the house during a violent episode • Finding excuses to avoid going home • Running away from home
Taking charge through caretaking	• Protecting brothers and sisters from danger • Being like a mother to brothers and sisters • Being like a mother to his or her mother
Reaching out for help	• Telling a teacher, neighbor, or friend's mother • Calling the police • Talking to siblings, friends, or supportive adults
Redirecting emotions into positive activities	• Taking up sports, running, fitness • Writing, journaling, drawing, acting, being creative • Excelling academically
Trying to predict, explain, prevent or control the behavior of an abuser	• Thinking "Mommy has been bad," or "I have been bad," or "Daddy is under stress at work" • Thinking "I can stop the violence by changing my behavior" or "I can predict the violence" • Trying to be the perfect child • Lying to cover up bad things (e.g., a bad grade) to avoid criticism and worse
	Disengagement coping strategies
Mental blocking or disconnecting emotionally	• Having numbing emotions or blocking thoughts • Tuning out the noise or chaos, learning not to hear it, being oblivious • Concentrating hard to believe they are somewhere else • Drinking alcohol or using drugs
Making it better through fantasy	• Planning revenge on abuser, fantasizing about killing him • Fantasizing about a happier life, living with a different family • Fantasizing about life after a divorce or after the abuser leaves • Fantasizing about abuser being "hit by a bus" • Hoping to be rescued, by superheroes or police or "Prince Charming"
Looking for love (and acceptance) in all the wrong places	• Falling in with bad friends • Having sex for the intimacy and closeness • Trying to have a baby or getting pregnant to have someone to love you
Crying out for help	• Making suicidal gestures • Causing self-injury • Lashing out in anger, being aggressive with others, getting into fights

Note. From *Helping Children Thrive: Supporting Woman Abuse Survivors as Mothers* (pp. 42–43), by L. Baker and A. Cunningham, 2004, London, Ontario, Canada: Centre for Children & Families in the Justice System. Copyright 2004 by the Centre for Children & Families in the Justice System. Adapted with permission.

thought they [police] were all screwed up. He assaulted my mom in front of them and got away with it. I guess 'cause she was really angry by then too. I thought he's invincible so I have to do it myself. They [police] wouldn't. I wanted to get my friends and dress in black and kill him so he couldn't hurt my mom. I'd just keep thinking about this. I even talked to one friend about it back then. He just thought I was crazy. (p. 96)

The caretaker role, of younger siblings and sometimes a mother, can give some teenagers a sense of control, as with Ivy's case quoted earlier. Ultimately, adolescents who see no hope of improvements in their lives can leave home, as this young woman did:

I learned to save my money and say to her [Mom] let's go . . . I'd always be outside—just didn't want to be home, didn't want to see. I tried to get [child protection] to take me and my sisters away. Finally, I just took off—I was 14 or 15. Mom says I was messed up and now I'm doing okay [because I am back home], but I was getting away from a mess. I left school—never went back. I became a Mom. (Cunningham & Baker, 2004, p. 94)

Youth who leave home early may be poorly equipped to negotiate the pseudoadult lives they create. They may career from one risk-filled situation to another and spend time with people who exploit them or otherwise take advantage of them.

Teens, even if they live in the same family, will likely adopt their own strategies to understand and cope with IPV. It helps them make sense of their world, align blame, and develop ways to manage intense emotions and thoughts. When working with teenagers, assessing their coping strategies can help identify which are problematic and concerning and which are helpful and can be encouraged. Mothers can be helped to identify their teenagers' coping styles and encourage healthy ways to cope with the violence their children have seen.

CONCLUSION

As helping professionals working with youth, we are likely to encounter adolescents who witnessed adult IPV at home, who experienced direct maltreatment, who perpetrated intimate violence against dating partners, who were victimized in a dating relationship, or all of the above. Understanding their perspectives on any violence they witnessed or experienced can inform the crafting of responsive interventions. Evaluating these interventions will provide the much-needed evidence base for practitioners working with adolescents exposed to IPV.

Even siblings growing up in the same home can have dramatically different memories and opinions about shared family events, so individual assessment is crucial. Accordingly, two frameworks were offered in this chapter for assessing the unique ways each teenager has been affected. The first is a model that takes into account how the optimal development of adolescents may be interrupted and distorted. The potential impacts include accelerated responsibility and precocious role exits, negative consequences associated with physical confrontation of abusive parent (e.g., arrest of the youth), suboptimal parenting and adult guidance, compromised school success, body-image distortions, and development of gender-role stereotypes.

The second framework derives from the work of Cunningham and Baker (2007), who proposed 10 ways a child can be adversely shaped by living with IPV. Six of these mechanisms were discussed here in relation to adolescents: exposure to abusive male role models, erosion of the mother–child bond, isolation of youth from helpful supports, evolution of unhealthy family roles, presence of co-occurring family adversities, and recourse of youth to problematic coping. Relevant interventions include psychoeducational groups, skill building, emotion coaching, learning about healthy relationships, encouragement of healthy coping, support for mothers, universal school-based programs, targeted school-based programs, and self-help and peer support. Assessment of coping styles and family roles presents opportunities for one-on-one therapeutic interventions. When the impact of exposure to IPV is so varied and variable, helping professionals must avoid recourse to one-size-fits-all approaches to both understanding and intervening in the lives of these young people.

REFERENCES

Arriaga, X. B., & Foshee, V. A. (2004). Adolescent dating violence: Do adolescents follow in their friends,' or their parents,' footsteps? *Journal of Interpersonal Violence, 19,* 162–184. doi:10.1177/0886260503260247

Baker, L., & Cunningham, A. (2009). Inter-parental violence: The preschooler's perspective and the educator's role. *Early Childhood Education Journal, 37,* 199–207. doi:10.1007/s10643-009-0342-z

Baker, L., & Cunningham, A. (2008). *Helping an abused woman: 101 things to know, say and do.* London, Ontario, Canada: Centre for Children & Families in the Justice System.

Baker, L. L., & Cunningham, A. J. (2004). *Helping children thrive/supporting woman abuse survivors as mothers: A resource to support parenting.* London, Ontario, Canada: Centre for Children & Families in the Justice System.

Baker, L., & Jaffe, P. (2003). *Youth exposed to domestic violence: A handbook for the juvenile justice system to enhance assessment and intervention strategies for youth from violence homes.* London, Ontario, Canada: Centre for Children & Families in the Justice System.

Bancroft, L. (2002). *Why does he do that? Inside the minds of angry and controlling men.* New York, NY: Berkley Books.

Bancroft, L., & Silverman, J. (2002). *The batterer as parent: Addressing the impact of domestic violence on family dynamics.* Thousand Oaks, CA: Sage.

Bilinkoff, J. (1995). Empowering battered women as mothers. In E. Peled, P. G. Jaffe, & J. L. Edleson (Eds.), *Ending the cycle of violence: Community responses to children of battered women* (pp. 97–105). Thousand Oaks, CA: Sage.

Bowlby, J. (1988). *A secure base: Clinical applications of attachment theory.* London, England: Routledge.

Bunston, W. (2001). *PARKAS manual: Parents accepting responsibility, kids are safe.* Flemington, Victoria, Australia: Royal Children's Hospital Mental Health Service.

Casanueva, C., Martin, S., Runyan, D., Barth, R., & Bradley, R. H. (2008). Quality of maternal parenting among intimate-partner violence victims involved with the child welfare system. *Journal of Family Violence, 23,* 413–427. doi:10.1007/s10896-008-9167-6

Crime Research Centre. (2001). *Young people and domestic violence: National research on young people's attitudes to and experiences of domestic violence.* Canberra, Australian Capital Territory, Australia: Commonwealth Attorney-General's Department.

Cunningham, A., & Baker, L. (2004). *What about me! Seeking to understand the child's view of violence in the family.* London, Ontario, Canada: Centre for Children & Families in the Justice System.

Cunningham, A., & Baker, L. (2007). *Little eyes, little ears: How violence against a mother shapes children as they grow.* London, Ontario, Canada: Centre for Children & Families in the Justice System.

Cunningham, A., & Baker, L. (2008). *Helping abused women in shelters: 101 things to know, say and do.* London, Ontario, Canada: Centre for Children & Families in the Justice System.

Davis, D. L. (2004). Group intervention with abusive male adolescents. In P. G. Jaffe, L. L. Baker, & A. J. Cunningham (Eds.), *Protecting children from domestic violence: Strategies for community intervention* (pp. 49–67). New York, NY: Guilford Press.

Dong, M., Anda, R. F., Felitti, V. J., Dube, S. R., Williamson, D. F., Thompson, T. J., . . . Giles, W. H. (2004). The interrelatedness of multiple forms of childhood abuse, neglect, and household dysfunction. *Child Abuse & Neglect, 28,* 771–784. doi:10.1016/j.chiabu.2004.01.008

Dube, S. R., Anda, R. F., Felitti, V. J., Edwards, V. J., & Williamson, D. F. (2002). Exposure to abuse, neglect and household dysfunction among adults who witnessed intimate partner violence as children: Implications for health and social services. *Violence and Victims, 17*(1), 3–1817. doi:10.1891/vivi.17.1.3.33635

Earley, L., & Cushway, D. (2002). The parentified child. *Clinical Child Psychology and Psychiatry, 7,* 163–178. doi:10.1177/1359104502007002005

Edleson, J. L., & Williams, O. J. (Eds.). (2007). *Parenting by men who batter: New directions for assessment and intervention.* New York, NY: Oxford University Press.

Fergusson, D. M., Boden, J. M., & Horwood, L. J. (2006). Examining the intergenerational transmission of violence in a New Zealand birth cohort. *Child Abuse & Neglect, 30,* 89–108. doi:10.1016/j.chiabu.2005.10.006

Finkelhor, D., Ormrod, R., & Turner, H. A. (2007). Poly-victimization: A neglected component in child victimization. *Child Abuse & Neglect, 31,* 7–26. doi:10.1016/j.chiabu.2006.06.008

Finkelhor, A., Turner, H., Ormrod, R., Hamby, S., & Kracke, Y. (2009). *Juvenile Justice Bulletin: Children's exposure to violence: A comprehensive national survey.* Washington DC: Office of Justice Programs, U.S. Department of Justice.

Finn, A. (2002). *Breathing underwater.* New York, NY: Harper Collins.

Fox, G. L., Sayers, J., & Bruce, C. (2001). Beyond bravado: Fatherhood as a resource for rehabilitation of men who batter. *Marriage & Family Review, 30,* 137–163.

Gewirtz, A. H., & Medhanie, A. (2008). Proximity and risk in children's witnessing of intimate partner violence incidents. *Journal of Emotional Abuse, 8*(1–2), 67–82. doi:10.1080/10926790801982436

Gjelsvik, A., Verhoek-Oftedahl, W., & Pearlman, D. N. (2003). Domestic violence incidents with children witnesses: Findings from Rhode Island surveillance data. *Women's Health Issues, 13*(2), 68–73. doi:10.1016/S1049-3867(02)00197-4

Goldblatt, H. (2003). Strategies of coping among adolescents experiencing interparental violence. *Journal of Interpersonal Violence, 18,* 532–552. doi:10.1177/0886260503251071

Goldblatt, H., & Eisikovits, Z. (2005). Role taking of youths in a family context: Adolescents exposed to interparental violence. *American Journal of Orthopsychiatry, 75,* 644–657. doi:10.1037/0002-9432.75.4.644

Graham-Bermann, S. A., Lynch, S., Banyard, V., DeVoe, E. R., & Halabu, H. (2007). Community-based intervention for children exposed to intimate partner violence: An efficacy trial. *Journal of Consulting and Clinical Psychology, 75,* 199–209. doi:10.1037/0022-006X.75.2.199

Groves, B. M., Van Horn, P., & Lieberman, A. F. (2007). Deciding on fathers' involvement in their children's treatment after domestic violence. In J. L. Edleson & O. J. Williams (Eds.), *Parenting by men who batter: New directions for assessment and intervention* (pp. 65–84). New York, NY: Oxford University Press.

Hanson, R. F., Self-Brown, S., Fricker-Elhai, A. E., Kilpatrick, D. G., Saunders, B. E., & Resnick, H. (2006). The relations between family environment and violence exposure among youth: Findings from the National Survey of Adolescents. *Child Maltreatment, 11*(1), 3–15. doi:10.1177/1077559505279295

Haynie, D. L., Petts, R. J., Maimon, D., & Piquero, A. R. (2009). Exposure to violence in adolescence and precocious role exists. *Journal of Youth and Adolescence, 38,* 269–286. doi:10.1007/s10964-008-9343-2

International, I. C. F. (2009). *Protecting children in families affected by substance abuse disorders.* Washington, DC: Children's Bureau, Office of Child Abuse & Neglect.

Indermaur, D. (2001). *Young Australians and domestic violence.* Canberra, Australian Capital Territory: Australian Institute of Criminology.

Indermaur, D., Atkinson, L., & Blagg, H. (2001). *Working with adolescents to prevent domestic violence: Rural town model*. Perth: Crime Research Centre, University of Western Australia.

Israel, E., & Stover, C. (2009). Intimate partner violence: The role of the relationship between perpetrators and children who witness violence. *Journal of Interpersonal Violence, 24*, 1755–1764. doi:10.1177/0886260509334044

Kwong, M. J., Bartholomew, K., Henderson, A. J., & Trinke, S. J. (2003). The intergenerational transmission of relationship violence. *Journal of Family Psychology, 17*, 288–301. doi:10.1037/0893-3200.17.3.288

Lenahan, P. M. (2009). Intimate partner violence: What do movies have to teach us? *International Review of Psychiatry, 21*, 189–199. doi:10.1080/09540260902747938

Lipschitz, D. S., Winegar, R. K., Hartnick, E., Foote, B., & Southwick, S. M. (1999). Posttraumatic stress disorder in hospitalized adolescents: Psychiatric comorbidity and clinical correlates. *Journal of the American Academy of Child and Adolescent Psychiatry, 38*, 385–392. doi:10.1097/00004583-199904000-00010

Martin, J., Langley, L., & Millichamp, J. (2006). Domestic violence as witnessed by New Zealand children. *New Zealand Journal of Medicine, 119*, 1–14.

Mathews, D. J. (1995). Parenting groups for men who batter. In E. Peled, P. G. Jaffe, & J. L. Edleson (Eds.), *Ending the cycle of violence: Community responses to children of battered women* (pp. 106–120). Thousand Oaks, CA: Sage.

Mayseless, O., & Scharf, M. (2009). Too close for comfort: Inadequate boundaries with parents and individuation in late adolescent girls. *American Journal of Orthopsychiatry, 79*, 191–202. doi:10.1037/a0015623

McDonald, R., Jouriles, E. N., Ramisetty-Mikler, S., Caetano, R., & Green, C. E. (2007). Estimating the number of American children living in partner-violent families. *Journal of Family Psychology, 20*(1), 137–142. doi:10.1037/0893-3200.20.1.137

McDonald, R., Jouriles, E. N., Tart, C. D., & Minze, L. C. (2009). Children's adjustment problems in families characterized by men's severe violence toward women: Does other family violence matter? *Child Abuse & Neglect, 33*, 94–101. doi:10.1016/j.chiabu.2008.03.005

McGee, R. A., Wolfe, D. A., & Wilson, S. K. (1997). Multiple maltreatment experiences and adolescent behavior problems: Adolescents' perspectives. *Development and Psychopathology, 9*, 131–149. doi:10.1017/S0954579497001107

Murray, C. E. (2006). Controversy, constraints, and context: Understanding family violence through family systems theory. *The Family Journal, 14*, 234–239. doi:10.1177/1066480706287277

National Film Board of Canada. (1988). *The crown prince* [Video]. Ottawa, Ontario, Canada: Author.

Ornduff, S. R., & Monahan, K. (1999). Children's understanding of parental violence. *Child and Youth Care Forum, 28*, 351–364. doi:10.1023/A:1021974429983

Peled, E. (2000). Parenting by men who abuse women: Issues and dilemmas. *British Journal of Social Work, 30*(1), 25–36. doi:10.1093/bjsw/30.1.25

Perel, G., & Peled, E. (2008). The fathering of violent men: Constriction and yearning. *Violence Against Women, 14,* 457–482. doi:10.1177/1077801208314846

Rothman, E. F., Mandel, D. G., & Silverman, J. G. (2007). Abusers' perceptions of the effect on their intimate partner violence on children. *Violence Against Women, 13,* 1179–1191. doi:10.1177/1077801207308260

Safe Start Center. (2009). *Healing the invisible wounds: Children's exposure to violence, a guide for families.* North Bethesda, MD: Author.

Salisbury, E. J., Henning, K., & Holdford, R. (2009). Fathering by partner-abusive men: Attitudes on children's exposure to interparental conflict and risk factors for child abuse. *Child Maltreatment, 14,* 232–242. doi:10.1177/1077559509338407

Shrimpton, B., & McKenzie, M. (2005). *What young people experiencing family violence have to say about Burstingthebubble.com.* Melbourne, Victoria, Australia: Centre for Program Evaluation, University of Melbourne.

Solomon, B. S., Bradshaw, C. P., Wright, J., & Cheng, T. L. (2008). Youth and parental attitudes toward fighting. *Journal of Interpersonal Violence, 23,* 544–560. doi:10.1177/0886260507312947

Sternberg, K. J., Lamb, M. E., Guterman, E., Abbott, C. B., & Dawud-Noursi, S. (2005). Adolescents' perceptions of attachments to their mothers and fathers in families with histories of domestic violence: A longitudinal perspective. *Child Abuse & Neglect, 29,* 853–869. doi:10.1016/j.chiabu.2004.07.009

Stith, S. M., Rosen, K. H., Middleton, K. A., Busch, A. L., Lundeberg, K., & Carlton, R. P. (2000). The intergenerational transmission of spouse abuse: A meta-analysis. *Journal of Marriage and the Family, 62,* 640–654. doi:10.1111/j.1741-3737.2000.00640.x

Vaillancourt, R., & Taylor-Butts, A. (2007). *Transition homes in Canada: National, provincial and territorial fact sheets 2005/2006.* Ottawa, Ontario, Canada: Minister of Industry.

Whitfield, C. L., Anda, R. F., Dube, S. R., & Felitti, V. J. (2003). Violent childhood experiences and the risk of intimate partner violence in adults: Assessment in a large health maintenance organization. *Journal of Interpersonal Violence, 18,* 166–185. doi:10.1177/0886260502238733

Winstock, Z., & Eisikovits. (2003). Divorcing the parents: The impact of adolescents exposure to father-to-mother aggression on their perceptions of affinity with their parents. *Journal of Emotional Abuse, 3*(1–2), 103–121.

Ziegler, R. G., & Weidner, D. A. (2006). Assessment and intervention with parents to stabilize children who have witnessed violence. *Journal of Family Violence, 21,* 209–219. doi:10.1007/s10896-006-9016-4

Zinzow, H. M., Ruggiero, K. J., Resnick, H., Smith, D., Saunders, B., & Kilpatrick, D. (2009). Prevalence and mental health correlates of witnessed parental and community violence in a national sample of adolescents. *Journal of Child Psychology and Psychiatry, and Allied Disciplines, 50,* 441–450. doi:10.1111/j.1469-7610.2008.02004.x

13

A CLINICAL CASE STUDY OF CADEN, AN ADOLESCENT BOY EXPOSED TO INTIMATE PARTNER VIOLENCE

ALYTIA A. LEVENDOSKY

Estimates of exposure to intimate partner violence (IPV) for adolescents vary from about 9% to 30% depending on whether the violence occurred anytime during development or only in adolescence and whether any IPV or only moderate/severe IPV is included (Kilpatrick, Ruggiero, Acierno, & Saunders, 2003; Straus, 1992). Adolescents in violent families are at risk of similar mental health problems as younger children, including posttraumatic stress disorder (PTSD), depression, anxiety, and externalizing behaviors (e.g., Evans, Davies, & DiLillo, 2008). However, adolescents also begin to go down new pathways of risk, including delinquent/criminal behavior (Herrera & McCloskey, 2001) and dating violence (Kim, 2009). In addition, some become violent to their parents or to their peers and/or siblings (Herrera & McCloskey, 2001; McCloskey & Lichter, 2003). These new pathways of risky behavior are specific to adolescence and may indicate particular vulnerabilities that are present in adolescence, such as hormonal changes, physical growth and maturity, and psychological changes, including interest in dating, that occur during pubertal development.

Despite the risk for adolescents in violent homes, there are relatively few studies on this age group. One reason is that it is difficult to recruit adolescents into these studies due to problems with compliance in this age group (see Chapter 11, this volume, for a fuller discussion). This means that we know much less about the effects of IPV for adolescents than for preschool- and school-age children and thus have less evidence upon which to base our interventions. The current chapter is a case study of an adolescent boy, age 14, who was evaluated due to exposure to IPV between his mother and his stepfather.

Caden was first seen shortly after he and his mother left the home where they lived with his mother's abusive partner. At the time of the evaluation, they were living in hiding with a family whom his mother knew through her work. The final incident before his mother left her abusive partner, described below, had been quite dramatic, and the police and the local news media were involved. Laura had come home from work only to find the door locked (with new locks). When she knocked on the door, she was told that she was being punished because she had sent home the wrong school records on Caden (her boyfriend, Jim, did not have access to these as he was not legally related to Caden but had previously demanded that Laura get them). An argument ensued in which Laura was begging to get in the house. At first Jim said she would have to spend the night outside due to her terrible error, but then he allowed her in. He proceeded to beat her badly with his fists by punching her abdomen and chest repeatedly, slapping her across the face, and stomping on her when she fell due to his repeated assaults.

Caden retreated to his room in fear, but since the door was slatted and opened into the hallway, he saw much of what then occurred. Jim moved Laura into the hallway and proceeded to cut off her clothes with a knife and then rape her. He handed Laura his gun and asked her to shoot him, stating that one of them had to die that night. When Laura refused, Jim grabbed his gun and went into Caden's room, locking it from the inside. Laura spent a terrified night outside of Caden's room, too frightened to use the phone to call the police for fear that he would hear her and pull the phone out of the wall, something he had done before. She waited until dawn, when she could hear Jim sleeping soundly. She crept out of the house and called the police, who then came with their hostage unit and negotiated with Jim to release Caden. His stepfather instantly relented and released Caden unharmed. The police immediately arrested Jim; however, he was released the following day with a trial set for 3 months hence.

Laura was now seeking help for her son, Caden, who began acting out in school, being truant, and being extremely angry at her. Caden was evaluated for individual treatment based on his reported behaviors and the traumatic event he had experienced.

THE EVALUATION

At the clinic, the evaluation process with children and families typically takes about four to five once-weekly sessions, which last 45 min. Typically, with an adolescent client, the therapist will meet with the adolescent prior to meeting with the parents or any other family members, in order to begin to establish therapeutic alliance. However, in this case, when the mother called and gave the initial information, she stated that Caden refused to come to a session unless she came with him. The therapist agreed to meet with them together for the first session.

During the first session, Laura described the above incident to the therapist and discussed their current situation, which entailed secretly living with friends and waiting to testify at trial—she said that the prosecutor had told her that both she and her son would need to testify to ensure a likely conviction. Caden appeared bored throughout the session, rolling his eyes and making noises to indicate his disagreement with his mother's interpretations of events. He occasionally interrupted his mother to state his interpretations of Jim's behaviors—for example, Jim wanted Caden's school records so that he could arrange for advanced math placement for him in high school and thus was reasonable in his anger toward Laura for not producing the needed records. He also said Jim would never have hurt him, and thus he was not afraid of him that night when they were in his room. At the end of the session, he glared at his mother and then turned to the therapist and said, "You see, she is the one who needs therapy—not me. Jim and I were fine! She screwed it all up." The therapist made the decision to meet with Caden alone for the second session to attempt to develop an alliance with him before proceeding to meet with his mother to obtain a developmental history and a detailed understanding of the presenting behavioral and clinical symptoms.

Theoretical/Empirical Basis for Assessment and Intervention

Caden's presenting problems were understood using an attachment-trauma framework (Bowlby, 1988). He had been betrayed by his stepfather, a man with whom he had a significant intimate relationship. He had witnessed severe violence perpetrated by this man toward his mother and sometimes toward himself since he was a young child. His internal working models of self and other were likely to have been significantly damaged by these repeated betrayals (Cicchetti & Toth, 1995; Levendosky, Huth-Bocks, & Semel, 2002). In addition, his exposure to chronic violence was likely to have led to dysregulation of his biological, affective, and cognitive systems (van der Kolk, 2005). Thus, the evaluation consisted of (a) interviews with his mother, to understand her parenting behavior and its potential contribution to his internal working models and to conduct a structured clinical interview—the Schedule for Affective Disorders and Schizophrenia for School-Age Children-Present and Lifetime Version (K-SADS-PL; Kaufman et al., 1997)—for Caden's clinical symptoms; (b) interviews with Caden that allowed the therapist to directly assess his capacity for engagement in a new relationship as well as his emotional dysregulation; and (c) behavioral symptom questionnaires completed by Laura, Caden, and Caden's school counselor in order to obtain situation-specific behaviors and severity of behavioral problems (Achenbach & Edelbrock, 1993).

Identifying Information

Laura was a 45-year-old Caucasian woman who had worked in an office as a secretary for the past 10 years. Her prior work history included other similar jobs in different organizations. Caden was her only child. She did not know Caden's father—she met him in a bar and became pregnant that night with their son and never saw him again. She met Jim when Caden was 3 years old, and he soon moved in with the family. Laura described him as loving with her and engaged and affectionate with young Caden. However, just months after he moved in, the troubles began. During a heated argument, he hit Laura so hard that she fell backward against the wall and had a brief concussion. This was the beginning of a pattern of frequent (almost daily) physical and psychological abuse that sometimes escalated to severe beatings and rapes. Laura maintained that Caden and Jim had a very positive relationship and that Jim had been his primary caregiver since he was about 5 years old. Jim had lost his job at that time and never got another one. However, she also said, in seeming contradiction, that Jim was sometimes physically abusive to Caden, such as standing on him, or pulling his arms behind his back until Caden cried out in pain. Although Laura was the only breadwinner, Jim controlled her income, giving her an allowance to buy groceries. He paid the bills, but intermittently, and had not allowed her to have a driver's license for about 8 years. He also paid the taxes irregularly. Due to his irresponsible money management, she had terrible credit. Finally, she also did not have her own bank accounts.

Laura said that Caden had always been an excellent student—at the top of his class—and that Jim often helped Caden with his homework. They were both very proud of how smart Caden was. He had always behaved well in school, and his teachers had only nice things to say about him. However, in the 3 weeks since the final incident, Caden had not done any homework—had refused to do it—and was skipping school. He had failed two tests and was seemingly uninterested in even bothering to try. Laura was very concerned that Caden was responding so negatively to their move out of the home, which she saw as protective for both of them.

Evaluation Sessions

The therapist met with Caden three times during the evaluation period and with Laura twice and then met with Laura and Caden together to provide feedback and treatment recommendations. In the first session following the initial joint meeting, Caden came into the therapist's office with a sullen look on his face. He barely responded to any comments or questions from the therapist except to reiterate that his mother was the one with the problems and that he really wanted to move back in with Jim. He also glanced anxiously at his watch about every 3 to 4 minutes to see if the session was almost over; he would ask, "Is it almost time yet?" even though he knew the length of the session and the ending time.

In the second session, the therapist used something Caden had indicated interest in during the first session—science fiction characters—and invited him to draw some for her. Caden drew his own figures—mostly male creatures with bulging muscles and large rounded phalluses. This invitation worked well as he was able to then engage with the therapist. When the therapist asked him to draw his family, he drew himself, his mother, and Jim—whom he stated was his father. Jim was drawn with bulging muscles, like his science fiction characters, but with no hands. All of his other creatures and humans had hands. He drew himself without bulging muscles, but with hands and with a clearly large rounded phallus, which his drawing of Jim notably lacked. During this session, Caden talked about his shame at school—how the other kids had all come up to him the day after the story was in the newspaper about the hostage situation and he was totally humiliated. He had been skipping large portions of school since then because of this shame. The therapist listened empathically and said that she could understand how much he would not want to talk about these terrible and sad experiences with other kids and how embarrassing it was to have his family issues in the newspaper. He seemed relieved at her response and then talked about how much he missed Jim. He cried, unashamedly, about how much he loved Jim and how Jim had been such a good father to him and had done so many fun things with him. He confessed that he was still talking to Jim on the phone on a regular basis, sneaking in phone calls from the home in which they were staying. He revealed that he had told Jim his address so that Jim would come and see him. The therapist was startled by this information, knowing it was Laura's intention to hide where they were living for fear of stalking and further violence. The therapist explained that his mother needed to know that he was talking to Jim for her safety (and his) and she asked if he wanted to tell her or if he wanted the therapist to do it with him present. He agreed to tell her, and the therapist brought Laura into the room, and Caden shared this with his mother. She was shocked but handled it well and responded that she knew how much Caden loved Jim so she could understand his need to talk to him.

In the third and final evaluation session, Caden continued to be more open with the therapist, telling her how guilty he felt that he had not done something about Jim. When the therapist asked what he could have done, he said that he had thought many times of taking an iron frying pan from the kitchen and hitting Jim over the head with it when he was hurting his mother. He felt ashamed and guilty that he had never done this—through all of the violence. The therapist talked about how helpless a kid can feel in this situation and that it was neither his fault that there was violence nor his responsibility to stop it—and that in fact, he could have been grievously hurt himself if he had interfered. He talked about how much he loved both his mother and Jim and how sad he felt. He talked about how he could not sleep well at night because he had terrible images of what had happened when he closed his eyes. He said that when he did fall asleep, he was frequently awakened by nightmares.

The themes of Caden's evaluation session demonstrated both his attachment difficulties and his trauma symptoms. He felt helpless and terrified and was showing signs of affective and biological dysregulation in the aftermath of the traumatic events. In addition, his internal working models of self and others were distorted, focused on victim–perpetrator relationships, and vacillating back and forth between himself as victim and as perpetrator.

During the first session alone with Laura, the therapist obtained a more detailed history of the violence with Jim and her previous attempt to leave him, as well as a developmental history of Caden. Caden had a normal developmental trajectory in terms of his physical, emotional, cognitive, and social development. He was born vaginally at full term and achieved developmental milestones in his first 2 years at normal rates. He learned to read early and loved reading. He and Jim would often read together, and they shared a love of science fiction.

She had tried to leave Jim when Caden was 6 years old after a particularly severe incident in which she had cuts and bruises up and down her back and anal area from being whipped with a belt and buckle and then anally raped. She had gone to the police and they had taken photographs. She moved out with Caden to her mother's home. However, when she spoke to Jim, he told her he would kill her and Caden when he got out of prison if she testified against him. So, she went to the judge and said that she had made up these charges—that she had fallen down the stairs and the bruises were from this incident. The judge charged her with false accusation and she was placed in jail. Jim bailed her out. She had felt trapped since that time.

She then reported that she had been sexually abused by her maternal grandfather, who lived with her family until she was 15 years old, and she told on him to her mother. He had been moved to a nursing home and died there about a year later. She currently had no contact with her family of origin because Jim cut off all contact with them about a year after he moved in. Her family had tried for years to get in touch with her, but she was too afraid of the consequences, for herself and Caden, so she never responded.

She also said that Jim had not allowed anyone to visit their home, so she and Caden never had friends over. Caden was occasionally allowed to go to friends' homes—but this was always up to Jim. He was in charge of all discipline and rules pertaining to Caden. She confessed that she felt very unsure of how to make parenting decisions, as she had not had to, or been able to, in so many years. At the end of this session, Laura signed a release of information for the therapist to contact Caden's teachers and school. Laura also completed an assessment of adjustment problems of Caden using the Child Behavior Checklist (CBCL; Achenbach, 1991).

In the second session with Laura, her CBCL for Caden was reviewed with her and compared with the one from the school counselor. Both indicated clinical levels of anxiety and delinquent behavior. In talking with the teachers and the school counselor, the therapist discovered that Caden was being verbally abusive to girls in his classes, calling them "sluts," "hot chicks," and "hot mamas." He also had tried to grab a girl's breasts and had successfully spanked another girl. He had been reprimanded for all of these incidents; however, the school knew about the current circumstances and was trying to be lenient until more time had elapsed. Still, Laura reported that he had been suspended for 3 days for these behaviors on the prior day. She also told the therapist that he had shoplifted over the weekend. She had made him return the gum and candy, and there had been no other consequences. The store owners were understanding and accepted his apologies and return of the items. The therapist also conducted the K-SADS with Laura to determine the types, severity, and frequency of Caden's clinical symptoms.

SUMMARY OF PRESENTING PROBLEMS
BASED ON EVALUATION

The following summary of Caden's presenting problems is based on the interviews with Laura and Caden; the parent, self-, and counselor CBCL reports; and a telephone interview with the school counselor.

Social Behavior

The damaged internal working models of self and other were manifest in Caden's new relationships with peers, in which he showed disregard for the feelings of others as well as a confusion about his own role in peer relationships. Longitudinal studies of attachment have confirmed a relationship between disrupted or damaged early attachment with caregivers and later attachment with peers and dating partners (Sroufe, Egeland, Carlson, & Collins, 2005). In addition, Caden showed confusion about his internal working models of his family relationships—drawing his stepfather with bulging muscles but no hands—perhaps suggesting an inability to effectively use his strength. His own view of male sexuality was also disturbed, as shown both in his attempts to sexually harass girls at school and in his drawings of the enlarged phalluses on his male figures.

Thus, based on his internal working models of self and others, it is not surprising that Caden was hostile and angry in his peer relationships and had no real friends. He was the center of attention at school for a couple of weeks following the incident at his home—and this caused him to feel tremendous shame and embarrassment. He responded with anger and hostility. In addition, the sexualized violence that he had experienced at home began to manifest itself in his behavior with girls in his classes, presumably as an identification with his stepfather as well as accompanying his anger toward his mother, whom he felt had destroyed his life by leaving the stepfather he loved. Caden was a terribly lonely adolescent, unsure of how to build positive relationships with either boys or girls, and he was now bereft of his primary companion, his stepfather.

Academic Assessment

Caden had always been an excellent student academically and was in advanced placement classes at school. He studied hard and tried hard to do well. He had worked for grades that would make his mother and stepfather proud of him. However, in the aftermath of the hostage situation and the end of his parent's relationship, Caden began to fail academically. He stopped doing his homework and started failing exams, at first seemingly out of depressed indifference and then later out of rebellion, expressing the feeling that he did not have to be the "good boy" any longer. He had worked so hard to keep Jim interested in him and proud of him and had not allowed himself to be free to act like a kid. Now that his stepfather was no longer in his life, he was angry and able to rebel for the first time.

Physical Health

Caden appeared to be in good physical health. He never had any significant health problems. However, his manner of dress suggested a more immature style, as it was not consistent with other teenagers and resembled more the dress of an elementary school child.

Family History and Functioning

This was a family history filled with trauma and abuse. Laura had struggled with a number of abusive family relationships over the course of her life. She had been sexually abused by her maternal grandfather who lived with her family until she was 15 years old. Her parents were uninterested in her complaints about him until her father walked in on her grandfather attempting to rape her. At that point, he insisted that his father-in-law move out. Laura married a man when she was 18 years old, mostly to escape an unhappy home. This man was 10 years her senior, and she soon discovered that he was an alcoholic. He was occasionally physically abusive to her while he was drunk, and when he was not drunk, he was often verbally abusive to her, frequently demeaning her. She left him during her mid-20s and spent many years alone. In her mid-30s, deeply despondent over not having a child, she went through a promiscuous phase, picking up men in bars, and then found herself pregnant. She was elated and did not date for 4 years, until she met Jim at a friend's barbeque. She was immediately attracted to him, partly because he was so engaging with her young son. They moved in together 3 months later. The abuse began several months after he moved in.

As part of Jim's controlling behavior, Laura and Caden had been cut off from her parents for the past 9 years. She contacted them again during the evaluation period, and they were planning a reunion. However, her parents seemed wary and distant. Laura was disappointed that they were not rushing to meet her and Caden with open arms.

Risk and Protective Factors for Caden

Caden was living in a new home with his mother and another family. He liked the boy in the family, an elementary-school-age boy, but he resented having to share a room with him instead of having his own space. Laura was exhausted, traumatized, and depressed from the years of abuse and the terrifying final incident that precipitated her departure. She was having difficulty managing discipline of Caden, who had previously not needed much discipline. She reacted fairly passively to the concerns raised by the school about his truancy and abusiveness toward girls.

In addition to these risk factors, Caden and his mother had little access to resources because of the terrible financial situation that his mother was in due to the control that Jim had exerted over their lives. Laura also had little idea how to manage in the world—for example, how to get a checking account, get her driver's license, or work with a lawyer to sort out her tax problems.

However, there were also some important protective factors for Caden. His mother realized that she and Caden both needed help and had sought help at the clinic. Caden was very bright and capable of excellent academic work. He had a good academic and behavioral record at school, and so his teachers were willing to give him some time to recover from the devastating incident and its consequences. Despite his lack of friends, and not understanding how to make friends, Caden was very appealing to adults and knew how to engage with them emotionally and intellectually. After his initial hesitation in the psychotherapy office, he then genuinely engaged with the therapist and was able to discuss openly his pain and fears.

DSM DIAGNOSIS AND FORMULATIONS

Several possible diagnoses were considered. Caden was diagnosed with PTSD. He fit the A criteria of the *Diagnostic and Statistical Manual of Mental Disorders* (4th ed.; American Psychiatric Association, 1994) due to his exposure to a life-threatening trauma and his feelings of helplessness as he watched his mother's rape. He had reexperiencing symptoms (nightmares and flashbacks), avoidance symptoms (restriction of feelings—only showing negative feelings, and avoidance of his former home), and arousal (easily startled).

He was given a rule-out diagnosis of major depressive disorder (MDD). He had feelings of worthlessness, concentration problems, sleep problems, and a lack of interest in things he used to enjoy. However, at the time of the evaluation, he did not report enough symptoms of MDD to warrant a diagnosis. He was also given a rule-out diagnosis of oppositional defiant disorder (ODD). Reports from his mother and his teacher indicated that he evidenced some of the symptoms of ODD, including frequent deliberate attempts to annoy others, blaming others for his mistakes, being mean to others. However, these symptoms had arisen in response to the recent traumatic event and thus were likely to be, in fact, "post" traumatic. Thus, ODD was considered a diagnosis to consider only once the traumatic reactions had been treated.

Caden had spent most of his 14 years in a violent and emotionally abusive environment. His stepfather humiliated him, controlled him, and hurt him. His mother did not protect him. Caden's depression and interpersonal difficulties were an indication of the inner turmoil that his environment had caused him. Caden appeared very needy in his relationship with the therapist, yearning for someone with whom he could identify, longing to feel connected because he felt displaced and alone in a confusing and scary world.

As he attempted to manage his fear and painful memories, Caden began to act out in school, attacking girls sexually and verbally—an identification with his stepfather. He hated his mother, and she, in turn, felt worthless and incompetent, something her abusive partner had worked to instill in her over many years. Caden's attitude toward her was in part another identification with his stepfather as well as a response to his feelings of betrayal and hurt that she had not protected him and herself from the frightening violence. Caden's attachment relationship with his mother had been damaged, and thus the emotional dysregulation caused by the traumatic history could not be regulated through a secure attachment relationship. Therefore, his distorted working models of relationships combined with his difficulty in self-regulation began to lead to challenging peer relationships.

Laura and Caden came to therapy in the midst of a crisis in their lives. Laura's history suggests that her internal working models of self and others were damaged during her early adolescence. Her adult relationships with abusive men served to further her feelings of worthlessness and helplessness. The very real damage that Jim did to her son also served to increase her feelings of incompetence and ineffectiveness as a mother. During the evaluation period, Laura showed a great desire to help Caden but little idea of how to connect with him and provide a secure base for him during this terrible transition and recovery from the trauma.

TREATMENT RECOMMENDATIONS

The therapist recommended a combination of individual treatment for Caden and supportive therapy/parent guidance for Laura. The individual treatment with Caden would focus first on healing from the traumas he had experienced within his family and help to prepare him psychologically to take the witness stand. A strong relationship between the therapist and Caden had begun to be established after a difficult first session. Following the trial, the individual treatment with Caden was broadly relational and specifically used an attachment-trauma framework with a focus on revising Caden's internal working models of self and others through the relationship with the therapist (e.g., Farber, Lippert, & Nevas, 1995). Relational intervention has demonstrated effectiveness in shifting internal working models (e.g., Levy, Kelly, Meehan, Reynoso, & Weber, 2006). Unfortunately, this is still experimental with traumatized adolescents as there have not been enough trials of relational therapies with this population to demonstrate whether it is effective (Wethington et al., 2008).

The work with Laura alternated between problem-solving work to help her set up a new life and prepare psychologically for the trial and parent guidance in her new role as the only parent in Caden's life. She also benefited from supportive work around her own traumatic experiences and PTSD. Finally, group therapy for IPV survivors was recommended for Laura, in order to gain support from others who had experienced similar situations. She needed others in similar circumstances who could support her emotionally in establishing her new life beyond abuse. Group therapy was also recommended for Caden because the therapist thought that he would benefit from being in a group of adolescents in which he did not have to feel shame for his family's unusual circumstances.

TREATMENT OUTCOMES

Caden was treated in a once-weekly individual relational psychotherapy, while his mother received weekly parent guidance, focused on supportive intervention for her and behavioral strategies for her parenting. The treatment lasted about 18 months. By the end of treatment, Caden no longer reported active PTSD symptoms and thus no longer fit criteria for this disorder. MDD and ODD were also ruled out as Caden's behavior and affects became more regulated and under his control. He had responded positively to the behavioral interventions his mother had used at home and was generally more cooperative with her. He had resumed his high level of academic success and had broadened his social networks—he had several genuine friends, both boys and girls, and frequently hung out with other high school kids after school in age-appropriate activities. He began several extracurricular activities that he had not been allowed to participate in while his stepfather was living with them, and these included theater and chess. Chess was of particular importance to Caden as his stepfather had taught him to play chess and they had spent many hours after school playing together. Caden found that he could hold onto these loving aspects of his stepfather even as he developed a life for himself that involved positive peer relationships and a more connected relationship with his mother. His mother, for her part, became less depressed, and her symptoms of PTSD also went into remission. She maintained her work and was able to develop a couple of close friendships with other women in whom she could confide about her prior experiences as well as her ongoing challenges as a single mother. She became more focused on parenting and was able to respond appropriately to Caden's changing developmental needs as a mid-adolescent.

REFERENCES

Achenbach, T. M. (1991). *Manual for Child Behavior Checklist/4-18 and 1991 Profile*. Burlington: University of Vermont, Department of Psychiatry.

Achenbach, T., & Edelbrock, C. (1993). *Manual for the Child Behavior Checklist and Revised Child Behavior Profile*. Burlington: University of Vermont, Department of Psychiatry.

American Psychiatric Association. (1994). *Diagnostic and statistical manual of mental disorders* (4th ed.). Washington, DC: Author.

Bowlby, J. (1988). *A secure base: Clinical applications of attachment theory*. London, England: Routledge.

Carlson, E. A., Sroufe, L. A., & Egeland, B. (2004). The construction of experience: A longitudinal study of representation and behavior. *Child Development, 75,* 66–83. doi:10.1111/j.1467-8624.2004.00654.x

Cicchetti, D., & Toth, S. L. (1995). Child maltreatment and attachment organization: Implications for intervention. In S. Goldberg, R. Muir, & J. Kerr (Eds.), *Attachment theory: Social, developmental, and clinical perspectives* (pp. 279–308). Hillsdale, NJ: Analytic Press.

Evans, S. E., Davies, C., & DiLillo, D. (2008). Exposure to domestic violence: A meta-analysis of child and adolescent outcomes. *Aggression and Violent Behavior, 10,* 131–140.

Farber, B. A., Lippert, R. A., & Nevas, D. B. (1995). The therapist as attachment figure. *Psychotherapy Research, 32,* 204–212.

Herrera, V. M., & McCloskey, L. A. (2001). Gender differences in the risk for delinquency among youth exposed to family violence. *Child Abuse & Neglect, 25,* 1037–1051. doi:10.1016/S0145-2134(01)00255-1

Kaufman, J., Birmaher, B., Brent, D., Rao, U., Flynn, C., Moreci, P., . . . Ryan, N. (1997). Schedule for Affective Disorders and Schizophrenia for School-Age Children-Present and Lifetime Version (K-SADS-PL): Initial reliability and validity data. *Journal of the American Academy of Child and Adolescent Psychiatry 36,* 980–988. doi:10.1097/00004583-199707000-00021

Kilpatrick, D. G., Ruggiero, K. J., Acierno, R., & Saunders, D. G. (2003). Violence and PTSD, major depression, substance abuse/dependence, and comorbidity: Results from the national survey of adolescents. *Journal of Consulting and Clinical Psychology, 71,* 692–700. doi:10.1037/0022-006X.71.4.692

Kim, J. (2009). Type-specific intergenerational transmission of neglectful and physically abusive parenting behaviors among young parents. *Children and Youth Services Review, 31,* 761–767. doi:10.1016/j.childyouth.2009.02.002

Levendosky, A. A., Huth-Bocks, A., & Semel, M. A. (2002). Adolescent peer relationships and mental health functioning in families with domestic violence. *Journal of Clinical Child and Adolescent Psychology, 31,* 206–218.

Levy, K. N., Kelly, K. M., Meehan, K. B., Reynoso, J. S., & Weber, M. (2006). Change in attachment patterns and reflective function in a randomized control trial of transference focused psychotherapy for borderline personality disorder. *Journal of Consulting and Clinical Psychology, 74,* 1027–1040. doi:10.1037/0022-006X.74.6.1027

McCloskey, L. A., & Lichter, E. L. (2003). The contribution of marital violence to adolescent aggression across different relationships. *Journal of Interpersonal Violence, 18,* 390–412. doi:10.1177/0886260503251179

Sroufe, L. A., Egeland, B., Carlson, E., & Collins, W. A. (2005). Placing early attachment experiences in developmental context: The Minnesota Longitudinal Study. In K. E. Grossmann, K. Grossmann, & E. Waters (Eds.), *Attachment from infancy to adulthood: The major longitudinal studies* (pp. 40–70). New York, NY: Guilford Press.

Straus, M. A. (1992). *Children as witnesses to marital violence: A risk factor for lifelong problems among a nationally representative sample of American men and women. Report of the Twenty-Third Ross Roundtable.* Columbus, OH: Ross Laboratories.

van der Kolk, B. A. (2005). Developmental trauma disorder: Toward a rational diagnosis for children with complex trauma histories. *Psychiatric Annals, 35,* 401–408.

Wethington, H. R., Hahn, R. A., Fuqua-Whitley, D. S., Sipe, T. A., Crosby, A. E., Johnson, R. L., . . . Chattopadhyay, S. K. (2008). The effectiveness of interventions to reduce psychological harm from traumatic events among children and adolescents: A systematic review. *American Journal of Preventive Medicine, 35,* 287–313. doi:10.1016/j.amepre.2008.06.024

EPILOGUE: CONCLUSIONS AND CHALLENGES

ALYTIA A. LEVENDOSKY AND SANDRA A. GRAHAM-BERMANN

This book demonstrates the importance of a developmental psychopathology framework for understanding the effects of intimate partner violence (IPV) on children's functioning. Research findings support a model of multiple developmental pathways in response to IPV exposure, including the potential for adaptation and maladaptation at many points across development. Interventions have been developed and tested that focus on children exposed to IPV at different developmental stages. Future research should continue to identify and understand mechanisms for pathways of risk and resilience to better develop interventions to target individuals on these differential trajectories.

In the past 10 years, the research methodologies examining the effects of IPV have vastly improved, including longitudinal studies, studies with large sample sizes, and multiple methods and multiple reporters. In addition, sophisticated analyses have allowed for examination of the variety of risk and protective factors, as well as of the multiple levels of child functioning. The state of the field suggests that we can make strong conclusions about the variety of impacts of IPV and the heterogeneity of outcomes in these exposed children. However, there remain consistent methodological issues with which the field must continue to grapple.

First, we must better define exposure to IPV. There are controversies around whether or not children must actually witness (i.e., see or hear the violence) or whether living in the household in which violence and its consequences are occurring counts as exposure. There are also controversies around whether IPV is only physical or sexual violence or also includes threats of physical or sexual violence. Many published studies do not make it clear how they handle each of these issues of definition, making comparisons across studies quite difficult.

Second, we must have more sophisticated ways to handle the very common co-occurrence of additional risk factors in families with IPV. These additional risk factors are inconsistently measured and/or used in analyses of data on children exposed to IPV. It is then difficult to interpret whether or not the findings are related to IPV or to the cluster of risk factors, including IPV, that plague some families.

Third, we need to have more culturally competent studies of children from ethnic minority backgrounds in the United States. Most of the studies reviewed in these chapters had predominantly Caucasian samples or sufficiently small samples that the researchers were unable to analyze the data by ethnic group. This limits our ability to understand whether ethnic or cultural background influences, positively or negatively, the developmental trajectories of risk from the exposure to IPV.

Fourth, we remain concerned that almost without exception the field of IPV research has focused on at-risk, low-income families. As a field of inquiry, we simply do not know much about the prevalence, the incidence, and the outcomes associated with IPV exposure for children in higher-income families. Further, we know little about the special needs, circumstances, and barriers to treatment for these women and their children.

Fifth, while there have been several longitudinal studies over the past 10 years, we have little information on the long-term effects of IPV, spanning all of childhood and adolescence. This dearth of information affects the development of adequate prevention and intervention efforts as we only have our best estimates of these long-term trajectories from our knowledge of the earlier childhood trajectories.

Using a developmental psychopathology framework, we can also discuss the interventions described and reviewed in this book. These interventions are evidence-based in that they were developed on the basis of the findings of the research in the field, as well as empirically supported by their evaluations of treatment outcomes. Based on the developmental period of the child, interventions are tailored to the unique needs of the child and the mother. Lieberman's infant–parent psychotherapy focuses on assisting the mother in practical ways due to the high role demands of this period. In addition, this treatment addresses the damaged representations that the mother has, which strongly influence her early parenting. Through these interventions, as well as others, this treatment has been shown in preliminary findings to improve the mother–child relationship in infants exposed to IPV. McDonald and colleagues' intervention, called Project Support, is tailored to the needs of the preschool child (McDonald, Jouriles, & Skopp, 2006). This intervention focuses on the mother and includes social and instrumental aid for mothers who still have high-role demands during this developmental period; secondly, it provides behavioral parent training to reduce aggression and oppositional behavior—behaviors that are particularly likely in this age group. Graham-Bermann developed the Kids' Club Program in response to the unique developmental needs of the school-age child, including the support and acknowledgement that children of this age can receive from peers. This program targets concerns found in this age group, including conflict resolution, as well as emotional expression. In Chapter 12 of this volume, Cunningham and Baker draw implications for interventions for treatment of adolescents exposed to IPV and make specific recommendations based both on the age-specific developmental trajectories of problematic coping and identification with abusive male role models as well as needs of adolescents, such as for peer involvement and authority figures outside the home.

The interventions described across the chapters herein use many of the assumptions of the developmental psychopathology model to best address the treatment needs of this population. For example, they all assume that psychopathology develops from successive deviations from normal development over time. Each of them is targeted to address the developmental deviations for their targeted age group. They also assume that change arising from an appropriately targeted intervention is possible. The positive evaluations of these interventions speak to their strengths. However, these interventions do less to address the issue of the multifinality/heterogeneity of outcomes, as discussed below. This potentially important implication of the developmental psychopathology framework is currently largely ignored in the intervention literature.

As the field of intervention evaluation develops for families with IPV, important next steps include developing new programs for children and comparing various kinds of interventions with one another to discern not only whether programs are effective for children of particular ages but also for whom a particular program might be the best. Although expensive, government support of modified, randomized control trials that compare interventions is needed to support such advancements in this field.

The multifinality and heterogeneity of developmental trajectories are well illustrated clinically by the four descriptions of amalgamated cases presented here. The cases of James, Chris, Alia, and Caden demonstrate the vulnerabilities of their developmental periods and suggest the heterogeneous pathways and functioning that may be seen by clinicians working with this population. All of these children live in families with additional risk factors, including poverty, sexual abuse, lack of education, and lack of resources. However, to the credit of each of their mothers, these children received evaluations and treatment that was able to move them from at-risk developmental trajectories to normal functioning for their ages. These clinical cases can serve as examples of the research findings as well as to suggest what further information is needed for clinicians serving this at-risk population. One area for further study to inform clinicians is the role of the ethnicity/culture of the mother and her child as she seeks treatment. How does their ethnicity/culture inform their understanding and interpretation of the impact of IPV in their lives and thus in the treatment? How do the ethnicity/culture and/or gender of the therapist influence the treatment seeking of these women and children and the treatment outcomes? These factors have been studied somewhat in the general treatment literature, but not in relationship to IPV specifically.

The interventions presented in this book, based on theory and evidence in their development and empirical support for their outcomes, are a giant step forward in the treatment of IPV exposure in children. However, problems in both intervention and implementation continue. First, the research and clinical case chapters in this book clearly outline the heterogeneity of outcomes in children exposed to IPV, yet many of the interventions are not designed to handle this heterogeneity. They have been developed primarily to address the most common problems associated with the particular developmental period, rather than the breadth of problems that may be experienced by children of a particular age. Given the research findings on children's profiles of adjustment, should treatment be tailored to meet the differing needs of children exposed to IPV, or is a more universal approach the best? More research needs to be done to tie the findings on the heterogeneous profiles of adjustment to the treatment success.

Second, while the Consort Standards for studies of medical interventions (Moher, 1998) set methodological standards for the field of intervention research, there are a number of reasons why it may not be possible to precisely follow the recommendations of these standards without modifications in studies of children exposed to IPV. For example, there are difficulties in using the use of clinical trial standards in the community setting. The differences between research standards and community practice are likely to be significant, and it is unclear who can decide how to settle them or how to even approach and ameliorate these differences. The Consort Standards were developed with the idea of testing a drug or intervention with patients with a diagnosed medical illness. Children exposed to IPV may differ in some ways from individuals with diagnosed medical illnesses and thus these standards may not be applicable. For example, the medical model assumes that the cause lies within the body of the patient, or at least, if environmentally induced, there is a biological change in the patient. For children exposed to IPV, there may or may not be biological changes and there may or may not be a diagnosable mental health response, for example, posttraumatic stress disorder (PTSD). Thus, their needs may be significantly different from those of medical patients. Further, special protections (i.e., protection from the abusive parent for both the child and the mother) may be needed for children exposed to IPV that may challenge the use of strict standards. Finally, in the Standards, comparison groups for treatment studies include no treatment and treatment-as-usual groups. However, in the treatment of children exposed to IPV, this means not offering treatment to some subset of the population. A question for intervention researchers is whether it is ever ethical to withhold treatment in order to study interventions for abused women and children.

Third, an important and underdeveloped field within IPV interventions is prevention work with children. Wolfe and colleagues have pioneered a dating violence prevention program with adolescents (Pittman, Wolfe, & Wekerle, 2000; Wolfe, 2006). This is an important step in breaking the intergenerational cycle of violence, but, in general, there are few programs that focus on prevention and little research on the effectiveness of prevention efforts, either for ameliorating future IPV or the wide range of behavioral symptoms and psychopathology that is found in these children. Intervention has been the primary focus because children come to the attention of mental health practitioners when they are already manifesting symptoms and difficult behaviors. Shelters may run groups for children who are living in them, but these have limited utility in preventing problems given their inherent very short-term nature (shelter stays are typically limited to 30–60 days) and the very transient and chaotic nature of the children's living situation during this treatment. However, given the now large body of research documenting the severity of children's developmental problems in the context of IPV, prevention efforts should be our next focus.

Finally, an exciting new development in this field of research of traumatized children may serve to better integrate research findings, clinical assessment and diagnosis, and interventions. In early 2009, the task force from the National Child Traumatic Stress Network (NCTSN) proposed diagnostic criteria for developmental trauma disorder (DTD)—a proposed new traumatic stress disorder for children in the forthcoming fifth edition of the *Diagnostic and Statistical Manual of Mental Disorders* (DSM; van der Kolk, 2005). This disorder is designed to address the very significant problem that most children exposed to traumatic events, including witnessing IPV, do not meet criteria for PTSD, even the modified criteria by Scheeringa, Zeanah, Myers, and Putnam (2003) for younger children. Instead, these children frequently receive diagnoses of generalized anxiety disorder, major depressive disorder, attention-deficit/hyperactivity disorder (ADHD), oppositional defiant disorder, and so on. Van der Kolk (2005) proposed that these disorders are in fact posttraumatic in origin, and thus children are being misdiagnosed and thus mistreated by treatments appropriate for ADHD or depression in the absence of traumatic origin. The A criteria for DTD include witnessing interpersonal violence and the disruptions of protective caregiving that can result from witnessing. The other criteria include symptoms of affective and physiological dysregulation, attentional and behavioral dysregulation, self- and relational dysregulation. In addition, the child has to have at least one symptom in two of the three PTSD clusters from the fourth edition of the *DSM*.

Within the context of a developmental psychopathology framework of risk and resilience, this disorder does not suggest that all children who are exposed to IPV develop psychopathology, only that those who do manifest disorders should be understood to have a traumatic origin to their pathology. This disorder can bring together the findings across the research chapters in this book that argue for hetereogeneity in outcomes as well as effects of IPV exposure on many levels of the child, including physiological, emotional, behavioral, and social. This disorder can help tie together the diverging branches of the tree (as in Sroufe's, 1997, description in Chapter 1 of this volume) by understanding that the trunk of the tree is suffering from a traumatic event. Thus, in fact, DTD fits neatly within a developmental psychopathology framework in that it suggests heterogeneity of developmental pathways and multifinality in the diagnostic outcomes of children exposed to IPV. Therefore, in addition to bringing together the research findings on children exposed to trauma, in this case, IPV, DTD also has important clinical implications. Children with psychopathology should be treated as posttraumatic, rather than viewing their ADHD or depression as arising from within, as in the typical medical model. Finally, interventions can be tailored to address the wide variety of dysregulation seen in the children with this disorder—thus targeting affective dysregulation as well as relational dysregulation, for example.

Using this disorder as a tool for assessment and diagnosis will allow many more children exposed to IPV and other traumas to receive treatment under current insurance conditions and to have treatment that is more appropriately targeted to the posttraumatic elements of their disorders. Currently, the treatments offered in this book are targeted at posttraumatic functioning, but this is not treatment as usual for children presenting in clinics, where they are much more likely to be diagnosed with an emotional or behavioral problem with the underlying trauma considered secondary or never even assessed. The credibility of a *DSM* disorder will bring treatment of children exposed to trauma more to the forefront of targeted interventions for children.

In conclusion, the developmental framework of this book on the outcomes of children exposed to IPV allows examination of the particular vulnerabilities on the basis of developmental stage. This was illustrated through the presentation of research findings, evidence-based interventions, and clinical cases for each developmental period. While there is still much to be done (e.g., development of prevention services and further refinement of our understanding of mechanisms involved in the maladaptive developmental trajectories), much knowledge has now accumulated that can be used to drive future research and intervention efforts. It is our hope and vision that this book will provide a basis for these endeavors, which will eventually significantly ameliorate the problems faced by children exposed to IPV.

REFERENCES

McDonald, R., Jouriles, E. N., Ramisetty-Mikler, S., Caetano, R., & Green, C. E. (2006). Estimating the number of American children living in partner-violent families. *Journal of Family Psychology, 20,* 137–142. doi: 10.1037/0893-3200.20.1.137

McDonald, R., Jouriles, E. N., & Skopp, N. A. (2006). Reducing conduct problems among children brought to women's shelters: Intervention effects 24 months following termination of services. *Journal of Family Psychology, 20,* 127–136.

Moher, D. (1998). CONSORT: An evolving tool to help improve the quality of reports of randomized controlled trials. Consolidated Standards of Reporting Trials. *JAMA, 279,* 1489–1491. doi:10.1001/jama.279.18.1489

Pittman, A. L., Wolfe, D. A., & Wekerle, C. (2000). Strategies for evaluating dating violence prevention programs. *Journal of Aggression, Maltreatment & Trauma, 4,* 217–238. doi:10.1300/J146v04n01_10

Scheeringa, M. S., Zeanah, C. H., Myers, L., & Putnam, F. W. (2003). New findings on alternative criteria for PTSD in preschool children. *Journal of the American Academy of Child and Adolescent Psychiatry, 42,* 561–570. doi:10.1097/01.CHI.0000046822.95464.14

Sroufe, L. A. (1997). Psychopathology as an outcome of development. *Development and Psychopathology, 9,* 251–268. doi:10.1017/S0954579497002046

van der Kolk, B. A. (2005). Developmental trauma disorder: Toward a rational diagnosis for children with complex trauma histories. *Psychiatric Annals, 35,* 401–408.

Wolfe, D. A. (2006). Preventing violence in relationships: Psychological science addressing complex social issues. *Canadian Psychology, 47,* 44–50. doi:10.1037/h0087043

APPENDIX: DISCUSSION QUESTIONS

I. Prenatal to Infancy

1. What are the implications for the findings from the Levendosky and Bogat study for the intervention program developed by Lieberman and colleagues?
2. Would you expect James to continue to have problems with development, with or without treatment? What kinds of problems might he have and why?
3. Should the primary emphasis of treatment during the perinatal period be on maintaining a violence-free home? Why or why not?
4. Why is attachment theory used by all of these authors to explain the consequences of intimate partner violence (IPV) during pregnancy through toddlerhood for mothers and children?
5. What other theoretical frameworks might be useful in explaining the effects of exposure to violence during this period?
6. Should Angela's mother have been included in the assessment of James's environment? Should substance use and abuse have been investigated here? Would the inclusion of either of these that have altered the treatment recommendation?
7. What do you think about the potential for father involvement in the intervention described by Lieberman and colleagues?
8. What part of the intervention program do you think was most effective in creating change for the mother and for the child? Without a comparison group that was followed over time but did not participate in the program, how do we know that it was the intervention program that was responsible for the changes in traumatic stress, parenting, and depression? What else might account for the findings?
9. How might a father's relationship (and attachment) to the child and the father-child dyad influence the diagnosis of relational posttraumatic stress disorder (PTSD)?
10. Why is there so little research on fathers of infants exposed to IPV? What are the challenges and pitfalls of doing this research?

II. Toddler to Early Childhood

1. During early childhood, many parents struggle with strains and stressors on the family. What do you suppose those stressors might be? How might these family-wide issues affect IPV severity or frequency?

2. Is the preschool period a sensitive period for exposure to IPV? Would we expect to see more long-term problems in these children as adolescents and adults compared with children first exposed to IPV at older ages (i.e., school age and adolescent)?

3. How are the effects of preschool-age children's exposure to IPV different from those of younger children? How can the heterogeneity of outcomes in preschool-age children exposed to IPV be explained?

4. Relatedly, should this heterogeneity be related to treatment recommendations? Should treatment programs such as Project Support be modified to address the wide range of outcomes in these children? How would that be done?

5. Given the developmental issues concerning young children's social and emotional development, how might the group aspect of the intervention program have assisted Chris in recognizing his feelings about the violence he had witnessed?

6. There is a range of programs offered for this age group—how would you choose one to use in your community? For example, if Chris and Sharon were to have entered Project Support instead of the Preschool Kids' Club and Moms' Parenting Empowerment Program groups, what could we expect the differences in treatment and outcome to have been?

7. What is the difference between and similarities among symptoms of PTSD and symptoms of attention-deficit/hyperactivity disorder in the preschool-age child?

8. Can mothers accurately report the symptoms of PTSD in their preschool-age children? Which ones would be most difficult to report on?

9. What would be needed in order to create measures of exposure to IPV and outcomes that are sensitive to preschool-age children's needs and developmental abilities?

10. Do you think that siblings are more of a source of risk or protection for children in families with IPV? Can you describe conditions under which siblings might add to a child's risk? Protection against developing problems?

III. School-Age Children

1. Alia's presenting problems were centered on changes in her academic performance and in socially appropriate behavior (e.g., her mother reported that she had temper tantrums and was bossy with friends; therapists reported that she used inappropriate language, such as swearing). What is there about PTSD that might contribute to the development of these behaviors?

2. What are the unique developmental issues of school-age children's exposure to IPV that differ from those of preschool-age children and infants?

3. Most developmental research studies have found that boys generally have higher rates of physical aggression than do girls. Why do you think that research on children exposed to IPV has failed to show this effect?

4. Why do you think there is such a broad range of outcomes for children exposed to IPV? Could it be related to aspects of the IPV that can vary tremendously across families? Or might it be due to differing constitutional strengths or vulnerabilities in the children? Or it is accounted for by different levels of other risk factors, for example, maternal mental health or parenting abilities? Or is it all of these?

5. How do the findings reviewed in Chapter 8 influence the development of treatment interventions such as the Kids' Club?

6. Should the theoretical frameworks used to explain the effects of IPV on school-age children inform treatment approaches? If so, how can they be used to inform treatment?

7. What do you think takes place in the Moms' Parenting Empowerment Program groups when one or more members are still living with their abusive partners? Would you consider this a problem? Why would mothers want or need to have their own group that is separate from the children's intervention program?

8. Should there be a parenting-oriented psychoeducational treatment group for abusive fathers that complements this treatment? In the case example, Alia's father is awarded significant time with his children, thus suggesting a need for parenting intervention for these fathers. What are the advantages and challenges in establishing such a program?

9. Some research suggests that mothers in IPV relationships often have multiple IPV relationships; how would the treatment effects hold up under the experience of subsequent violent family interactions?

10. What are the special considerations in doing efficacy trials with at-risk children? Are there some things that should not be asked? Under what conditions do we ask children about their exposure to violence?

IV. Adolescents

1. Given what we know about power and gender issues involved in IPV, what issues might it raise for Laura and then for Caden had the evaluator been a male rather than a female psychologist?
2. Do you think that the therapist had to inform the mother that Caden had revealed the telephone number and address at their new living arrangement to the abusive stepfather? Why or why not?
3. What are the possible social, cognitive, physical, and emotional vulnerabilities of adolescents such as Caden who have been eyewitness to severe IPV? For example, how do the hormonal changes at adolescence influence the developmental trajectories of children exposed to IPV?
4. Adolescents may have only been exposed to IPV during their early childhood, or only during their adolescence, or chronically, across their development. Would we expect there to be different developmental trajectories of risk based on timing of exposure to IPV? If so, what would we expect?
5. What are the factors that make adolescents exposed to IPV vulnerable to becoming involved in violent dating relationships?
6. Based on the research literature, what is the likely prognosis for Caden without intervention? With intervention?
7. Based on treatment model described in Chapter 12, what kind of treatment approach do you think would be most successful with Caden?
8. Should treatment of adolescents exposed to IPV include an assessment of the role that the adolescent plays in the family and then be tailored to the specific consequences of that family role?
9. Given the review of the research literature, and the theory that boys learn aggression tactics from observing the modeling behavior of fathers and male father figures, what could explain the findings of many studies that girls exposed to IPV are more likely than boys to be physically aggressive during adolescence?
10. If adolescents exposed to IPV are at risk for early pregnancy, which increases their risk for violence in intimate relationships, when is the best time in the life cycle to intervene?

INDEX

meta-analyses on, 156–159
perpetrated by women, 50
psychoeducation about, 54, 219
as risk factor for school age children, 166–167
school-age children understandings of, 170–171
tactics of, 197
timing of, 33, 170
Intimate terrorism, 164
IQ (intelligence quotient), 92–93
Isolation, 253, 257–258

Jaffe, P. G., 157, 181
Jakupcak, M., 187
Johnson, M. P., 163–164
Johnson, V. K., 99
Jouriles, E. N., 93, 159

Katz, L. F., 98, 192
Kenny, E. D., 88
Kerr, M. A., 192
The Kids' Club Program, 179, 184–199
and age group developmental needs, 289
efficacy trial design and outcome measures, 194–199
and Moms' Parenting Empowerment Program, 192–194
for preschoolers. See Preschool Kids' Club Program
program design, 185–186
school-age children interventions, 184–199
session goals of, 187–192
theoretical basis for, 186–187
Kilpatrick, D. G., 228
Kilpatrick, K. L., 88
Kitzmann, K. M., 88, 157, 158, 165, 166
Koss, M. P., 192

Lamb, M. E., 158
Language barriers, 51
Larieu, J. A., 91
Lazarus, R. S., 92
Lee, V., 157
Levendosky, A. A., 26, 91, 98, 142, 168–169, 230
Lieberman, A. F., 35, 36, 93, 92, 99
Life span, 88, 248

Life Stressor Checklist-Revised (LSC-R), 52
Lilly, M., 100
Limitations, 198–199
Longitudinal studies, 25, 161–162, 288. *See also* Mother Infant Study
Low, S. M., 98, 192
Low self-esteem, 233
LSC-R (Life Stressor Checklist-Revised), 52
Luthar, S. S., 172

Major depressive disorder (MDD), 282
Male aggression, 164–165
Massage, infant, 55
Masten, A. S., 169
Maternal parenting behavior. *See* Mothers
Maternal representations
effects of IPV on, 31
infant–parent case study, 74–76
interventions that target, 35–36
in Mother Infant Study, 28–31
postpartum, 23–24
prepartum, 22–25
stability of, 29, 30
Mayes, L., 23
McCloskey, L. A., 192, 235
McDonald, R., 93, 159, 162, 289
McFadden, M. E., 187
McIntyre-Smith, A., 157
MDD (major depressive disorder), 282
Measures
of aggression, 232
culturally appropriate, 193
of intimate partner violence, 164–165
Mother Infant Study, 27–28
of outcome, 169, 194–199
for Perinatal CPP intake assessment, 52–53
Medhanie, A., 248
Media influence, 251
Mediators, 110, 198
Medical patients, 290–291
Mega-analysis, 158–159
Mental health
of mothers, 161–162
preschool case study, 137–139
services for pregnant women, 50

Shame, 189–190, 252, 278
Shapiro, D. L., 98
Shelton, K. H., 192
Sibling play therapy, 121–122
Siblings, 262
Small group formats. *See* Group formats
Smiler role, 261
SNS. *See* Sympathetic nervous system
Social behavior, 215, 279–280
Social competence, 97
Social context, 239
Social learning theory
    aggression, 167
    intergenerational violence, 254
    Kids' Club Program, 186
    Moms' Parenting Empowerment
        Program, 134
    peer aggression, 234
    preschool-age children, 111–113
    Preschool Kids' Club, 134
Social support
    isolation from, 252, 257–258
    Project Support, 117–118
    and well-being, 142
Socioeconomic status, 288
Solomon, J., 22
Spontaneous disclosure, 188, 200
SS (Strange Situation) procedure, 20–21
Stability, 22, 29–33
Steinberg, L., 226
Stereotypes, gender, 191–192
Stern, D., 81
Sternberg, K. J., 96, 158
Stover, C. S., 93, 99
Straatman, A., 237
Strange Situation (SS) procedure, 20–21
Straus, Murray, 228
Stress
    chronic, 115
    traumatic, 54–55, 90–92
Stressors, 240
Stress response systems, 168
Subjective experiences, 74–76
Sullivan, C. M., 182
Support services, 49–50, 179
Swank, P. R., 159
Sympathetic nervous system (SNS), 90,
    95, 168

Symptoms
    in adolescents, 240
    trauma theory on, 187
    of traumatic stress, 90–92
Systemic approach, 102

Taxonomy of exposure, 166
Teachers, 125
Thapar, A., 192
Theran, S. A., 30
Therapy sessions, 58–62
Threats, 113, 288
Timing, 33, 170
Trajectories
    developmental, 289–290
    of recovery, 100–102
Trauma, 24, 231. *See also* Trauma theory;
        Traumatic events
Trauma-focused treatment, 48–49
Trauma Symptoms Checklist (TSC), 231
Trauma theory
    cognitive functioning, 116
    with ecological theory, 168–169
    school-age case study, 209
    spontaneous disclosure, 200
    symptoms and behaviors, 187
Traumatic events
    and cognitive functioning, 92–93
    and maternal representations, 24
    physiological response to, 90
    trauma theory on, 187
Traumatic stress, 54–55, 90–92
Treatment
    assessment of, 53
    course of, 142–148
    father participation in, 56–57
    fidelity of, 184
    modalities for Perinatal CPP, 53–56
    outcomes, 162–163, 220, 284
    systemic approach to, 102
    wait-list, 183
Treatment manuals, 184
Treatment recommendations
    in adolescent case study, 283–284
    infant–parent case study, 80–82
    preschool-age children case study,
        141–142
    school-age case study, 219–220
Trials, randomized controlled, 117–120

ABOUT THE EDITORS

Sandra A. Graham-Bermann, PhD, is a professor of psychology and psychiatry at the University of Michigan, Ann Arbor, where she has been researching the ways in which different forms of violence affect children's adjustment, including their traumatic stress reactions and resilient coping. She has studied children ages 3 to 13 in a variety of contexts, such as preschools, community settings, and shelters for abused women. As part of this program of research, she has developed new measures of children's fears and worries, their symptoms of traumatic stress, attitudes and beliefs about violence, family stereotyping, and conflicts in sibling relationships. With support from the Centers for Disease Control and Prevention, the Department of Health and Human Services, and state and local foundations, she has studied multiple forms of violence in the lives of children and designed and evaluated interventions for women and children exposed to domestic violence. These programs have been adopted for use in five countries and 27 states. Dr. Graham-Bermann is author of more than 50 research journal articles, and she is coeditor with Jeff Edleson of *Domestic Violence in the Lives of Children: The Future of Research, Intervention, and Social Policy* (2001).

Alytia A. Levendosky, PhD, is a professor of psychology and director of clinical training at Michigan State University, East Lansing, where she studies the intergenerational transmission of violence, specifically focusing on the prenatal effects of intimate partner violence. The goal of her research program is to develop a comprehensive model of the psychological, physiological, and neurological mechanisms through which prenatal exposure to intimate partner violence affects the mother–child relationship and children's developmental outcomes. With colleagues at Michigan State University, she has followed a cohort of 200 children from pregnancy through age 10. Her research has led to an understanding of the mother–child attachment relationship in the context of intimate partner violence. She has received support for her research from the National Institute of Justice, the Centers for Disease Control and Prevention, the National Institute of Mental Health, and the National Institute for Child Health and Development. She is author of more than 45 research journal articles, and this is her first book.